ISSUES & SKILLS

NEW EDITION

ISSUES & SKILLS

FOR
A-LEVEL ENGLISH

PETER
TURNER

NEW EDITION

Hodder & Stoughton
A MEMBER OF THE HODDER HEADLINE GROUP

Orders: please contact Bookpoint Ltd, 39 Milton Park, Abingdon, Oxon OX14 4TD.
Telephone: (44) 01235 400414, Fax: (44) 01235 400454. Lines are open from 9.00 - 6.00, Monday
to Saturday, with a 24 hour message answering service. Email address: orders@bookpoint.co.uk

British Library Cataloguing in Publication Data

Turner, Peter, 1946–
  Issues and skills for "A" level English
  1. English language – Usage   2. English literature
  I. Title
  428

ISBN 0 340 688319

First published 1997
Impression number   10 9   8   7   6   5   4   3
Year   2004   2003   2002   2001   2000   1999   1998

Typeset by Wearset, Boldon, Tyne & Wear.
Printed in Great Britain for Hodder & Stoughton Educational, a division of Hodder Headline Plc,
338 Euston Road, London NW1 3BH by Scotprint Ltd, Musselburgh, Scotland.

Contents

Acknowledgements

I would like to thank my colleagues at Bournemouth and Poole College of Further Education for their advice and assistance in preparing this edition, in particular Maureen Griffin, Martin Price, Sara Southerden, Linda Turner and Mike Wedge. For their cheerful willingness to act as guinea-pigs and critics, thanks are due to my A-level students at Bournemouth and Poole College, particularly Penny Pearson, who allowed me to plunder her essay on 'Dubliners', and Jeanette Moore, who wrote the marginal notes on 'The Sisters'. I would also like to thank my friends Paul Ashley, Lyn Gerrey, Melanie Gerrey, Mikki Nanowski and John Randall for their help and encouragement; for their patient assistance in the final preparation of the manuscript I would like to thank Elaine Baker and Glenys Stechman.

I would also like to acknowledge the friendship and support of Rich Tetenbaum in the earlier incarnations of this book. Tet died tragically on 2 June 1996, and the book is dedicated to him.

Preface

This book is designed specifically for the AEB 623 A-level English (Language and Literature) examination. It covers every aspect of the syllabus, providing a thematically integrated approach to language study, and detailed guidance on studying and writing about literature.

Part I concentrates on techniques and practice in discussion essay and narrative writing, summary and comprehension, and exercises are set in the format of the AEB examination.

Each chapter of Part II, except for the last, covers a single major social, political or cultural issue of the late 20th century. The issues are ones which appear frequently in the continuous writing section of the AEB exam. The chapters all provide a comprehension and analysis or a summary skills exercise, and a series of extracts designed to present a wide range of viewpoints and information on the issue under consideration. Suggestions for discussion, research and further written work are built into the chapters, and lists of essay titles and additional stimulus material are added at the end. Each chapter also contains a final section dealing with problems inherent in some aspect of written work. The last 'issues' chapter deals with three additional themes more briefly, providing, overall, for two full-scale discussion and writing sessions per term for the first five terms of a two-year course. This central section of the book would be of value for general studies as well as English A level.

Part III deals with the study of English literature texts. It is focused on the requirements of the AEB 623 examination, and covers all aspects of literature study from initial note-taking to final examination preparation. It deals in detail with techniques of analysis and essay writing on literary texts, both for whole-text questions and for questions which require depth analysis of sections of text. Overall, the book is designed to enable students to develop qualities of writing and thinking which are transferable between the different parts of the language and literature course.

The language essay and narrative writing titles are all taken from AEB English examination papers.

About the author

Peter Turner is an English Lecturer and adviser on higher education at Bournemouth and Poole College of Further Education in Dorset, where he teaches AEB English 623. He has also been an examiner for this syllabus. He has taught at secondary schools in Devon and Leeds, and in a college of technical and further education in Sydney, Australia. He gained a B.A. degree at Hull University, and an M.A. at the University of Waterloo in Canada, where he specialised in Shakespeare studies, and taught undergraduate courses. He has written for the magazine *New Internationalist*.

Language Writing Skills

1 The Discussion Essay

General preparation for essay writing

Essay writing is an ancient art form, and many of the great imaginative writers of the past have used it as a vehicle for expressing their ideas directly. The essay is also, of course, the essential vehicle for testing academic subjects at Advanced level. At this level, as practised by people like you, it is a formal exercise, with relatively rigid conventions. The purpose of this chapter is to explore the conventions and offer advice on essay preparation.

Let us begin, then, with some general approaches to preparation for advanced English discussion essay writing. A study of past examination papers over the previous few years will give you a good idea of the kinds of topics favoured by the examination board. You will probably find that most of the issues covered in this book feature in past examination papers. During your course you will almost certainly be involved in class discussions or debates on the issues, and jotting down ideas which interest you from these sessions is a start. But the material contained in the book is obviously not intended to provide the last word on any topic. To be adequately informed you must read further into the topic before the discussion takes place, and each chapter contains suggestions for preparatory reading.

Early on in your course it would be advisable to make a list of the most important issues which recur in past examination essay questions. This should guide your reading. It is not enough, of course, if you are preparing for an examination which includes questions requiring analysis of current issues, simply to learn about the topics covered in this book. The examination paper you eventually sit may include none of them. Wider reading is therefore essential. A quality Sunday newspaper is a valuable source of information, and periodicals and good daily papers can also be useful. Simply *reading* informed analysis is bound to develop your own ideas and understanding, but newspapers and magazines are by nature ephemeral; before they reach the waste bin you are likely to have forgotten the details. If you cut out and keep useful articles and collect them, perhaps in the form of a scrapbook, then you will be able to *learn* some of their contents and to refer back to them as you would to books. You could draw up a list of 20 or more themes and make a collection of pieces relating to each.

If you follow this advice, you should find at least one question on your examination paper about which you have prepared some material. But there is no guarantee. It is quite possible that none of the topics you have researched will appear in any form at all on your final examination paper. Will it matter? It may, or it may not. You cannot be expected to have a specialist knowledge of any subject area on the language essay paper, so a carefully thought out argument, with only a few 'hard' facts to back it up, can form a perfectly adequate essay. Much depends on whether you have thought about the issue on which you choose to write before you start writing. Working out your ideas as you go along almost inevitably results in a laboured and unconvincing essay. Thus, breadth of reading and thinking is the only certain safeguard in examinations which are as unpredictable as general English essay papers.

Planning and writing a discussion essay

Let's look at a hypothetical situation. You are faced with an examination paper which contains no topic on which you are specifically prepared. You therefore choose the question with which you feel most comfortable. Let us imagine that the title you have chosen is: ' "Cars are not a blessing but a curse!" What are your views?' Let's now go back a little to fundamentals.

You will almost certainly have been told to make notes and a plan before beginning an English essay. The same principle applies to more advanced essay work. But if you have only got an hour, or less, for an essay, you can't devote much of it to detailed planning. The 'continuous writing' question in the AEB English examination allows an hour and a half for preparing and writing, however, so you can afford to spend up to 20 minutes on planning. The examiner will expect to see a set of notes.

How you set about planning your essay is obviously a personal matter. The simplest and probably the most effective approach for most people is to just start thinking about the subject, and jot down ideas as they come into your mind. They may or may not follow a logical pattern of development, but at the initial planning stage it does not matter. An overall approach to the topic will probably occur to you after a few minutes, and the more-or-less random notes can be organised into a paragraph scheme, once you have worked out a sufficient range of ideas. Some people seem to be able to write well-balanced and logically-developed essays off the top of their heads, but for the majority, detailed planning makes a crucial difference.

Specimen answer   Here is an example of an essay planned and written in an hour and a half. You should perhaps be warned that the viewpoint it adopts is deliberately provocative!

'Cars are not a blessing but a curse!' What are your views?

Random notes

2 Convenience – buses take longer in and between towns
         – annoyance of using buses when car breaks down
2 Reorganised public transport system
3 Using up world's scarce oil
3 Need to do without petrol-driven car if oil gives out
3 Noise pollution
3 Greenhouse Effect
3 Ozone layer
4 Accidents – major cause of death
         – drain on Health Service
         – danger to cyclists/puts people off cycling
5 Garage bills and other costs
4 Motorways – pollution of environment
         – destroy countryside
3 Air pollution – carbon monoxide, especially Tokyo and Los Angeles
4 Destruction of towns – flyovers and bypasses
         – motorways go right into cities
1 Intro. – origins of car
         – are cars a blessing?
4 Effects on people – adds to isolation
         – stress: traffic jams/rushing through traffic
5 Conclusion: main advantage – speed and convenience
         could cars be done away with?
         effect on unemployment

Plan

1 Intro – historical perspective
2 Advantages: convenience → reorganisation of transport system
3 Disadvantages: pollution and depletion of resources
4 Disadvantages: destructive effect on people and places
5 Conclusion: cost and summing up

Essay

In 1885 a German, Carl Benz, produced the first petrol-driven vehicle, which proved to be the forerunner of the modern car. Few people in those days realised what a monster had been spawned. If they had foreseen the extent to which the automobile has come to dominate life in the Western world a century later, would they have looked on Herr Benz's achievement with approval?

To many people at the end of the twentieth century, a car has come to seem an indispensable part of daily life. The extent to which I myself have become dependent on my car is highlighted whenever it breaks down and I have to use buses. By the time I have walked to the bus stop, which is some distance from my house, and waited for twenty minutes in the pouring rain for a bus which leaves me with a twenty-minute walk the other end, the car does indeed seem a blessing. In a town like Bournemouth, the public transport system is so run-down that cars tend to be the only comfortable and efficient mode of travel. Does this have to be the case?

Many people feel that the days of the car are numbered, that the world's reserves of oil will be exhausted within a generation, and the petrol-driven car will have to be phased off the roads. What will happen then? The answer which many have suggested, a full-scale reorganisation of the public transport system, shows that the car is not necessarily such an indispensable asset as we tend to assume. If everyone used buses instead of cars, then public transport could be run efficiently, with a regular, rapid network of routes in every town and city in the country, and with no traffic jams! There could be express buses, stopping only at major points along the route, even within cities. However, cars are fast and efficient, except in rush hours, so what, apart from slowing down the depletion of oil reserves, would mankind gain from the loss of the motor car? Is it really a curse?

You have only to travel to Tokyo or Los Angeles to realise the appalling effects of cars on the environment. Traffic police in Tokyo have to wear masks and carry oxygen, or they would collapse because the air is so polluted with carbon monoxide from cars. Cars produce other, more insidious types of pollution. Perhaps the most deadly threat facing mankind is the global warming resulting from the Greenhouse Effect and the destruction of the ozone layer. Cars are considered by scientists to be the major contributors to this potential catastrophe. On a less cataclysmic scale, noise pollution, caused by the ceaseless roar of engines and honking of horns, is a further cause of stress in major cities. Actual death from these causes at the moment, however, is rare. The car is, nevertheless, a major killer.

One of the principal causes of premature death in the Western world is from car accidents. Thousands of people are killed on the roads every year in Britain. Thousands more are injured and maimed, which results not only in indescribable suffering, but also in a serious drain on the resources of the National Health Service, with precious space in hospital wards taken up, for months or years, by the car's victims. Not only human life is destroyed by the ubiquitous car. Towns and cities are ruthlessly knocked about to build flyovers and bypasses which destroy the character of our urban areas; motorways destroy the peace and beauty of the countryside.

Clearly the car has come to dominate human life to an unhealthy extent. Can the monster be killed off, without too much pain? Car workers will say 'no'. Unemployment would soar if the motor industry folded up. But is the saving of jobs a strong enough reason for the destruction of human life and the environment? With an efficient public transport system, the only real blessings of the car – speed and convenience – would be rendered insignificant, and the death of the private car would make the world altogether safer and less stressful.

Technical analysis of the specimen answer

This would gain a high grade as a general English language essay, despite the fact that, as you can see, it contains little 'hard' factual information. One of its advantages, of course, is that it contains no errors of spelling, punctuation or grammar! Perfection in the essentials of written English is not expected, even for an *A* grade at A level, but an examiner will not give an essay a top grade without a high level of formal accuracy, as the examiners' marking scheme at the end of this chapter shows. However, our concern is with content and the presentation of ideas. Let's analyse the content.

How many 'hard' facts does the essay actually contain? The opening sentence presents precise historical detail, and the argument of paragraph 4 is backed up by references to problems in particular cities. Are even these facts absolutely necessary? The introductory reference to 'the first petrol-driven vehicle' gets the essay off to a stylish start, but has no particular value as information. What about the references to Tokyo and Los Angeles in paragraph 4? If you knew generally about the problems of atmospheric pollution, but could not give any specific details, would the argument be weakened? Such facts certainly add colour and an air of authority to the arguments, but the points could be made without them.

The essential requirement is to have thought about the issues themselves. Paragraph 5, in fact, conspicuously fails to provide any precise facts and figures. The vague 'thousands' is not particularly convincing; exact figures would add potency to the argument. But the analysis is still valid, despite the vagueness in the details.

The one crucial feature of any successful discussion essay is a coherent argument, and for this, obviously enough, you must have a definite viewpoint. The key idea of this essay is developed in paragraph 3: it does not have to be stated immediately. A careful build-up to the central argument is always more effective than a bald statement of attitude at the beginning, which tends in any case to pre-empt the argument. You will, what is more, be expected to show that you realise that there are two sides to any argument, and at least passing reference to the opposing point of view is essential.

Paragraph 2, the first main paragraph after the brief introduction, develops one of the major arguments *in favour* of private cars. It leads, in the last sentence, directly into the central argument about the reorganisation of public transport. Thereafter, the essay concentrates on arguments against the use of private cars. There is nothing wrong with such heavy weighting of your argument. In fact, one common weakness of discussion essays is a lack of direction, presenting first one side of the case, then the other, and leading nowhere. Showing that you understand the opposition's case does not mean that you have to be unbiased, unless the question specifically asks you to 'discuss arguments for *and* against' something. Careful organisation of your ideas into paragraphs, however, is essential. Let's look in more detail at the planning of essays.

If you look at the random notes for the essay above, you will notice numbers before each point. The numbers are written in *after* the paragraph plan has been worked out, and refer to the paragraph into which each point will fit. This is simply a convenient way of picking out the ideas which are relevant to a particular paragraph, swiftly working out the order in which they are to be used, and checking that you have not missed any points. You may find the technique useful if you have not tried it before.

As stated earlier, the actual paragraph plan will probably not fit into place in your mind until after you have started making random notes. Similarly, the plan may well be modified when you actually begin writing your essay. There is no need at all to feel that you *must* follow your plan. It is, after all, for your benefit. If you look again at the essay, you will notice that it does not even contain the same number of paragraphs as the plan indicates. What in fact occurred when the essay was being written was that the argument about the reorganisation of public transport assumed a greater importance after the essay had been started than had been envisaged at the planning stage, and instead of developing directly from the discussion of the advantages of private motorised transport, it earned a paragraph for itself. If the original paragraph scheme had been followed, paragraph 2 would have been twice as long as others, which is, in any case, structurally unsatisfactory. New ideas will always come to you when you start writing, and as long as they are directly relevant to the paragraph on which you are working, they can be accommodated perfectly easily. If they are not immediately relevant, they can be added to the random notes and incorporated where they do fit in.

If you do think of new ideas as you go along, however, you may come up against the eternal bugbear of examinations – time. Trying to develop every idea that occurs to you can result in you running out of time before you have managed to follow through your prepared structure properly. Therefore, it is essential to *pace* yourself. Good ideas may have to be discarded if time is getting short; other ideas, which you would like to develop, may have to be stated much more briefly than they might be. The final sentence of paragraph 5, for instance, glosses very briefly over two ideas which could have been embellished and made much more compelling with examples. However, this would have been at the expense of an adequate conclusion, which is an essential requirement of a properly constructed essay.

Not all the random notes are included in the essay. The last but one of the points in the random notes list, about individual isolation and stress caused by queues of cars with single occupants, was left out. The ideas are just as valid as many that *are* included, and might have been illustrated interestingly by referring, for instance, to a Ray Bradbury science-fiction story called *The Pedestrian* about a time in the near future when pedestrians in the Western world are almost unknown and everybody uses cars. But it would have taken too long to explain the point of the story. The reference to bicycles is also missing. When ideas are flowing freely, self-discipline is sometimes required! No illustration of a single idea should, in any case, take up too much space, and more crucially, you should *never* include ideas just because you have thought of them. Your essay must have direction, and every idea must be plainly relevant to the theme of the paragraph in which it appears.

So, although there is no need to adhere rigidly to your original plan, it should provide a clear overall structure for your essay, and a reasonably full set of random notes to refer back to will almost certainly make the writing of the essay much easier. As well as achieving coherence within paragraphs, you should try to dovetail neatly from one paragraph to the next. If you look once more at the essay, you will notice that the first three paragraphs all end with a question. As long as it is not overused, this can be a reasonably simple and effective technique by which to achieve links between paragraphs. The final sentence of paragraph 4 also leads, by a statement this time, directly into the theme of paragraph 5. Thus the argument develops with an air of naturalness and inevitability. The conclusion, though quite short, is firmly stated; this too is essential. It must also, however, like the introduction, be interesting, which a bald statement of opinion, or a brief rehash of some of the earlier arguments would not. Before the final statement of opinion in this essay, reference is made to an argument against the abolition of private cars, which was not mentioned earlier. There is no reason why you should not include new material in your concluding paragraph, provided it does not obscure the conclusion itself.

Additional points

There are a number of general questions which often arise with reference to language discussion essay writing. Let us consider some important ones.

- Should you refer to yourself and your own experience in a formal discussion essay?

If you look back at the specimen essay, you will notice that paragraph 2 draws entirely on personal experience to elaborate the point. As long as you do not fall into the classic logical flaw of arguing from the particular to the general (see 'Further Advice on Writing: Illogical argument in essays', page 175), a personal anecdote can add interest and variety to an essay. The examiners are, in fact, instructed to look for a 'personal voice', which inevitably involves the use of the pronoun 'I'.

- Will it jeopardise your chances if you adopt an unconventional viewpoint which the examiner disagrees with?

The answer to this question is again illustrated by the essay. Most people, examiners included, would probably disagree with its viewpoint. Perhaps the writer was even playing devil's advocate to some extent, for the sake of producing an interesting discussion! This would certainly not prevent the essay from gaining a high grade. The examiner is not looking for the 'right' answer, but for clarity of expression, of ideas and of organisation, and these are the qualities you must strive to develop as you progress through your course.

- Do the introduction and conclusion need to be the same length as the other paragraphs?

The short answer to this is 'no'. The main purpose of the introduction is to define the terms of the question, if necessary, and to explain the approach you are taking to it. It only needs to be a few lines long. The same applies to the conclusion, the purpose of which is to round off your argument with a final, definitive statement. Much time can be lost trying and failing to make an impressive start to an essay. It is far more important to get quickly into the 'body' of the essay, after a short introduction, for this is the core of the essay, on which the quality of your thinking and essay structuring can be demonstrated.

- How important is spelling and punctuation?

The answer to this is 'very'. The marking scheme which follows indicates the stress placed on formal accuracy of expression in the discussion essay, and the same applies to continuous writing exercises generally. You must take positive steps to sort out any difficulties you are experiencing with spelling, punctuation and sentence structure. To quote from the 1995 AEB English Examiners' Report: 'poor expression and grammatical uncertainty restrict candidates to the lower mark bands, whatever the quality of their ideas and however creatively they can write' (see 'Further Advice on Writing: preparing for the exam', page 215).

Examiners' marking scheme for the discussion essay

To understand how your discussion essay would actually be marked, if you chose to do one in the exam, here is the AEB English marking scheme for the discussion essay. The first two mark bands both approximate to a grade A, the next five reflect the standards necessary to gain grades B to N, and the last three may be considered to reflect work which would be ungraded.

Exploratory, Discursive and Factual Writing

27–30: The highest quality of writing in this category which can be expected to be produced in examination conditions.

24–26: Very good work, consciously crafted, with a sense of personal style. Vocabulary and expression accurate, well-controlled, with variety and range. Material and argument organised to provide logical and interesting exposition. Content will have been carefully selected, and will be entirely relevant to the demands of the question and the approach chosen by the candidate. It is unlikely that there will be many technical errors in work at this level.

21–23: Good work, revealing some perception, cogency or balance of argument, based on a range of appropriate information. Effective writing with generally controlled accuracy of expression and very few mechanical flaws. Some variety in vocabulary and syntax; effective paragraphing; overall structure controlled.

18–20: Sound work, showing a willingness to develop a point of view, attempting discussion, analysis or exploration based on relevant information. Overall control of expression; evidence of understanding of paragraphing, sentence structure, spelling and punctuation. Appropriate vocabulary; few mechanical flaws.

15–17: Sensible cover of the major aspects of the topic, but possibly some uncertainty about shape, form or ideas. Understanding and relevant treatment, but without sophistication either of thinking or expression. Apt information and vocabulary. Expression may be lacking in flexibility and precision, but adequately handled. There may be some mechanical flaws but no repeated gross error.

12–14: Acceptable understanding and straightforward treatment, with an awareness of structure, if an inability to handle it successfully. There may be a number of mechanical flaws and occasional gross error, but on the whole the work demonstrates an underlying ability to use syntax, spelling and punctuation correctly. Some appropriate information; vocabulary may be limited.

9–11: Basic response with some relevance, though work in this bracket is likely to vary in consistency, focus and control of expression, and may be marred by gross error. There are likely to be flaws in writing skills, characterised by problems with syntax, spelling and punctuation. The work can be identified as a serious attempt to respond to the task and to construct a piece of writing which conveys some ideas and uses relevant, if limited, information.

6–8: Uncertain grasp and lack of ability to organise material effectively. There may be irrelevance and/or repetition, limitations in basic writing skills and gross error. Argument and factual material may be appropriate but presented poorly.

3–5: Weak work, incoherent, very poorly expressed. There may be an attempt to write at some length, but totally without control.

0–2: Chaotic, ill-planned, totally incoherent writing.

The following note to examiners is appended to the marking scheme, explaining the distinction between 'gross error' and 'mechanical flaw':

'Gross error' refers to inability to structure sentences, lack of subject–verb agreement, persistent spelling errors, especially of homonyms and basic words (their/there/they're, where/were), lack of understanding of how or where to use common punctuation marks and apostrophes. Be alert to the candidate whose writing generally proves that the basic structures are understood and in place, but who makes an occasional slip. This should not be regarded as *gross error* but as *mechanical flaw*.

A further note to examiners explains how the overall mark for Paper 1 (continuous writing and summary skills) is arrived at:

This paper is marked out of 50, and the marks are scaled up by computer. In effect, every mark either awarded or withheld is worth two marks when the final totals are decided.

Further advice on writing: varieties of essay question

When you are given seven or eight titles to choose from for a lengthy piece of continuous writing in exam conditions, making the right choice can be a problem in itself. You need to feel confident that you can write for an hour and a half on a subject.

There are five types of prose writing question which might feature on your exam paper: discussion, narrative, personal, factual and descriptive, plus a possible poetry-writing option. The second of these is dealt with in detail in the next chapter. The third, the personal essay, is obviously one in which you focus your writing on personal experience, analysing your feelings about the topic, based on that experience. A factual essay is informative in content; the subject is considered from various angles, and information and reflections on each are offered. A descriptive essay is simply a long physical description or series of descriptions. The poetry option is dealt with in the 'Further advice on writing' section at the end of Chapter 2.

Most titles are likely to offer no alternative to the formal discussion essay. Titles which ask you to 'discuss' or 'consider' or 'argue/present a case for or against' something, or are posed in the form of a question on some issue, require arguments. It is with this type of question that this book is primarily concerned.

On the other hand, you may find that the title is more open, and allows for more than one type of approach. Titles such as 'The right to strike' or 'In defence of discipline and order' or 'The problems posed by hunger strikes', whilst most obviously encouraging discussion essays, could also be treated as titles for stories. Titles which consist simply of a word or short phrase, like 'Hope', 'Paradise', 'Silence', 'Swimming against the current' or 'The river', could be treated in a variety of ways. Each of them could be used as the title of a short story. 'Hope', 'Paradise', 'Silence' and 'Swimming against the current' could also be treated as personal essays, either focusing on one particular episode in your life, or offering a more general analysis of your experiences in relation to the topic. 'Paradise' could also be treated as a factual essay, in which you explain different people's or cultures' visions of paradise. 'The river' could be treated as a factual or descriptive as well as a narrative title. One particular river, or several, could be dealt with factually.

The main danger with the personal essay is triviality. If the most vivid experiences of 'Hope' that you can think of, for instance, are on the level of hoping to pass an examination or win a prize, you are unlikely to produce a very interesting or thoughtful personal essay. You must be able to convey a sense of genuine personal involvement in the experiences you are relating, for a personal essay to be successful. Personal and narrative essays, of course, are often indistinguishable, and a story about a single personal experience which is relevant to the title can make a very effective answer.

The danger with factual essays is dullness. Essays which begin: 'There are many types of . . .' and which go on to explain laboriously how 'the river' can be used for leisure, sport, transportation and so on, are almost invariably turgid. Extended descriptive essays tend to ramble and run out of steam, and are probably best avoided unless you have a real flair for this kind of writing.

2 Narrative Writing

If the choice of titles for continuous writing contains a narrative option, this can be a good alternative to the conventional essay for students with a flair for creative writing and a vivid imagination. In examinations which contain both essay and story questions, the highest marks are often gained by those who choose to write a story. However, there tend to be more pitfalls in narrative than in essay writing, and the lowest marks also tend to be scored by story writers.

Before we look at some of the common ingredients of successful narrative writing, then, we shall look at some of the dangers of choosing the story option.

Pitfalls of narrative writing

Probably the main reason why students score particularly badly when they attempt a story is that there is a tendency to treat it as a 'soft option'. You don't have to *know* anything to write a story! A student who decides that he or she does not have enough ideas or information about a discussion or personal essay topic, and chooses the story out of desperation, has every chance of failure. Rambling and incoherent stories score very low marks.

A story *has* to capture the reader's interest and appeal to his or her imagination from the start. It has, therefore, to have a structure: it must develop towards some kind of coherent climax. Probably the major pitfall of examination story writing is the failure to map out the storyline in your mind before you start writing. If you think the story out as you go along, without knowing how the plot is going to unfold and how the story is going to end, you are likely to end up with a weak and shapeless narrative.

The most damaging pitfall of all is the failure to make clear the relevance of the narrative to the question. The title theme *must* be an integral part of the story, and must not just be loosely fitted in somewhere. However effective a story may be otherwise, if the reader cannot work out fairly early on how it relates to the title, it will fail badly.

Even if the story is well thought out and interesting, there is another pitfall which is peculiar to narrative writing. The time limitation of the examination is much more of a potential problem with narrative than with any other kind of writing. If a story is developing effectively and convincingly, you cannot simply 'wind it up' in the last ten minutes if you find yourself running out of time. A rushed ending can be disastrous in a story, and pacing yourself is therefore especially important. Too much incidental detail can slow the story down fatally. Stories do tend to need time to unfold, and an examination room is not the ideal setting for an exercise of the creative imagination.

Dullness is, of course, a fatal flaw in a narrative piece. You cannot hope to gain a high mark if your storyline, characters and descriptions fail to capture the reader's interest. For example, a simple story, based on a personal experience which is of no particular intrinsic interest, with a straightforward linear structure and characters who are impossible to visualise or relate to, and in which the ending is an anticlimax, is likely to be marked down more than a pedestrian answer to a discussion topic. Conversely, an unconvincing adventure story, packed with detail, but with little structure, with cardboard characters and a contrived ending, is likely to score even fewer marks.

Nevertheless, if you find you have a good idea for a story when you read through the titles in the examination, and you possess some flair for creative writing, the story can be an excellent choice.

An example of a short story

Let us look at a story, written in 1988 by a 17-year-old college student, Kim Carty. It is a fine example of how to make even the most bizarre story realistic and believable, even though the ending may not be to everyone's taste.

Three Little Piggies

Andrea flopped down, relieved, into a welcoming armchair. The Wilsons had just left and now she was all alone, save for the two sleeping children upstairs. She smiled secretly to herself as she pictured Helen Wilson, still looking fabulous at 38, fussing with her hair in the hallway mirror.

'The children are already asleep, so help yourself to anything you want to eat,' Helen said, trying to find her lipstick.

'Hurry along Helen!' Mr Wilson called, as he started up the engine.

'How do I look?' Helen asked, turning to face Andrea.

'You look wonderful,' Andrea replied.

Helen smiled thankfully. 'Right, where's my coat?'

'Here,' Andrea answered, laughing. Mr Wilson sounded his horn in annoyance.

'Better go. Oh, by the way, I've left a number by the phone upstairs and in the lounge in case you get into any difficulties.'

Andrea smiled and nodded. She had heard these instructions at least a thousand times!

'We should be back at half-past-one,' Helen confirmed, as she stepped out into the cold night.

'Have a good time,' Andrea called. She watched silently as the large estate car pulled away. Turning around, she entered the house, shutting the huge oak door.

Stepping out of her high red shoes, she padded into the kitchen. It took her a good ten minutes to find the jar of coffee. As usual, it was in the place she was least expecting. Armed with a mug of steaming coffee and a packet of Hob-nobs, she headed towards the lounge, switching off the light with some difficulty.

The kitchen was immediately shrouded in darkness. Outside, the moon shone bright and clear, sending ominous shadows dancing across the driveway. No one, including Andrea, noticed the enormous, slightly stooped figure of a man. Nor did they notice him moving slowly towards the house, holding something large, which gleamed in the moonlight.

She sat, relaxed by the warmth of the fire, sipping her drink. For some reason she began to feel incredibly tired.

No, she thought, she must not give in to the welcoming, slowly enclosing blackness, she must . . . The sudden shrill ring of the phone jolted her to her senses.

Damn it! she thought, as she pulled herself up to answer it. 'Hello,' she answered, hoping it was a wrong number. The phone went dead.

'How funny!' she thought, as she replaced the receiver. She no longer felt like sleeping; instead she reached for the remote control and switched on the television. The room seemed to come to life, and feel more cheery. This made her feel safe and not quite so alone.

Changing channels, she settled down to watch a film, starring Kirk Douglas. It was not even ten minutes before the phone rang again. Placing down her mug, she answered the phone.

'Hello. This is five-seven-four-double-two . . .'

The sudden insane laugh made her nearly drop the phone.

'Who is this?' she asked, startled and annoyed.

'There were three little piggies. Oh what fun! Two were disembowelled, then there was one.'

The voice, cracking in places, sounded evil and menacing. Again the insane and hysterical laughing commenced.

'Go to hell!' Andrea yelled, slamming down the receiver. She searched frantically for her cigarettes. The calls had made her nervous and she desperately needed a cigarette to calm her down.

The slow entry of nicotine in her lungs helped to soothe her fraught nerves.

Luckily, the children had not been awoken by the phone or her raised voice. How strange! she thought. Feeling a sudden boldness, she strode towards the kitchen in order to make herself another coffee. The fearful ring stopped her dead in her tracks. It was almost a mixture of instinct and habit now which made her raise the receiver.

This time she did not recite the number or say hello; instead she listened as the slow, gruff voice commenced. 'I know you're alone, and I'm gonna get you! You hear? Get you, get y . . .'. She slammed the hand set down before he had time to finish. Who the hell was it? she thought. A drunkard? A pervert? Picking the receiver up again she dialled the operator. The voice sounded distant but reassuring.

'Hello, can I help you?'

'Yes,' Andrea answered. Her body heaved, and she was close to tears. 'Could you trace an outside call for me? The number is five-seven-four-two-two-five.'

'Are you alright?' the lady asked, concerned.

'I'm fine. It's just a drunk keeps ringing me up and making threats,' Andrea replied.

'I see. If he rings again keep him talking. This will enable me to trace the call quickly. I'll ring you back if there are any results.'

Feeling relieved, Andrea settled back into the chair and began watching the film. The phone came to life almost immediately. Panic gripped her as she gingerly reached towards the phone. The man's voice sounded frightful to her ears.

'There was one little piggy, oh what fun!

Her throat was slit, then there was none.'

'You're nothing but a pervert, a damn pervert!' she screamed, as she let the receiver fall back into place.

Lighting up a cigarette, she paced the room, watching the phone. Suddenly it came alive, filling the room and her ears with its persistent call for attention.

She grabbed the hand-set ready to listen, again, to the abuse.

'Listen quickly.' The operator's voice sounded disturbing.

'Tell me,' the operator continued, 'do you have another phone in the house?' Andrea, confused, could not think for a minute.

'Why yes, there's a phone upstairs with the children.' Her voice was awkward and slow.

'Whoever has been calling you has been using the phone upstairs. For heaven's sake, get out quickly!'

The phone went dead. Sobbing, she stumbled towards the door. Opening it, she ran quickly towards the stairs and front door.

The sight which met her bulging eyes sent her vomiting into the corner. On the middle part of the stairs stood a huge and grotesque-looking man. His eyes, filled with mad frenzy, bore down on her. His clothes and face were drenched in blood, and in his right hand he held a blood-spattered chopper. It was what the man held in his left hand that made her faint. It steamed slowly, giving off a hot and sickly smell. The children, or what was left of them, were lying at the top of the stairs. They had been disembowelled and their insides completely 'cleaned' out. Slowly he let the warm, soft, glistening entrail slip from his hand as he made his way towards Andrea.

Analysis of 'Three Little Piggies'

One of the interesting features of this story is that, although the climax is dramatic and even lurid in the extreme, the opening is extremely leisurely and uneventful. This contrast goes a long way towards explaining the success of the story. The simple domestic details of the opening create a sense of normality and everyday reality to which almost anyone could relate. When the phone starts ringing and the panic begins, the reader believes completely in the character and situation, and the steady build-up towards the ghastly climax is entirely convincing.

The dialogue at the beginning of the story is, in fact, a flashback to what happened just before the story opened. It could hardly be less dramatic. What it does is to establish a realistic, utterly ordinary domestic situation, and an impression of both the central character, Andrea, and the children's parents. Natural dialogue such as this is far more effective in conveying a sense of character than statements telling us *about* the characters. Tiny details, such as the line: 'Mr Wilson sounded his horn in annoyance', add greatly to the sense of everyday reality and the illusion that we are reading about real people. The dialogue serves another important function: it enables us to share Andrea's impressions of the Wilsons, and thus we are able to identify more easily with her. The ability to create identification with and concern for a story's central character is a crucial aspect of the story-teller's art. It might be a useful exercise to try rewriting the second paragraph of the story without using any dialogue, and compare the two versions.

Once the Wilsons have left, a series of very precise details is given of Andrea preparing to settle down for the evening. They do nothing in particular to advance the plot, but are of great importance in increasing our identification with the character. Tiny details like her search for the coffee, and her choice of Hob-nobs, make her seem entirely believable. These are things with which everyone can identify. Similarly, her sudden sleepiness just before the phone rings for the first time, and her switching of the channels afterwards, and selecting a Kirk Douglas film, all help us to visualise the situation. It is surprising how much difference even the simplest use of precise details, such as the mention of Kirk Douglas, makes to the aura of realism in a story. You could perhaps find other examples, and try reading the passages in which they feature, with the details left out to show the difference.

Between the description of Andrea switching off the light and of her relaxing in front of the fire, a paragraph is included which suddenly changes the nature of the story, with the approach towards the house of the shadowy figure with the gleaming implement. From this point on, the story becomes one of suspense. We know something awful is going to happen to Andrea, and she does not. It might be interesting to consider whether the introduction of suspense at this point is successful: might the story have had even more impact if surprise had been employed instead of suspense, so that we have no more idea than Andrea that there is an intruder?

Once the first 'three little piggies' message has been given, the pace of the story picks up considerably, and the events move rapidly towards the climax. It is even more important now to use convincing details of everyday life, to prevent a sense of unreality creeping in. The writer does this through the description, for instance, of Andrea's frantic search for her cigarettes after the first horrible shock, followed by the sentence: 'The slow entry of nicotine in her lungs helped to soothe her fraught nerves.' This sentence is in fact a complete paragraph. It is worth noting the effect of the paragraphing here. By placing this sentence apart, Kim Carty has actually captured a sense of the soothing, slowing-down effect of the nicotine. In narrative writing, the rules of paragraphing which were analysed in Chapter 1 do not apply. In a story, paragraphing can be used purely for effect, as this one-sentence paragraph illustrates.

Andrea's reactions to the insane telephone calls are once again entirely believable; we can identify completely with her, in her panic and anger. The excitement builds up rapidly, and the syntax adds to the sense of tension: just before the final, climactic paragraph, a sequence of three short, dramatic sentences vividly captures the panic and desperation of the terrified girl.

Then comes the climax. We may well feel that the grotesquerie is gratuitous, but we cannot feel that the ending is in any way contrived; the story has been building up inexorably towards some sort of horrific culmination, however distasteful we may find it.

A final comment on the style of the story. It is written in a very natural way, but this does not mean that the words are not chosen with care and conscious effect. A sentence near the beginning will illustrate this: 'Stepping out of her high red shoes, she padded into the kitchen.' From this description we can picture exactly not only what she was wearing but also how she walked; it is the choice of precise verbs in this case which creates the sense impression. It might be worth reading through the story again and picking out phrases which capture a sense of people, atmosphere and incident particularly vividly.

One final, general point. The inspiration for this story was the film, *The Babysitter*, which has a similar story-line. There is absolutely nothing wrong with such mild plagiarism. You will not be marked on the basis of your story being entirely original; what is being tested is your ability to write an interesting story, convincingly and well.

Narrative writing technique

Let us now attempt some generalisations about narrative writing. Before we do so, however, it must be made clear that this is not an attempt to lay down rules. To talk of rules for short-story writing is, in a sense, absurd. Truly creative writing cannot be circumscribed by convention. The only meaningful test of the success or otherwise of a piece of narrative writing is whether or not it *works*; if it arouses and sustains the interest of the reader, then it has succeeded. A story can work brilliantly with or without dialogue, with or without detailed setting and characterisation, and so on. The vogue towards the end of the 1980s for 50-word mini-sagas clearly illustrated the fact that none of the conventional features of narrative writing are actually necessary for stories to be effective.

However, it is possible to talk of features or techniques which are *commonly* found in successful short stories, and which *tend* to add interest and effectiveness to narrative writing. We will look at the most important of these techniques.

An arresting start

A lengthy introductory explanation of the situation and the main characters in the story is generally a poor way to start. The opening of a story is more likely to capture the reader's interest if it is arresting.

If the story begins with an actual incident, rather than an explanation, the reader is involved from the start. A passage of dialogue inevitably creates immediacy, and can make an effective opening. Another generally effective technique is to open with an incident some way into the actual story, followed by an explanation of how the situation arose and who the characters are, possibly dealt with through flashbacks as the story unfolds.

Here is a very basic example of a story opening which is immediately arresting. These are the opening few lines of a story called *The Five-Forty-Eight* by John Cheever:

When Blake stepped out of the elevator, he saw her. A few people, mostly men waiting for girls, stood in the lobby watching the elevator doors. She was among them. As he saw her, her face took on a look of such loathing and purpose that he realised she had been waiting for him.

The story is immediately under way: we want to read on!

A powerful climax

The focal point of most successful stories is the climax, towards which everything has been leading. It normally comes close to the end of the story, and is followed by a brief 'dénouement' in which the loose ends are tied up. A well-constructed story usually has a single climax, which clearly stands out as the major incident. Too many dramatic events earlier in the story can, in fact, reduce the impact of the climax, and damage the story. There is certainly no need to write complicated plots with a wealth of incident; a simple storyline, with a powerful climax, can make a perfectly effective story. The essential thing to avoid is making it too obvious how the story is going to end. If the climax is too predictable, it becomes an anticlimax.

A popular narrative technique is that of the final, unexpected 'twist' at the very end of the story. The technique was developed to the point of becoming a formula by the American comic story writer O. Henry, and tends nowadays to be somewhat derided. However, a skilfully handled 'twist' can create a very memorable ending.

The ultimate expression of this technique is to leave the 'twist' or revelation until the very last sentence. A good illustration of the technique at its most gruesomely dramatic is *The Boarded Window*, a short story by the late 19th-century American writer, Ambrose Bierce. A brief summary of the story is needed for the twist to be appreciated:

The wife of an American frontiersman of the early 19th century has just died of a fever. The couple had lived contentedly in a lonely cabin in the woods, and the man is described preparing his wife's body for burial. His task finally completed, he lays the body out on the kitchen table and falls asleep, exhausted, as a long wailing sound is heard in the woods surrounding the cabin. He awakes, hours later, in pitch darkness, as the table, on which he is slumped, shakes, and he hears the sound of bare feet on the floor. A heavy body seems to be hurled against the table, which seems to be empty. The man grabs his rifle and fires randomly into the darkness. This is how the story ends:

By the flash which lit up the room with a vivid illumination, he saw an enormous panther dragging the dead woman towards the window, its teeth fixed in her throat! Then there was darkness blacker than before, and silence; and when he returned to consciousness the sun was high and the wood was vocal with songs of birds.

The body lay near the window where the beast had left it when frightened away by the flash and report of the rifle. The clothing was deranged, the long hair in disorder, the limbs lay anyhow. From the throat, dreadfully lacerated, had issued a pool of blood not yet entirely coagulated. The ribbon with which he had bound the wrists was broken; the hands were tightly clenched. Between the teeth was a fragment of the animal's ear.

Bringing people and places to life

A more-or-less essential feature of effective narrative writing is the ability to capture the essence of a character or setting in a few words. If the reader cannot visualise characters and places, his or her interest in them is considerably lessened. Detailed descriptions are generally unnecessary, and excessive detail is likely merely to clog up the story. But one or two well-chosen phrases, creating a visual impression of the appearance of a person or place, generally increase the reader's involvement in the story considerably.

Here are two examples of how skilful writers can create a vivid picture of a character or setting in a few words.

In his story *A Little Cloud*, James Joyce introduces a character thus: 'Ignatius Gallaher took off his hat and displayed a large, closely cropped head. His face was heavy, pale and clean-shaven. His eyes, which were of bluish slate colour, relieved his unhealthy pallor and shone out plainly above the vivid orange tie he wore.'

Susan Hill, in *Ossie*, paints this word-picture of one of the story's settings: 'I was shocked by the gloomy, dingy house, and by his room at the top of it. There was a smell of sour milk, and the window looked onto a wall, so that he was obliged to keep the light on the whole time – a muddy, low-watt bulb. He had plenty of furniture – huge, dark oak furniture, cluttered into the small space. On the table was a brown suitcase and a woman's blonde, curly wig.'

We have an instant visual impression from these descriptions, which thus make the character and setting three-dimensional for us.

The use of dialogue

Perhaps the simplest way to bring an incident to life and create immediacy is by the use of dialogue. The way people talk gives strong character clues, and inventing conversations for your characters is a more effective way of conveying an impression of them than by definitive statements.

One of the cardinal rules of creative writing is 'showing, rather than telling'. Instead of simply making statements about people, situations and events, it is always more subtle and interesting to *reveal* them to the reader, by incident and dialogue.

One danger should be mentioned here, though. Dialogue is notoriously difficult to punctuate accurately. You should make sure that you check carefully how dialogue is punctuated before you use it in a story.

Choosing evocative words

In all forms of writing it is necessary to choose your words with care. This is particularly true of creative and narrative writing. Although adjectives should not be overworked – if every noun has an accompanying adjective the result is likely to be a feeling of artificiality and stiffness – well-chosen and colourful adjectives and adverbs can add greatly to the effectiveness of your writing. The use of imagery, especially of the figures of meaning and sound analysed in chapter 13, can enhance the vividness of your writing still further, though again, such techniques should not be overworked.

Narrative titles

a Intolerance.
b Hope.
c 'To travel hopefully is better than to arrive'.
d Write a short story designed for a volume of short stories entitled 'Suspense'.
e The River of Life.
f Leaving.
g Danger.

h Write a story involving a family, a foreigner, a boat, a horse and sunflowers.

i Write a fairy tale about growing up.

j Swimming against the current.

Examiners' marking scheme for narrative writing

Here is the AEB English marking scheme for Narrative. As with the marking scheme in the previous chapter, the first two mark bands can be roughly considered to represent grade A, the next five grades B to N, and the last three U (ungraded).

Narrative

27–30: The highest quality of writing in this category which can be expected to be produced in examination conditions.

24–26: Highly crafted. Content and form, vocabulary and style will have been deliberately selected and controlled. The reader's interest will be completely engaged in events, characters, description, story-line. Overall and internal structures will be successfully handled. The writing will be entirely appropriate for its audience. It is unlikely that there will be many technical errors in work at this level.

21–23: Well crafted. Very accurate writing, with a minimum of technical error. Original and interesting work, clearly aimed at its audience, which successfully holds the reader's attention. Form and style appropriate to the given task. Evidence of the writer's enthusiasm for and engagement with the writing task.

18–20: Carefully crafted. The writing has little technical or mechanical error; presentational aspects such as the layout of dialogue are confidently and correctly handled. Structure, material and approach appropriate to the task and the audience, but may not always be evenly sustained. Enjoyable.

15–17: Adequately crafted. The writing has clearly been structured to provide a recognisably sustained narrative, and the writer has the audience in mind. Some aspects, such as characterisation, handling of events, description, may not be entirely successful, but have been seriously attempted. The writer shows an awareness of the conventions of punctuating and presenting dialogue, though may not always do so correctly. There may be some mechanical flaws but no gross error.

12–14: Acceptably crafted. A straightforward, relevant approach, demonstrating an awareness of structure, appropriate vocabulary and content for audience. May lack originality, and be of limited interest, but a clear attempt to respond to the task in a sustained and controlled manner. There are likely to be a number of mechanical flaws and an occasional gross error.

9–11: Work in this band will demonstrate an attempt to respond relevantly, and show basic awareness of appropriate narrative structure and techniques. Audience awareness may be limited or poorly sustained. The writing may be naïve, derivative and/or banal. There are likely to be flaws in writing skills, characterised by problems with syntax, spelling, punctuation, and some gross error.

6–8: Work in this band is likely to be badly constructed, banal and lack any audience awareness. It will be characterised by poor spelling, punctuation and control of syntax.

Vocabulary will be impoverished. It may show a very limited awareness of the demands of the task. It is likely to be tedious to read.

3–5: A wholly unsuccessful attempt, lacking any apparent control, ideas or structure. It may appear mainly irrelevant to the set task. A serious, but flawed, attempt, should be in a higher band.

0–2: Chaotic, ill-planned, totally incoherent.

For an explanation of the distinction between mechanical flows and gross error, and of how the mark bands translate into grades, see pages 8 and 9.

Further advice on writing: writing a poem

The invitation to write a poem, as an alternative to writing a story, has become a fairly regular feature of the Continuous Writing exercise. A length of about 20 lines is sometimes suggested as a guideline. It can easily seem like a soft option. It is easy to write 20 lines of free verse or unmetrical rhyming verse, without worrying too much about presentation, in half the time allowed for the exercise. This often happens, and it results in extremely low marks. Before you even contemplate writing a poem in the exam, you would be well advised to take careful note of the AEB English marking scheme, and the 'additional guidance on the assessment of poetry' which is provided by the Board to help examiners decide on a mark for poetry, both of which are included at the end of this section. You would be inviting disaster if you decided to write a poem in the exam because it seemed easier than writing an essay or a prose narrative, without having previously practised writing poetry with the A-level criteria in mind. Poetry is assessed as rigorously as any other kind of writing. If the poem you write shows no signs of identifiable crafting, it will fail. The examiner will be looking for an accurately punctuated poem, with at least one initial draft, using specific techniques of writing which can be objectively judged as poetic. This does *not* necessarily mean that you *must* write a poem with a conventional metre and rhyme scheme. Free verse *is* acceptable, as are other contemporary verse forms, such as rap. What is not acceptable is a poem which shows no evidence of conscious crafting in the rhythmic flow of the lines, or a poem which uses rhyme but has no regular metrical pattern.

A couple of quotations from the poetry of Philip Larkin should help to clarify why rhyme must be accompanied by regular metre. The following extract is the first half of a poem from the *Whitsun Weddings* collection, and it seems at first to contradict what has just been said:

Self's the Man

Oh, no one can deny
That Arnold is less selfish than I.
He married a woman to stop her getting away
Now she's there all day,

And the money he gets for wasting his life on work
She takes as a perk
To pay for the kiddies' clobber and the drier
And the electric fire,

And when he finishes his supper
Planning to have a read at the evening paper
It's put a screw in this wall –
He has not time at all

With the nippers to wheel round the houses
And the hall to paint in his old trousers
And that letter to his mother
Saying 'Won't you come for the Summer.'

The poem is written in rhyming couplets, yet there is no attempt at metrical regularity. If a famous poet can publish poetry like this, why can't a student get away with it in an exam? The answer is in the nature of the poem. What is being portrayed in the excerpt? What kind of language is employed? How accurate are the rhymes? As you may have worked out by now, it is about a man who can't impose any control over his fairly chaotic life. The disjointed metre fits in with the consciously colloquial, unpoetic language and the slapdash rhyming ('supper' not quite rhyming with 'paper', 'houses' with 'trousers', 'mother' with 'summer'.) In other words, the lack of metrical control is deliberate. You can only write verse with no metrical crafting if you can convince the examiner that there is some deliberate purpose behind it.

This is a more typical example of Philip Larkin's rhyming verse, a complete poem this time, taken from the same collection.

Home Is So Sad

Home is so sad. It stays as it was left.
Shaped to the comfort of the last to go
As if to win them back. Instead, bereft
Of anyone to please, it withers so,
Having no heart to put aside the theft

And turn again to what it started as,
A joyous shot at how things ought to be
Long fallen wide. You can see how it was:
Look at the pictures and the cutlery.
The music in the piano stool. That vase.

The mood this time is whimsically melancholic, the language much more conventionally poetic, and the metrical pattern is completely controlled. Count the syllables in each line. As you should have noticed, the rhythm is as regular as the rhyme scheme. The poem is, in fact, written in iambic pentameters, the metre that Shakespeare used.

Here is the AEB marking scheme for poetry, and the 'additional guidance' that is issued with it. The meaning of the marks in terms of grades is explained on page 8.

Poetry

27–30: The highest quality of writing in this category which can be expected to be produced in examination conditions.

24–26: Highly crafted work. The writer will have selected a poetic form entirely appropriate to content, ideas, mood and tone, and employed a range of poetic techniques to produce work which is both original and shows a confident personal style. It will fully engage the reader's interest. It is unlikely that there will be many technical errors in work at this level.

21–23: Well crafted. Form and content carefully controlled, the poetic techniques employed are appropriate and interesting. A personal voice which engages the reader. Accurate writing, with a minimum of technical error. Evidence that vocabulary has been carefully chosen and punctuation applied purposefully.

18–20: Carefully crafted. This writing shows evidence that poetic techniques are understood and consciously employed but may not always be entirely controlled. Appropriate form, tone and vocabulary, thoughtfully punctuated. Enjoyable. Very few mechanical flaws.

15–17: Adequately crafted. This writing shows an understanding of some poetic techniques and an attempt to use them appropriately, but there may be some lapses in the handling of both form and content. There may be signs of some of the qualities of the higher bands, but unsustained. Some evidence of an active choice of vocabulary and style, and an awareness of the necessity to use appropriate punctuation. No gross error, but there may be some mechanical flaws.

12–14: Acceptably crafted. A relevant approach, showing a conscious attempt to use and sustain poetic form. Work in this category may be derivative, strive too hard for effect, and have content of limited interest. It will be evident, however, that the candidate is making active choices and attempting to control the writing. Some mechanical flaws, possibly occasional gross error.

9–11: Work in this band will show a basic awareness of crafting but an inability to control or sustain it effectively. It may be naïve, derivative and/or banal. Content, form and vocabulary will be appropriate to the title, but treatment inadequate. There are likely to be some flaws in writing skills and there may be some gross error.

6–8: Work in this band is likely to be banal both in content and technically. There may be some striving for form, but this may result in doggerel: if it has no other virtues, such work should be placed in this band. Very limited writing skills, and some gross error. Look carefully for merit in work which may immediately present itself as fitting this description; if there are signs of original thinking and real crafting, consider a higher band.

2–5: A wholly unsuccessful attempt, lacking any apparent control. Unstructured. It may appear mainly irrelevant to the set task. If it is a serious, but flawed, attempt, consider a higher band.

0–1: Chaotic, ill-planned, totally incoherent.

Additional guidance on the assessment of poetry
Candidates may provide some notes or comment on their poetry, which may explain the ideas behind the work, their chosen approach, or give other relevant information. Examiners may find this adds little to their understanding of the work and their response to it; conversely, there may be instances in which such information is revelatory, and positively affects their assessment. In such cases such reactions should form part of the comment made to justify the mark.

Most candidates will produce one or more drafts before the final submission. Examiners should look at the process of drafting, which may provide evidence of the thought processes behind the content, and the methods of crafting. Again, if this has been a factor in the final mark, a note should made to explain this.

Since the option of writing poetry has appeared on the paper, more candidates have offered poems each year, and the spread of quality of such writing has been very similar to the spread of quality of other kinds of writing. Candidates may choose to follow the suggested length of poem, but many write at greater length. Poems shorter than 20 lines, or poems which are over-long and rambling, cannot normally expect to gain high marks, but examiners must make very careful judgement in these cases, and award marks for the merits which they find. For example, a well-crafted sonnet should be rewarded on its merits, though it must, by its nature, be considerably shorter than 20 lines.

A very wide range of styles and techniques has been employed successfully by candidates, from rap rhythms to carefully measured quatrains, sonnets or free (but consciously crafted) verse form. A successful poem will show evidence of deliberate choice and use of a variety of techniques: assonance, alliteration, onomatopoeia, rhyme, metrical and stanzaic form, as well as appropriate vocabulary. It should show an awareness of the importance of punctuation in the construction of a poem. It may experiment with language, create images, offer a narrative or explore a theme. Examiners should be open to all possibilities which they may encounter, and judge each poem according to its success in responding to the given title and the relative quality of its crafting.

3 Summary Skills

Introduction

Summary work involves picking out the essence of a piece of writing, or a speech, or a meeting, or a broadcast, and re-expressing it in continuous sentences or notes. The traditional summary exercise, which was generally referred to as 'précis', involved reducing an entire passage to about a third of its length. Summary nowadays involves a wider range of skills than mere précis-writing. The extent of the reduction required can vary greatly, and the exercise is likely to necessitate the selection only of those points which are relevant to a particular issue or aspect of an article or piece of writing, and to write in a style and format which are suitable for a particular audience and purpose. Although it is likely that formal writing, in continuous sentences, will be asked for, it is possible that all or part of the answer will have to be written in note-form.

The opposite extreme from the traditional one-third, full-sentence summary would be the very highly condensed notes which a minuting secretary would take from a meeting. This would be difficult to set as an exercise in examination conditions, but you may quite possibly be given a word limit of as little as a tenth of the passage, or possibly even less.

Summary technique: general

Whatever form the summary exercise takes, certain basic techniques need to be applied, and we will consider these first, before looking in more detail at approaches to different types of summary question.

The first stage in any summary work is to achieve as full an understanding as possible of the passage to be summarised. This will probably mean reading it through two or three times before even picking up your pen. On your initial reading, the sense of much of the passage may well be obscured by the presence of difficult words. You should learn not to let yourself be thrown into a state of panic by this! It will be possible, after a couple more readings, to understand what the writer is saying, without necessarily knowing what is meant by every word he or she uses.

On the second reading, you should have the set task in mind, and begin focusing your reading on it. If you decide on a third familiarisation reading, you could try to start thinking about how you are going to deal with the presentation requirements. Then you can start working on the passage.

Preparing for a first draft can be tackled in various ways. The simplest is to read through the passage once more, this time underlining sentences and phrases which you feel to be important to the set topic or theme. If the question requires reordering the material, you can start thinking about this, and perhaps numbering the points in an order which seems logical. You can then begin writing a draft in continuous sentences, without making notes, and with the word limit in mind. Some people advocate deliberately keeping your first draft short, and building it up to the word limit in the second, whilst others favour the inclusion of everything of major or minor relevance in the first draft, and cutting down in the second. It is purely a matter of personal preference. A more time-consuming general approach is to make full notes of the points to be included, before writing them out in sentences. You will discover soon enough whether you can manage to complete a set of notes and two drafts within the time limit, and which general technique suits you better. The second draft should be your perfected answer in the number of words stipulated (or as near as you can possibly manage).

Some further general points need to be made, before analysing specific types of summary exercise. Whatever form the question takes, you must make sure that you summarise each relevant section of the passage in terms of *ideas* rather than sentences. If you attempt to summarise sentence by sentence, you are likely to end up with at best a stilted and at worst an incoherent piece of writing.

You should, as far as possible, try to write your summary in your own words, even if you are not specifically asked to adopt a style suitable to a specific audience. This does not mean that you should try to find a different way of expressing every word in the original, and the copying of words or short phrases may sometimes be essential if there are no obvious alternatives. You certainly must make sure that you do not distort the meaning of an idea in the passage, even slightly, by rephrasing it. But you must not simply copy chunks from the passage.

You should never repeat ideas, even if they are repeated in different words in the passage, and you should never add ideas of your own which do not appear in the passage.

Selective and note-form summaries

It is extremely unlikely that you will be asked to summarise a complete extract. The exercise will almost certainly be specific in terms of *what* and *how* you summarise. An important summary skill which you should develop, therefore, is the careful *selection* of material which is relevant to a specified aspect of the passage. As regards the *way* in which you write your summary, you are likely to be expected to write in continuous sentences, but all, or more likely part, of your summary may have to be written in note form. Let's look at an exercise which combines selection and writing in notes. Here is the passage:

Hypocrisy vividly laid bare

THEATRE

Mrs Warren's Profession
Citizens, Glasgow

Giles Havergal's new production of Shaw's *Mrs Warren's Profession* at the Citizens finally gives the lie to that old gibe at the theatre, that patrons come out whistling the sets. Instead of relying on sumptuous designs for effect, as the company did for its recent cycle of Wilde plays, Havergal turns the emphasis of Shaw's play on the acting.

There are only a few pieces of rehearsal furniture, battered tables, chairs and door frames, with the odd tatty couch or a garish parasol, registering all the more effectively in their drab surroundings. The actors wear modern clothes with minimal Edwardian touches. Apart from the women's dresses, the costumes could still be worn today. It gives the play a chilling relevance.

Quite why this should be is hard to determine. Most of the actors have worked at the Citizens before and Havergal is practised in the stripping down of plays, but seldom have the elements of a production welded themselves so effortlessly together. My guess is that it owes much to the presence of Ann Mitchell. Mrs Warren could have been written for her.

From our first glimpse of her at the back of the stage looking slightly demure in a vaguely Edwardian hat dominated by a pair of bird's wings, she looks like the vulgarian she admits to being. She is slightly blowzy but motherly too, and this is the key to her power over men like Frank.

Mitchell's Mrs Warren reverts to her native Cockney accent with the subtlety and precise calculation which underlie everything she does. Her performance throws new light on the character and universalises the relation between mother and daughter. She is a mother, a bad and demanding one. Now that there is unlikely to be any frisson about her profession as the owner of the best little whorehouse in Brussels, we can see clearly what Shaw actually wrote: a drama about the power politics between parents and children as much as any critique of the hypocrisy of society. As Vivie Warren says, we know all that. This interpretation is infinitely more provocative.

This Mrs Warren, however, is not a one-woman show, and the rest of the cast match Mitchell perfectly. Debra Gillett as Vivie, looking unsettlingly modern, is the prototype of the fanatical meritocrat denying all need for emotion. Despite her privilege she spouts cant about choices in life being available for all.

As Sir George Crofts, Michael MacKenzie is hideously recognisable as the baronet who would now be living in tax exile behind a number of offshore companies. Derwent Watson makes the silly-ass rector Samuel Gardner vicious as well as funny. Tristram Wymark, looking like a raddled cherub, works perfectly with Ann Mitchell to make the scene in which he attempts to seduce Mrs Warren alive with sexual tension.

The programme quoted Shaw on the exaggerated effect that scenery has on a play. Shaw was talking about the fondness of the Edwardians for stage decoration rather than a design which complements the play. But by going against tradition the Citizens has produced the most illuminating production of Shaw there has been for many years. A lady behind me told her friend rather indignantly that this was not the way they would have done it at Stratford. More fool Stratford.

Alasdair Cameron, *The Times*,
4 September, 1990

This is the exercise:

List in note-form the *factual* information we are given about the production, ignoring the reviewer's comments and opinions. You should make between ten and twelve points.

Before reading on, you could perhaps attempt an answer, as far as the end of the fifth paragraph. You should allow yourself 20 minutes. Now look at the specimen answer in Appendix A on page 264.

Let us now consider the techniques involved in approaching this kind of summary exercise.

Analysis of the specimen answer

The most immediately obvious feature of the answer is the way that it is set out. Generally speaking, unless the instructions are more specific, a note-form answer simply requires you to set down each new point on a separate line, perhaps with sub-points set out a little further to the right, with a dash before each. Writing in note form implies that sentences are unnecessary. Your concern should be to get the point across as briefly as possible, which means that you can ignore, in particular, definite and indefinite articles, personal pronouns, (especially 'it') and past and present tenses of the verb 'to be'.

With regard to the distinction between fact and opinion, we will look at the first three paragraphs in detail. The opening sentence of the first paragraph repeats the information given immediately above as to the location of the production, and names the director. This is obviously factual. The second sentence is more problematic. Is the reviewer's statement about the production's non-reliance on 'sumptuous designs for effect' an incontestable fact or not? Might some other reviewer view it differently? This is the question you must always ask yourself when attempting to differentiate between facts and opinions. The opening sentence of the second paragraph provides the clue. The reviewer describes the set in some detail, establishing beyond doubt that the production does not rely on 'sumptuous designs'. There is no need to list the features of the set. A further difficulty arises with the final clause of the opening paragraph. Could the reviewer's statement that the director 'turns the emphasis of Shaw's play on the acting' be merely a comment, with which another reviewer might disagree? Since he establishes that there is no reliance on 'sumptuous designs', or costumes (which is obviously also factual), we are probably safe in assuming that the emphasis is, in fact, on the acting, and treat the statement as fact. The final observation in the second paragraph, that the set and costumes provide a 'chilling relevance', is obviously an opinion. In the third paragraph, the only statement which is not open to question is the one about the actors having worked at the Citizens before. The reviewer's remark about the elements of the play welding themselves 'effortlessly together', and his 'guess about' the presence of 'Ann Mitchell' is clearly a personal opinion.

You might look at the rest of the passage and specimen answer, and/or attempt a similar analysis to the one above.

Presentation for a specified purpose and audience

It is virtually certain that at least half the marks for the summary skills exercise will be allocated for content. The remainder of the marks, possibly up to half, are likely to be for presentation. Presentation may mean some or all of the following:

- the layout of your summary on the page in a way which fits the audience and purpose for which it is intended;
- using a register and style of writing appropriate to the audience;
- clarity and accuracy of expression;
- keeping within the word limit.

The target audience may be a specified age group (ten- to 12-year-olds, 15-year-olds) or a special interest group: school governors, A-level students. The purpose may be, for example, a leaflet, a magazine article, a tabloid newspaper article or leader (editorial), a formal business letter.

Let us look in a little more detail at how to tackle questions on presentation for a particular audience and purpose. The style and register which would be suitable for a specified audience is generally fairly obvious. If the audience is adult, you are generally required to do no more than write in accurate, formal English. For a younger audience you would need to simplify your vocabulary and syntax according to the age group; the use of colloquial language and slang would be accepted by the examiner as a valid stylistic choice for the target audience. The summary would probably need to be set out in an eye-catching way as well.

Here is an example. An exam summary skills exercise based on a newspaper article about smoking was worded as follows: 'rewrite the material in the article so that it becomes suitable for 13-year-olds, setting out clearly the risks of smoking'. This is the first paragraph of the article:

Ifs and Butts

A gruesome but lesser-known fact about smoking is that it makes your legs fall off. Arterial disease, which restricts the blood flow to the legs and feet, is much more common among smokers. Eventually gangrene may set in, making amputation necessary. Nearly ten times as many people lose legs because of smoking as do so in accidents.

This is obviously relevant to the theme of 'the risks of smoking' and should therefore be included. But how should it be presented? A technical explanation, referring to 'arterial disease' and 'amputation' is unlikely to be very appealing or even comprehensible to 13-year-olds. But if you just write 'smoking makes your legs fall off', without explanation, it sounds like a joke. It would make a punchy and comprehensible start if you summarised the paragraph something like this: 'Lots of people lose their legs through smoking. It causes gangrene, and their legs have to be cut off'. As regards layout, a series of catchy sub-headings would help to arouse interest and persuade the audience to read the article.

A somewhat more precise style and register requirement would be to ask you to summarise a broadsheet newspaper article in the manner of a tabloid. Here is an example. This is the question:

> Write an article for a tabloid newspaper of your choice with the intention of showing how British food shoppers get a bad deal.
> USE NO MORE THAN 200 WORDS.
> Select appropriate material from *The Sunday Times* article and present it in such a way as to be suitable for its new audience and purpose.
> Give the article an appropriate headline. Name the newspaper you are writing for.
> 20 marks will be given for content and 20 marks for presentation, accuracy and fitness for audience and purpose.

The article on which this question is set presents arguments and statistics to suggest that British supermarket food prices are excessive in comparison with those in other countries in Europe and the USA. This is how the article begins:

Supermarkets push British food prices to top of league

SHOPPERS in Britain's supermarkets are paying up to twice as much for basic foods as customers in other Western countries do.

Stores that consistently boast 'special' offers and the lowest prices are increasingly uncompetitive compared with overseas companies. Figures published this weekend reveal they are trailing behind foreign supermarkets, which have smaller profit margins and more aggressive pricing policies.

The findings follow the announcement last week by Tesco that it is cutting the price of more than 500 products by up to 50% in its biggest 'own-label' marketing initiative.

Statistics produced by the European commission in Brussels show that the cost of British food has gone up by a third since 1985, significantly more than in other northern European countries. In a separate study, the United States was found to offer the best value.

Yesterday leading experts said Britain's food was unreasonably expensive. Raymond Blanc, chef and owner of Le Manoir aux Quat' Saisons in Oxfordshire, one of the country's top restaurants, said, 'Raw produce such as fresh meat and vegetables is becoming as costly as convenience food, and the consumer has much less choice than anywhere on the continent.'

Before attempting to answer a question like this, you would be well advised to study the 'Newspapers' section of Chapter 11, especially pages 179–182 and 185–187, which deal with tabloid journalism.

Here is a worked example of how the extract quoted might be rewritten for a tabloid newspaper, taking the word limit into consideration. It should be borne in mind that before the draft was written, relevant phrases from the extract were selected, and the order in which the points were to be made was decided upon. If the whole article was being summarised, the points would have to be divided into sections, and arranged under tabloid-style sub-headings.

Supermarket Swindle

British shoppers are being RIPPED OFF! Figures published this week show that housewives are paying up to TWICE AS MUCH for basic foods in this country compared with other Western countries. And top chefs say we have LESS CHOICE than anywhere on the continent! While foreign supermarkets go for price wars, British supermarkets go for profit margins. And American supermarkets come out the cheapest of all.

Now let us look at a complete exercise involving presentation for a specified audience and purpose. This is the AEB Summary Skills exercise set for the summer examination in 1995. The question appears first, followed by the article on which the question is set.

The article below appeared in the *Independent* on 14 April 1993 as part of the newspaper's media coverage.

Your task is to use material from the article as the basis of an entry entitled 'Forty Years of Children's Television' in an encyclopaedia which deals with cultural and social aspects of 20th-century Britain, and is aimed at a non-specialist adult readership.

Use no more than 200 words.

20 marks will be given for content.

20 marks will be given for organisation and presentation of material, fitness for purpose and accuracy.

Looking back, it doesn't seem quite so good

From 'Twizzle' to 'Tiswas' and the 'Thunderbirds' revival: a young person's television history

IT IS usual to look back on the television of our own childhood as somehow better than that on offer to children today. Measured against the tacky game shows and endless cartoons lapped up by children in the Nineties, how could *Watch With Mother* and *Muffin the Mule* fail to appear more reassuring and altogether nicer?

In fact, there remains a solid core of programmes offering innovative drama, story-telling and information. And many of them are more than simply technically superior to those of the Fifties and Sixties.

Like many children of that era, I have fond memories of Sunday tea in front of *Armand and Michaela Denis On Safari* and *Twizzle* at my best friend's because my family didn't have ITV. But take off the rose-tinted specs and it all looks rather wooden, very slow and terribly worthy.

Children's lives were very different 40 years ago, not least because television played such a minor role in their daily routine. The first children's producers were able to rely on a captive audience who would watch almost anything because television was such a novelty.

Yet the arrival of ITV in 1955 had a dramatic effect. With a shameless schedule of Westerns and adventure series like *Lassie*, *Roy Rogers* and *The Adventures of Robin Hood*, starring Richard Greene, ITV won a child audience three times the size of the BBC's. The BBC fought back with *Champion the Wonder Horse* and other American series, but ITV kept its glamorous edge.

Since the Sixties, children have grown up accepting television as part of the furniture. They go to bed later and have sets in their bedrooms. In the Nineties, a combination of television itself and computer games has accustomed them to a pace of presentation that would have bemused previous generations.

Satisfying such a sophisticated audience is a daunting task. The first concern of children's programme-makers now is to treat children as equals; any tendency to over-protect or patronise has been stamped on. Anna Home says this is in line with a general change in attitudes: 'The way people talk to children and how much they tell them has changed over the years and I think we reflect that. In the early days, children's producers wouldn't have dreamt of doing hard news stories about Ethiopia or Yugoslavia as *Newsround* does. *Children's Newsreel* in the Fifties was very much morris dancing, animals and items about royalty.'

The same change in attitude was evident in the earliest junior soaps. *Grange Hill*, first broadcast in the Seventies, reflected life in contemporary schools – sex abuse, drugs, teenage pregnancy – and all from the children's viewpoint. Until then, television's portrayal of education had remained solidly public school, with series like *Jennings* and *Billy Bunter*.

The relationship between presenter and audience, both at home and in the studio, has also become much less formal. On *Crackerjack* (1955–84), a schoolmasterly Eamonn Andrews, in suit and tie, talked at rather than to contestants, who all wore school uniform. 'And it was *a girl* who knew it, too!' he would exclaim at a correct answer. The studio audience shrieked 'Crackerjack!' but only on cue.

A much more anarchic, anti-adult style was spearheaded in the Seventies by *Tiswas*, introduced by Chris Tarrant and featuring Lenny Henry. It was one of the first of the Saturday morning programmes for children that saw off the ritual of Saturday-morning cinema.

Today's presenters have developed the *Tiswas* style. At one extreme, bright young things with loud shirts and relentless smiles are on nudgingly familiar terms with young participants and the audience at home. At the other, they're rather bossy – as in 'Buy jumble-sale clothes to save the environment'.

Delivery has become so informal that it seems they're constantly making mistakes. Children are everywhere on the screen, marking a deliberate change of policy made in the mid-Eighties. Before then, it was thought that the audience at home disliked watching their contemporaries. The overall effect has been to reduce the impression of adults delivering a service to children.

There have always been cartoons on television, although *Mickey Mouse* was stopped in mid-stream when BBC television closed down for the war in 1939. Some parents have always complained that animation is neither uplifting nor informative. But it is relatively cheap – and a sure-fire way to build ratings. The flood of cartoons from the United States and the Far East since the Eighties has done little to improve the image. It's not just because of violence. They often last longer – half an hour rather than a harmless five minutes – and many are terribly bland.

Parents are more tolerant of a distinctively British style of animation that started with the primitive *Captain Pugwash* in the Fifties (you could almost see the hand rocking the paper boats) and developed with puppets like the *Clangers* in the Sixties, *Paddington* and *The Wombles* in the Seventies and *Postman Pat* in the Eighties. The style is similar to that of *The Magic Roundabout*, which provided a perfect coda to *Children's Hour* from the mid-Sixties to the mid-Eighties and which was revived in 1991.

The biggest surprise for producers and parents has been the new generation's enthusiasm for revivals of Sixties classics like *Thunderbirds* and *Dr Who*. It's also rather reassuring. The special effects may look ridiculous to Nineties eyes, but children don't seem concerned. For all the sophistication children have acquired at the hands of television, what still matters most of all to them is a good story, well told.

from the *Independent*

Before reading on, you might attempt to write your own answer. You should spend an hour on this exercise. You might then look at the specimen answer below.

Forty Years of Children's Television

Early years
Children's television in the early 1950s was slow and artificial, largely because the BBC had a monopoly and therefore an undiscriminating audience. This changed suddenly in the mid-50s with the arrival of ITV, offering adventure and western series, and easily outstripping the BBC's audience ratings.

Changes in the 70s
Until the 1970s, children were patronised in programmes designed for them, and there was little attempt at spontaneity. Beginning with *Tiswas* in the 70s, a more anarchic style has emerged, the presenters treating the child studio audiences much more as equals, reflecting a general change in social attitudes towards children. The school series *Grange Hill* in the 70s introduced realism and the presentation of contemporary issues.

80s developments
In the mid-80s, a change of policy in children's programming occurred, with children themselves playing a much more important role. News programmes for children began dealing with world issues. Another 80s development was the flood of bland or violent foreign cartoons.

Conclusions

Children have become increasingly sophisticated over the past four decades, but it is interesting that sixties classics have become popular with 90s children, suggesting that a good story rather than sophisticated techniques is what children respond to most.

(199 words)

Analysis of the specimen answer

The immediately obvious feature of this answer is that it is set out under sub-headings. Such an approach is not essential in this particular question, since 'an encyclopaedia entry' could just as well be set out in paragraphs without sub-headings. If you do use sub-headings, they must be brief, because they are included in the word count.

What *is* essential is to create a clear sense of structure and organisation in your answer. The wording of the question gives you clear clues about this. You must think very carefully about the meaning and implications of these clues. You are asked to write 'an entry entitled "Forty Years of Children's Television" in an encyclopaedia'. This implies that the focus of your summary should be on *changes* over the period spanning the 1950s to the 1990s. The question is even more precise, however: the encyclopaedia for which you are writing 'deals with cultural and social aspects of 20th-century Britain'. This makes it clear that what you should be looking for is *the points made about the programmes* in terms of cultural and social developments, rather than the programmes themselves. Only two programmes are in fact specifically mentioned in the answer, and these were chosen because they are programmes which established new trends in children's television, and are therefore especially important.

The answer is structured to focus on the main developments in children's television over the four decades, in historical sequence. The result is a substantial re-ordering of some sections of the passage. Let us see how this re-ordering has actually worked.

Section 1: 'Early years'

This section draws on material from paragraphs 3 to 5 of the article, which concentrates on children's television in the 50s and 60s. The order of points in the summary follows that of the article, where statements about the general situation in the earliest period, in paragraphs 3 and 4, are followed by a paragraph about developments which began in 1955.

Section 2: 'Changes in the 70s'

This section is based on material in paragraphs 7 to 10. The order of points in the summary is quite different from that in the article. The summary concentrates on following a chronological development, which is not the case in the article. Paragraph 9 talks about 'the relationship between presenter and audience' in the days of *Crackerjack* (1955–84), and this is where the second section of the summary starts. The summary goes on next to draw material from paragraph 10, which explains the development of a new style 'in the 70s with *Tiswas*'. This is followed with material from the first part of paragraph 7, which talks about 'the first concern of children's programme-makers now'. This section of the summary ends with a sentence about changes in the *content* of programmes in the 70s, based on paragraph 8.

Section 3: '80s developments'

The three sentences in this section are drawn from paragraphs 12, 7 and 13, all of which refer to developments which began in the 1980s.

Section 4: 'Conclusions'

This section is drawn from paragraph 6 and the final paragraph of the article.

It should be clear from this analysis that you need to concentrate as much on the 'organisation and presentation' aspect of the question as on the content, and that the two are inextricably linked. It is a very different kind of exercise from précis, in which you summarise a whole passage without altering the order of the points.

A glance at the marking scheme below will show the vital importance of careful organisation in this question. To gain even 4 marks out of 10 you need to have shown 'some attempt at organisation'. To gain 7 marks, your summary must be 'well organised'. As regards the target audience for this question – 'a non-specialist adult readership' – a straightforward, formal piece of writing is all that is required. The style should be neutral. Any use of colloquialisms in this exercise would be out of place. You will notice that the summary is by no means entirely in the writer's own words. Words like 'anarchic', 'sophisticated' and 'bland' have been borrowed from the article. As mentioned earlier, this is perfectly acceptable. What you must try to avoid is lifting whole phrases from the passage.

Here is the Examiners' Marking Scheme for this exercise.

0623/1 June 1995: Question 2

A thorough handling of this exercise will draw on both the social and the programme detail contained in the article. The specified purpose/readership is fairly neutral, and the register and tone of the writing should reflect this. Examiners should look for a clear and well-balanced presentation of the main facts which appear in the original article.

These are the main points which should be included.
Award 1 mark for the inclusion of up to ten of these ideas.

a early television was cosy/technically limited/a novelty
b the coming of ITV in the mid-50s brought changes, with Westerns/adventure series
c ITV gained majority audience for children's programmes
d since the 60s television has been a household item
e 70s brought anarchy/anti-adult style/and Saturday-morning programmes (which displaced cinema)
f 70s saw the start of junior soap operas/programmes reflecting contemporary problems (from child's viewpoint)
g children regularly seen on screen by mid-80s
h by the 90s greater demands made by a more sophisticated/computer-literate audience
i changing attitudes demanded more hard-edged programmes/that children be treated as equals by programme-makers
j the relationship between presenter and audience became less formal
k cartoons have been a constant feature (despite parental complaints)
l imported cartoons long/violent/bland
m parents prefer British animation

n   animation techniques have improved since early programmes
o   revivals of 60s programmes in 90s indicate children's appetite for
    stories/unconcern with sophisticated techniques

NB: Dates do not have to be included or repeated if the approach makes the era or the
    time-scale clear.
    Titles of programmes, where included, should be used as examples. They cannot
    carry the point without explanation.

Award the second mark using the scale given below. Consider the category and mark
for the summary as carefully as you do the grade band for question 1. Remember that
the mark that you award is eventually doubled to give the final mark, and that every
mark awarded or not awarded is, in fact, worth two marks. Look for the positive merits
of this piece of work and reward it accordingly. Slovenly, inaccurate and ill-presented
work cannot gain high marks, but do not be afraid to reward good work highly.

0–1   a submission longer than 215 words
2–3   some relevant material
        basically sound expression
        not more than 215 words
4–6   logically chosen material
        sound expression
        some attempt at organisation
        reader-friendly
        no more than 205 words
7–8   material entirely appropriate
        very few flaws in expression
        well-organised
        interesting and inviting to read
        within word limit
9–10   thoroughly inviting and interesting, with some individual style and sparkle;
        publishable
        within word limit

Additional guidance on the marking of summaries

Count the number of words used, placing a double line after 200 words, and a further
line after 215 words. You cannot reward any points made after 200 words. Write the
number of words at the end of the summary. You do not need to count further than
215: if that number is exceeded, write '215+'.

All correctly-hyphenated words (eg: 'programme-makers') to be counted as one word.
All numbers, either written as words or numerically, to be counted as one word,
including contractions (eg: 1955–84).

The title is not part of the word count, but sub-headings, if used by the candidate,
should be counted.

Style comparison questions

If you are asked to compare your answer with the set passage in terms of
style and effectiveness of communication, there are certain points to make
which will be of general application.

The most obvious one is that your piece of writing will inevitably be dry, and lacking in individuality, compared with the original. To create interest in what he or she has to say, a writer will almost always include examples, illustrations and comparisons, or historical and other details, or quotations or references. He or she will also shape the piece, and attempt to infuse it with vitality. When your sole concern is abbreviation, all of this has to go.

The way to answer a question calling for stylistic comparison, therefore, is to briefly *quote* examples of the features of the original which are missing in your summary, and attempt to explain what is lost by missing them out.

Additional points

1 You must take the word limit *very seriously*. Even if you are only a few words over the limit, your mark is likely to be drastically affected. This means counting your word total very carefully, and allowing yourself time to cut out excess words if necessary. The examiners are instructed to count the words in every summary script. If you are many words under the limit, on the other hand, the chances are that you have missed some relevant points, and you should expand your summary.

2 If you are asked to supply a title for your summary, try to keep it short (no more than ten words at most) and think of a phrase which represents an encapsulation of the theme of the whole summary. You are not expected to include the title in your final word count.

3 There is no point in wasting words by introducing your points with phrases like 'the writer says/goes on to say that . . .'. Simply write your summary as if it is an original piece of work.

4 You should not waste time trying to enhance the appearance of your summary by the use of graphics, different coloured inks or highlighter pens. You will gain no credit for such devices, which have no relevance to an English-language exercise.

5 It is best not to use abbreviations of any sort, except in a note-making exercise, since a summary is a piece of formal prose, and abbreviations are a rather unfair short-cut to word saving.

6 When your summary is complete, you should check carefully for spelling and punctuation errors, since technical accuracy will play a part in your overall mark.

Passages for summary

1 The passage which follows was published in 1965, in a book called *The Popular Arts*. The television programmes and government reports referred to are now outdated, but the arguments presented are still considered to be valid. You have been asked to summarise the essential arguments, leaving out the illustrations, so that a version of the passage, with up-to-date illustrations, can subsequently be written. Your summary of the arguments should be made in no more than 150 words. (The passage contains 806 words.)

The question of violence looms large in any discussion of the mass media among educationalists. When the Pilkington Report set out to analyse the causes of public 'disquiet about television', it was obliged to begin with violence. Yet this question of violence in the media is more complex than appears at first sight. There may certainly be some point in the complaint that there is too much traffic in violent themes. But this complaint should be seen for what it is: a criticism of the balance of content in the media generally, and not a qualitative judgement on the particular kinds of violence treated, nor an informed opinion on their various effects. We must deal with the general question first. But since violence, death and human suffering have always been the subject matter of at least some great art, we must go on to draw the more complex distinctions between different kinds of violence: between, say, the violence of the BBC series of Shakespeare history plays on television, *Age of Kings*, and that of *Sunset Strip*, *Wagon Train*, *Whiplash* and *Gunsmoke*. Such distinctions are impossible without some attention to questions of style and treatment. We shall have to understand the different qualities expressed in these programmes, trying to decide how they work as dramatised experiences, and what their psychological impact is.

First, then, in general terms, so far as television is concerned, we are faced with problems of timing and volume. What is suitable for adults in the late evening may not be considered suitable for young children in the afternoon – always supposing that the television providers are alive to their educational responsibilities here, and that a time limit or boundary can be established. When, in a debate on the issue in Parliament in 1962, the Postmaster General said that the BBC assumed children were in bed by nine o'clock, a wise but unidentified backbench voice commented, 'They're wrong'. As for sheer volume, the Pilkington Report remarked simply that 'there was too much violence on television'. Few would disagree with this.

When an incorrect programme balance is combined with the general effects of repetition, the judgement is strengthened. Repetition is crucial. The steady networking of badly produced, low-level dramatised series – many of them American in origin or feeling – is one aspect of this saturation process. The 'competition' between the BBC and ITV for the peak viewing figures is probably another. Both the Nuffield Report (1958) and the Pilkington Report (1962) present disturbing evidence on this score.

Although it seems that only the child who is already emotionally disturbed will actually learn violence from a particular television programme (the evidence on this score seems fairly conclusive, in both *Television and the Child* and the comparable American study *Television in the Lives of our Children*), it is certainly true that we gradually become habituated to certain attitudes and situations if they are repeated often enough. The danger here is that we develop a permissive attitude towards the existence of violence in the world, come to regard it as a 'natural' solution to difficult social problems, or accept it as part of the background to life. This is what the Pilkington Report meant by the danger of a 'callous indifference'. The fear is strengthened when the whole balance is wrong, and when counter-images and attitudes, which enhance life or ennoble gentleness, kindness and love, are so difficult to evoke and often appear so trite and banal set beside the tension and vigour of the rougher scenes.

As the *Guardian* observed in an editorial: 'An isolated murder which strikes the viewer with horror is less corrupting than the incessant suggestion that murder is a bagatelle'. But the programmes in which this 'incessant suggestion' is made are those in which nothing seems to exist on the screen except the moment of violence – many of the television crime serials, for example, in which characters are, at most, two-dimensional stereotypes, the settings simply a procession of expensive penthouses, and the only visual moments of climax those when bodies slump to the floor. As the Pilkington Report commented:

'Many submissions recorded the view that it [violence] was often used gratuitously, that it often did little or nothing to develop plot or characterisation and that it was, presumably, thrown in "for kicks". Another common opinion was that it was often unnecessarily emphasised by being shown in close-up and by being lingered over. The damage was not necessarily repaired by ensuring that, in the end, the good were seen to win and the bad to lose, and that crime did not pay: conventional endings of this sort did not penetrate to the level at which the portrayal of violence had its emotional effect. What mattered was that violence provided the emotional energy, the dramatic content of the programme.'

Stuart Hall and Paddy Whannel

2 Read the following review of the film, *A Room with a View*, and answer the questions which follow:

CINEMA

A Room with a View

('PG'. Curzon, Mayfair)

Pictures from Italy

The film has all the makings of a genteel elegance, from the carefully ironic credits at the beginning – 'Judi Dench: Eleanor Lavish, a novelist' – to the carefully modulated sense of loss at the close. It is a deliberate period piece, in other words, and with such attention lavished upon costumes and interiors that it acquires a slight museum-like air. One could almost feel the older members of the audience in Mayfair hugging themselves with pleasure at some of the wonderfully constructed Edwardian scenes.

The actors play up to their surroundings by putting on their best faces – in other words, by adopting the persona which has over the years best suited them. Denholm Elliott is once again the slightly eccentric, warm-hearted party with more than a suspicion of a cockney accent.

Maggie Smith is sinewy and difficult, Simon Callow rubicund and ebullient. And then there are the assorted elderly actresses who are adept at playing English ladies in their lavender twilight years.

A Room with a View, then, verges on parody – not so much a parody of Forster or even of Edwardian society, but rather of the cinematic versions of that period. Of course this is not deliberate and the film-makers, Ismail Merchant and James Ivory, are well known for both their carefulness and their genius for cinematic adaptations of literary works. But carefulness can create a sense of artificiality, and adaptations often seem contrived. There are compensations, however: practically every scene shows such an elaborate orchestration of visual effects that, just as an exercise in composition, the film demands to be looked at.

The plot itself will be known to any one with the remotest knowledge of E. M. Forster – a dwindling minority, perhaps, but those who have not read this particular novel will still be able to follow the story of certain English people who 'come alive' at the impress of Florence on their inchoate souls. The film-makers are even more helpful than usual by interpolating Forster's arch chapter headings.

And the acting is excellent: leaving aside the slight tendency towards self-parody (which the director perhaps encouraged), the film contains a series of excellent performances. Judi Dench, as the female novelist, brought a certain majesty to the pseudo-romantic imagination; perhaps next time she should play E. M. Forster. And Helena Bonham-Carter, as the young heroine, looked absorbingly preoccupied and intelligent – she is one of those actresses whose thoughts the camera seems to photograph. All the way through, Maggie Smith quivers (there is no other word for it) with suppressed passion. And so, after a while, the elements of parody and artificiality no longer matter; *A Room with a View* may lack a certain continuity of rhythm (and this largely because the imposition of chapter headings tends to turn the narrative into a number of carefully modulated scenes) but it has the bravura which comes equally from creative conviction and from tight formal control.

It could be said, in fact, that this adaptation is almost too faithful. Merchant and Ivory (as well as Ruth Prawer Jhabvala, their screen-writer) have earned their large reputation principally by taking on the works of the more 'sophisticated' or elaborately humanistic Western novelists – subdued, complicated novels, the realism of which is finally touched by lyricism but is generally enmeshed in the obliquities of class or caste. It would be difficult to imagine them adapting Dickens, for example; he is too grotesque, too large. Henry James is their metier.

As a result they have a definite vision, but it is one filtered through a certain kind of literature about a certain kind of life – it is admirable, but even as one responds to it, one cannot but feel and recognise the constrictions which press down upon it. But of course *A Room with a View* itself is concerned with those very constrictions, and on this occasion the film-makers have been able to use their carefully balanced scenarios precisely in order to render more vivid their images of violence or fragility. One of the most interesting aspects of this production is the way in which the elaborate tonalities of the English dialogue are placed against the soaring grandeur of the Florentine architecture – thus setting up a tension which the rest of the film explores. And so, when the scene returns to England, there are some wonderful moments largely concerned with the social embarrassment of everyone concerned. An episode of nude bathing is almost wilfully interrupted by two ladies, and there are various nerveless tea-parties at which Maggie Smith's manner is the star attraction.

Peter Ackroyd, *The Spectator*

a List in note form the *factual* information we are given about the film and its making. (*10 marks*)
b In not more than 100 words of connected prose say what you understand the film to be about from what the critic writes. (*10 marks*)
c What are the opinions of the critic about the film? Your answer should be no more than 150 words in length. (*20 marks*)

3 Your task is to use the information contained in the article below to produce an information sheet for competitors in a junior tennis tournament, advising them about what they should eat and drink during the course of the event.
Work on the assumption that the average age of your reader is 15.
Your presentation should be appropriate to the task and to the intended readership.
Your writing must not exceed 200 words.
20 marks will be awarded for the selection of relevant information.
20 marks will be awarded for presentation, accuracy and fitness for purpose and audience.

Jenny Bryan says sensible snacking could make the difference between winning at Wimbledon and losing

Yes, do have those bananas

AS TENNIS stars unpacked their bags by the umpire's chair at Wimbledon this week you'd be forgiven for thinking that some had come for a picnic. Under the favourite racquets and lucky sweatbands were the bananas, biscuits and muesli bars that players increasingly rely on to boost their flagging energy levels at the end of tough matches. And, as the pace hots up next week, the snack boxes will begin to bulge.

'I can show you players at the end of a five-set match who have lost because they didn't eat and drink sensibly during the game,' says Iona Smeaton, state-registered dietician to the Lawn Tennis Association. 'At the US Open last year so many players dropped out because of heat stress that a nine-point advice sheet was put up in the men's changing room to remind them how to avoid getting ill during matches,' she adds.

Dehydration is a tennis player's biggest enemy. A few years ago players could be seen drinking all manner of magic potions brewed in the secrecy of their hotel rooms. But most now recognise that you can't do much better than plain water, perhaps with a pinch of salt.

Trained athletes sweat twice as much as unfit people. Men sweat more than women, who rely on radiation to get rid of excess heat. That's why women players tend to get redder in the face than men. But both need to preload their stomach with $\frac{1}{2}$ to $\frac{3}{4}$ pint of water before they go on court and then top that up with a cupful of liquid every 10 to 15 minutes during their match.

It's important to keep drinking even during the warm-up and the first few nervy opening games because dehydration quickly dulls the concentration and slows the legs. Athletes don't need to add much salt to their drinks because their sweat is remarkably dilute, says Dr Craig Sharp, chief physiologist at the British Olympic Medical Centre in Middlesex.

They conserve salt much better than someone who is unfit because their sweat glands work differently, he explains.

He believes the various commercial drinks designed for sportsmen and women have little or no advantage over water, and he knows of no special ingredient in orange or lemon barley water that could be responsible for its appeal at Wimbledon.

Making drinks very sweet would be counter-productive, says Iona Smeaton, because this actually slows the rate at which water is absorbed.

'A drink that contains more than 12 per cent sugar can actually make you dehydrated. It would have so much sugar in it that the body would need to pull back some water into the intestines to help the sugar get absorbed,' she points out.

So a tennis player may take a swig or two of cola but they'll quickly follow it with several gulps of water to dilute it.

They do need glucose for energy, though, and that's where bananas come in. The American player Michael Chang was one of the first to popularise bananas, and he's been known to get through three or four in a match. There's no magic ingredient to a banana, but about a fifth of its weight is carbohydrate. It contains a good mixture of sugars, some of which will slip quickly into the muscles to boost energy levels and some more slowly to give a prolonged effect. It also tastes good and is easy to digest.

Tennis players rely on bursts of speed so their muscles run on glucose. In the days before a competition they will bolster the fuel supply in their muscles by

eating a carbohydrate-rich diet of bread, pasta and rice.

For a straight sets match under a dull sky, the energy stores they have built up pre-match will probably be enough to see them through. But there's no predicting when they will come up against a player who is determined to upset the seedings and put even the Boris Beckers and Steffi Graffs of the championships through an unexpectedly long and gruelling match.

The picnic basket is especially important for the players who compete in the doubles and mixed doubles as well as the singles during the Wimbledon fortnight. They may have to play twice in a day and their energy stores will almost certainly run low.

Iona Smeaton advises young British hopefuls to replenish their energy supplies as soon as they come off court. 'There is evidence that in the first half an hour to an hour after exercise the muscles are most geared to refuelling. So players should eat immediately after they come off court. People who refuel most effectively can start their next match with 20 to 30 per cent more energy in their muscles than their opponent,' she says.

In the last painful minutes of a three- or four-hour match, that could mean the difference between posing with the famous Wimbledon trophy and going down in the record books as a gallant loser.

from *The Guardian*, 26 June 1992

Specimen answers to all the summary skills exercises in this chapter can be found in Appendix A on pages 264 and 265.

4 Comprehension and Analysis

Varieties of question

The traditional comprehension exercise tests the student's understanding of a passage of prose, and the ability to express ideas contained in the passage in his or her own words. This is still an integral part of comprehension. However, modern comprehension exercises at Advanced level also test the student's skill at analysing the *presentation* of ideas and argument, both in terms of content and of expression. The student may be expected to comment on the persuasiveness of the argument in a piece of discursive or polemical writing, and to analyse the means by which the writer's case is presented. This may include the identification and assessment of the writer's bias. An analysis of the effectiveness of the writer's style, and of the tone of the passage, may also be required, and the student may be asked to show how all of these aspects of the writing offer clues as to the target audience.

The passages set for comprehension are unlikely to be from works of fiction; newspaper articles, extracts from reviews and biographies, or autobiographical writing are the likeliest sources.

Initial approach to a comprehension exercise

Just as with summary skills exercises, the first essential in preparing to answer comprehension and analysis questions on a passage is to read it through once or twice to gain some sense of what the passage is about. It may be a good idea to read through the questions first, and to start focusing on them as you re-read the passage.

When you begin answering the questions, you may find it useful to underline key phrases in the passage which are relevant to the question you are answering, as long as you either rub out your underlinings when you've finished your answer or write in the margin the number or letter of the question to which your underlining refers.

You should always be careful to check the number of marks allocated for each question, as this will give you a fairly clear idea of the amount of detail required in your answer. It is foolish to spend a lot of time on questions for which there are only two or three marks. In fact, since you are not required to answer the questions in order, it may be best to leave questions which carry few marks till the end, in case you run out of time.

Content questions

Traditional comprehension questions, requiring explanations of ideas or information contained in the passage, or of the writer's attitude to something which is described or analysed, test a student's ability to understand what a writer is saying, and to articulate this understanding.

In general, such questions will refer to a particular idea or ideas, sometimes with reference to specific paragraphs or lines, and the answer will normally be found within one paragraph or section of the passage. This is not always the case, however, and some questions may refer to an idea which is developed in more than one paragraph. Care must be taken to check whether an idea is developed or information presented in more than one section of the passage, before attempting an answer. In either case, you should try, if possible, to include all relevant details in your answer.

On occasions, you will find that words or phrases are so specialised or precise as to be impossible to re-express without altering the sense, in which case it is acceptable to copy them.

Questions requiring explanation of phrases

In the case of questions which ask for explanations of vocabulary used in the passage, a brief answer is all that is required. There is no need to explain the context of the word or phrase, and your answer should not contain many more words than are contained in the phrase itself.

Style questions

Questions requiring evaluation of the style of a passage may take a variety of forms. You may simply be asked to 'comment on' or 'examine' or 'identify the characteristics of' the style, or the question may be more precise. You may, for instance, be asked to give your opinion as to whether the passage is 'well written', or exhibits 'good writing', in which case you are quite likely to be asked to explain your criteria for judging the writing style. Similarly, you may be asked to 'evaluate the effectiveness' of the style of writing.

You may also be instructed to consider particular aspects of the style, such as language/diction/vocabulary, syntax, register and imagery. A brief explanation of these essential elements of writing style may be useful.

Language (or diction or vocabulary)

A piece of writing may be consistent in the type of language it uses, or it may not. The first thing to look for is evidence of variations from the predominant language type; you should be prepared to quote and explain the purpose or effect of such variations.

A passage may be written in highly formal or highly informal language, or any variation in between. Formal language is likely to contain a fairly high proportion of complex or multisyllabic or abstract words. This does not, of course, necessarily make the style dull, and therefore ineffective. What you are essentially looking for, in terms of the effectiveness or otherwise of the language, is *freshness* of expression. Highly *in*formal language may contain clichéd expressions, which tend to destroy the sense of freshness in the writing.

Informal language will tend to be more simple and concrete, and its effectiveness can be gauged by its immediacy of appeal: it may be colloquial (employing the kind of phraseology normally associated with spoken rather than written language) or colourful (appealing to the imagination in the choice of words, particularly of adjectives and adverbs) or emotive (having a powerful emotional appeal).

Syntax (or sentence structure)

The syntax of a piece may be essentially complex or simple. Generally speaking, the more intricately argued and formal the writing, the more complex its syntax is likely to be. You should look out in particular for sophistications of syntax, such as the proliferation of subordinate clauses within sentences, or the use of colons and semicolons.

Long and complex sentences, however, need not necessarily equate with good style, and can occasionally obscure the sense, though with skilled writers this is rare. It is perhaps a little risky to criticise a writer's syntax in terms of obscurity, since you may merely be revealing your inability to understand a carefully reasoned argument.

Less formal writing tends to use shorter sentences and simpler syntax. Again, this proves nothing about the comparative effectiveness of the writing. Very short sentences, however, are worth picking out from a passage and commenting on, since they inevitably stand out simply by the nature of their shortness, and tend to create a direct, 'punchy' or even dramatic effect.

In writing which employs largely complex syntax, you should look out for occasional examples of short, simple sentences, and be prepared to comment on the effect they produce. The same applies with occasional complex sentences in passages in which the syntax is generally simple.

Other features of syntax which you might look out for and comment on are the use of questions instead of statements, rhetorical repetition, balanced phrases in two separate parts of a sentence, and the deliberate use of ungrammatical or incomplete sentences.

An example of complex, sophisticated syntax is the following sentence from *Washington Square* by the American novelist Henry James, who is famous for writing long, complicated sentences such as this one, describing the character of the novel's heroine, Catherine Sloper, and her reactions to her lover's visits:

As I have tried to explain, she was not eager and exacting; she took what was given her from day to day; and if the delightful custom of her lover's visits, which yielded her a happiness in which confidence and timidity were strangely blended, had suddenly come to an end, she would not only not have spoken of herself as one of the forsaken, but she would not have thought of herself as one of the disappointed.

The sentence, as you will have noticed, is broken up into sections by the use of semi-colons. After the second semi-colon, the main statement is interrupted by a subordinate clause ('which yielded . . . strangely blended'), and the sentence ends with a pair of balanced, symmetrical phrases, the first of which contains a double negative ('she would not only not . . .') which further complicates the syntax.

Register

The register in which a piece is written reflects its subject matter or the social situation of its writer or the audience for which it is intended. In the broadest sense, writing itself is a register, as distinct from speech. Again very broadly, we can differentiate between formal and informal registers in both speech and writing. More precisely, the immense number of dialects of English are all registers: for instance, we can talk of a Jamaican English register, or a black American English register, or a northern working-class English register.

These registers can, of course, be represented in writing as well as speech. The same person can, and in fact, inevitably does, adopt different registers, depending on the audience. In a committee meeting, a learned register might be adopted, or else one reflecting the professional jargon of his or her peers; this would be quite different from the informal, colloquial register used with friends. In writing a report of the meeting, he or she would employ a vocabulary, syntax and mode of punctuation designed to highlight his or her professional expertise and seriousness of intention; the style most probably would be formal, the vocabulary learned, the syntax complex and the punctuation strictly accurate. In a letter to a friend, however, the same person would be likely to eschew formalities, and write simple sentences, consciously ignoring the formal rules of punctuation by, for instance, using dashes, and adopting a style of writing more akin to speech.

Register, therefore, encompasses not only the type of language used, but also the sentence-structure and the mode or style of writing in general. A writer's intentions, and target audience, can normally be gauged from the register he or she chooses.

In the following extract, contrasting registers are illustrated by the deliberate mixing of registers within sentences. The extract is from an article entitled 'White English in Blackface, or Who Do I Be?' by Geneva Smitherman, and it illustrates her argument that formal White (American) English [WE] is different, but not necessarily less effective as a means of communication, from informal Black (American) English [BE]. It should be easy to distinguish which is the WE and which the BE Register!

I say without qualification that we cannot talk about the Black Idiom apart from Black Culture and the Black Experience. Nor can we specify educational goals for blacks apart from considerations about the structure of (White) American society.

And we Black folks is not gon take all that weight, for no one has empirically demonstrated that linguistic/stylistic features of BE impede educational progress in communication skills, or any other area of cognitive learning. Take reading. It's don been charged, but not actually verified, that BE interferes with mastery of reading skills. Yet beyond pointing out the gap between the young brother/sistuh's phonological and syntactical patterns and those of the usually-middle-class-WE-speaking-teacher, this claim has not been validated.

Imagery and figures of sound

For a detailed analysis of imagery (simile, metaphor and personification) and figures of sound (alliteration, assonance and onomatopoeia), you should turn to Chapter 13 ('Literary Style'). You should familiarise yourself with these figures of speech as part of your preparation for comprehension and analysis exercises as well as literature essays.

As a broad generalisation, imagery can be divided into two classes: fresh and stale. Fresh, original images can greatly enhance writing, providing an extra dimension and imaginative focus on an idea. Stale imagery tends merely to reveal the writer's lack of originality. A constant feature of the popular press in Britain is the use of clichés, which are really overworked, 'dead' metaphors and similes.

Questions on tone

'Tone' and 'language' are difficult to separate, and questions which ask for analysis of tone are frequently posed in terms of 'language and tone'. One way of defining tone would be 'the emotional temperature of the language used'. A writer's feelings about a topic are revealed through the tone he or she adopts.

The tone of a passage, as well as its language, may vary. An expository passage, in an essentially neutral tone, may contain touches of humour, employing, for instance, a whimsical tone. Such variations should be illustrated, and the effects explained.

There is an immense range of tones in which a writer can express his or her feelings. These might be broadly categorised, and illustrated, as follows:

Neutral tones

Much formal writing is largely *neutral* in tone, conveying no impression of emotion. The tone of such writing might even be *detached*, where the writer creates no feeling of personal involvement whatsoever in the writing. When a writer is attempting to convey an impression of balance and reasonableness, the tone might be described as *measured*. It might, on the other hand, be *didactic*, making assertions which the reader is expected to accept as the truth.

Angry tones

When a writer is arguing against some perceived abuse or folly, emotions of anger are likely to be displayed in the choice of language. The tone is quite likely to be *bitter* or *disparaging*, *mocking*, *scornful*, *abusive* or even, at the furthest extreme of anger, *vitriolic*.

A bitter tone is also likely to be exhibited when the writer sees no likelihood of the unsatisfactory situation which he or she is analysing being rectified; in these circumstances, a *heavily ironic, sarcastic* or *sardonic* tone is also likely. At the extreme, in this case, the tone may be *despairing*.

Humorous tones

Sarcasm, of course, is a form of humour, and can also be used in more light-hearted writing. Writers frequently resort to a *gently sarcastic* tone to poke fun at their targets. More light-hearted pieces of writing frequently exhibit a more lightly humorous tone: for instance, a *whimsical, wry* or *lightly ironic* tone.

Tones reflecting strong conviction

If a writer is pursuing a crusade, and is determined to persuade the reader of the correctness of his or her views, the tone employed may be *hectoring*, in which he or she seems to be attempting to enforce acceptance of the views expressed. Subtler appeals to the reader may be made through a *familiar* tone, in which the reader is addressed as a like-minded individual who is certain to share the writer's attitudes; such an approach may, as its worst, employ a *patronising* tone, in which the writer talks down to the reader.

Enthusiastic tones

If the writer wishes to show his or her enthusiasm for something, the tone used may be *laudatory*, employing language ringing with praise, or *passionate, jubilant* or even *triumphant*.

Whatever you perceive the tone of the passage you are analysing to be, you must make sure that you quote illustrations from the passage of the language displaying the tone.

To test your recognition of differences of tone, you might now attempt a simple exercise. Write down ten different sentences, each containing the phrase 'shut the door.' Then read some of them out loud, conveying the tone intended with your voice. The class can then define the tone of each.

Questions on effectiveness of argument

To answer questions on methods of argumentation and the persuasiveness or otherwise of arguments, you will need to look both at the way the argument itself is presented and at the manner in which it is written.

Perhaps the most important consideration in assessing argumentation is the presence or absence of *adequate supportive evidence*. Factual evidence, possibly including *figures and/or statistics*, is essential to provide a basis on which to judge the validity of the argument. Precise evidence, with up-to-date information, gives the necessary substance to an argument; without it, the case rests on unsubstantiated assertion. You should check to see if the evidence is *overly selective*, ignoring evidence which might invalidate the case. You should bear in mind that statistics are notoriously easy to misuse. If the writer uses statistics to back up an assertion, you should attempt to assess whether or not they are put to valid use.

Personal, inside knowledge is a useful way of adding an air of conviction to an argument and giving the impression that the writer 'knows what he or she is talking about'. A *personal anecdote* can also make the argument seem more 'real'; but here you should think carefully about the use made of the anecdote; *arguing from the particular to the general* (see 'Further Advice on Writing: Illogical argument in essays', pages 175–178) is one of the classic logical flaws. *Comparisons* are another useful tool in argument, where the writer presents a parallel or comparable case to back up his or her position. The comparisons must, of course, be relevant; *irrelevant analogies* are another basic error of logic.

As for the actual mode of writing, several factors should be looked for in terms of the effective presentation of an argument. A sense of a *personal, individual 'voice'* tends to predispose the reader towards acceptance of a viewpoint in contrast to a bland, abstract, impersonal series of propositions. *Emotive language*, as long as it is not overdone, helps to create a sense of personal conviction, especially a tone of scorn, anger or sarcasm, and *colloquial language* personalises the case. The use of *humour* can also be an effective way of giving credence to a viewpoint: the reader is more likely to accept the attacks on the writer's target by being made to laugh at them.

Syntax can also play a part: *short, punchy, statements* tend to create a particularly strong impact as long as they are not overused; *rhetorical questions* encourage the reader to share the writer's conviction in what he or she is saying. The *use of questions*, generally, is an effective tool of argumentation, forcing the reader to think for him/herself about the issues being raised.

Questions on bias

Much of what has been said in the above discussion of methods of argumentation is relevant to bias. These are the essential features to look for:

- lack of adequate supportive evidence;
- presenting only evidence which supports the writer's case, and ignoring valid counter-evidence;
- providing only a single piece of evidence, and falsely basing a general contention on it;
- misuse of statistics;
- irrelevant personal anecdotes;
- suggestions by the writer that he or she knows best, and those who disagree are either ignorant or wilfully misleading;
- attempts to cajole the reader into agreement by suggesting, for instance, that any sensible person would view the issue the way the writer does;
- appeals to naked prejudice, such as racial or sexual chauvinism;
- use of mocking, abusive, etc. tones;
- use of emotive language to influence the reader against something.

Questions on target audience

If you are asked to identify the kind of audience for which a piece of writing might have been intended, you should offer evidence both from the style and the content of the piece.

Vocabulary, syntax, register and tone all offer clues as to the readership at which it might have been targeted. You should consider the subject matter and the attitude which the writer takes towards it, the political stance (if any), the degree of sophistication of the arguments, and the level of cultural, historical and general awareness that a full understanding of the article requires. These factors will provide convincing evidence as to the age range, social class, political viewpoint, degree of education and sophistication, special interests, etc., of the target audience.

Answering comprehension and analysis questions

The exercise and specimen answers which follow are designed to show you how to tackle questions of the analytical type which we have been considering above.

Comprehension and analysis | Read the following passage which appeared in the *Independent* and answer the questions:

Curse of the day-glo dazzlers

St Thomas Aquinas was fond of saying that the man who was free only in his leisure time
5 was a slave. Aquinas lived a long time ago in Italy, however, and what he said is clearly anathema to the British in 1990. The British
10 believe in leisure. Leisure (along with shopping) is the new religion and its devotees work hard to take it easy.
15 Among other things, they have caused the building of vast new temples of a type never seen before: the shopping mall, the theme
20 park and the leisure centre. These buildings are the cathedrals, monasteries and hospices of our day.

If you find the leisure
25 creed repugnant, you can escape the theme park and the leisure centre. It is more difficult, however, to avoid the vast shopping mall and
30 its mesmerising air-conditioned nave, aisles, chapels and clerestories with their expensive offerings of luxury goods.
35 But it is impossible to escape from the habits – the clothes as well as the gum-chewing, burger-stuffing and soft-drink suckling – of
40 the leisure era. In dignified city streets, in country lanes, in shopping arcades up and down the country, in churches, airports and coun-
45 try houses, leisurewear is all intrusive.

A whole nation seems to be dressed, notably at weekends, in man-made fabric
50 representations of the contents of a packet of liquorice allsorts. The strident acid colours of leisurewear dominate every
55 view of every British street, lane and public building.

Architects trying to build even the most sensitive modern building are given a
60 hard time by interfering local planning committees. Anyone, however, can don a garish polyester-nylon

tracksuit and waddle
65 shamelessly along a much-
loved street lined with
beautiful buildings, without
fear of censure. Yet
leisurewear is visual pollu-
70 tion of the highest order.

It is also damning evi-
dence of a slob culture that
seeks to undermine urbane
and civilised values. For
75 leisurewear means never
having to think about
appearances. Leisurewear
means never having to
straighten a tie or polish a
80 pair of shoes. Leisurewear
means never having to step
out of your pyjamas.
Leisurewear means free
advertising for manufactur-
85 ers: shoes, jeans and T-
shirts decked with tags,
labels and transfers cele-
brating company names.

Why do people pay for
90 these clothes? Surely they
should be paid for their
role as animated bill-
boards? Traditionally, a
good English suit hides its
95 label – if it has one – in the
lining of an inside pocket.

Today's tracksuits, bomber
jackets, trainers and
hooded 'mugger' tops are
100 emblazoned with their
makers' names, like crests
on medieval soldiers'
tunics. Many carry crude or
insulting messages.

105 How are you meant to
respond to a fat, ill-shaven
slob strolling around a
National Trust house in the
Cotswolds wearing a garish
110 and very sweaty sweatshirt
that reads: 'If I wanted to
listen to someone talking
out of his arse, I would
have farted.'?

115 If, however, a Cotswold
resident wants to build a
very small addition to the
back of their house – one

Leisurewear dominates every British street

that cannot be seen from
120 the road – it will be refused
planning permission unless
it is designed in a style and
materials that ape what
went before.

125 But what is more offensive? A dignified new building that cannot be seen or a
T-shirt that will pollute a
hundred streets, malls and
130 railways stations?

Leisurewear is meant to
be noisy. Its supposedly
relaxed nature cannot con-
ceal a strident heart. If you
135 go skiing today, you need
dark glasses or goggles, not
just to shield your eyes
from the sunlight, but to
protect them from the
140 kaleidoscopic glare dazzling
off polychrome ski outfits.
These outfits are designed
to draw attention to the
individual skier, to say
145 'Hey! Look at me!'.

Traditional ski outfits
were designed in colours
that blended with winter
mountain scenery. The skier
150 appeared a small part of a
much bigger creation.
Today, the leisure skier has
no such modesty.

The joy of traditional
155 clothing – which can range
from the most fogeyish city
suit to an innovative cou-
ture dress – is that it
enhances wearer, onlooker
160 and surroundings.

If you stroll along a street
in the City of London, you
will still find clothes, taxis,
buses, police and buildings
165 working together to ani-
mate a scene harmoniously.
On a country walk, it is still
possible to find parts of
Britain in which walker,
170 country clothes, dog, horse,
farmyard and scenery work
together.

As soon as you see some-
one dressed in day-glo
175 leisurewear in a city street,
however, that civic har-
mony is upset.

As soon as you clap eyes
on an acolyte of leisure on
180 a country walk, natural harmony is luridly sabotaged.
Because it demands very
little of people, leisurewear
is infectious. Increasingly,
185 people in uniformed jobs
adapt their costume to
accommodate the dictates
of Leisure.

British Rail workers and
190 bus staff have become
famous for their scruffy
appearance. They have
done away with the tie, jet-
tisoned the cap and
195 replaced polished shoes
with 'Levis for Feet'.

The point about a uniform
is that it identifies public
servants. It singles out the
200 person who can be turned

to for information or when
something goes wrong.
When the driver of a train
or the conductor of a bus is
205 dressed Blade Runner-style
– a cross between a
shopped-out Saturday shopper and a jogger with a beer
gut – are you sure you want
210 to turn to him for help? His
clothes suggest he doesn't
really care about his job.

Perhaps the saddest thing
about leisurewear is that it
215 denies great chunks of
British society the right to
walk with dignity when they
lose their youthful looks.
Old men confined to
220 leisurewear (through habit
or because, at the price
most can afford, the market
offers little else) looks particularly undignified.
225 Dressed in jacket, tie and
hat, the most creaky old
man looks good. That can
be tested out by ambling

through any Italian town.
230 Perhaps old people are
accorded greater dignity in
Italy than they are in
Britain, not because Italians
are, on the whole, a more
235 sociable lot than the British,
but because they *look* dignified.

Leisurewear is unlikely to
go away just yet. Anything
240 easy is preferable to anything that requires effort,
and that goes for dressing as
much as it does for most
British architecture and
245 design of today.

Grandfather is unlikely
ever again to don ironed
shirt, tie and cap to prune
the rose bushes. His dignity
250 gone, he really doesn't mind
looking like a liquorice allsort well past its sell-by
date.

Jonathan Glancey, the *Independent*

a Give an evaluation of the style of the passage, concentrating especially on language, register, syntax and imagery. *(12 marks)*

b Show how the writer's attitude to his subject is revealed through his tone. *(10 marks)*

c By what means does the writer attempt to convince you of the validity of his viewpoint? *(12 marks)*

d What kind of audience would you consider this piece to have been directed at? *(8 marks)*

e To what extent do you accept the writer's attack on contemporary fashion? *(8 marks)*

(Total of 50 marks)

Now study these specimen answers.

*a   **Give an evaluation of the style of the passage, concentrating especially on language, register, syntax and imagery.***

The passage is written in a lively and entertaining style. The tenor of the piece is personal, creating the impression that the writer is addressing the reader directly. An educated vocabulary, with words like 'clerestories', 'strident', 'urbane' and 'luridly sabotaged' is mixed with colloquial language, with the occasional use of slang words like 'slob', 'scruffy' and 'beer gut', to create a register which gives the impression of an infuriated academic deliberately slipping into the style of the mass culture which he derides. A particularly good example of this mixing of registers is in the phrase 'clap eyes on an acolyte of leisure'. The language of the passage as a whole is essentially concrete, and full of precise illustrations.

The syntax also reflects the mixing of registers. It is frequently used to help create the accents of speech, as in the sentence: 'Traditionally, a good English suit hides its label – if it has one – in the lining of an inside pocket', with its informal use of dashes. Few of the sentences are complex in construction, though it is rare to find sequences of short sentences. The paragraph beginning 'Traditional ski outfits were designed . . .' (line 146) is an exception in this respect, consisting of three simple sentences. The paragraphs are mostly short. Rhetorical repetition is a device used to add forcefulness to the writing, as in the sequence of sentences beginning in line 74: 'For leisurewear means . . . Leisurewear means . . . Leisurewear means . . . Leisurewear means . . .'. Rhetorical questions are also used, to personalise the writer's appeal to the reader, as in the sentence: 'Why do people pay for these clothes?' and the sentence beginning 'How are you meant to respond to a fat, ill-shaven slob . . . ?')

The imagery used in the passage creates a humorous effect. The comparison of people dressed in 'strident acid colours' with 'the contents of a packet of liquorice allsorts' is amusingly apt, as is the simile of 'crests on medieval uniforms' to mock the wearing of 'makers' names' on leisurewear. The style can be extremely expressive at times, as in the phrase 'the gum-chewing, burger-stuffing and soft-drink suckling', making effective use of assonance in 'gum', 'stuffing' and 'suckling', creating an overall onomatopoeic effect. At its best, the writing can capture a vivid sense impression through its mixture of styles, notably in the phrase: 'the kaleidoscopic glare dazzling off polychrome ski outfits'.

b   *Show how the writer's attitude to his subject is revealed through his tone.*

The writer's attitude to 'day-glo' fashion is one of anger and resentment; he feels that this particular aspect of 'leisure creed' is a crude and frequently offensive intrusion into everyday contemporary life. This attitude is expressed through the tone, which is consistently angry, and becomes bitterly vituperative at times, as in the paragraph beginning in line 106, with its 'fat, ill-shaven slob . . . wearing a garish and very sweaty sweatshirt' with its obscene motto. Phrases like 'pollute a hundred streets' and 'luridly sabotaged' display a tone of intense anger, and this is frequently mixed with a savagely contemptuous tone in descriptions such as 'gum-chewing, burger-stuffing and soft-drink suckling' and 'slob culture'. Even when the tone is humorous, it is sardonic humour, as in the description of a whole nation '. . . dressed . . . in man-made fabric representations of the contents of a packet of liquorice allsorts'.

c   *By what means does the writer attempt to convince you of the validity of his viewpoint?*

This is a polemical article, in which the writer expresses his disgust at an aspect of modern life which he finds repugnant. His intention is therefore to encourage the reader to view the situation through his eyes, and share his repugnance.

He does this partly by direct, powerfully emotive assertions, such as: 'Yet leisurewear is visual pollution of the highest order'. The sense of outrage he conveys is allied to a sense of humour, by which the reader is invited, for instance, to laugh at the idea of the grandfather 'looking like a liquorice allsort well past its sell-by date'. He uses rhetorical questions to encourage acceptance of his viewpoint, such as: 'But what is more offensive? A dignified new building that cannot be seen or a T-shirt that will pollute a hundred streets, malls and railway stations?'

He offers a wide variety of illustrative evidence of the fashions which he is deriding, and quotes a particularly offensive example of sweatshirt emblems in lines 111–114. He uses extended illustrations of his points at times, as in the section on 'British rail workers and bus staff' (line 189 onwards), and is not afraid to employ exaggeration for comic effect, as in the description of the British rail official 'dressed Bladerunner-style – a cross between a shopped-out Saturday shopper and a jogger with a beer gut.' He also employs comparisons to add substance to his argument, as in the contrasting picture of the appearance of old people in Italy compared with Britain, and offers a parallel situation to create a feeling of injustice, in the section on the 'Cotswold resident' beginning in line 115. He offers an ideal against which to measure the situation which he is attacking, in the passage about 'a country walk' (lines 167–172).

d   What kind of audience would you consider the piece to have been directed at?

The passage is clearly directed at a relatively educated audience, who would be expected to understand words like 'anathema' and 'acolyte'. However, he gives the impression that he suspects some of his readers to be barely above the level of the 'slob culture' he derides. After mentioning a saying by St Thomas Aquinas, for instance, he patronisingly adds 'Aquinas lived a long time ago in Italy.' The target audience is likely to be traditional in their values, people who favour 'traditional clothing' and who could be assumed to share the writer's revulsion at 'fat, ill-shaven slobs' wearing sweatshirts with 'crude or insulting messages'. The passage seems to be principally aimed at those who 'find the leisure creed repugnant'. Socially and politically the target audience could be assumed to be conservative, middle-class and probably middle-aged people who would be likely to nod in agreement when the writer presents value judgements masquerading as facts, like 'British Rail workers and bus staff have become famous for their scruffy appearance'.

e   To what extent do you accept the writer's attack on contemporary fashion?

I feel that the writer overstates his case in his attack on contemporary fashion. It is perfectly true that 'leisurewear' is ubiquitous in Britain: T-shirts and especially trainers have become the normal clothing outside working hours for large numbers of British people. However, it is not true to suggest, as the writer does, that a high proportion of old men are 'confined to leisurewear' and have therefore lost their 'dignity'. The great majority of old men dress relatively formally, and although jeans have been the norm amongst young people for decades, the 'day-glo' fashions which he derides are not as all-pervasive as he suggests. I personally find casual dress comfortable and relaxing, whilst ties in particular are uncomfortable and restricting. I find it hard to feel completely relaxed in a suit, and hard not to in a T-shirt and shorts. As for emblems on T-shirts, these are more often amusing than offensive, and the example he gives, though admittedly gross, is very much the exception rather than the rule.

Comprehension and analysis practice exercises

The exercises which follow are designed to provide practice in the full range of comprehension and analysis skills discussed in this chapter.

You are advised to spend about one and a half hours on each exercise.

1   The first extract which follows is an article which appeared in *The Sunday Times* in October 1990, and the second is an abridgement of a letter which appeared in the magazine *English* in November 1990. Read both extracts carefully, and answer the following questions:

a Do you consider Norman Stone's article a 'good' piece of journalism, in which he presents his case convincingly? *(10 marks)*

b Comment in some detail on the tone of Norman Stone's article. *(8 marks)*

c Give a precise explanation of the relevance of the picture which accompanies Bob Bibby's letter to the contents of the letter, and consider whether the wolf-child story adds to the persuasiveness of his argument. *(6 marks)*

d Each writer refers to the idea that standards in English are declining; the one treats it as a fact whilst the other describes it as a 'myth'. Do you find the one more convincing than the other and for what reasons? *(9 marks)*

e In paragraph 6 of his letter (beginning in line 139), Bibby makes an implicit defence of GCSE against the old O levels, and paragraph 11 of Stone's article (beginning in line 199) explicitly attacks GCSE. Basing your answer on the arguments presented and on your own educational experience, say with which writer you are more inclined to agree. *(8 marks)*

f Comment on Stone's remarks about A levels in the light of your experience so far as an A-level student. *(9 marks)*

(50 marks total)

Pulling out A levels will not cure education's toothache

The team that produced a preposterous national curriculum is out to cause more havoc, warns Norman Stone

A cruel and not inaccurate description of the British monarchy is 'a gold filling in a mouthful of rotting teeth' – a remark made, I recall, by Lindsay Anderson. There are other institutions to which you can apply it: and one of them is under fire at the moment. We all, by and large, agree that our educational system is the worst in Europe. Its crowning element is the A level, in theory a rather testing examination for 18-year-olds, who are supposed to show a high degree of knowledge in two or three specialist subjects.

In the old days it certainly was a testing business: if you did French, for instance, you had to work through a stack of Racine, and the vocabulary was hard work. (To this day, thanks to a brilliant teacher at Glasgow Academy, I can still defeat my colleagues in French when it comes to words such as 'itinerant scissors-grinder' or 'maidenhair fern'.) Pressures are now mounting for the abolition of the A level. The team that snowed our teachers under with a preposterous national curriculum is now working out ways to wreck the rest.

Now, it is true that there is something wrong with the A level. It is, in many ways, a glossy, antiquated flagship galleon in a flotilla of bumboats. Nowadays, people with A levels in, say, English, history and economics will not have more than primitive French, and no other languages, let alone decent maths. No other country of my acquaintance encourages such narrow specialisation at an early age: on the Continent, the higher school leaving certificate requires knowledge of half a dozen subjects, which is no doubt healthy.

Again, the origins of the A level are strange. We never really had public systems of examination: in the

19th century, they came from private initiatives, usually from churchmen. The done thing in those
70 days was to specialise in classics, and you bashed away to a high degree. The argument for this now looks strange, but there is
75 in my opinion much to be said for it: that the classics, properly taught, gave you a highly adaptable mind, capable of absorbing any-
80 thing else.

In any event, modernisers, by 1900, muttered that we were falling behind the Americans because our
85 education was not practical – in today's jargon, giving 'skills'. The higher certifi-cate (the nomenclature of A levels did not come until
90 later) therefore catered for other specialisations: his-tory, modern languages, etc., to begin with, then economics and, in our own
95 day, modish things such as sociology or political sci-ence (we have only just been spared 'peace stud-ies', though no doubt
100 women's history will come along some day).

The old system had much to commend it. In the first place, it relieved the uni-
105 versities of the burden of teaching elementary things, so that the English (as dis-tinct from the Scottish) uni-versities could in-and-out
110 their students in three years. Then again, the spe-cialisation did not really inhibit people from learn-ing other things: this was
115 done informally, and it was quite usual for boys of 17 at a good public or grammar school just to sit about reading.
120 Of late, the system has

declined, rather. In some subjects, standards are still high, demonstrably so with the 'quantifiable' ones, such
125 as maths or physics. In oth-ers, they are obviously not what they once were. I doubt if an A level in English nowadays amounts
130 to much; instead of the great stacks of classics which once you had to know, many of the boards supply modish pap; spelling
135 has badly declined; and in any case there is a very modern-English problem with examiners, in that they are swamped in scripts,
140 marking which is demand-ing on the nerves, and are paid comical money per script (£1.83 and the like).

An examiner in these cir-
145 cumstances cannot be blamed if, with his 500 or 600 three-hour scripts con-taining mis-spelt effusions on, say, the plays of Edward
150 Bond, he dishes out the beta-alphas with a pepper-pot. These marks are now known, all too frequently, to be unreliable.
155 Voices are now raised for the abolition of this system. The Higginson Report spoke for something like the Scottish Highers, a
160 multi-subject leaving certifi-cate, not so highly spe-cialised. One consequence of this could be that the uni-versity course would have
165 to be lengthened to the Scots' usual four years and maybe even to most conti-nentals' five and more. Another consequence,
170 which deterred the Prime Minister herself from endorsing the report's sug-gestions, would be to weaken the flagship qualifi-
175 cation. But more voices are

now raised, not to abolish the A level, but to build into it some 'vocational' element – 'skills', in other words.
180 Most school pupils after 16 will stay on in some form of education and get some A level or equivalent at the end, to include something
185 that employers allegedly want.

That is tripe. Employers are not interested in grades: they just know if someone
190 can read, write, count and be honest. Then again, a great part of our working-class culture does not fit with schooling beyond a
195 certain age: if at 16 you can get a job earning £200 a week, schooling is not going to be attractive.

In any case, the new pro-
200 posals suffer from that crip-pling English guilt about 'class'. In order to avoid class-discrimination and supposed hurt-feelings on
205 the part of the non-acade-mic, we have to devise an examination to fit everyone. This was done, in effect, when the old O levels were
210 replaced by GCSE, an examination regarded with ribaldry and contempt by almost every teacher whom I have consulted. Most of
215 them say that it could be, and has been, passed even by a bright 10-year-old. If A levels are diluted in the same way we shall end up,
220 as was rightly said the other day, in a country which pro-duces neither brain sur-geons nor plumbers.

There are many things
225 wrong with A levels, and they are not what they were. But they still represent a standard of some serious-ness, at a time when stan-
230 dards elsewhere have

slipped. They are also part of a culture, which is not going to be altered simply by tinkering away at its manifestations.

If you abolish or water down the A level, then you would also have to extend university courses, rope trade unions into apprenticeship schemes, and make it compulsory for Sharon and Tracey to stay on at school instead of heading for a job in a boutique or a hairdressers.

In other words, you would have to be a German. There, the unions, in enlightened fashion, have just agreed that wage rates in East Germany can be flexible; they will help out with extending apprenticeships, too. The German school-teachers' union (and the lecturers' union) appealed to the voters in the recent local elections to vote only for parties that agree to 'pluralism' in education, i.e. without compulsory comprehensives.

None of these things, sadly, apply in England. Therefore, we cannot get a sensible system of vocational training for the non-academically-inclined. The problem would only be worsened if we now try and use the battered old A level for a purpose remote from it. You do not cure the rotten teeth by pulling out the gold filling.

Norman Stone, *The Sunday Times*, 21 October 1990

Crying Wolf

Bob Bibby *urges the new Secretary of State not to fall prey to the myths of declining standards*

When I was a young teacher, there was a story current in the neighbourhood where I worked of a young woman who had given birth to a child with a wolf's head. No one had ever actually seen this child but the story was widely believed. I have since encountered this story, and variations of it, in other neighbourhoods in other times and have heard from colleagues that it crops up in other parts of the country too. The story is, of course, a myth, no doubt arising from subconscious fears within the human psyche, but nevertheless it is a powerful myth and all the more so because it will not go away.

There exists an equally powerful myth about English in our schools which says that standards are falling. The myth has been propounded regularly throughout the quarter of a century I have been a teacher (and, of course, for at least 100 years before that). It has given rise to two major government inquiries into the state of English teaching which resulted in the 1975 Bullock Report, *A Language for Life*, and the 1988 Kingman Report, not to mention the Cox Report which has subsequently been translated into the National Curriculum for English. Each of those two inquiries was in response to panic about supposed falling standards. The myth's current manifestation will be telling you that standards of reading and spelling are falling. My worry is that you will fall prey to those myths rather than seek proper evidence.

For the evidence tells a very different story – a story of considerable success. It is there in the published reports of your Inspectorate, who state quite unequivocally in *The Teaching and Learning of Language and Literacy*, their survey of inspections carried out in primary schools between 1983 and 1988:

'The basic skills of reading and writing continue to receive a great deal of time and attention. The standards achieved are generally good and continue to improve.'

It is there in the published reports of the Assessment of Performance Unit (APU) which was set up in response to a previous panic and which summarised its sampling operations in schools by stating in 1988:

'Very few children appeared to have problems decoding the printed word. The initial stages of literacy have been

passed by all but a tiny minority of 11-year-olds.'

90 It is there in the statistics which demonstrate a dramatic improvement in the achievements of 16-year-olds in English at GCSE and
95 of 18-year-olds at A level.

I also have to tell you that the myth does not match with the reality I experience daily in my work as an
100 English adviser, visiting classrooms and witnessing dedicated teachers at work, and as Chair of NATE, talking with and listening
105 to teachers discussing their practice. From them I rediscover the excitements of learning, such as when a five-year-old finds for the
110 first time that he can read a whole story to his teacher, or a non-reading eight-year-old discovers she can hold a group of secondary
115 pupils enthralled with a story she has made up, or a 12-year-old can recognise the difficulty of explaining a playground game to a
120 group of infants, or a 16-year-old can feel the confi-

dence to write a letter to the Prince of Wales, following the latter's criticisms of
125 the state of English teaching, which concludes:

'May I respectfully point out to your Highness that some people are 'cursed'
130 with poor spelling. I am one of these disadvantaged few, but I have found that rechecking my work irons out these small discrepan-
135 cies. If your staff have the same problem, why not tell them to check spellings with a dictionary?'

Sadly, I also find that
140 many of these committed, conscientious and caring teachers feel bewildered by the constant media attacks on them. They know that
145 what they are helping their pupils to achieve is way beyond what you or I were expected to achieve at a similar age. They know that
150 they are helping their pupils to become truly skilled language users whose making of meaning will contribute massively to their present
155 and future identities as

members of our society. They know that what they do, at their best, is more likely to produce youngsters
160 who will 'be able to participate effectively in a democracy' (to quote the Kingman Report) than prodding them through the sorts of
165 decontextualised exercises in grammar and spelling and reading that you and I passed through and forgot.

So let me end this letter
170 where I began, with a plea to you in your new role as Secretary of State for Education. The plea is twofold: first, that you
175 eschew the myths about English teaching that inevitably you will be exposed to and instead seek evidence of what is really
180 happening; and second, that you refuse the easy option of blaming teachers of English for the failings of the nation and instead find
185 words of praise for what they are enabling their pupils to achieve.

Bob Bibby, *English*, November 1990

2 Read the following article carefully and answer the questions on it.

a Briefly explain the 'two incidents' referred to in paragraph 5, and show why the writer considers them to be of 'the utmost relevance'. *(8 marks)*

b Examine the writer's claim that 'in modern society, paintings investigate, as nothing else but literature and religion can, the great questions of suffering, hope, love, death and redemption' (lines 119–125). Show the ways in which you personally feel that literature can 'investigate' the 'great questions' mentioned. *(12 marks)*

c Explain, in your own words, the arguments which the writer puts forward for asserting that 'Individuals, like nations, need to contemplate Piero and Rubens' (lines 125–127). *(6 marks)*

d To what extent do you find the writer's arguments against introducing admission charges for public art galleries in Britain convincing? You should consider the methods by which he attempts to convince you. *(10 marks)*

e Give a brief evaluation of the style of the article, concentrating on the use of language. *(8 marks)*

f Explain what you understand by the quotation from Lord Clark in the final paragraph, and say why you feel that the author concluded his article with this quotation. *(6 marks)*

Charge that would be self-defeating

Neil MacGregor, director of the National Gallery, opposes any financial barriers between the public and its treasury of pictures

In the spring of 1918, at one of the bleaker moments of the First World War, the government resolved to make a special grant for the British nation. This allocation of extraordinary funds was voted not for munitions or food, which were indisputably in short supply, but for paintings, to enable the Trustees of the National Gallery to bid in Paris at the great sale held in March of that year of the pictures owned by Degas. With these funds, the Trustees acquired for the nation Delacroix's portrait of Baron Schwiter, three works by Ingres, a Gauguin still-life and the monumental fragments of Manet's *Execution of the Emperor Maximilian.*

Twenty-three years later, in March 1941, when the United States was preparing to intervene in the Second World War, President Roosevelt accepted, on behalf of the American people, the National Gallery of Art in Washington, given by Mr Andrew Mellon, enriched by the gifts of Messrs Kress and Widener, and modelled in every material respect on the National Gallery in London.

Like its sister institution in Trafalgar Square, the Washington National Gallery was to be maintained at public expense, to present the highest achievements of Western art and to be open to all free of charge: access to great art was one of the defining characteristics of a free nation.

In a striking phrase, President Roosevelt argued that 'great works of art have a way of breaking out of private ownership into public use'. And that use, he went on, was to stand as 'symbols of the human spirit and of the work the freedom of the human spirit made'.

These two incidents are, I believe, of the utmost relevance today. Anglo-Saxons are not, as is often alleged, Philistines, nor have we ever been. On the contrary, the peoples of Northern Europe and North America have set the standards in public access to art.

The great achievement of the British Museum, the National Gallery and our other national collections has been envied and emulated abroad: the complex of Smithsonian museums and art collections in the Mall in Washington is, like our public collections, a tangible result of the Enlightenment ideal that every citizen should have the right of access to the highest. And that ideal is today a reality not only in London and Washington, but in Glasgow and Leeds; Forth Worth, St Louis, Cleveland and Malibu; Copenhagen and Berlin.

In recent years there have been critics of this achievement. They argue that the cost of free galleries is too high, or that things not paid for are never fully appreciated. They would have us follow the example of Paris or New York. They argue that financial conditions in the United Kingdom are now such that we should abandon the tradition of two centuries, remove from the public the right of easy familiarity with their paintings, and charge for entrance. The suggestions are seriously made and must be seriously considered.

Wartime insistence on the central place of art is of course inspiring, but it is in no sense surprising. In modern society, paintings investigate, as nothing else but literature and religion can, the great questions of suffering, hope, love, death and redemption. Individuals, like nations, need to contemplate Piero and Rubens for exactly the reasons they need to read Dante and Shakespeare: in joy or in distress, the unconsidered life is no life at all. Our art galleries have the crucial task of allowing people to take themselves seriously. They exist that we may not only have life, but have it abundantly.

And not just on one free day a week. Anyone who has used a gallery for respite knows the importance of even a brief visit – indeed, especially of a brief visit when the opportunity occurs. From the very foundation of the National Gallery, the significance of free entry and easy access for all was stressed. The gallery was to be situated not in a pleasant, leafy suburb (although that might have been better for the pictures than the sulphurous centre), but 'in the very gangway of London', so that all might reach it with ease. And the prime minister responsible for its foundation, that arch-Tory Lord Liverpool, was from the beginning insistent that even babes in arms should be allowed in; for if babes were excluded, so would be all parents without servants to tend them.

I find it hard to believe that the need for access to beauty in daily life is less now than it was 170 years ago. During that time, around 1,300 of the National Gallery's paintings have been given to the nation, while the other 700 or so have been bought for it. They were given or purchased (like those bought in 1918) on the understanding that they would be available to all, and in normal circumstances all are on view.

Galleries exist, as Roosevelt said, for public use. Each person uses them in his or her own way, but to use a gallery, you must visit it. If we reduce the number of visitors by 40 per cent (and the evidence from art museums suggests that this would be the minimum effect of introducing a charge of any sort), then we reduce by the same proportion the use the public makes of its collections.

The value of a visit to a museum or gallery is, of course, unquantifiable. We cannot know how many lives have been affected, or in what degree, by contact with great paintings. What we can quantify is the number of people who use the gallery, and that has now climbed to well over three million a year: to accommodate and serve them better, we are opening the Sainsbury Wing in 1991. What they gain from their visit only they know, but the numbers, and the numbers of those who return, suggest it is something of great value.

We should be proud to have led the world in the tradition of free museums and galleries.

The economic aspects of this question are peripheral. Since 1824, the National Gallery has been outstandingly fortunate in its friends, and never more so than in the last five years. Charging for admission is, nonetheless, always an option to be considered, given the huge sums required to put the building to rights or to buy paintings worthy of the collection.

At best the National Gallery might raise a net £500,000 a year from entrance charges. We already earn nearly twice that much each year from our shop (the proceeds of which recently bought the Caspar David Friedrich *Winter Landscape*), and gifts to the gallery in cash and in kind exceeded £5 million last year. Customers in the shop are visitors to the gallery, and their numbers would dwin- dle if they were made to pay for entrance.

There can be no doubt that benefactors want their pictures to be seen and enjoyed by as many people as possible. In the same way, our sponsors would like as many as possible to enjoy the fruits of their sponsorship. If shop receipts, gifts and sponsor- ship are jeopardized, the net gain – £500,000 at the outside – is likely to be con- siderably less than we shall lose.

Even so £500,000 repre- sents less than 5 per cent of our annual expenditure. Of course, the National Gallery must do what it can to raise money, but all our experience suggests that the money can be raised in ways that do not keep the public from their pictures.

Disraeli once remarked that it is private life that governs the world. This argument concerns free access to one of the most important things in private life. One of my predecessors at the National Gallery, Lord Clark, memorably observed: 'You ask me what is the purpose of art? I can only reply, what is the pur- pose of love?'

Neil MacGregor, *The Times*, December 1989

(50 marks total)

3 The passage below is from *Eminent Victorians*, written by Lytton Strachey, which was published in 1918. It is about Florence Nightingale's work during the Crimean War (1854–1856).

Read the passage, and answer the following questions.

Mark allocations are shown in brackets.

a Explain in your own words the problems caused by the arrival of a large number of sick and wounded men.   *(8 marks)*

b Using the evidence provided by the passage, explain why Florence Nightingale said that nursing was 'the least important of the functions into which she had been forced.'   *(8 marks)*

c What effect did Florence Nightingale's presence have on the sick and wounded men?   *(6 marks)*

d What do you think is Lytton Strachey's purpose in writing this account, and how successful do you think he has been?   *(10 marks)*

e Examine the techniques used to contrast the behaviour of the authorities with that of Florence Nightingale. Your answer should concentrate on language, syntax and structure.   *(10 marks)*

f Imagine that present-day tabloid newspapers existed when the events described in this passage took place. Write an editorial of approximately 75 words, with an appropriate heading, in which the newspaper's attitude is expressed.   *(8 marks)*

All at once, word came from the Crimea that a great new contingent of sick and wounded might shortly be expected. Where were they to go? Every available inch in the wards was occupied; the affair was serious and pressing, and the authorities stood aghast. There were some dilapidated rooms in the Barrack Hospital, unfit for human habitation, but Miss Nightingale believed that if measures were promptly taken they might be made capable of accommodating several hundred beds. One of the doctors agreed with her; the rest of the officials were irresolute: it would be a very expensive job, they said; it would involve building; and who could take the responsibility? The proper course was that a representation should be made to the Director-General of the Army Medical Department in London; then the Director-General would apply to the Horse Guards, the Horse Guards would move the Ordnance, the Ordnance would lay the matter before the Treasury, and, if the Treasury gave its consent, the work might be correctly carried through, several months after the necessity for it had disappeared. Miss Nightingale, however, had made up her mind, and she persuaded Lord Stratford – or thought she had persuaded him – to give his sanction to the required expenditure. One hundred and twenty-five workmen were immediately engaged, and the work was begun. The workmen struck; whereupon Lord Stratford washed his hands of the whole business. Miss Nightingale engaged two hundred other workmen on her own authority, and paid the bill out of her own resources. The wards were ready by the required date; 500 sick men were received in them; and all the utensils, including knives, forks, spoons, cans and towels, were supplied by Miss Nightingale.

This remarkable woman was in truth performing the function of an administrative chief. How had this come about? Was she not in reality merely a nurse? Was it not her duty simply to tend the sick? And indeed, was it not as a ministering angel, a gentle 'lady with a lamp', that she actually impressed the minds of her contemporaries? No doubt that was so; and yet it is no less certain that, as she herself said, the specific business of nursing was 'the least important of the functions into which she had been forced'. It was clear that in the state of disorganization into which the hospitals at Scutari had fallen, the most pressing, the really vital need was for something more than nursing; it was for the necessary elements of civilized life – the commonest material objects, the most ordinary cleanliness, the rudimentary habits of order and authority. 'Oh, dear Miss Nightingale,' said one of her party as they were approaching Constantinople, 'when we land, let there be no delays, let us get straight to nursing the poor fellows!' 'The strongest will be wanted at the wash-tub,' was Miss Nightingale's answer. And it was upon the wash-tub, and all that the wash-tub stood for, that she expended her greatest energies. Yet to say that is perhaps to say too much. For to those who watched her at work among the sick, moving day and night from bed to bed, with that unflinching courage, with that indefatigable vigilance, it seemed as if the concentrated force of an undivided and unparalleled devotion could hardly suffice for that portion of her task alone. Wherever, in those vast wards, suffering was at its worst and the need for help was greatest, there, as if by magic, was Miss Nightingale. Her superhuman equanimity would, at the moment of some ghastly operation, nerve the victim to endure and almost to hope. Her sympathy would assuage the pangs of dying and bring back to those still living something of the forgotten charm of life. Over and over again her untiring efforts rescued those whom the surgeons had abandoned as beyond the possibility of cure. Her mere presence brought with it a strange influence. A passionate idolatry spread among the men: they kissed her shadow as it passed. They did more. 'Before she came,' said a soldier, 'there was cussin' and swearin', but after that it was as 'oly as a church.' The most cherished privilege of the fighting man was abandoned for the sake of Miss Nightingale. In those 'lowest sinks of human misery', as she herself put it, she never heard the use of one expression 'which could distress a gentlewoman'.

Lytton Strachey

5 The Third World

More than half the people in the world are living in serious poverty, undernourished, or at best malnourished, and hence prevented from having any hope of achieving their full potential. One in every three is living in absolute, abject poverty[1]: underfed and, as a consequence, lacking in vitality and highly prone to disease; ill–housed; most probably underemployed and illiterate. Many millions of people in Latin America, Asia and Africa are destitute. It is to the majority of countries in these areas that the term 'Third World' applies. Every day, on average, 15,000 people there starve to death.

The purpose of this chapter is to explore the crisis of world hunger, and perhaps provoke some discussion of tentative solutions. The passage for comprehension is a 'utopian' solution to the world crisis in general. Then follows a glimpse of individual lives of some of the world's poor. The remainder of the chapter presents the two main schools of thought on the crisis of world hunger: first, that the root of the problem is the 'population explosion', and secondly, that it lies in the unequal distribution of the world's food and resources. Each of these views will be explored largely through selections from works by two influential writers.[2]

Comprehension and analysis

The passage which follows was written by the English novelist and social critic, H. G. Wells, in 1931. Entitled 'Our world in 50 years' time', it was reprinted in *The Observer* 50 years later on 28 December 1980. Read it carefully, and answer the questions. You are advised to spend about one and a half hours on this exercise.

1 According to the International Labour Office, quoted in Paul Harrison, *Inside the Third World*, pp. 405–6.
2 It is perhaps worth mentioning that this chapter is closely related to the one which follows, on the environmental crisis. The two chapters can be taken together, and treated at length, over two or three sessions, as a single topic: 'The World in Crisis'. Some of the essay questions and the debate suggestion at the end of Chapter 6 invite this treatment.

a Explain what Wells means when he says 'the abolition of distance . . . has made all the governments in the world misfits'. (lines 5–6) (*4 marks*)

b Why are 'peoples' (line 15) and 'modern democracy' (line 31) in inverted commas?   (*3 marks*)

c Explain in your own words Wells' view of politicians and the nature of international politics.   (*6 marks*)

d What, according to Wells, would be needed to reverse the drift towards 'catastrophe'?   (*5 marks*)

e Explain briefly, in your own words, Wells' vision of the future of the world, if his ideas were accepted and put into practice.   (*7 marks*)

f Write an evaluation of Wells' style of writing in this passage, with particular reference to his uses of language, syntax and imagery.   (*10 marks*)

g How persuasive have you found this piece of writing?   (*8 marks*)

h In your opinion, have recent world events tended to indicate that Wells' pessimism was justified or not?   (*7 marks*)

(*50 marks total*)

Instead of progress there is crisis everywhere. There is no government, not even the American, which has now the manifest fixity of the 'Great Powers' of the 1880s. There is a growing scepticism whether any existing government is as necessary as it ought to be. All contemporary governments have been outgrown – physically and mentally –
5   by the needs of mankind. The abolition of distance, foretold fifty years ago, is achieved. That has made all the governments in the world misfits. Seventy-odd sovereign governments, all acting independently and competitively, all jammed together by that abolition of distance, are trying to carry on the affairs of our race, which now, under the new conditions, would be far more conveniently and
10 successfully dealt with as one world business. Human life has become a world-wide thing, but governments remain cramped and partial things.
     More and more people are coming to realise this. Yet none of us knows clearly how to change over to a more comprehensive and securer way of running the world.
     While we puzzle over the riddle, armaments go on, and the old – and now utterly
15 stupid – tradition of malevolence between sovereign governments and their 'peoples' is maintained. International politics still consist largely of idiotic attempts on the part of these seventy-odd governments, amid which our affairs are entangled, to get the better of their rivals, to maintain a flaming prosperity within their borders while restricting and injuring the welfare of all other peoples.
20   The old game goes on because the world lacks the mental energy to call it off. So we are all drifting through needless and wasteful economic war towards actual military war. Some years ago I wrote that the salvaging of civilisation was a race between education and catastrophe. Nowadays I am forced to add a qualification. Catastrophe indeed travels briskly; tariffs strangle trade; gold – the life blood of trade – is being
25 hoarded against some fresh day of reckoning; armaments increase; the friction between states intensifies. The new air war is being prepared. The new gas war is being prepared. But education has not even started yet. There is no race. It looks like a walk-over for catastrophe.
     In the schools of Britain, America, France, Germany, Italy, Japan today the school-
30 teachers are still doing the fundamental work of mental armament. There are few exceptions. And the hundreds of millions of 'modern democracy' show as much ability to protect their minds from subjugation and arrest the advancing disaster, which will enslave, torture, mutilate and destroy the greater proportion of them, as a trainload of hogs bound for Chicago.

35   Gladly would the prophet prophesy pleasant things. But his duty is to tell what he
sees. He sees a world still firmly controlled by soldiers, patriots, usurers and financial
adventurers; a world surrendered to suspicion and hatred, losing what is left of its
private liberties very rapidly, blundering toward bitter class conflicts, and preparing for
new wars.

40   The economic machine is stalling in every country in the world. The decline is
going on under our eye. Production is diminishing, trade is declining; presently we
shall find even our present educational and hygiene services too costly for our existing
methods of payment. Few people realise yet how flimsy are the liberties and securities,
the plenty and the leisure, we still enjoy.

45   The prophet must say what he sees. It is as if I was watching a dark curtain fall
steadily, fold after fold, across the bright spectacle of hope with which the century
dawned. The way toward a great world state of power, freedom, and general
happiness is still plainly open to mankind. We have been brought to the very borders
of the Promised Land of Progress. And the amount of visible human determination to
50 cross those borders and escape from the age-long sequences of quarrelling, futile
insufficiency, wars, and wasted generations that fill the blood-stained pages of history
is contemptible.

There is no inevitability in the approaching catastrophe. I confess I see no signs
whatever of any such awakening as might save us, but who can tell what may be
55 happening among the young, among the intelligent and wilful, outside one's range. It
would need nothing superhuman to avert the decline. We are not being beaten in an
honourable struggle; we are loitering and rotting down to disaster. A few thousand
resolute spirits, the tithe of a tithe of the misdirected heroism that went to waste in the
Great War, a few hundred million dollars for a world campaign for the new order,
60 might still turn the destinies of mankind right round toward a new life for our race.

It needs only that the governments of the United States, Britain, France, Germany
and Russia should get together in order to set up an effective control of currency,
credit, production and distribution; that is to say, an effective 'dictatorship of
prosperity' for the whole world.

65   The other sixty-odd states would have to join in or accommodate themselves to the
overruling decisions of these major powers. It is as simple a business as that, which
our presidents, potentates, statesmen, kings of finance and so forth, do not even
realise they could carry through, with human decay and disaster plain before them!

They just fumble along. The bands play and we 'troop the colours'. The party men
70 twaddle about debts and security. They cant patriotism. They love their countries so
that they would rather see them starve than let them co-operate with nasty
foreigners. They do their best to reassure the world – and do, it seems, succeed in
reassuring the world – that this skimped, anxious, dangerous life we lead is the best
that can be done for us. These rulers and leaders and statesmen of ours get in front of
75 the cameras at every possible opportunity to put their fatuous selves on record, while
Death, the Ultimate Creditor, and Collapse, the Final Stabiliser, add up their inexorable
accounts.

But given that wave of sanity, that sudden miraculous resolve to stop this foolery,
and what sort of world might we not have before another half century has passed?
80   Everyone alive might be by then a citizen of the whole world. All of us would then
be free to go where we would about this fascinating and sometimes so lovely planet,
which would have become our own. For most of our lives we should be released from
toil. All the necessities of the human population – food, abundant transport, clean,
fresh and beautiful housing and furniture, adequate health services, education, social
85 security – could be supplied now under modern conditions by something between 12
and 20 years of not too arduous work on the part of everyone. The town, the
countryside would be undergoing constant revision and improvement: the world city

would be constantly more gracious and pleasant; the world garden constantly more beautiful. The layout of industry could be as exciting as a game.

90   These are not the assertions of an 'imaginative writer'; they are possibilities proved up to the hilt by economists and by the scientific examination of these matters. Some 15 or 20 years of growth, education and preparation there would have to be for everyone, and the rest of life would be free for creative work, for graceful living, for movement and experience.

95   There is no need why any human being now should be underfed or ill-clad, badly housed or sickly. The whole world could be run as one concern and yield a universal well-being.

And it is no good mincing matters when it comes to saying why we have not this universal well-being at the present time. Most of our rulers and directors are, to put it

100 plainly, narrow-minded, self-centred, mentally indolent, pompous and pretentious creatures of the past; and we others are fools enough to tolerate their mismanagement. These ruling and controlling people have got enough for themselves, they stick to the controls like barnacles, they live in relative comfort and immense dignity, chiefly engaged in the defence of their own conceit, and the mass of us lacks

105 the spirit, will and understanding to call them to account.

A thousand million human beings are leading lives of want, limitation, humiliation and toil, scores of millions are in immediate danger of the futile tortures of war, and these dull, self-protective folk in control of things do nothing of what they might do and pose for our respect and admiration with infinite self-complacency.

110   But in another 50 years after that renascence – if, after all, it should occur – things will be different. For an ignorant world we shall have a soundly educated world, aware of its origins, capable of measuring and realising its possibilities, and controlling its destinies.

Every human being born into that world of plenty will learn from the beginning of

115 the varied loveliness of the life before it, and of the expanding drama of human achievement in which it has to play its part. Its distinctive gifts will be developed. It will be taught another history than that of kings and conquerors and armies. It will do its fair and definite share in the productive or other necessary service of mankind, and for the rest it will be released to accomplish whatever possibilities it has of innovation,

120 happiness, and interesting living.

That wide fine life is within reach of mankind; it is there for the taking. But mankind is not taking it. The curtain is falling. When the Promised Land is cut off forever, 'Homo sapiens' will be readily convinced there never was a Promised Land. The last thing we human beings will produce is concerted effort; only under the spur of greed

125 or panic do we produce that. We shake our heads sagely at the 'dreamers'. As long as possible we will go on living the close, ignoble lives of thieves, bullies, and drudges to which we are accustomed. We will snuffle our satisfaction that we are not in any 'fantastic Utopia'.

And when presently the rifles are put into our hands again, we shall kill. The whips

130 will be behind us and the 'enemy' in front. The Old History will go on because we had not the vigour to accept the new.

H.G. Wells

Themes for discussion

Some of the issues raised by H. G. Wells in this passage are perhaps of sufficient importance to warrant fuller discussion and analysis. Three of these issues are selected here. The first is of particular relevance to the world of the late 20th century, the second has been relevant since the dawn of mankind, and the third is of at least academic relevance to you, as a student.

1 The world economy	Is Wells' idea of a world government, or a 'dictatorship of prosperity', possible, or desirable? What factors continue to prevent it from happening?
	Which countries are currently most in debt to the West? What are they, and the creditor nations, doing about it?
	What is the IMF, and what does it do to help bring about world prosperity?
2 War	Wells talks about the 'now utterly stupid tradition of malevolence' between nations. Is war always 'utterly stupid', or are some wars essential?
	Are there any circumstances in which it is right to be a conscientious objector?
	What international wars are being fought at the moment? What civil wars are being fought in which other nations have significant military or economic involvement?
	For what reasons were wars generally fought in the past? Are the motives of warring nations today fundamentally different, on the whole?
3 Worldwide education	In which sense can it be argued that only 'education' can save the world from 'catastrophe', as Wells says?
	How many people in the world are still illiterate? How might their lives be improved if they became literate? Is literacy always desirable?
	Does it make any real difference to you if you read essays and works of fiction by creative writers such as H. G. Wells, or is literature simply 'art for art's sake'?

Preparing for discussion

Discussion, if it is to be more than a matter of 'sounding off' ideas, or 'letting off steam', needs to be informed. A fully effective discussion of some of the issues raised above will probably require at least some of the students in the class to do more than merely read the H. G. Wells passage. Here are some suggestions for preparing for such a discussion:

1 Read through the discussion questions and think about them before the class.
2 Look out for and collect items from newspapers and magazines on the discussion topics.
3 Be prepared to introduce this material into the class discussion.
4 In the case of very specific questions, such as the role of the IMF, and the situation of debtor and creditor nations, interested students, with advance warning of the discussion, should be prepared to undertake private research, and to report their findings to the class when the discussion takes place. It should be possible to find passages from books, magazines and newspapers, or to jot down details from television and radio programmes, which are relevant to the issue which they are researching. Students who specialise in or have studied other disciplines than English – economics, history and sociology in the case

of the three themes suggested above – should be in a particularly strong position to provide factual information to help with the discussions.

Creative essay

Write an essay of about 750 words on one of the following titles:
a What do you imagine the world will be like 50 years from now?
b Write the essay on 'the condition of humanity' which H. G. Wells might have written if he had been alive today.

The global situation approaching the millennium

In an article in *The Observer* in July 1996, Martin Jacques discusses a recent UN report on global growth and inequality. The following extracts provide an overview of the world situation at the approach of the millennium.

The wealth of the world's 358 billionaires exceeds the combined annual incomes of countries with nearly half the global population. The gap between rich and poor countries is growing. Since 1980, 100 countries have had stagnant or declining incomes, reducing living standards for a quarter of the world's population – or 1.6 billion people.

The losers fall into four main regional groups: sub-Saharan Africa, where decline mostly began in the late 1970s; Latin America and the Caribbean, although several here began to recover in the late 1980s; many Arab countries, which suffered from declining oil prices in the 1980s; and Eastern Europe and the countries of the former Soviet Union, where per capita income has fallen on average by a third since the mid-1980s.

[But] over the last 25 years, income per head in East Asia, which contains over a quarter of the world's population, has grown by more than 7 per cent a year – the most impressive performance in history.

The key to East Asia's success was a relatively equal distribution of public and private assets. Land reform was one key factor, the emphasis on mass education another.

East Asia has proved that it is possible, however far you are behind, to take off and close the gap with the West. But there is no denying that countries representing a quarter of the world's population have, in the last 15 years, fallen further behind. If present trends continue, the growing polarisation of wealth will be exacerbated: sub-Saharan Africa's share of world GDP would decline from 1.2 per cent in 1993 to 0.4 per cent in 2010.

The new knowledge-based economy creates the possibility of countries doing extraordinarily well, like East Asia, or extraordinarily badly, like sub-Saharan Africa.

The dilemma facing sub-Saharan Africa, Latin America and the Arab countries is how to end the cycle of decline. The biggest questions of all surround Africa. It is not difficult to explain the continent's lack of success: rising population, a delicate agrarian eco-system, poor and corrupt government, immense disparities of wealth and low levels of literacy. Africa needs a few success stories that can inspire other countries. But amid the gloom there are some encouraging signs: Uganda is doing relatively well and so, until recently, was Ghana, while Botswana rivals even East Asia.

We are moving into an era in which the disparity between winners and losers will be greater than ever before. Overtaking and leap-frogging will be the reward for those countries that get it right: isolation and marginalisation the fate of those that get it wrong.

Martin Jacques, *The Observer*, July 1996

Life in the Third World

Now let us see what it means in everyday reality to be an ordinary person who was born in a country in which the large majority of the population live in extreme poverty. Here are three glimpses into the lives of the Third World's poor.

In the first extract, Domitila Barrios de Chungara, the wife of a tin miner in Bolivia, describes her family's circumstances:

Our houses are very small, that is, we have a little room measuring four by five or six metres. That little room has to be living room, dining room, pantry, and bedroom. In some houses there are two little rooms, and one of them is the kitchen; they also have a little corridor. This is what the company housing is like, only the four walls, without any water or sanitary installations. And that's how we have to live, with our children, all crowded together. In my case, we set up three beds in the room; that's all that will fit. That's where my seven children sleep, that's where they do their homework, that's where we eat, that's where the kids play. In the little back room I have a table and a bed where I sleep with my husband. The few things we have just have to be piled one on top of the other, or hung from the ceiling, in the corridor. And the babies, well, some of them have to sleep in the beds and some of them under the beds. Wherever ...

For some hours during the day and all through the night we have electric light in the camp which the company gives us.

We also have drinking water. But not in the houses. In the neighbourhoods there are public water pumps. You have to line up to get water.

So you see, we don't have too many comforts. For example, we don't have a bath in the house. Of course, there are public baths, but there are 10 to 12 showers for everyone, for so many people, and these showers are for the whole camp. So the showers are open on alternate days; one day for the women and one day for the men. The showers only work when there's oil. Because the water is heated by oil.

Not only that, but there are only sanitary facilities, latrines, in the houses of the company's technical personnel. There aren't in the workers' houses. There are public latrines but only about ten of them, for a whole neighbourhood. For a whole neighbourhood! They get dirty very fast and there's no running water. In the mornings the company workers assigned to the job clean them; but afterward, all day long they're very dirty. And if there's no water, they're dirty for several days. Even so, we have to use them. Just like they are.

There are plenty of problems with water, especially in the non-company villages. They suffer there more than we do. They have to stand in long lines. They have to come from very far away to get their water. And in these villages they don't have electric light like us. Their life is really hard.

Domitila Barrios de Chungara

For the landless peasant's family the struggle is often a hopeless one. Here the English journalist and writer Paul Harrison illustrates the cycles of despair through which such people travel. The passage describes a family he met in Brazil:

Francisco's mother Fatima is small for her age. She is visibly weak, distant, yet easily irritated by the children. Years of pregnancy and menstruation, along with an iron-poor diet of maize, have made her chronically anaemic. Her husband Jaime is a landless labourer, with a low, erratic income barely enough to keep them all alive and clothed. No one eats enough, and when there's not enough to go round Fatima goes without, even when she's pregnant. And that is frequently, as the couple use no form of contraception. They have had ten children, six of whom survived to adulthood.

Fatima went through several periods of undernourishment while Francisco was in her womb. There were times when Jaime could not get regular work and everyone went hungry. Fatima also had several attacks of stress and anxiety when Jaine beat her. Francisco probably suffered his first bout of growth retardation, both mental and physical, before he even saw the light of day.

He was born underweight, and his brain was already smaller than normal size. For the first few months he was breast-fed and suffered few infections, as he was partly protected by the antibodies in his mother's milk. Then he was weaned onto thin gruels and soups, taken off the breast and put onto tinned evaporated milk, thinned down with polluted water from the well. His diet, in itself, was inadequate. Then he started to get more and more infections, fever, bronchitis, measles and regular bouts of gastro-enteritis. With well-fed children these pass within a few days, but in his case they went on for weeks and sometimes a month or more. In these periods he could tolerate no milk and few solids, and so was given weak broths, tea or sugar water. By now he was 25 per cent underweight. Because of poor nutrition, he was even more susceptible to infection, and each time he was ill, he lost his appetite and ate even less. Then he got bronchitis which developed into pneumonia.

But Fatima borrowed money off a relative, went to town and got antibiotics for him.

So he survived. But malnutrition made him withdrawn and apathetic. His mother got no reward for playing with him, so he received little of the stimulation his brain needed to develop properly. As he grew older, infections grew less frequent, but by the time he went to school, aged eight, he was already a year behind normal physical development and two years behind mentally. The school, in any case, was a poor one, with only three classes, no equipment, and a poorly qualified teacher. As Francisco was continually worried about whether and what he was going to eat that day, he was distracted, unable to concentrate, and seemed to show little interest in schoolwork. The teacher confirmed that he was a slow learner, and could not seem to get the hang of maths or reading and writing. As the family was poor, they did not want to keep him on at school. He was doing so badly anyway that there seemed no point. He did a year, then was away for three years helping an uncle who had a farm, then did another year, then left for good, barely able to read or write more than a few letters. He soon forgot what little he had learned. So, like his father, he began tramping round the local ranches asking for work. Without any educational qualifications or skills, that was all he could ever hope for. And because so many were in the same boat, pay was low. When he was 22 he married a local girl, Graciela, aged only 15. She too had been undernourished and was illiterate. She soon became pregnant and had to feed another organism inside her before she herself had fully developed. Graciela had heard about family planning from a friend, but Francisco would not let her use it and anyway she was not sure she wanted to. So by the age of only 25, Graciela already had five children and had lost two. The children had every prospect of growing up much as Francisco and Graciela did, overpopulating, underfed, in poor health and illiterate.

Paul Harrison

At the very bottom of the pile are the destitute. Paul Harrison met many people without work or hope in the Indian city of Calcutta. He describes some of them:

And there are the street dwellers . . .

The street dwellers are variously estimated to number anything from 40,000 to 200,000. You see them curled up on a straw mat or a piece of cardboard by the odd aluminium pot, along the staid colonial shopping arcades, under the subways, camped on a roundabout by the gigantic pylons of Howra bridge. A random line of them under a high wall by the riverside warehouses of Strand Road: a family of three living in a tiny shelter of torn khaki canvas slung over bamboo poles, not more than four feet square. A woman dreaming on her charpoy string bed, baby at her side with a tattered shirt over its face, pots, pans and boxes stuffed under the bed. A large family of eight under an awning, their tea cups neatly hanging from a string tacked to the wall. All this in full gaze of passers-by and a noisy flow of traffic. Street life is, by definition, a life lived in public.

Each of these faces hides a personal disaster: a 15-year-old boy whose parents died of cholera four years earlier. His uncles neglected him so he left his home village for Calcutta, and he earns two rupees a day collecting rags and scrap paper. A 25-year-old woman whose husband deserted her, so she had to move out of their bustee room. Now she lives on the pavement near the railway station, working as a domestic servant in the daytime and at night as a prostitute. A widow of 40 with five children: when her husband died she couldn't work the family smallholding and bring up the children, so she fell into debt and had to pay it off by selling house and land. Now she lives on a platform at Ballygunge railway station where she has to pay protection money to thugs to stop them driving her away. She supplements her meagre servant's pay by begging.

Paul Harrison

Suggestion for writing

Write a story, or a brief biography, about the life of either the 15-year-old boy or the 25-year-old woman in Calcutta referred to above.

The population explosion

Two writers who argue that the population explosion is the fundamental problem to be tackled, before world hunger and want can be eased, are the American environmentalists, Paul Ehrlich and Gordon Rattray Taylor. These extracts are taken from Ehrlich's *The Population Bomb*, published in 1968, and Taylor's *The Doomsday Book*, published in 1972. Despite the passage of a quarter of a century or more, the situation these writers describe is fundamentally the same as the end of the century draws near.

What the 'population explosion' means in simple terms is that the world's population is expanding at a rate vastly greater than at any previous period in human history and at a faster rate than resources and living space are likely to expand.

Recent projections of world population growth are contained in an article by Sanjay Kumar, entitled 'Too many people spoil the planet', published in the magazine *New Scientist* on 6 November, 1993.

Even according to conservative estimates, the global population of 5.5 billion could double within the next half century. The worst scenario puts the population at 19 billion by 2100 and 28 billion by 2150.

The global implications of population growth are variable, depending on the degree of development of the countries where the growth occurs, as the same *New Scientist* article indicates:

Britain's 0.2 per cent annual growth rate adds 116,000 people per year to its population. By contrast, Bangladesh, with a 2.4 per cent growth rate, adds 2.7 million. But every person in Britain uses more than 80 times as much fossil fuels as a Bangladeshi, so Britain's population growth effectively contributes 3.5 times as much carbon dioxide to the global atmosphere as Bangladesh's.

Rich and poor in Latin America

The immediate implications for countries like Bangladesh are graphically suggested by Paul Ehrlich on the front cover of *The Population Bomb*:

> 'While you are reading these words four people will have died of starvation. Most of them children.'

The principal reason for the explosion in world population is the vast increase in the proportion of people surviving infancy:

Around 1800, when the standard of living in what are today the DCs (Developed Countries) was dramatically increasing due to industrialisation, population growth really began to accelerate. The development of medical science was the straw that broke the camel's back. While lowering death rates in the DCs were due in part to other factors, there is no question that 'instant death control', exported by the DCs, has been responsible for the drastic lowering of death rates in the UDCs.[3] Medical science, with its efficient public health programmes, has been able to depress the death rate with astonishing rapidity and at the same time drastically increase the birth rate.

Paul Ehrlich

The fact that so many more people are surviving infancy results in an increasing proportion being at or near child-rearing age, which in itself accelerates the 'population explosion'.

It is already the case that in the under-developed world, about half the population is under 15 years of age.

Gordon Rattray Taylor

A rapidly expanding population in the 'Third World' has many repercussions in addition to malnourishment and starvation amongst the poor:

More people with more technology spells more pollution, more environmental distortion and less privacy. Much of the damage will come from attempts which will necessarily be made to feed the ever-increasing number of mouths, and to house their owners. The crash of falling timber, as forests are felled, will be echoed by the thunder of explosives, as canals and harbours are blasted into existence.

It is obvious that this process cannot continue for ever: when will the poison-point come? Some maintain the world could support 15,000 million people, one or two have put the figure as high as 30,000 million. The earlier figure could come in the lifetime of those now living, so the question is not an academic one.

Gordon Rattray Taylor

Think what it means for the population of a country to double in 25 years. In order just to keep living standards at the present inadequate level, the food available for the people must be doubled. Every structure and road must be duplicated. The amount of power must be doubled. The capacity of the transport system must be doubled. The number of trained doctors, nurses, teachers and administrators must be doubled. This would be a fantastically difficult job, say, even in the United States – a rich country with a fine agricultural system, immense industries, and rich natural resources. Think of what it means to a country with none of these.

Paul Ehrlich

The problems of providing schools and teachers become immense . . . In some African countries, already, despite unprecedented programmes of school-building, the percentage of children receiving education is falling: children are born faster than schools can be put up to receive them.

Gordon Rattray Taylor

In developing countries, cities are growing at a terrifying rate ... The extreme instance of city growth is expected to be Calcutta.[4] ... Already it is in a state of social disorganisation. The Metropolitan Planning Commission says that it sees 'no prospect' of housing the population over the next 25 years. At the moment, open-sided sheds are being built to provide some sort of shelter. Twenty or 30 people share a single cold tap.

3 Under Developed Countries, referred to later in this chapter as 'developing countries'.
4 At the beginning of the 1990s the city with the fastest growth was Mexico City: in 1950 its population was 3.05 million; by 1982 it was at 16.0 million, and the UN projection for 2000 is 26.3 million. (Figures taken from *Our Common Future: The World Commission on Environment and Development*, 1987.)

Sewage runs in open gutters in the streets, and at times of river-flood may be washed anywhere. People wash their clothes and themselves in the polluted water. Other parts of the city, of course, are highly civilised – but the disorganised sector is growing ...

New York, with a much longer experience, finds it hard enough to function at 12 million. Cities like Calcutta can hardly avoid becoming jungles, in which crime cannot be controlled, in which health standards cannot be maintained and in which people die on the pavement without the fact even being remarked ...[5]

In short, it seems certain that the mushrooming cities of the immediate future will be plagued by crime and mental disturbance of various kinds.

Gordon Rattray Taylor

Whilst population growth in developed countries like Britain has slowed to zero with the help of easily available birth control methods, the same methods in countries like India have had negligible effects, despite the fact that India has had an official birth control programme since 1952. The main reason is poverty:

Large families are a response to high death-rates in infancy and childhood. In many oriental countries the figure is ten or 12 children born, of whom formerly only two or three would survive. Now that death rates have been cut dramatically, people begin to attempt to limit their families, but not by the full amount required. Custom is important, and a family of two seems ridiculous in a culture geared to 12. Experience shows that it takes several generations for people to make a full response. The first generation cuts back from ten to seven or eight; the next to five or six and so on. But the period we are looking at is little more than one generation ...

Unfortunately, it is not the case that, when people are poor, they try to restrict the family to a size they can afford. Sometimes they hope their position will improve; sometimes they see their children as an asset, able to work in the fields or support them when they are old. There is thus little hope that the provision of contraception will, of itself, make much impact. The prime need is to convince people that two is the best family size.

Gordon Rattray Taylor

Writers such as Ehrlich and Taylor see hope only in controlling the world's birth-rate.

Basically, then, there are only two kinds of solution to the population problem. One is a 'birth-rate solution', in which we find ways to lower the birth-rate. The other is a 'death-rate solution', in which ways to raise the death-rate – war, famine, pestilence – find us ...

Men do not seem to be able to focus emotionally on distant or long-term events. Immediacy seems to be necessary to elicit 'selfless' responses. Few Americans could sit in the same room with a child and watch it starve to death. But the death of several million children this year from starvation is a distant, impersonal, hard-to-grasp event. You will note that I put quotes around 'selfish' and 'selfless'. The words describe the behaviour only out of context. The 'selfless' actions necessary to aid the rest of the world and stabilise the population are the only hope for survival. The 'selfish' ones work only towards destruction ...

Remember, above all, that more than half of the world is in misery now. That alone should be enough to galvanise us into action, regardless of the exact dimensions of the future disaster now staring 'Homo Sapiens' in the face.

Paul Ehrlich

5 The work of Mother Teresa of Calcutta alerted the world to the extent of the breakdown of normal human life in this city at the beginning of the 1990s.

The situation described in these extracts has shown little sign of improvement over the past quarter of a century.

In 1990, Paul Ehrlich, together with his wife Anne, published a follow-up to *The Population Bomb* called *The Population Explosion*. This book analyses the ways in which the picture presented in 1968 has changed. Here are some extracts.

When *The Population Bomb* was written, we and our colleagues were enormously worried about the course that humanity was on. Yet it is sobering to recall that the book appeared *before* depletion of the ozone layer had been discovered, *before* acid precipitation had been recognized as a major problem, *before* the current rate of tropical-forest destruction had been achieved, let alone recognized, *before* the true dimensions of the extinction crisis had been perceived, *before* most of the scientific community had recognized the possibility of a nuclear winter, and *before* the AIDS epidemic.

The size of the human population is now 5.3 billion, and still climbing. In the six seconds it takes you to read this sentence, 18 more people will be added. Each hour there are 11,000 more mouths to feed: each year, more than 95 million. Yet the world has hundreds of billions *fewer* tons of topsoil and hundreds of trillions *fewer* gallons of groundwater with which to grow food crops than it had in 1968.

India suffered greatly from hunger in the early 1970s. In 1987, environmental analyst R. N. Roy of the Catalyst Group in Madras described the outlook succinctly: 'With two-thirds of India's land threatened by erosion, water shortages and salinity, and with the added threat of pollution and increasing urban industrial demand, the country appears to be facing a catastrophic problem in the 1990s, if not earlier.' And don't forget: with an annual population growth rate of 2.2 per cent, India must somehow feed an additional 16 million people each year.

Since 1968, food production per person in Africa south of the Sahara has declined by some 20 per cent. Tropical African nations are too poor and debt-burdened to make up for all of the deficit with imports, and far too little food has been made available for donation. The result has been a continuous erosion of the nutritional status of Africans. Remarkably little has been accomplished in population control in the 20 years since *The Population Bomb* appeared. Global population growth has slowed a little, but nearly all of that slowdown is due to fertility reductions in two principal regions: China and the industrialized nations, especially the West. A few other developing nations have achieved significant fertility declines, but most are growing as rapidly as before.

Paul and Anne Ehrlich

Discussion suggestion

Assuming that the 'population explosion' *is* a serious world problem, you might discuss how the 'birth-rate solution' could be made more effective. You could consider such options as:

- wider early education about birth control and family limitation;
- free distribution of the pill or other birth-control devices, and education in their use;
- free abortion on demand;
- financial or other penalties for families which have more than, say, two children;
- government encouragement or enforcement of late marriage;
- compulsory sterilisation.

Some of these suggestions may seem grotesque, but all have been tried out somewhere in the world. Whether you find them acceptable or offensive, you should be able to explain why. Wide reading by one or more selected students will, of course, assist the discussion.

Note-taking

As well as jotting down interesting points brought up in class discussion, it can be a useful exercise to make summary notes of relevant articles and extracts which you have read. It is much easier to remember information and ideas if you have made notes on them.

As a preliminary exercise in note-taking, you could try listing, in note form, the main general points covered in the preceding section ('The population explosion') under the following five headings:

- Meaning
- Causes
- Effects
- Reasons for failure of policies
- Future prospects

Distribution of resources

Over the past couple of decades, a shift of emphasis in the analysis of world poverty has been noticeable. Many writers on population and global politics tend now to stress the unequal distribution of wealth as much as overpopulation as the principal cause of starvation and malnutrition.

This alternative analysis of world poverty is again represented by extracts from two books by influential writers: *How the Other Half Dies*, by the American writer Susan George, published in 1976, and *The Creation of World Poverty*, by the British writer Teresa Hayter, published in 1981.

Rich and poor: the global situation

The extent of world poverty and destitution today, and the contrast between rich and poor countries, is suggested by Teresa Hayter:

Wage rates in underdeveloped countries are often one twentieth to one thirtieth of those in the richer countries, for the same type of work . . .

Today the World Bank says that there are about 800 million people, or almost 40 per cent of the population of the so-called developing countries, who live in 'absolute poverty': 'a condition of life so characterised by malnutrition, illiteracy and disease as to be beneath any reasonable definition of human decency'. In some countries one child in four dies before the age of five. Millions of people live in houses or huts made of corrugated tin, cardboard boxes and other 'impermanent' materials. They have no running water and no toilets. Electricity is a luxury. Health services are rarely within walking distance, and have to be paid for. Primary education may be available and free, but often children are needed to work. There is generally no social security or unemployment pay, and many people, some 300 million, according to the ILO (International Labour Organisation), are without any kind of employment.

Teresa Hayter

Susan George also quotes from a statement by a representative of the World Bank (the major lending organisation):

World Bank figures show that 'on average the one billion people in the countries with per capita incomes below $200 consume only about 1 per cent as much energy per capita as the citizens of the United States'. The Bank's Mr McNamara also hopes that 'once the people of the United States understand that they, with 6 per cent of the world's population, consume about 35 per cent of the world's total resources, and yet in terms of economic assistance as a percentage of GNP rank 14th among the 16 developed nations . . . [they will not] turn away in cynicism and indifference'.

Susan George

The moral implications of this are starkly suggested by Rene Dumont, quoted by George:

'The rich white man, with his overconsumption of meat and his lack of generosity for poor people, behaves like a veritable cannibal – an indirect cannibal. By consuming meat, which wastes the grain that could have saved them, last year we ate the children of the Sahel, Ethiopia and Bangladesh. And we continue to eat them this year with undiminished appetite.'[6]

Susan George

Hayter sees low income, more than overpopulation, as the principal cause of destitution in the countryside, in the Third World:

The most likely explanation for probably increasing impoverishment in rural areas is not to be found in population increases, but rather in an increasingly unequal distribution of income.

Teresa Hayter

Division between developed and developing countries

It is easy, and consoling, to assume that the developed Western nations have no responsibility for the plight of the other half of humanity, that 'charity begins at home', and that it is somehow their own fault that the world's poor and destitute have to wage a bitter struggle simply to survive; that they should sort out their problems for themselves.

Writers such as George and Hayter point out, however, that the imbalance between rich and poor nations owes a great deal to the process of colonisation which began five centuries ago:

One of the results of colonial policy in dependent territories seems to have been, in many cases, actually to produce hunger where it did not exist before, as self-sufficient farming gave way to cash crop production for export to the colonial nation, and local industries were deliberately held back and destroyed in the interests of the export of raw materials to and of finished products from the controlling power.

Susan George

As early as the 17th century, when the British began enacting the protective Navigation Acts, colonies were prohibited by law from turning to any industry which might compete with the industry of the mother country. For example, the North American colonists were forbidden to manufacture caps, hats, woollen or iron goods. They were expected to send the raw materials for these products to England to be manufactured and then to buy them back from England.

Teresa Hayter

Hayter quotes from a report by Lord Cromer, governor of Egypt from 1883 to 1907, which provides a startling illustration of the way in which

6 Rene Dumont, *Population and Cannibalism* (UN Development Forum).

colonialism benefited the ruling country to the detriment of the ruled. Explaining Britain's policy of running down Egyptian industry and forcing Egyptian industrial workers back into agriculture, Lord Cromer stated proudly, looking back on his career:

'The difference is apparent to any man whose recollections go back some ten or 15 years. Some quarters (of Cairo) that formerly used to be veritable centres of varied industries – spinning, weaving, ribbonmaking, dyeing, tentmaking, embroidery, shoemaking, jewellery-making, spice-grinding, copper work, the manufacture of bottles out of animal skins, saddlery, sieve-making, locksmithing in wood and metal, etc. – have shrunk considerably or vanished. Now there are coffee houses and European novelty shops where once there were prosperous workshops.'

The destructive effects of cash crop plantation are vividly illustrated by a quotation from the Latin America writer, Eduardo Galeano:

'Early chroniclers told of travelling across all of Cuba in the shade of giant palms and through forests abounding in mahogany, cedar and ebony. Cuba's precious woods may still be admired in . . . Madrid, but in Cuba the sugarcane invasion sent the best virgin forests up in smoke. In the same years it was destroying its own timberlands, Cuba became the chief purchaser of United States timber. The extensive plunder-culture of sugarcane meant not only the death of the forest but also, in the long run, the death of the island's famous fertility. With forests surrendered to the flames, erosion soon did its work on the defenceless soil and thousands of streams dried up.'[7]

Why mass poverty continues in the post-colonial era

For most of the nations of Latin America, colonial exploitation ended in the early 19th century, whilst most countries of Africa and Asia were ruled by European governments until the 1950s and 1960s. Though almost all of them are now independent, however, desperate poverty on a mass scale persists, as we have seen.

This can partly be explained by the positions in which the developing countries were left after independence. The general pattern in Third-World ex-colonies is that local élites and landowners, left behind (and often originally created) by the colonial country, are still in control and still largely dependent on cash crop and raw material export for their income, instead of concentrating on producing food for consumption by their own people.

Third World governments and people are thus still at the mercy of fluctuations in the worldwide market for their commodities:

The fluctuations in commodity prices can be dramatic. They are accentuated by speculation on commodity markets, many of them in London, which are of course outside the control of the underdeveloped countries. In the mid-1970s, the price paid for sugar dropped from 64 cents a pound to 6 cents a pound in 18 months.

Teresa Hayter

The system by which the great majority of the land is owned by a small number of rich landowners makes the life of the rural poor precarious in the extreme:

In India, peasants have become deeply indebted to landowners and traders who are able to force them to sell their crops cheaply in order to obtain further credit. Such

7 Eduardo Galeano, *The Open Veins of Latin America: Five Centuries of the Pillage of a Continent.*

traders hoard food and sell it in times of scarcity at prices that peasants cannot afford.

A. K. Sen gives evidence to show that the famines in Ethiopia in 1973 and 1974, which were responsible for the deaths of between 50,000 and 200,000 people, were not the result of overall food shortages in Ethiopia as a whole, but of a terrible decline in the purchasing power of people in the areas affected by the famines . . .[8]

Massive unemployment and migration from impoverished rural areas into cities have become the most obvious features of current forms of underdevelopment.

Teresa Hayter

This migration from the countryside into the cities accounts, in part, for the situation in cities like Calcutta, described earlier.

Recent changes in relations between developed and developing countries

Since the mid-1970s, the World Bank, and groups of Western politicians such as those who produced the 'Brandt Report', and the 'Bruntland Commission on the Environment', have become conscious of some of the factors outlined above, and called for a more responsible attitude from the governments of developed countries towards developing countries.

Susan George quotes Robert McNamara, former president of the World Bank, who argued that the governments of the developed countries must not only increase their aid, but also link it to land reform and redistribution in the recipient countries if it is genuinely to help the poor.

'The average citizen of a developed country enjoys wealth beyond the wildest dreams of the one billion people in countries with per capita incomes under $200 . . . We must . . . give as much attention to promoting the inherent potential and productivity of the poor as is generally given to protecting the power of the privileged . . . Land reform is not exclusively about land. It is about the uses and abuses of power and the social structure through which it is exercised.'

Yet as Hayter points out, loans continue to be given regardless of whether they benefit the poor or not. She quotes the example of Brazil:

Brazil is one of the biggest recipients of World Bank loans, but its record on income distribution is one of the most notoriously bad. Between 1960 and 1977, according to Brazilian official sources, the share of national income of the poorest half of the population fell from 17 per cent to 13 per cent, while the share of the richest one per cent rose from 12 per cent to 18 per cent, or more than the poorest half receive.

Teresa Hayter

In fact, aid is rarely given to underdeveloped countries with the aim simply of helping the poor, and with no strings attached. Hayter quotes a statement by Hubert Humphrey, who was later to become Vice-President of America, made in 1957, which puts the issue of aid with unusual frankness:

'I have heard . . . that people may become dependent on us for food. I know that was not supposed to be good news. To me, that was good news, because before people can do anything they have got to eat. And if you are looking for a way to get people to lean on you and be dependent on you, in terms of their co-operation with you, it seems to me that food dependence would be terrific.'

8 A. K. Sen, *Ingredients of Famine Analysis.*

The developed world has recently begun to affect the economies of the underdeveloped countries in another significant way, through the operations of multinational companies which, according to Hayter, 'today control between a quarter and a third of all world production'. Increasingly, 'labour-intensive' manufacture is being located in underdeveloped countries, 'in order to take advantage of the extreme cheapness of the labour there'. Once again the benefits generally are not experienced by the poor; the profits go to the shareholders of the companies and the élites in the countries where they are operating.

A partial, short-term solution to the problems of Third-World poverty put forward by writers like George and Hayter is that of 'intermediate technology', a term invented by Ernst Schumacher, meaning small-scale, low-cost technologies which can be developed independently of Western expertise and financing, producing goods of immediate use to the local community. George feels that the governments of underdeveloped countries should make it *public policy* to seek out and produce intermediate, low-cost solutions to their problems involving maximum participation on the part of the rural poor themselves.

Written or oral comprehension

A good way to check whether you've fully understood and assimilated material you have read is to test yourself on it. You could try *briefly* answering the following questions, *without* looking at the book, either in the form of a written test, or as a series of oral questions round the class. Try to explain the ideas in your own words rather than learning parrot-fashion 'definitions'.

1 What is 'absolute poverty'?
2 List six ways in which 'absolute poverty' is revealed in practice.
3 What is the explanation given for 'increasing impoverishment in rural areas'?
4 How did 'cash crop production' help to widen the gap between rich and poor nations?
5 What generally happened to the raw materials and the industries of colonised countries?
6 How do 'fluctuations in the world-wide market' affect the economies of Third-World countries?
7 What are the two main results of 'the system by which the great majority of the land is owned by small numbers of landowners'?
8 Explain the term 'strings' as applied to aid to developing countries.
9 What is the normal policy of multinational companies towards developing countries?
10 What is the meaning of the term 'intermediate technology'?

Themes for discussion

What do you imagine happens to Third World families in which the breadwinner has no regular paid employment?

Do you think that Robert McNamara was being over-optimistic when he expressed the hope that 'the people of the United States . . . will not turn away in cynicism and indifference' when they realise the problems of the

Third World? Do you think the people of the USA or Britain are generally aware of these problems *yet*? If not, why not? Does it matter?

Do you think that developed countries such as Britain and the USA are still, in any respects, to blame for Third World poverty?

Why do you think so little progress has been made towards land reform and income redistribution in most Third World countries since independence?

Is there anything that Western governments and aid agencies can, or should, do to encourage reforms?

Do you think that major worldwide fundraising efforts like the Live Aid, Sport Aid and Comic Relief campaigns have any significant effect? What happened to the money they raised?

Are there any signs that Third World governments are attempting to diversify their economies to counter the effects of market fluctuations in their dominant export commodity?

Do you think that the general situation of the poorer half of the world's population has improved or worsened in the last 25 years?

Suggestions for debate

If the issues in this chapter are to be tackled by means of formal debate rather than informal discussion, here are two debate motions:[9]

a 'Charity begins at home.'
   We should solve the problems in our own country before we start worrying about the problems of others.
b Enforced sterilisation is the only answer to the problems of countries like India.

Essay titles

Essays on global problems are frequently fairly general, so that an answer might well be concerned equally with the material contained in the next chapter, on environmental issues, as with population and poverty. You may wish therefore, to write an essay only after dealing with *both* chapters.

Here are three titles which relate specifically to this chapter:
a 'We must share the world's resources more fairly than we have done in the past, even if we reduce the standard of living in the Western World.'
b What suggestions do you have to offer the world community in tackling famine?
c Should governments provide money for overseas aid while there are pressing demands on limited financial resources in their own countries?

---

9 A further debate topic, taking in the issues of Chapters 5 and 6 as a whole, is suggested on page 94.

Bibliography

Books

Barrios de Chungara, Domitila, with Moema Viezzer, *Let Me Speak!: Testimony of Domitila, a woman of the Bolivian mines*, Stage 1, 1979

Clark, John, *For Richer, For Poorer*, Oxford, 1990

Ehrlich, Paul R., *The Population Bomb*, Pan Ballantine, 1972

Ehrlich, Paul R. and Anne H., *The Population Explosion*, Hutchinson, 1990

Galeano, Eduardo, *The Open Veins of Latin America: Five Centuries of the Pillage of the Continent*, Monthly Review Press, 1973

George, Susan, *How the Other Half Dies: the real reasons for world hunger*, Penguin, 1976

Harrison, Paul, *Inside the Third World: the anatomy of poverty*, Penguin, 1993

Harrison, Paul, *The Third Revolution*, Penguin, 1992

Hayter, Teresa, *The Creation of World Poverty*, Pluto Press in association with Third World First, 1981

Lappé, Frances Moore and Collins, Joseph, *World Hunger: twelve myths*, Earthscan, 1988

Taylor, Gordon Rattray, *The Doomsday Book*, Panther, 1972

World Commission on Environment and Development, *Our Common Future*, Oxford, 1987

Periodicals

New Internationalist

Additional materials

Various resources, ranging from free pamphlets to photopacks, slides, videos and films, are available from the major organisations concerned with alleviating hunger and poverty in the Third World.

Catalogues, resources and suggestions can be obtained from the following:

CAFOD (Catholic Fund for Overseas Development)
Romero Close
Stockwell Road
London SW9 9TY

CWDE (Centre for World Development Education)
Regents College, Inner Circle, Regents Park
London NW2 6NB

Christian Aid
PO Box No 100
London SE1 7RT

Oxfam
274 Banbury Road
Oxford OX2 7DZ

Speakers can often be booked to visit schools and colleges to show videos and films, and discuss the issues.

Further advice on writing: choosing a question

The right choice of question on a language essay paper is of fundamental importance. If you realise after half an hour that you do not know enough about your chosen subject to continue writing authoritatively about it, then you cannot expect to do well. A reasonably detailed plan, with a paragraph scheme, should prevent this from happening. Your plan should enable you to establish quickly whether you can write convincingly about the subject for the length of time allocated. Scrapping an essay after five minutes' unsuccessful planning is better than struggling to think of ideas when it is too late to start a different essay. During the planning stage, you should try to think out fully the implications of and possible approaches to the question, and make sure that you have sufficient information and ideas about the topic.

It is quite likely that at least one of the 'continuous writing' questions will concern a comparatively current issue. We will look at one or two such questions, and consider valid approaches to them.

The issue of terrorism has been prominent in the news for some years. Let us therefore take the question: 'Can terrorism ever be justified?' If you have read newspaper reports and analyses, and watched television news and/or documentary programmes about IRA bomb attacks, then this might be a good question to attempt. However, if this is the only example of terrorism you can think of, your answer is certain to be too narrow. A discussion of suicide bombing in the Middle East, or the kidnapping of tourists/hijacking of planes, with the threat to kill the hostages if the terrorists' demands are not met, would show that you are aware of terrorism as an international problem. Furthermore, if you have only a vague knowledge of the situation in Northern Ireland, you are unlikely to be able to write convincingly about it. Your essay would be further broadened if you could go on to discuss 'State terrorism', the use of torture, murder and 'disappearances', for example, as a means of terrorising populations into acquiescence. Some knowledge of *where* all these things have happened would be needed, to avoid your essay seeming vague.

Similarly, if the question you chose read: 'Weapons of war are obsolete. We should abolish them', you would be expected to focus on a *range* of aspects of war; its necessity or otherwise in different circumstances would have to be discussed, as well as the practical feasibility of abolishing weapons. It would obviously be relevant, in the light of the ending of Soviet control over Eastern Europe, and the subsequent planned destruction of the Soviet and American nuclear arsenals at the beginning of the 1990s, to discuss the question of whether or not nuclear weapons are obsolete, and could ever be entirely abolished. However, if you focused too heavily on this one aspect of the question you would score poorly. A discussion of civil war, such as that in Bosnia, would broaden the scope of your answer, as long as you made sure that you related it to the question of retaining/getting rid of weapons of war.

Vagueness is one of the most serious failings in language essays. If you write in generalities when the question invites specific illustration, you will lose quite a lot of marks. If the question, for example, was, 'Do we owe a greater debt to the artists than to the scientists?', you would be expected to cite a reasonably wide range of both. If you can only think of one or two writers whom you happen to be studying in literature, then you will merely be displaying your ignorance. Again, if the question was, 'Given a Time Machine, to which past age would you like to return, and why?', you would be expected to display a fairly detailed knowledge of life in your own chosen era. If your historical memory is sketchy, then it would be best not to attempt the question. Similarly, if the question was, 'Modern dramatists apparently enjoy expressing violence; they should look for more positive values in our society', then you would be expected at least to display a knowledge of the works of a variety of dramatists who express violence, and ideally be able to cite one or two whose messages you consider positive.

You must make sure, therefore, that you fully understand the implications of a question before attempting to answer it, that you can discuss it in depth, and that you can illustrate your answer adequately, if illustrations seem to be called for.

Ten Issues

6 The Environmental Crisis

Poverty and overpopulation have an immediate effect on the day-to-day lives of hundreds of millions of people in the developing world. The destruction of the world environment, by contrast, has a less obvious impact on human life; yet in the long run it may prove to be the greatest threat of all to humanity.

The subject of environmental decay is vast and complex, requiring, for an adequate understanding, a study of ecology, which is a far more ambitious task than can be undertaken here. All that can be attempted in a brief survey is to indicate some of the problems which are considered by experts to pose the greatest threat to our environment and the future of the human race.

The chapter begins with a summary exercise on the rainforests.

Summary skills

The article and accompanying 'Fact File' which follow appeared in *The Guardian* newspaper on 8 December 1989.

After reading the material carefully, answer the following questions:

a Write a set of notes, with sub-headings, under the general title: 'The Value of the Rainforest'. You should use no more than 40 words in total, including the sub-headings. You may wish to use the following as a guide:

The Value of the Rainforest
  Use values
    Source of timber   (*8 marks*)

b In no more than 130 words, summarise the arguments for conserving the tropical rainforests, based on 'existence value'.   (*20 marks*)

c Taking any eight of the ten points in the 'Rainforest Fact File', write eight brief newspaper headlines (no more than ten words per headline), capturing the essence of the information in headline style.   (*12 marks*)

You are advised to spend about one hour on this question.

Options for the forest

Governments and conservationists are split on how to save the world's rainforests. Should there be a total ban on logging or is the problem one of underdevelopment? **David Pearce**, the economics adviser to Christopher Patten and author of the Pearce Report, outlines his views.

Despite the popular attention given to big dams as agents of environmental destruction, they are in fact very minor causes of deforestation. Something like 7.3 million hectares of tropical forest were being destroyed annually in the early 1980s. Updated estimates are expected soon, and may well be larger. Almost all of this clearance is for agriculture. Perhaps another 4.4 million hectares are selectively felled every year for timber, all of it, bar a trivial amount, unsustainably. At these rates, all tropical forests would be cleared in about 170 years. But for some countries, such as Ivory Coast, Sri Lanka, and Costa Rica, virtual extinction of tropical forests will come in 20–30 years. Is it all necessary? Must development be at the expense of these unique, beautiful ecosystems?

There is a strong moral case for calling a halt to most deforestation. But appeals to moral principles are not always very persuasive among the powers-that-be who have to balance what they see as immediate needs for food, land, energy, minerals and foreign exchange against the concerns of much richer people in far-off lands, many of whom hardly offer an example in terms of their own environmental record.

Economic arguments can be marshalled to defend the tropical forests. Environmental economists speak of the 'total economic value' of a natural resource. This is made up of use and non-use values. Use values include the worth of the forest as timber resource; as the source of many other forest products; as a food source for indigenous peoples; as a repository of germ-plasm for medicinal and crop-breeding uses; as a facility for 'ecotourists'.

Indirect use values include the watershed protection functions of tropical forests – the role they play in containing erosion and sedimentation, and in the cycling of nutrients which would otherwise be released as pollutants to aquatic systems. Perhaps the most widely discussed indirect use function is carbon fixation, the role of forests as a 'carbon sink' to contain the greenhouse effect.

Beyond the use value lies what economists call 'existence values'. These are the values many people have for conserving tropical forests regardless of any direct use they make of them now or in the future. Existence value is what is being expressed when money floods into environmental charities aiming to save the whale, protect the panda and conserve the elephant.

But it is an issue of getting the 'signals' right. That means the true worth of conservation must be demonstrated. It also means that there has to be fairer treatment of the less powerful who, all too often, have no secure land and resource rights to enable them to combat the forest colonists.

Existence value provides one of the other major arguments for tropical forest conservation. Environmental economists have researched what people are willing to pay for unique species of animal or habitat. By adopting sophisticated questionnaire techniques, it is possible to get sensible individual valuations. No one has yet, to my knowledge, done this for a tropical forest. But, interestingly, values for blue whales, California sea otters and other species can be shown to cluster around $8 per adult. Values for the bald eagle and the grizzly bear are higher still, as one would expect of American respondents. Values for the visibility of the Grand Canyon were $22 per adult. It hardly seems feasible that existence values for say Amazonia will be less.

Even at $8 per adult for the richest countries in the world, we would have an hypothetical conservation fund of $3.2 billion. To get a feel for the significance of this sum, the entire contribution by the Amazon area to Brazil's Gross National Product (GNP) is around $6 billion. Since many of the uses of the area are wholly consistent with conservation, existence value alone could be used to compensate Brazil for not engaging in destructive developments.

Of course the numbers are speculative. It is not the exact

size that matters. Rather it is the principle that conservation values, in economic terms, can be very large indeed.

But big existence values won't mean much to Brazil, Malaysia or Indonesia if they cannot be converted into cash or kind. Yet this is exactly what must now happen if the forests are to be saved. No small part of their conservation value accrues to us in the rich world, in the form of appreciation of the wonder of a tropical forest, in plant-based drugs that we use, as educational and scientific resources, as carbon sinks. Their value to the people of the nations that own the forest is also increasingly appreciated, something we may not always recognise. If we all gain from tropical forest conservation we have to retreat rapidly from the stance that it is somehow all their fault and that we should not have to pay. A little less of a moralistic stance and more of an economic approach will work wonders.

David Pearce is Professor of Economics at University College and Director of the IIED Environmental Economics Centre.

David Pearce, *The Guardian*, 8 December 1989

Rainforest Fact File

- Tropical rainforests play a critical role in regulating the climate and what is called the greenhouse effect. They act as the earth's lungs by producing vast quantities of oxygen and using up carbon dioxide during photosynthesis.
- Burning the forests sends at least two billion tonnes of carbon dioxide per year into the air. This increases global warming. The practice of burning fossil fuels currently adds around 5.6 billion tonnes to this per year.
- Forest cover is disappearing at a rate of more than 200,000 acres a year in Brazil, Colombia, Indonesia, Mexico, Thailand, Ivory Coast, Ecuador, Nigeria, Peru and Malaysia. All these countries lie wholly or mainly in the tropics.
- Constant media references to tropical rainforests suggests that all forests in the tropics are rainforests and consist of an extremely complex and fragile web of flora and fauna. This is not true. Not all moist tropical forests are evergreen, nor are all tropical forests moist.
- Commercial logging is directly responsible for only 20 per cent of the deforestation in tropical forests. But related activities, including road building and damage to other trees as logs are pulled clear, increase the toll.
- More critically, road construction in logging areas opens up huge tracts of forest to the landless poor who then move in to practise a version of the traditional method of cultivation that has been carried on for years. However, these 'shifting cultivators' do not leave the forest soil long enough for it to recover its fertility before returning to clear the trees and farm again.
- Radical environmentalists say that commercial development of the forests is the root of the destruction. The World Bank says that lack of commercial development, by creating armies of landless poor, is to blame.
- Drier and more open tropical forest formations, together with the shrubland into which they merge (and which falls under the definition of forest) are even more acutely threatened and their shrinkage should give cause for concern.
- Since 1945, 40 per cent of the world's rainforests have been destroyed. As a result, over 50 species of plants and animals become extinct every day.
- Rainforests cover only 6 per cent of the total land surface but contain at least 50 per cent of all species of life on earth.

From *The Guardian*, 8 December 1989

How to save the world

One of the most thorough analyses of the environmental crisis is contained in *World Conservation Strategy*, published by the three major international conservation agencies.[1] This vast document is summarised for the general reader in a book called *How to Save the World* by Robert Allen, published in 1980. During the decade which followed the publication of this book, the problems which it analyses have become more pressing, and are at last beginning to be taken seriously by world leaders.

Each of the problems has been addressed by various international bodies at the highest level, culminating in the Earth Summit, held in Rio de Janeiro, Brazil, on 3–14 June, 1992. The Rio Summit led to the formulation of Agenda 21, a programme for sustainable world development, integrating environmental and developmental issues, which was adopted by 178 governments. Agenda 21 carries a moral obligation on the signatories to implement it, but no legal obligation. The extent to which this so-called 'last chance to save the world' will eventually be seen to have succeeded remains in doubt.

According to an article in *The Observer* of 8 September 1996, entitled 'Loggers in rainforest chainsaw massacre':

The unbridled plunder of the world's forests by giant timber firms is increasing at an alarming rate, with Japan's Mitsubishi topping the league of forest 'rapists', according to the Environmental Investigation Agency. World leaders, it says, are failing to stem the increase in deforestation despite the worthy aims of the United Nations Earth Summit in 1992.

The following extracts from Robert Allen's book explore the most serious environmental concerns which were addressed at Rio.

The worst environmental problems

Loss of soil
The bottom is dropping out of the world's breadbasket. Prime farmland is being obliterated by roads and buildings. Croplands and grazing land are being mutilated on a huge scale by farming methods that more resemble mining than good husbandry. Wild and traditional crop varieties, the main weapons against pests and diseases that could wipe out harvest after harvest, are vanishing . . .

Not only is farmland disappearing at an alarming rate, but much that remains is being heavily degraded by bad farming practices. As much as one-third of the world's cropland will be destroyed in the next 20 years if current rates of land degradation continue.

Spreading deserts
The creation of new desert areas is happening on a colossal scale. All over the world people are busy making life more difficult than it already is. They are turning semi-desert into desert and desert into extreme desert, transforming the barely productive into the unproductively bare . . .

---

1 International Union for Conservation of Nature and Natural Resources (IUCN); United Nations Environment Programme (UNEP); Worldwide Fund for Nature (WWF).

The vulnerable areas are the drylands. Drylands, where rainfall is low and evaporation and transpiration are high, cover about a third of the earth's land surface. They are extremely prone to desertification (the process by which land becomes desert) unless used with care and skill, and they represent the most extensive ecological problem area on this planet.

It is estimated that almost 80 million people are immediately threatened by a desertification-induced drop in productivity of the land on which (directly or indirectly) they depend. Regions already in the grip of desertification or at very high risk cover 20 million square kilometres (nine million square miles), or an area twice the size of Canada . . . Most of it is in Africa and Asia.

Deforestation

Forests are the prime example of natural areas that contribute heavily to human welfare by acting as environmental buffers . . . Removal or degradation of watershed forests and pastures can cause great human suffering. Without the sponge-like effect of their vegetation, which retains moisture and releases it slowly, the flow of water becomes erratic, leading to both floods and water shortages. The increased rate of water run-off causes additional damage by stripping the soil away, depriving agriculture of nutrients while clogging reservoirs, irrigation systems, canals and docks with silt, and smothering coral reefs . . .

Badly organised timber operations are degrading the forests as effectively as expansionist agricultural and settlement schemes. In a given forest section, only a few species . . . may be considered of commercial value. Yet to reach them, 75 per cent of the surrounding canopy is destroyed. The *apparently* endless supply discourages caution . . .

In many parts of South America . . . large tracts of forest are being burned down and converted into ranchland. The beef is raised cheaply enough to satisfy demand in the United States, Canada and Europe, but it is a destructive business; the pasture is invaded by scrub so rapidly that after a few years it becomes uneconomic to maintain and is abandoned.

We are at the point now where what goes now is gone forever. Once destruction is widespread, tropical rainforests can no longer be reconstructed . . .

Destruction of tropical rainforests may have serious climatic effects well beyond the tropics. Tropical forests contain in their wood, leaves, litter and humus, an enormous store (estimated to be 340 thousand million tonnes) of carbon. Carbon is burned when fossil fuels are destroyed and it accumulates in the atmosphere ... The likely consequence of the accumulation of carbon dioxide in the atmosphere is that the global climate will become warmer, and that the warming will be greater at the poles than between them. Nobody knows the effects of this uneven warming, but it is quite possible that one of the effects would be a general drying of the wheat areas of North America. Another possible effect is an increase in sea level if the western ice sheet in Antarctica were to melt, as it did in earlier geological times during a similar warm period.

Overfishing and sea pollution

The world's most valuable wild animals are almost certainly shrimps. Their closest rivals are cod and herring. The total annual value of exports of fresh and frozen shrimps from developing to developed countries is already close to $1000 million . . . Unfortunately use of fisheries is often not sustainable and their contribution to national diets and incomes is likely to diminish . . . At least 25 of the world's most valuable fisheries are seriously depleted. Many more are now so fully exploited that they can expect to become depleted within a decade or so, because of the effects of exploitation either alone or in combination with those of pollution and habitat destruction . . .

Over-exploitation is waste: the substitution of relatively small short-term gains for much bigger medium or long-term losses. A sobering measure of this wastage is the conversion over the years of poor people's food into rich people's food. There was a time in the UK, before over-exploitation and pollution did their work, when oysters and fresh salmon were a monotonously common feature of the poor person's diet. This is no longer the case and both are now beyond the pocket of the average family. Now the cod ... seems to be going in the same direction.

Discussion points

What are the effects of the destruction of cropland and the spread of deserts worldwide?

What would be likely to happen if the wheat areas of North America dried?

Why are the world's rainforests being burnt, sawn and bulldozed down?

What are the effects of rainforest destruction?

Why are overfishing and pollution of the sea such serious problems?

Global warming

Scientists are now virtually unanimous in declaring that global warming is the principal threat to mankind's continued existence. In the extracts which follow from the book *It's a Matter of Survival* by the Canadian environmentalists, Anita Gordon and David Suzuki, published in 1990, this threat is explored.

The danger

The 'Big Warming' we expect is the result of human activity. We release heat-trapping molecules of such gases as carbon dioxide and methane as the byproducts of our civilization; carbon dioxide from burning coal and oil, driving our cars, and heating our homes, and from the destruction of forests; methane from cattle herds, and from rice paddies ...

We also add heat-trapping gases like CFCs from the consumer products we have made part of our lives: spray cans, air conditioners, and refrigerators. Like a pane of glass in a greenhouse, all these molecules let lots of sunlight in but prevent a large amount of heat from escaping the Earth's atmosphere into outer space ... With global warming will come a rise in sea level of as much as 1.5 metres (5 ft) ...

Something in the order of a third of the world's population and more than a third of the world's economic infrastructure are concentrated in coastal regions with altitudes below 1.5 metres (5 ft). 'All that is at risk over the next 40 to 60 years,' says McNeil.[2] Whole nations are at risk ... The temperature of the planet is higher than it's been since record keeping began ...

Food scarcity is emerging as the most profound and immediate consequence of global environmental degradation. It is already affecting the welfare of hundreds of millions of people. Every day around the world 40,000 people die of hunger. That's 28 human beings every minute, and three out of four of them are children under the age of five. And that is the toll in times of relative plenty ...

2 Jim McNeil, secretary general of the 1987 Brundtland Commission on the Environment.

Malaysian rainforest destroyed to make way for agricultural development

Perhaps a billion or more of the world's people already spend 70 per cent of their income on food. For many in this group, a dramatic rise in the cost of grain is life-threatening . . .

The specter of Ethiopia is abroad. The television images are haunting: an 18-year-old Eritrean, driven out of her homeland because of starvation, stands and gives birth to an emaciated infant. Do we want that quality of human life?

The principal causes

The disappearance of the rainforest would be nothing less than an incalculable disaster for the whole planet. The rainforests are, in effect, 'the lungs of the planet,' helping to regulate the exchange of oxygen and carbon dioxide, just as our own lungs do. In the Amazon region alone, 75 billion tons of carbon are filtered out of the air by trees . . . As those trees are cut or burned, they release their carbon into the air as carbon dioxide, exacerbating the greenhouse effect.

Perhaps the hardest question of all that we must face is whether, given the state of the world, there can be a future for the automobile . . . The automobile is proving itself to be incompatible with human survival and the well-being of the planet. It destroys our quality of life, the air we breathe, our crops and our trees with toxic emissions. It destroys the ozone layer. It is responsible for the paving over of our cropland and wilderness. Every time we climb into a car and put our foot on the gas, we're jeopardizing our family's future . . .

More than 400 million vehicles clog the world's streets today, and the production and use of fuels for automobiles accounts for an estimated 17 per cent of all carbon dioxide released from fossil fuels . . .

China and India together account for 38 per cent of the world's population, and at this point, they own scarcely 0.5 per cent of its automobiles . . . Imagine one billion Chinese deciding they all want to have a car. It could happen . . .

The heart of the dilemma is energy, the world's reliance on fossil fuel ... The industrial countries' fossil-fuel emissions are going to heat the atmosphere for the whole world ... And the route the Third World takes to industrialization could determine the future for the whole planet ...

One North American does 20 to 100 times more damage to the planet than one person in the Third World, and one rich North American causes 1,000 times more destruction.

The profligacy of the United States has already put us in grave peril; if the Third World follows our example, it will finish us off.

What needs to be done

Twenty per cent of the world is living an orgy of mindless consumption, and the rest struggle to survive by destroying the life-support systems of the planet. Each one of us is responsible for the carnage of the rainforests as surely as if we were to take an axe or a match to the forests ourselves ... The goal of development, for rich and for poor, must be to create conserver societies; that basically means the rich must live more simply so the poor may simply live ... There is no quick fix for the environmental crisis; however, each of us has the power to make a crucial difference to the mounting odds against survival ... In the world of garbage management, recycling is one of the three Rs – recycle, reuse, and reduce. Glass bottles, aluminium beverage cans and newspapers can be ground up and reprocessed and then recycled, as a real energy saving ...

If recycling glass bottles to be ground up and remade uses 25 per cent less energy than creating a bottle from virgin material, imagine the energy saving, not to mention the pollution that isn't being created or the resources that aren't being used up, if those same glass bottles are simply washed out and reused for pop or milk. Standardizing glass containers for food would go a long way toward creating that kind of saving ...

Reuse is heading in the right direction, but the journey is futile without restraint: the most efficient way to avert the looming garbage crisis is to avoid producing garbage at all ...

Starting with Berkeley, California, in 1987, a number of municipalities have joined the rush to ban plastics and packaging ... [However], for survival's sake, we must add a fourth R to the garbage-management primer – *rethink* – and that, in the end, is what will save us ... What we've got to rethink is our consumer society.

As the car overruns us, more and more people are becoming convinced that the true solution is much more brutal than fuel efficiency and alternative fuels. We must restrict our driving ...

Stockholm may become the first European capital to charge for road use, with the money collected devoted to improving public transport ... The major policy of the Western world has to be 'to virtually eliminate dependence on fossil fuels overall, as fast as is humanly possible to achieve'[3] ... Not only are we going to have to cut carbon emissions by as much as 80 per cent, we're going to have to do it in this decade if we want to avoid a hothouse future; yet, as of this writing, not a single national government has implemented a plan to reduce CO_2 emissions ...

Now that we are faced with this greenhouse apocalypse, it is extraordinary to discover that there are – researched, developed and ready to go – technologies that could clean up the First World's mess and provide the Third World with an alternative route to development. We must tell our legislators at every level that they must lead us into this new world, with hope and with vision, and we must speak with one voice:

3 The author is quoting Stephen Lewis, former Canadian ambassador to the United Nations.

- If our leaders must legislate us into a new era of renewable energy, then do it.
- If they must redistribute the pie to help Third-World countries so we all survive, then do it.
- If we must be legislated out of our cars, then do it.
- If industry must be legislated in order to become environmentally responsible, then do it . . .

Our own cheap road to prosperity is leading to the end of global civilization; there is no future via that route. Even if a fraction of the remaining 80 per cent of the planet headed down the same highway, the ecological chaos could bring all our civilizations tumbling down . . . In June 1990, faced with new research that showed the ozone layer was deteriorating much more rapidly than previously predicted, the 56 nations that had signed the original Montreal protocol[4] voted to establish a world fund. They pledged US $240 million to help the developing world to stop producing and using chemicals that damage the Earth's ozone layer . . . 'Why is it that our generation in the 1980s and 1990s has the right to reach back through millions of years of geologic time to get deposits that fuel our civilization, and then quickly transform them into pollution that will be here for thousands and hundreds of thousands of years into the future?' asks US Senator Al Gore. 'Don't we need to think about those who come after us? That's really the bottom line, isn't it? How do we get up in the morning and look our children in the eye and tell them that we spent their future?' . . .

This is the test of humanity. Will we degenerate into territorial creatures struggling for power, land and survival, or will we emerge with a new collective image of ourselves as a species integrated into the natural world?

In times of crisis, people have pulled together and forgotten their mistrust and petty rivalries. They've sacrificed and worked to change their lives. There has never been a bigger crisis than the one we now face. And we are the last generation that can pull us out of it. We must act because this is the only home we have. It is a matter of survival.

Anita Gordon and David Suzuki

Questions for discussion and analysis

What do you imagine will happen if the sea level rises to the extent predicted in these extracts?

What is the relationship between global warming and food scarcity? What other factors cause severe famine and malnutrition?

What is meant by describing the rainforests as the 'lungs of the planet'?

In what ways can the automobile be regarded as the single most significant contributor to global warming?

In what ways can it be said that people in North America do between 20 and 1,000 times more damage to the planet than the Third World's poor?

How practical do you consider the ideas for recycling and reusing throw–away containers to be?

Do you think plastics and packaging should be banned by law?

What is your reaction to the suggestions for courses of action that 'we must tell our legislators' to take?

4 An international agreement, signed in 1987, aimed at halving most CFC emissions by 1998.

How can the Western world persuade the developing world not to follow the environmentally disastrous 'road to prosperity' which the industrialised world has taken?

Pollution in the Third World

Millions of the Third World's poor live their lives amidst pollution on a scale unimaginable to most people in Britain. A glimpse of the impact of atmospheric pollution at its worst is provided in the following article by Sue Branford, which appeared in a 1985 edition of *The Times*:

Sirens, similar to those used in Britain during the Second World War, are being installed in the town of Cubatao on the coast of Brazil to warn the population, not of an imminent air raid, but of a more insidious enemy – toxic chemicals and inflammable oil derivates.

Cubatao is a town of 100,000 about 35 miles from the industrial metropolis of São Paulo. Conveniently situated about eight miles from the port of Santos, Cuabatao has taken on dirty servicing tasks for Brazil's industrial sector. Using largely imported crude oil, it produces fertilisers, petrochemicals and oil derivatives, as well as steel products.

This concentration has turned Cubatao into probably the most polluted city in the world.

Cubatao achieved temporary international notoriety in February 1984, when petrol leaked from one of the huge pipes taking oil derivatives over the mountain to São Paulo. The petrol went up in flames in the middle of the night, setting fire to a large shanty town. An unknown number of people, possibly as many as 1,000, were killed.

Since the fire, there have been other leaks of toxic or inflammable products. The most serious, of ammonia, led to the evacuation in the middle of the night of another shanty town, perched outside the gates of one of the factories. It is hoped that the system of sirens, to be used with loudspeakers, will reduce the level of panic.

Sue Branford

Discussion points

Do you know of any other cities where pollution is particularly severe?

Why do countries like Brazil allow pollution to reach the level of cities like Cubatao?

Have we in the Western world any responsibility for such environmental horrors?

Research and discussion

One way of organising a discussion of such a wide-ranging issue as pollution is for individual students or small groups to choose an aspect of the subject on which to research, and report briefly to the rest of the group. Students who have studied geography and biology might well take a lead in this research.

Research might be useful on:
1 river pollution
2 lead pollution
3 noise pollution
4 insecticides and the ecological balance
5 nuclear waste and radiation

A research 'pot-pourri'

As a way of developing conciseness and confidence in public speaking, students might be asked to deliver a five-minute prepared speech on one of the following topics:

acid rain; bilharzia (or schistosomiasis); cesium; CFCs; eutrophication; food chains; 'Green Revolution'; kwashiorkor; ozone layer; PCBs; World Wide Fund for Nature.

Final thoughts

So what chance do we have of achieving the objectives of the Rio Earth Summit, and restoring the health of the planet? In the final section of his award-winning book *The Third Revolution: Population, Environment and a Sustainable World*, published in 1992, from which the following extracts are taken, Paul Harrison offers his assessment:

On the eve of the Third Millennium, we are in the embrace of an environmental crisis that is coiling around more and more regions and ecosystems. Accelerating deforestation in the south, forest death in the north, red tides, the ozone hole, the threat of global warming: underlying them all is the long attrition of biological diversity, and the progressive degradation of land.

These problems arose when perhaps no more than 1.4 billion people were consuming at levels of at least moderate material affluence.

Yet ahead lie four decades of the fastest growth in human numbers in all history . . .

The human race is not like Oedipus. We are not inescapably doomed, whatever we do. But we are very much like Hamlet. We may be doomed if we carry on procrastinating.

In almost every case, we have let environmental problems reach the stage of crisis before doing anything about them. Blue and humpback whales were hunted close to extinction before whaling was banned. Forests had to start dying before acid rain – first raised as a problem in 1872 – was taken seriously. An ozone hole of 14 million square kilometres had to appear to galvanize international action on chlorofluorocarbons.

The lessons of our past are not encouraging. They seem to suggest that catastrophic damage must occur, or obviously impend, before we are shaken into taking decisive action . . .

Is this how it will always be?

Will global temperatures have to rise by three or four degrees to make us act on global warming? Will half our forests have to die before we cut our use of private cars? How many toxic red tides must occur before chemical fertilizer use is controlled? Does desertification have to eat up a third of a village's lands before the village will act?

Will we stagger on like this for ever, acting only when we have to, diminishing the future's options, even risking the absence of a future?

Can we shake the Hamlet syndrome? Can we learn to act before we are forced?

It seems almost an inexorable law of history that we only respond to environmental crises when we have to. But history has another, less pessimistic lesson. It is that there are no inexorable laws of history. The rise of communism was not, as Marx and Lenin claimed, the inevitable result of iron laws. It was the outcome of determined action that succeeded against all probabilities. Nor was the collapse of communism the result of any contradicting set of laws. The system could have teetered on for decades, but for Gorbachev's bold break with 70 years of history.

The exercise of free will has altered history. Human determination can transcend determinism . . .

We must break the fatal habit of acting too late.

To do so means working to reduce population growth and excess consumption, and to change damaging technologies for benign . . .

We must strengthen our institutions to shorten the delays in perceiving and acting on environmental problems. We must improve our capacity to monitor changes in the environment. We possess the technology to do so: what we need is the commitment of funds and manpower . . .

We must increase security of tenure or ownership over land. And for forests, rangelands, rivers, oceans and atmosphere, we must strengthen community, national and international control . . .

Finding and spreading appropriate technologies is the final stage of the process. We must give far higher priority to research into environmentally benign technologies, especially in energy production and in agriculture . . .

Adjustment will occur. Sooner, with less damage, if we are wise. Later, with more damage, if we are not . . . But environmental problems are the outcome of individual actions multiplied millions of times. That is one reason why they are so intractable, but at the same time it is a source of hope. Many changes in environmental behaviour do not have to pass through the whole political system to become effective. Of course political action helps: not just campaigning for wider changes, but for local ones. Anyone can change their own behaviour straight away, as an individual, as a member of a family, of a local community and a workplace. We don't have to wait till collective disaster forces us to change on a collective scale.

We can turn lights off when we leave a room, starting now. Lower heating or air conditioning controls. Insulate the home. Walk, cycle or use stairs where we can. Wash hands in cold water. Next time we renew a light bulb or an appliance, make sure it is the most energy efficient we can afford. Choose a car for maximum fuel economy, not maximum power to impress.

Use consumer power to change what manufacturers provide. Eat organic, fresh and unprocessed foods if you can afford them. Eat less red meat. Recycle what you can. Refuse unnecessary packaging. Don't buy canned drinks. Buy recycled goods. Use things till they wear out. Repair anything that can be repaired. Don't trash anything that someone else could make use of. Have no more than two kids.

Try to break the habit of impressing other people through conspicuous consumption. Status should be determined by how little we damage the earth, or how much we enhance it, not by how much we contribute to its spoliation. Excess consumption should become a matter of scorn and shame, not pride.

The list is endless, and we can add to it each day. Every new addition is a new victory. For it is a war – one that will go on until we finally achieve a sustainable balance with our environment . . .

And the future will judge us harshly if we do not change. For we risk being remembered as the generation that in the space of only three or four decades closed up the horizons, hemmed in our children's freedom, left them a duller, uglier, poorer world ...

The time is out of joint. Like Hamlet, we were born to set it right.

Should we succeed, the present age will be known as the age when human numbers, consumption and technologies were shifted into sustainable balance with the environment. When we developed social arrangements to keep us in balance, despite inevitable and permanent change. When the needs of living humans, of future humans and of other species were reconciled.

In all of human history, no generation has ever borne such a responsibility on its shoulders.

Paul Harrison

Suggestion for debate

The following debate motion assumes that Chapters 5 and 6 are treated as a single topic:

> For the next decade, the rich nations should devote 20 per cent of their Gross National Product to solving the problems of poverty and pollution in the Third World which they have helped to create.

Essay titles

a Do you think that too much effort and money is spent on persuading individuals and governments to conserve wildlife and the natural environment, and too little on the needs of deprived people?

b What do you think will be the major ecological problems in the first quarter of the next century, and what suggestions do you have for dealing with them?

c You have been asked to produce two pieces of journalism, one for a quality newspaper and one for a tabloid newspaper, on the topic of solutions to pollution problems. Using the same basic information for both, write the two articles. Give each piece a title, and make it clear which newspapers you are writing for.

d 'I have often heard it said that posterity must look after itself. I can think of no more callous viewpoint.'

e The importance of international co-operation.

f 'Science solves problems and occasionally creates them.' What do you consider is the major scientific problem today and how do you think it can be solved?

g How far do you agree that despite man's attempts to control Nature, Nature has found very successful ways of controlling man?

h Many people are concerned to protect our environment. Do you support the conservationists or do you think they overstate their case?

Bibliography

Books

Allen, Robert, *How to Save the World: Strategy for World Conservation*, Corgi, 1982

Durrell, Lee, *State of the Ark: An Atlas of Conservation in Action*, Bodley Head, 1986

Gordon, Anita and Suzuki, David, *It's a Matter of Survival*, Allen and Unwin, 1990

Gribbin, John, *Hothouse Earth*, Black Swan/Bantam Press, 1990

Harrison, Paul, *The Third Revolution: Population, Environment and a Sustainable World*, Penguin, 1992

Lamb, Robert, *Promising the Earth*, Routledge, 1996

Lovelock, J.E., *Gaia: A New Look at Life on Earth*, Oxford University Press, 1987

McKibben, Bill, *The End of Nature*, Viking, 1989

Myers, Norman, *The Gaia Atlas of Future Worlds: Challenge and Opportunity in an Age of Change*, Penguin 1990

Porritt, Jonathan, *Where On Earth Are We Going?* BBC, 1990

World Commission on Environment and Development, *Our Common Future*, Oxford University Press, 1987

World Resources 1997–98, *A Report by the World Resources Institute, in Collaboration with The United Nations Environment Programme and the United Nations Development Programme*, Oxford University Press, 1997 (updated annually)

Periodicals

The Ecologist
New Internationalist

Audio-visual materials

Several commercial companies produce good videos, film-strips and tape-slide material on the environmental crisis. Here are some companies from which catalogues can be obtained:

Audio-visual Productions
Hocker Hill House
Chepstow
Gwent NP6 5ER

Diana Wyllie Ltd
1 Park Road
Baker Street
London NW1 6XP

Friends of the Earth (UK)
Education Section
26–28 Underwood Street
London N1 7JQ

Concord Films Council
201 Felixstowe Road
Ipswich
Suffolk

Visual Publications
The Green
Northleach
Cheltenham GL54 3EX

Further advice on writing: essay writing – use and misuse of information

Many students fare badly in the discussion essay through lack of ideas and information. The possession of an encyclopaedic knowledge of facts and factors relevant to a question, on the other hand, is no guarantee of success. You have still got to know how to use that information effectively to produce a well-structured, coherent and relevant essay.

One of the most ruinous pitfalls in language essay writing is, in fact, irrelevance. Though it is uncommon for A-level students of English to miss the point of a question completely, there are nevertheless many snares into which you can fall – with possibly fatal consequences – while *seeming* to be answering the question.

Let us look at a question for which the material contained in Chapter 5 and 6 would be ideally suited, and see what can go wrong! Read through the following essay plan, and try to work out its failings as an embryonic answer to the question:

'The world will not live in harmony so long as two-thirds of its inhabitants find difficulty in living at all.'

Paragraph 1 – Introduction
living conditions in developed countries compared with those in Third World countries

Paragraph 2 – Poverty
  'absolute poverty' in Third World
  unequal distribution of resources in Third World countries, e.g. Brazil
  imbalance in affluence between developed and developing countries

Paragraph 3 – Population explosion
  causes: developments in medicine and lack of birth control
  effects: doubling of populations requiring doubling of resources
  description of situation in Calcutta to illustrate horrors of poverty and
    population explosion

Paragraph 4 – Effects of poverty and population explosion on
environment
  deforestation
  spreading deserts and soil erosion
  overfishing and sea pollution

Paragraph 5 – Conclusion
  Gap between rich and poor nations is widening. Adequate birth
    control policies and redistribution of resources in Third World
    countries needed if starvation and malnutrition not to increase further

All of this is relevant, *potentially*. But an essay based on this plan would not score very high marks. The points outlined are simply not related sufficiently closely to the question. Had the question been more general, had it been worded, for instance: 'While a third of the world's population lives in comparative luxury, two-thirds find difficulty in living at all', the plan would have been perfectly adequate. The core of the question, however, lies in the phrase about the world living 'in harmony', and unless the analysis of the global imbalance of wealth is specifically related to this idea, the essay will merely skirt around the central issue.

A useful exercise would be to try to relate this plan more closely to the title, making any additions and alterations necessary, but retaining as many of the points as possible. Alternatively, you could ignore the above plan altogether, and write one of your own.

A still more damaging failing in language essay writing can spring from the attempt to twist a question to fit material which you have learnt. An ingenious student can often manage this successfully, but skill and confidence are needed for such adaptation to be convincing.

A case in point might be the question about 'the major scientific problem today' in the list of essay titles. The 'scientific problem' treated could be pollution, and the entire essay could be successfully based on it. A question which reads: 'The successes and failures of technology', on the other hand, would require broader treatment, and a too heavy concentration on the issue of pollution would result in a seriously unbalanced essay. Similarly, if the question was: 'Should the "haves" support the "have nots"?', it would be valid to treat Britain and the Western World as the 'haves' and the Third World as the 'have nots', but if you interpreted the title *only* in this way, your essay would be too limited. You would also need to show some awareness of poverty and deprivation *within* Britain and the Western World.

7 Education

What is education for? At the time when Forster's Education Act introduced universal education to Britain in 1870 the answer was simple. The act was a response to the requirements of an increasingly industrialised society for an educated workforce. No such certainty about the purposes of education exists today. The nurturing of interests and aptitudes for life and leisure, as well as for employment; the development of social and personal awareness; the goal of social cohesion: all these take their place beside the original concentration on literacy, numeracy and skill learning, in the thinking of modern educationalists.

The chapter begins with an exercise combining summary skills and analysis, on the age-old issue of declining educational standards. A full comprehension exercise, specifically on the teaching of English, can be found in Chapter 4, on pages 51–55.

Summary skills, comprehension and analysis

The following report appeared in *The Times* newspaper in June 1990.
Read it carefully, and answer the following questions:
a Summary Skills: summarise the points made about the teaching of
   English and history in not more than 100 words.   (*20 marks*)
b Comprehension and Analysis: give a detailed personal response to the
   points made about A-level English, on the basis of your study of
   English language and literature.   (*20 marks*)
You are advised to spend about one hour on this exercise.

Public school heads attack government over 'easy' A-level exams

Senior staff at top public schools are to challenge the government's claim that educational standards among 18-year-olds, and the quality of A-level candidates, are improving.

Heads of department from 25 leading schools, including Eton and Rugby, will next month hold an unusual joint meeting, with A-level standards top of the agenda.

The move is expected to be the first in a sustained campaign to persuade examination boards and the government to stop further changes to the exam, which the schools say is becoming less rigorous.

The decision follows last week's publication of A-level results for the first generation of teenagers to have moved on from the new-style GCSE. They appeared to show a small improvement in standards and were enthusiastically welcomed by the government.

Michael Fallon, the junior education minister, said he was delighted with an A-level pass rate that had gone up to 77 per cent in a year when a record number of pupils had entered for the examination.

But a comparison with A-level papers 30 years ago shows that in the 1990s pupils study more opinion and less fact.

In 1961, candidates in the Associated Examining Board's English paper were expected to write a fluent précis, in 250 words, of a 750-word essay on archaeology. This year, the exercise was replaced by a 'test of skills of summary writing' in which pupils were asked to list in a table the main points of a newspaper article.

Thirty years ago, English literature students were asked factual essay questions about poetry, such as: 'In what ways does Wordsworth utilise the themes of youth and old age?'. In 1990 the questions are much more likely to be subjective: 'Is Wordsworth, in your view, too much like a teacher? If he is not a teacher, then what is he?'

Instead of being asked historical facts, pupils today may be given an extract from a contemporary account and asked to assess the 'validity' of the writer's point of view.

Such changes, according to senior teachers such as Jonathan Smith, add up to a drop in standards in the past two years as A-level examiners fall into line with the more informal methods of GCSE.

Smith, head of English at Tonbridge School, Kent, said: 'There is far less emphasis on precise knowledge of the meaning of words, and more on interpretation. In the past they would ask you to explain the meaning of lines 17 to 22 of Hamlet's soliloquy; now they ask you how Hamlet felt about it.'

Smith believes it will soon be possible to pass A-level English literature without studying Chaucer, Wordsworth, Milton and Dickens. Next year the Oxford and Cambridge board, which Smith uses, will drop compulsory questions on Chaucer.

Fred Marsden, head of science at Tonbridge, said: 'There is no doubt that the content of the A-level syllabus has been substantially diluted since the advent of the GCSE. Every year A levels become a bit easier, despite the exam boards' denials. The goalposts are being moved.'

Marsden said that in recent years, 15–20 per cent of the factual content of Oxford and Cambridge chemistry papers had been removed, making the exams easier to pass. He has written a letter of protest to John MacGregor, the education secretary.

Critics say the changes are taking place in spite of government assurances that A levels will remain as they always have been – academically rigorous. Vivian Anthony, secretary of the Head Masters Conference of top public schools, and an economics chief examiner, blames the School Examinations and Assessment Council, a quango that oversees exam syllabuses, for a 'behind the scenes' alteration.

The Centre for Policy Studies is so concerned about standards that it will call this autumn for an exam for high-flyers to supplement A levels. Dr Sheila Lawlor, deputy director, said: 'A-level papers are shrinking in content. An independent inquiry should be held to investigate the claim that the A-level results today are the equal to those in the past.'

Michael Durham, *The Times*, June 1990

The views of students

The reflections of a large number of students in British schools on different aspects of their education were collected by Edward Blishen and published in 1969 in a book called *The School That I'd Like*. At that time, students at 16 took either GCE 'O' level or CSE, which equated roughly with the Foundation and Higher Tiers at GCSE, and tended to place a greater emphasis on knowledge rather than skills.

In the extracts which follow, six students express their feelings about the value of their personal experience of education. It might be interesting to compare your own feelings with those of this collection of students from three decades ago.

Three cheers for the GCE and this product of the examination system: a stuffed puppet, reeling off facts and dates and predigested ideas, at the pull of a string, wondering if it was worth it and if this really is intelligence.

Boredom. Twenty-eight pairs of vacant eyes regarding with a hollow stare the woman at the front of the room who does the churning. Twenty-eight minds too apathetic to think, and 28 bodies, too lethargic to do anything except scrawl over desks and carve names, with infinite care, on the lids.

This is education. This is the way in which a child's enthusiasm for learning is quelled to a point of non-existence. Is it surprising that so many escape after O level, the climax of the whole ludicrous system?

Elizabeth, 16

Teachers and pupils are bogged down, from 13 and 14 onwards, in the heavy mire of accumulation of often undigested and unrelated knowledge which can be spewed out as a turgid mark-gaining mess during the examination. The whole school week becomes geared to the GCE and all extra-curricular activities are forced to prostrate themselves in front of this almighty God.

This, surely, is not our ideal British education?

Kenneth, 17

In secondary education today the emphasis is on passing O and A levels. Half-educated children emerge from school clutching their exam certificates, having been filled to capacity with information about T.S. Eliot and Plato. They believe themselves to be 'educated'. To some extent they are, I suppose. But are they equipped to understand and live with their fellow human beings? Moreover, has their education encouraged them to think creatively and originally? Isn't this what education should be about?

Anthony, 18

But what is the main purpose of schools – to educate young people so that when they go out into the world they will be prepared for it? But are they? We learn our mathematics, English, physics, etc., but what do we learn about sex, marriage and things like this? These are just as important, but we don't learn very much about them.

David, 15

We ought to be taught the meaning of local government and how elections work. We should be told of the difference between the different parties, and the people they represent. We should also be taught about other countries' politics and have discussions on which is the best method used to govern the countries.

Ruth, 13

I hope that all the schools of tomorrow will primarily have much more freedom and variety than those of today. By freedom I mean much more time to work individually on subjects or aspects of subjects the people find interesting; and by variety I mean more flexibility in the weekly programme of lessons.

Gillian, 14

Themes for discussion

Do you think that GCSE tends to lead to 'an accumulation of undigested and unrelated knowledge which can be spewed out' in an examination?

Do you think that the English system of specialisation at A level is a good thing, or do you think a broader-based post-16 education is preferable?

Do you think your education has encouraged you 'to think creatively and originally'? Which aspects of your education have been the most creative and stimulating?

Do you think your education has prepared you sufficiently for adult life?

Do you feel that you should have learnt more about politics and current affairs at school? Is it right for teachers to deal with controversial political issues in the classroom?

What changes would you have liked to see in the curriculum of your secondary education?

Teaching and learning: purposes and methods

Guidelines for the future of secondary education in Britain were set out in *The Newsom Report: Half Our Future*, published in 1963. Here is a key passage from this seminal government report:

Skills, qualities of character, knowledge, physical well-being are all to be desired. Boys and girls need to be helped to develop certain skills of communication in speech and in writing, in reading with understanding, and in calculations involving numbers and measurement. These skills are basic, in that they are tools to other learning, and without some mastery of them the pupils will be cut off from whole areas of human thought and experience. But they do not by themselves represent an adequate minimum education at which to aim.

All boys and girls need to develop, as well as skills, capacities for thought, judgement, enjoyment, curiosity. They need to develop a sense of responsibility for their work and towards other people, and to begin to arrive at some code of moral and social behaviour which is self-imposed. It is important that they should have some understanding of the physical world and of the human society in which they are growing up.

Since Newsom, a bewildering variety of views have been expressed as to how these objectives can be attained, and even as to the possibility of attaining them within the limitations of the normal classroom. Since the mid-60s a revolution has occurred in the entire system of secondary schooling, with comprehensive schools largely replacing the old selective system of grammar schools and secondary moderns. This development in itself has become an issue again in the 1990s, with many people advocating a return to the grammar/secondary modern school divide, and even to single-sex schools.

Child-centred teaching methods, involving group work, have, to a considerable extent, replaced the teacher-centred, 'chalk and talk' methods which were the norm in the 1950s, with interactive learning and project work taking the place of whole-class instruction by a teacher standing at the board in front of rows of children.

With mounting evidence that Britain is falling behind many other countries in its levels of educational attainment, the issue of group work versus whole-class teaching has become a major educational debate once again as the 20th century draws towards its close, with calls for a return to the methods of the 1950s. The debate is far from new, as the following two extracts, both from books published in 1971 reveal. The first is taken from an article published in *The Black Papers on Education*, edited by C. B. Cox and A. E. Dyson.

The importance of discipline

No one would wish to return to the days when junior school children were rigidly confined to their rows of desks and learnt long lists of largely unrelated facts. But what is happening now? The restrictions of the old 11+ have almost disappeared, but the resulting freedom has been used in a multiplicity of ways. The children moving on to secondary schools present a bewildering problem even among the brightest groups.

Some at 11 can write fluently and imaginatively, paying due attention to paragraphing, punctuation and spelling, with none of their enthusiasm dampened. Others, of comparable intelligence, write illegibly, have no idea of arrangement of work and are thoroughly frustrated.

According to some present-day psychologists, all teaching of young children must be child-centred: the teaching must grow from the child's interests and not be limited by any timetable division. Freedom of expression is all important and the method of conveying it is relatively unimportant. So far so good, but at what point should the child learn that correctness and accuracy have their place? All may be well at the junior-school stage, but the freedom of the look-and-say method of teaching, of the outpouring of ideas without arrangement or plan has disastrous results at a later stage. For instance, when learning a foreign language, one incorrect letter may well alter the whole meaning of a sentence.

Some of my friends in junior schools tell me that marking and correcting is a thing of the past as it may bring a sense of failure to a child. So one sees mistakes becoming firmly implanted in the child's mind. Many schools arrange projects for their children and some begin through this to learn the excitement of independent research and the joy of exploring in the library. Others undertake the work but do little more than copy passages from the encyclopaedia and stick cut-out pictures in their books.

It is interesting to find that the children who, by the age of 11, have mastered the skills of the three Rs have gained a freedom which enables them to extend their horizons without the frustrations felt by those who at this stage realise the limitations imposed on them by the lack of disciplined thought . . .

Attitudes and behaviour in the country as a whole, of course, exert great pressure on our young people, but the schools must take a share of the blame. At the very heart of the problem is the need for self-discipline, for freedom within certain defined limits, for the security resulting from a realisation of cause and effect, from having certain decisions imposed and being able to enjoy the peace and security that comes from an ordered life.

The world is a noisy, chaotic and restless place, yet in schools we see the same lack of quiet encouraged. It is putting a great strain on young children to leave them constantly to make decisions with rarely any time in the day when they are quiet and listening. This feeling was expressed in a delightfully naïve manner by a little 11-year-old, beginning life in an ordered secondary school, who said she liked her new school because discipline was allowed.

A child who has always followed his own inclination finds it hard to sit down and learn his French and Latin verbs or his tables and yet, this knowledge acquired, he has the freedom to make rapid progress towards the exciting discoveries awaiting him at a more advanced stage. How comforting it is to know that, whatever distress there may be among the nations, two and two still make four.

The child who has been free to wander in his junior school much as he pleases, fails to see at a later stage why he should not wander further afield. Many children who come before juvenile courts have committed their offences during school hours, although the truancy is rarely known at the school. The boy has been present for registration and then has disappeared . . .

Many of my colleagues who are working in secondary schools would agree that the children who are the most well-balanced and who make the steadiest progress are those who come from the junior schools where the children have had plenty of opportunity for independent, free study, but who have learnt the importance of listening and concentrating and who have found the satisfaction which comes from doing something, at whatever standard, really well.

It is generally accepted that the home is the strongest influence on a child's development, so the child from the inadequate home, more than any other, needs security, an ordered school life, sensible discipline and quiet.

C.M. Johnson

The second extract is taken from a book by the educationalist John Holt, called *The Underachieving School*.

The importance of active involvement

A child is most intelligent when the reality before him arouses in him a high degree of attention, interest, concentration, involvement – in short, when he cares most about what he is doing. This is why we should make schoolrooms and schoolwork as interesting and exciting as possible, not just so that school will be a pleasant place, but so that children in school will act intelligently and get into *the habit* of acting intelligently. The case against boredom in school is the same as the case against fear; it makes children behave stupidly, some on purpose, most because they cannot help it. If this goes on long enough, as it does in school, they forget what it is like to grasp at something, as they once grasped at everything, with all their minds and senses.

The child who wants to know something remembers it and uses it once he has it; the child who learns something to please or appease someone else forgets it when the need for pleasing or the danger of not appeasing is past. This is why children quickly forget all but a small part of what they learn in school. It is of no use or direct interest to them; they do not want, or expect, or even intend to remember it. The only difference between bad and good students in this respect is that the bad students forget right away, while the good students are careful to wait until after the exam. If for no other reason, we could well afford to throw out most of what we teach in school because the children throw out almost all of it anyway . . .

The alternative – I can see no other – is to have schools and classrooms in which each child in his own way can satisfy his curiosity, develop his abilities and talents, pursue his interests, and from the adults and other children around him get a glimpse of the great variety and richness of life. In short, the school should be a great

Discovery or discipline in the classroom; two very different approaches

smorgasbord of intellectual, artistic, creative and athletic activities, from which each child could take whatever he wanted.

Some proponents of a return to whole-class instruction in the 90s have pointed to the educational advances made in some Far Eastern countries, such as Taiwan, where whole-class teaching is the norm. Research by Professor David Reynolds, of the University of Newcastle, seeming to show the benefits of whole-class maths teaching in Taiwan and Hong Kong, has been used to back up the case against interactive group work. In a report in the *Independent* on 6 June 1996, Professor Reynolds' views on the issue are presented.

Whole-Class Teaching or Group Work?

Professor Reynolds, of the University of Newcastle, said, 'There is no evidence to support what the traditionalists are saying about the effectiveness of whole-class instruction. It is whole-class interactive instruction that is the key. Going reactively towards whole-class instruction is as silly as going to group work as a reaction against whole-class teaching.'

His report will say that the low proportion of whole-class teaching in Britain's schools is not the only reason for low standards. British teaching methods are also too complicated. They can cause 'chaos', with teachers switching from whole-class teaching to groups based on ability in one subject to a mixed-ability group in another. Another complication is that there may be several adults, such as parents and classroom assistants, in a classroom whom the teacher has to manage. The report will also emphasise that some of the reasons for Taiwanese success are cultural, not educational. Taiwanese pupils are more successful because their culture is geared to hard work.

Professor David Reynolds, the *Independent*, 6 June 1996

In the same issue of the *Independent*, Fran Abrams reports on a visit to Taiwan to observe teaching methods there at first hand and she describes a typical lesson.

A School Lesson in Taiwan

When the teacher enters a Taiwanese classroom, some of the pupils are already working, finishing off earlier lessons. Within 45 seconds they are all paying attention, facing the front and ready to begin work. The teacher explains an element of arithmetic, using a cake to demonstrate division, for example. The lesson is fast moving and even slightly anarchic, with several children shouting at once in answer to a question. All the children are fully involved, coming up to the front to give their answers and writing them on the board. Sometimes six or seven of the 40-plus pupils in the class are on their feet. Once or twice during the 40-minute lesson, the teacher asks the pupils to do a sum in their text books, but within a few minutes the whole class has completed the task and is facing the teacher again. But for at least nine-tenths of the time, the teacher talks. While the pupils have their heads down, she walks up and down the neat rows of desks, picking out the slower pupils for a little extra help. In some classes, every child waits until the last one has finished a piece of work before moving on.

A class of seven-year-olds might be found doing number work just as they might in London or Manchester, but they would concentrate on basic sums rather than on the ways in which they might be applied. And the Taiwanese pupils are ahead of their British counterparts. Large quantities of subject matter are covered in a single lesson. Parents of middle and low-achieving children in Taiwan are usually very happy with the system, which aims to bring everyone up to a minimum standard. Those with very bright children tend to feel less happy because pupils with problems can expect to get more of the teacher's attention.

Fran Abrams, the *Independent*, 6 June 1996

The development of the Internet, the CD–ROM and whatever further new technology may emerge in the years to come, will, according to many, render debates about classroom teaching methods largely obsolete by the end of the first decade of the 21st century, as supported self-study increasingly takes over from classroom lessons. A glimpse of the possible future of education is provided by Alan Burns, in his book *The Microchip: Appropriate or Inappropriate Technology?*

Learning in the 21st Century

Teaching machines ranging from hand-held dictionaries to complete classroom systems will, to a great extent, replace the human teacher. Schools themselves may decline in importance when the home information system supplements, or even supersedes, traditional methods of education. It is not, however, only the children that will need or require education; all ages in a rapidly changing society will be demanding retraining and refresher courses. This demand will be impossible to satisfy if the potential of automated computer-aided teaching is not fully utilised.

Alan Burns

Themes for discussion

Do you agree with C. M. Johnson that learning is best carried out in an environment of order and strict discipline and comparative silence, or do you agree with John Holt that enforced silence leads to boredom and only short-term retention of knowledge?

Has your experience of project work been good, on the whole?

What do you think Professor Reynolds means by 'whole-class interactive instruction'? Is it more or less effective than interactive learning in groups?

Are there any other teaching and learning methods that you have found effective?

Have you found it difficult to adjust to different teaching methods between one lesson and the next? Should there be greater uniformity of teaching methods?

How do you react to the description of the school lesson in Taiwan? Could such lessons happen in Britain?

How do you feel about the kinds of development described by Alan Burns?

The Education Reform Act

In 1988, the British government introduced a new body of legislation for education in Britain, the first major reform of the entire education system since the 1944 Education Act.

In the following extracts from an article in the *Independent*, in July 1988, the main provisions of the Act are summarised, together with a cross–section of viewpoints on it.

A framework has been set for the future of educa-tion that could last for half a century. Kenneth Baker, Secretary of State for Education, sees it as an attempt to raise standards by freeing schools from professional and bureaucratic straitjackets, to create a service that responds to its consumers' needs. Many crit-ics, pointing to Mr Baker's 415 new powers, see it as an irre-versible shift of power to the centre, the biggest attack on local democracy made this cen-tury. Others, pointing to the application of market forces, see it as a charter for the rich and powerful, reversing the 1944 principle that children should enjoy equality of opportunity, perhaps even paving the way for a privatised education service.

So what are the main points of the Bill?[1]

National Curriculum
Described by Mr Baker as the cornerstone of his reforms, the

curriculum requires maths, English, science, history, geog-raphy, technology, music, art and physical education to be taught to children of all ages, a modern foreign language to children of 11 to 16 and Welsh to children in Welsh-speaking schools. The Secretary of State will lay down programmes of study, with attainment targets and assessment for children of 7, 11, 14 and 16.

What it means. Primary schools will need to pay more attention to science and technology. Secondary schools will need to ensure that all children follow a balanced curriculum until 16; it will no longer be possible for pupils to drop, say, modern lan-guages or science at 13 or 14. The national curriculum is expected to take at least 70 per cent of the timetable for 14- to 16-year-olds.

Religious Education
Though religious education is not included in the national cur-

riculum, a school must provide it for 'all registered pupils'.

What it means. In some respects, schools will have more freedom than under the 1944 Act. Though a daily act of worship is still required, it can take place at any time of the day, not just at the beginning, and it need not involve all pupils simultane-ously.

Opting out
Schools will be able to opt out of local authority control and become grant-maintained schools, funded directly from Whitehall.

What it means. All secondary schools and those primary schools with more than 300 pupils (about 10 per cent of the total) are eligible for grant-maintained status.

Though the paymaster will be different, grant-maintained schools will receive the same money for current spending as

1 The article appeared the day before the act became law.

they would receive under local authority control.

Open Enrolment

Parents will be able to enrol their children at any school that has physical capacity for them, provided this is appropriate for the age and aptitude of the child.

What it means. In many areas, the Bill will make little difference. But some, mainly urban, authorities have been setting maximum admissions limits below a school's physical capacity, in order to give all schools a fair share of pupils. Such authorities will have to change their procedures and the danger is that less popular schools will be trapped in a spiral of decline, with falling numbers of pupils and dwindling resources. Another danger is that white parents will manipulate their rights to keep their children out of schools that have large numbers of ethnic minority children, thus creating racial segregation.

Local management of schools

All secondary schools and primary schools with more than 200 pupils will receive budgets from the local authority, which they will be free to spend as they wish. The budget will cover the vast majority of their running costs, including staff salaries. Governors will have 'hire and fire' powers over staff.

What it means. Authorities will remain technically accountable for spending ratepayers' money. But the schools will decide whether it goes on extra teachers or new staff-room furniture; at present, most have such flexibility only on day-to-day costs such as books and equipment.

Schools will operate rather as if they were small businesses. Income will depend on success in attracting custom.

Inner London Education Authority

The authority will be abolished and its powers transferred to the 13 inner London boroughs.

What it means. The ILEA has always involved a large-scale transfer of resources from richer boroughs, such as Westminster, to the poorer ones, such as Tower Hamlets. So the main danger is that schools in disadvantaged areas will get less money and fewer teachers than now; overall ILEA spending was already being reduced by the Government's rate-capping powers. The future of London-wide services, such as special needs, careers and child guidance, adult and further education, is uncertain. Parents, however, will still be able to choose schools across borough boundaries.

Polytechnics and colleges

All polytechnics, and those colleges with most of their work in higher education, will be taken out of local authority control. They will become free-standing corporate institutions, funded by a new Polytechnics and Colleges Funding Council.

What it means. The polytechnics and colleges will be in charge of their own payrolls and will have to set up financial control systems.

from the *Independent*, 28 July 1988

In an article which appeared in *The Times* in February 1988, John Clare reported an interview which he had held with the Secretary of State for Education responsible for the Education Reform Act (ERA), Kenneth Baker.

Here are some extracts from the article, in which Kenneth Baker explains his rationale for the National Curriculum:

'Our biggest mistake has been to demean and dismiss technological education as something to do with greasy overalls and dirty hands. That's where we missed out, by chilling the hopes and expectations of all those who would never be good at Latin or write great prose but who had an awful lot to offer.'

It leads him to one of his favourite Shakespearean quotations: 'The fire i' the flint shows not till it be struck'. 'One of the purposes of education is to strike the fire from the flint. Every boy and girl has something in them to be brought out, something they can do really well. But too many flints have not been struck. That's the real dreadful waste.'

That, says the Secretary of State for Education, is why he put computers into schools. That is why he is so proud of his nascent network of city technology colleges. And that is why technology is to be 10 per cent of every pupil's timetable under the National Curriculum.

'I was given some carpentry lessons at school and a bit of metalwork, but you dropped them as quickly as you could because other things were supposed to be more important. Now, thanks to the Technical and Vocational Education Initiative [TVEI] you see bright 16-year-olds who will be going on to university bending metal and making things that work.

'That's what I want all young people to have: a technological ability' . . .

Technology is far from all Baker wants. He gladly subscribes to the thesis propounded by Chicago's Professor Allan Bloom that there is a core of knowledge all educated citizens should possess and which schools have a duty to impart.

'Part of it is teaching certain basic skills: literacy, numeracy and oracy. But over and above that, children should have an understanding of the literary and artistic background of this country as well as of the historical and geographical roots from which they come.

'That is why we must have a national curriculum. But there's nothing 1984-ish about it. One of the difficulties of the past 30 years has been that curriculum development has been too free-form, everyone doing their own thing. I sense a yearning among teachers for a more explicit framework, one which will limit the subjects pupils can drop.'

The subjects that worry Baker most are the three that will form the core of the National Curriculum: English, mathematics and science. He describes English teaching as very patchy: 'There are too many young people who can read and understand only the simplest newspapers. That's very depressing.'

'I'll tell you what's wrong: not enough rigour, not demanding-enough teaching.' He quotes Browning on the 'reach exceeding the grasp, the grasp exceeding the reach'. 'Children must be extended and made to operate at the edge of what they think are their capabilities. Then they suddenly discover that it's not the edge, that they can do more than they thought.

'But that's not the way they've been taught. Instead, they're all roped together on the side of the hill to ensure that no one falls down and no one gets on the top. It's the convoy philosophy: keep them together instead of allowing them to go at their own speed and achieve things in their own way.

He says: 'It's like that other great struggle between those who think education is the acquisition of knowledge and those who say it's the application of that knowledge to life. But it's a false distinction. The basic skills have got to be taught first, and if they're taught intelligently you soon get into problem solving. Good teaching makes that transfer, bad teaching doesn't. It's that simple.'

from The Times, 18 February 1988

Discussion points

What are your feelings about the so-called 'core curriculum'?

Do you think that compulsory testing of all children at key stages of their education has been a welcome development?

Why do you think such strong emphasis has been placed on technological education? Is the emphasis right?

Do you agree with the setting up of city technology colleges?

Do you agree with the principle of schools being allowed to opt out of local authority control?

Do you agree with the principle of parental choice over the school to which their child goes?

Can you see any pitfalls in the Local Management of Schools section of the ERA?

Do you feel that you have been extended enough in your education? If not, in what respects do you think you could and should have been extended more?

Writing/ discussion suggestion

Devise your own 'ideal school', considering such issues as:
- the question of streaming, setting or mixed–ability classes
- the degree of pupils' control over which subjects they should study
- the relative merits of public examination and continuous assessment courses
- the degree of stress on academic competition, through school exams, prizes, competitive marks for classwork, etc.
- the importance of fostering integration between pupils of different academic ability and home background
- the importance of individual attention in the classroom, and pastoral care outside it
- the role of senior pupils in maintaining discipline
- the wearing of school uniform
- the importance of regular school assemblies.

The educational performance of boys and girls

Many children in Britain complete 11 years of education with nothing tangible to show for it. Since the mid–1980s, boys have performed significantly less well than girls.

A report by the Equal Opportunities Commission in 1996 shows how wide the division is between the educational attainment of boys and girls. Various surveys and research studies have been conducted in which school children have been interviewed and videoed, in an attempt to shed light on the reasons for this phenomenon. The issue was taken up in *The Times Educational Supplement* on 28 June 1996. Here is an extract from one of the articles, written by Alan Evans.

Perils of ignoring our lost boys

For ten years now boys have been slipping further behind girls in terms of their achievements at secondary school. In 1994/95, girls gaining five or more GCSE A–C grades outnumbered boys by 9 per cent.

According to a report prepared for the Equal Opportunities Commission, boys' performance in GCSE is such that they have fallen behind in English, humanities, arts, modern languages and technology, whereas girls, who traditionally have trailed boys in mathematics and science, have almost caught up in both these core subjects.

During 1985–94, the performance of both boys and girls has improved, but boys have improved at a much slower rate than girls. In some schools, the extent of boys' under-performance has become so serious that twice as many girls are getting five GCSE grades A–C. Moreover, in single-sex schools, girls have realised higher overall grades than boys in single-sex schools, irrespective of type of school. In areas where the schools serve socially and economically deprived communities, the relative superior performance of girls is even more marked, and the difference is often as high as 15 to 20 per cent.

In order to obtain a fuller picture than that offered by the commission's report, consideration should be given to the survey, carried out at the University of Keele, of attitudes and behaviour of 30,000 students in the compulsory secondary school age group. This research shows that:

- The motivation of boys falls from Year 8 onwards.
- By Years 10 and 11, some 40 per cent of pupils belong to three school groups known as the disappointed, the disaffected and the disappeared, and schools have little or nothing to contribute to the development of these pupils' self-esteem and self-respect. These three groups are comprised predominantly of boys.
- It is not 'cool' for boys to work at their studies and, even if they do, they hide the fact.
- Boys are 'out' four nights a week and girls are out one night a week.
- Boys do their homework in the minimum of time, and girls spend as much time on it as the task requires.
- Boys do not go back over assignments which were not satisfactorily accomplished whereas girls endeavour to do so.

The overall impression arising from the Keele study is that from the age of 11 years upwards, the girls have a more positive attitude to school work and a better image of themselves as young learners. In short, girls are good students and a substantial minority of boys are not.

For the disappointed, school is to be endured with the minimum of aggravation for the sake of peer friendship, identity and a congenial home life; for the disaffected, it provides a theatre for their unfriendly energies; and for the disappeared, school is no longer an institution of any significance.

This serious and debilitating state of affairs will not be self-correcting. Unless major priority is given to combating the under-achievement of boys, the new millennium will herald a bleak future for hundreds of thousands of young men because they are unable to secure employment, because they lack qualifications and equally seriously, because they lack the confidence and application to take advantage of post-school training and educational opportunities.

The prospect of up to half the young men between the ages of 18 and 30, who live in urban areas in Britain, being unemployed, on probation or in jail is one which no civilised society should contemplate. Yet unless the Government, policy makers and the teaching profession take action as a matter of urgency, that prospect inevitably awaits us.

Alan Evans

In another article in the same edition, Clare Dean reports on a conference, which had just taken place, on the gender factor in exams. Here is an extract:

Dr Mel Vlaeminke, a lecturer at Leicester University, which organised the conference in conjunction with the local authority, said, 'We have got to find out what is going wrong. It is not uncommon for nearly twice as many girls as boys to gain five or more grades A–C at GCSE and for boys to dominate the figures for exclusions and special needs. Is it that girls are more intelligent – or that their early upbringing makes them better socialised for school life or better equipped to use language, enjoy reading and organise their work better? Do boys get caught up in a peer group culture which tells them that hard work isn't macho but messing about is?

Clare Dean

In March 1996, the Dearing Report on 16–19 Education recommended that disaffected 14-year-olds should be given the option of studying at a college or workplace. The statistics behind this recommendation can give little cause for complacency with relation to either boys or girls. According to Sir Ron Dearing, quoted in the 29 March 1996 issue of *The Times Educational Supplement*, '20 per cent of kids don't get GCSE grade G in English and maths. That means that they are not at the level of an average 12-year-old'. Nicholas Dike, in the same issue, sums up the general situation at the lower end of the educational spectrum: 'It is felt that there is a lack of basic literacy and numeracy for all but the élite of British school leavers, a large proportion of whom end up without qualifications, employment or training.'

Discussion points

How do *you* explain the fact that girls have begun to outperform boys in education? What is the likely social consequence, if the trend continues?

Why do you think that by Years 10 and 11, perhaps up to 40 per cent of pupils have become 'disappointed, disaffected or disappeared'? What is the likely consequence for these people?

What is your attitude to the Dearing Report recommendation with relation to 14-year-olds who are failing at school?

Can you think of any action that the Government policy makers or the teaching profession could take to halt the drift of boys, from Year 8 onwards, towards educational failure?

Questionnaire

A questionnaire on education might be an interesting project for a few students to undertake. The questionnaire could be prepared and analysed, and a report on it written and printed for the rest of the class to discuss and evaluate, along the guidelines explained on pages 111–112. Here are a few possible questions for inclusion in a questionnaire:

1 What are the most important purposes of education:
    a   to develop interests for later life;
    b   to prepare for public examinations;
    c   to develop skills which will be useful in later life;
    d   to develop imagination and creativity?
    List in order of importance.
2 Which school subject do you find:
    a   the most interesting;
    b   the least interesting?
    Say why.
3 Do you think that discipline should be more, or less, strict in the school you attend(ed)? Say in what way.
4 Do you think that homework is useful or not?
    Do you think you should get more, the same amount, or less homework than you do?

(Some of the questions on page 108 could also be framed for inclusion in the questionnaire.)

Essay titles

a Write the talk you would give to students at the start of their A-level studies if you were asked to advise them about how to approach their work.

b Write an article for your local newspaper about your own experience of education and give advice to your readers about what they can gain and lose from being educated further.

c There are frequent debates about education, and from time to time the government sets up an all-party select committee to investigate the topic and to advise about legislation. Write a report in the form of a letter to your Member of Parliament who is a member of such a select committee arguing for those reforms to the education system which *you* feel to be most important.

d Is educational equality a myth?

e What changes would you like to see in the educational system of this country?

f How far do you think students should have a say in the running of the school or college which they attend?

g Do schools try hard enough to develop pupils' creativity?

h Bearing in mind current trends, what kind of an education would you plan for a child born today?

Bibliography

(The topic of education is so broad, and so many books have been written on it, that there seems little point in attempting to make any specific suggestions for further reading. The bibliography, therefore, simply lists the books referred to in this chapter.)

Blishen, Edward, *The School that I'd like*, Penguin, 1969

Cox, C.B. and Dyson, A.E., *The Black Papers on Education*, Davis Poynter, 1971

Holt, John, *The Underachieving School*, Penguin, 1971

Further advice on writing: preparing and presenting a questionnaire

For a questionnaire to yield meaningful results, a number of factors must be taken into consideration.

Before you begin to prepare the questionnaire, you must be absolutely clear about your aims, and be able to explain them clearly both when conducting the interviews and when writing up your report.

You must choose your sample carefully, as this is likely to influence the results of the questionnaire. For instance, you can only draw conclusions about the community in general from your data if the sample represents a cross-section of the community. Alternatively, you may wish to concentrate on particular groups, such as social-class groups or year groups in a school, and correlate answers with these groups.

You might include a mixture of open- and closed-ended questions.

The simplest form of closed-ended question just demands a 'yes'/'no'/'don't know' response. If you are collecting opinions or attitudes, the interviewees might be given a statement and asked to respond in one of a number of given ways, the usual format being: 'strongly agree'/'agree'/'undecided'/'disagree'/'strongly disagree'. These can be numbered for ease of analysis. In the case of open-ended questions, interviewees are free to answer in any way they want. It is important that the questions are clear and unambiguous, and it is a good idea to show your completed draft questionnaire to someone else, to ensure that there is no ambiguity, and re-draft it if necessary.

When you are conducting your survey, it is important to explain to each interviewee exactly what it is about. A sample of 50 is generally considered to be the minimum required to achieve meaningful results, especially if it is to be subdivided into different groups.

The analysis of your questionnaire and the presentation of your report are likely to take much longer than the collection of your information. When you are analysing the answers to each question, it is simplest to put the questionnaires into separate piles according to the replies.

Your report should start with an explanation of the object and aims of your research, and of your research procedure. You should go on to explain the sample in terms of numbers and groupings. Each question should then be quoted, and the percentage response to the questions given. Significant trends in the answers should be explained, and particularly interesting answers to open-ended questions could perhaps be quoted. Finally, you should try to draw some conclusions from the questionnaire as a whole.

Ten Issues

8 Crime and Punishment

S everal aspects of the theme of crime and punishment are explored in this chapter: the viewpoints quoted are those of criminologists, psychologists, journalists, hooligans, prisoners, politicians and Jesus Christ. The chapter begins with a comprehension exercise on a provocative piece of journalism on the police.

Comprehension and analysis

Read the following article carefully and answer the questions below. You are advised to spend about one and a half hours on this exercise.

a Explain, in your own words, the 'lesser matter' introduced in the third paragraph.   *(3 marks)*

b Give your response to paragraph 5 of the passage.   *(6 marks)*

c Comment on each of the following aspects of the article, showing your reaction to them and how they are likely to influence the reader: the headline, the sub-heading, the picture and caption.   *(9 marks)*

d Consider carefully the language and tone of the passage to show:
  (i) its attitude to the Metropolitan police;   *(7 marks)*
  (ii) its attitude to the Police Complaints Authority and Scotland Yard.   *(6 marks)*

e Explain what the writer has to say about 'power' in paragraph 7.   *(4 marks)*

f Why does the writer describe Scotland Yard's statement in paragraph 10 as 'shabby, deceitful words'?   *(5 marks)*

g Write a letter to *The Times* offering your opinion of Bernard Levin's article.   *(10 marks)*

                                                          (50 marks total)

When there's more to black and blue than the bruises

Bernard Levin explains how racist thugs in uniform can be made to think twice before putting the boot in

Last week, the general; today, the particular. Four black men have been paid damages in a civil process, totalling £20,000, by the Metropolitan Police. They had sued for assault, false imprisonment and malicious prosecution, and the Met settled out of court; the plaintiffs said they had been racially abused as well as physically ill-treated. In what has become standard conduct in policemen who have done wrong, the victims had earlier been prosecuted in the criminal courts; the magistrates dismissed all the charges as soon as the prosecution had finished; so obviously bogus were the cases there was no need for the defence to be called.

These upright benchers milked the Met for £7,500 in costs; the Met had to shell out another £3,000 in costs at the end of the civil action. There goes £10,500; not a bad rate I suppose, for an evening's entertainment, particularly since it is the taxpayer who has to foot the bill.

Before I explore the more significant aspects of these cases, there is one lesser matter to be considered. I do not know whether there is more police wrongdoing where racial matters are involved, or whether it only seems so because there is more public reporting and comment on such incidents. But there is disturbing evidence that the corner-cutting policemen are getting more stupid, a most dangerous combination.

The evidence for my claim lies in the nature of the people they pick on; not long ago I went into detail about a shocking case in which a black man was awarded a record £100,000 (reduced on appeal to £65,000) for having had drugs planted on him. The stupidity lay in the fact that the chosen victim turned out to be a teetotal, non-smoking lay preacher. But the coppers in the more recent case went a good deal further; the men they nicked were not only Seventh Day Adventists (you can't get more respectable than that), but they were returning from a religious retreat (there is reason to believe they were actually praying, in their van) when Plod decided to have his fun.

Don't misunderstand me; I like fun as well as any man, nor do I feel that the way I get it should be the only way permitted. If the Force like to while away an evening knocking a few darkies about, it is not for me to insist that they should give up the practice and try Wagner. But could not their superiors suggest that before kick-off they should pause to scrutinise the quality and identity of the kickees more closely?

Few will be surprised to learn that the policemen involved are still in the Met, and that the Police Complaints Authority may be ready to give its adjudication some time in the reign of King Charles the Fourteenth. But some may be surprised to learn that the total damages awarded in such cases quadrupled in 1988, and increased again by a third in 1989. The overall total of the three years amounts to not much less than a million. And that is the damages only; costs must be added to the figure. It would be naïve to suggest that the damages should come out of the wages of the miscreants and their superiors, but a compromise might be found; perhaps after such a case one of their helicopters or other expensive toys should be taken away from them.

Anyone with power will be tempted to extend it, and since there are people with weak characters in any organisation, there will be policemen who succumb to the temptation to extend their power. Anyone with extended power will likewise be tempted to abuse it, and since the same test governs the greater temptation, there will be policemen who abuse their increment of power. Anyone who abuses power is standing on a cliff-top of corruption, and it is well known that many of those who go near such cliff-tops lose their footing and fall over.

I do not know how to cure the disease of which these cases are the symptom, but I can see one form of treatment, widely applied, which so far from effecting a cure is making the disease worse. This poisoned pill was doled out lavishly in the case of the Seventh Day Adventists, as it has been in many other similar scandals. It is time for the authorities to insist that the prescribing of it must cease, and any surplus supplies returned to the dispensary.

When the four black men had received their damages settlement and their costs, Scotland Yard put out a statement saying that the payments were made 'without any admission of guilt', and that it will be borne in mind that' it is only necessary for the plaintiffs to prove a case on the balance of probabilities, and in considering whether an action should be settled, many matters are taken into account.'

These are shabby, deceitful words. Are we invited to believe that the Met shelled out £30,000 from nothing but a charitable impulse? Every word and nuance of that statement testifies to the extent of the rot, and a police force content to rely on such evasion of the truth has forgotten what truth is. There was no need for the Yard to say anything at all; yet it went out of its way to dig itself further into the mire. That, not the guilty policemen, constitutes the disease and the fatal prescription alike. How do the Met's leaders expect to restore public confidence in the police – a confidence that in recent years has suffered a catastrophic fall – if they demonstrate so clearly their inability to understand why such conduct erodes the confidence even further?

There is an obvious reply, but it is dangerous, and the Met takes care it will remain dangerous. It is for those who have been wronged, and who have been offered compensation with the grubby string of 'no guilt' attached, to refuse a settlement which denies culpability. The danger, of course, is in our system of civil law; if a plaintiff refuses a sum offered and the defendant pays into court more than a jury subsequently awards, the plaintiff must pay the costs, often wiping out the damages.

There is, however, a way round that problem, and it has the extra merit of testing the Met's good faith. Let the Commissioner announce that from now on, if a plaintiff refuses to take a proffered settlement without admission of guilt, the question of damages shall be left entirely to the jury, with no attempt at a pre-emptive paying-in. The judges cannot be commanded; but I trust that the use of such weasel words would, when the plaintiff won, encourage the bench to increase the damages.

This will not by itself stop policemen ill-treating respectable black men for no better reason than that they haven't ill-treated one since the Thursday before last. But even that problem is soluble, if heed is paid to the advice I gave a few paragraphs back, where I urged the Met's higher ranks to persuade the men on the beat that they should have a good long look at the next man whom they feel like clouting. Otherwise, they will sooner or later march into the station dragging a black man 5ft 2in tall wearing very peculiar clothes, only to discover, after explaining that the prisoner had got his swollen eye, torn lip and lost front teeth from a misdirected conker, that they have booked, not to say bashed, Archbishop Tutu.

Bernard Levin, *The Times*, August 1990

Juvenile crime

In the newspaper article on the next page, the sports journalist, Dudley Doust, reports an interview with a young Scottish football hooligan.

The article appeared in *The Sunday Times* in 1975. Over the years which followed, violence inside football grounds increased in frequency and intensity, until it died down again at the end of the 1980s, partly as a result of the 'closer surveillance' and the 'cages for fans' which 'Bobby' anticipates in the article. In other essential respects, the piece could have been written two decades later.

It all ends with a kick in the face

Scotland's defeat in Czechoslovakia last week was reason enough to get drunk, and Bobby McTear didn't rouse himself until noon next day. Gazing idly at the Ulster Volunteer Forces' poster and the King Billy portrait on the bedroom wall, he dressed and then drifted down to the local pub near Bridgeton Cross in Glasgow. It was Bobby's first day back since he was jailed and fined £40 for assault and breach of the peace at the Aston Villa–Rangers match in Birmingham.

'Pleasure? No pleasure in throwing a bottle, man. Revenge is the word for it. When you throw the bottle, you hope you'll hit some bastard, a polis, or a Catholic, a guy who's given you some shit about the Orange or Rangers or Glasgow.' His accent was as thick as porridge. 'There's always going to be fighting at Rangers matches. Aye, it's a good feeling to kick some guy in the baws. He's down and he's useless, and so you kick him in the face after that. That ends it.'

Bobby McTear is not the lad's real name, but his story is true. He is 17 years old. He looks younger. He has a spray of facial pimples and wears a scab, much like a signet ring, on his left little knuckle. He has also a knife-wound which, in the quiet of a nearby library reading room, he later pulled off his shirt to display; an ugly red welt under the shoulder blade.

'Parkhead,' he said. 'I didn't know what happened to me until I got home and was changing my shirt. Then I saw all this blood, and I went to the Royal Infirmary and got seven stitches. A week later we played the Celtic bastards again, and 16 of us got two guys on the London Road and we done 'em in. I took an open razor and did a guy's jaw. Seventeen stitches.'

In two seasons Bobby has been convicted on 11 charges of assault or breach of the peace following football matches. He has served two short spells in prison. 'I had my first football fight when I was 13,' he said. 'I was standing on the railway station after the Rangers–Aberdeen game, and a guy went like this to my dad, and told him to get out of the road. So my dad starts fighting him and I hit the guy over the head with a bottle. Out cold. Thirteen stitches.'

Bobby was born in Bridgeton Cross, one of Glasgow's gloomy Victorian slums. His mother was born a Catholic in Northern Ireland, and down the years her husband, who is sometimes a long-distance lorry driver, has fought with her Catholic brothers. 'We all go to the Orange Order,' said Bobby. 'I'm a Protestant, and I'll always live up to my religion. I'll live up to it until the day I die.'

Rangers hooligans – indeed, even most of their orderly fans – have found comfort in the unblinking bigoted policy of the Rangers Football Club. During its 103-year history the club's proud tradition has been not to sign or play a Catholic in the side. That suits Bobby. Further, it is unlikely that he was shaken later when the club announced it was to drop its sectarian bias.

'A Catholic playing for Rangers?' he laughed. 'You gotta be joking. You'll never see a Catholic in the side, and if you do, you won't see me supporting Rangers.' He sensed the irony of this ultimatum. 'Maybe that would be a good thing. Maybe if they brought in a Catholic on the side there'd be a lot less trouble because we guys, the trouble-makers, would be finished with Rangers.'

Bobby, however, foresaw a closer surveillance of alcoholic liquor at Ibrox; perhaps identity cards, cages for fans and even a lock-out for himself and his hooligan friends. He would like to see lounges and proper seating, he said, and then, in the way of a

Glaswegian, he delivered a sudden, soft, piercing throw-away line – '. . . and give us more respect.'

Bobby left school abruptly at 15. 'If I'd finished school, I might have been in some better place than this one,' he said with neither self-pity or remorse. 'I got expelled. I hit the teacher with a case of books.' He trained briefly as a bricklayer but, he says, due to his many criminal convictions, he has been unable to get work. He drifts, steals, does a bit of house-breaking and, best of all, fights at football matches.

'I'm doing it because there's nothing else to do. There's not even a cinema or a dance hall down here at the Cross. Things might be a wee bit different if I had a job.' He smiled. 'But I'd still go to games and have a battle.'

The Villa battle followed a familiar pattern. Bobby and his mates, joined by three girls and half-a-dozen Rangers supporters from Belfast, boarded a chartered coach (£6 return) at Bridgeton Cross, at seven o'clock on Saturday morning. They had their standard battle gear: razors, screw-top bottles of beer, bottles of sweet Old English wine, blue and white Rangers scarves and, scattered across the occasional breast, the badge of the Red Hand of Ulster. 'If you don't have your gear ready, they'll be ready before you.'

The coach arrived at Villa Park just before noon. Bobby and his mates sent their girls into a pub with the purpose of enticing young Villa fans to the coach. The waiting Scots ambushed and 'mingled' the luckless English. Bobby stole £1.50 from one victim. 'You got to be half-drunk when this happens. If we weren't drunk? That's a hard question. I'll tell you, I wouldn't do it alone unless I had a bottle of wine in me.'

At the turnstiles, Bobby says, a young Villa fan taunted him: 'Go back to Glasgow, you yellow Orange bastards.' Bobby swung, missed and hit a brick wall. Trouble later broke out when Rangers went two down. Bobby and his mates swept into the passages under the stands. They smashed open a kiosk, went for the beer when 'this big polis started waving a stick at us. Then he dropped his stick and we jumped in and give him a battering.'

Bobby was arrested outside the ground and after appearing in court on Monday ('fined £3 a week and I'm not paying it'), he wandered the Birmingham streets that night, stealing £20 from a newsagent and finally jumping on a train back to Glasgow without paying the fare. He slept under the seats to avoid the guard. What did his parents think of all this? 'They don't know. They don't know anything. My father just says, 'If you do daft things, it's your own fault.'

Bobby one day may kill somebody. Would he be happy to kill anybody? 'No,' he said. 'I don't want to kill anybody. I want to hurt him bad, really mark the bastard, but I don't want to kill him. He has to go home to his mother and father. Same as me.'

Bobby was restless. He wanted to leave the library. But it was past 2.30 in the afternoon and the pub would be closed. So he went to a nearby snooker hall. One look at his face, and the attendant stopped the turnstile. The boy wasn't wanted. Bored and barred, Bobby walked back towards the street, pausing to urinate against the big oak door.

Dudley Doust, *The Sunday Times*, August 1975

Putting the boot in

In this extract from a *Times* article, the psychologist, Dr Sybil Eysenck, argues for harder sentencing of violent juvenile offenders.

My fear is that the escalation of crime, due to our unwillingness to take a firm stand and really enforce our laws, is leading to a far greater danger. This is the new public attitude to the police. For many generations there has been a strong unspoken rule concerning the police; nobody dared argue with them, never mind strike them. This taboo has slowly seeped away and assaults on the police are now not uncommon.

Where the sight of a blue uniform once made a would-be criminal run, the new attitude is confrontation. Instead of chasing their suspects the police now reckon to have to put up a fight to restrain them.

There cannot be many people who did not feel truly alarmed by the riots in Bristol recently during which the police left the citizens to their own devices for four hours. If we expect police to protect the public, surely we should give them far more support and rather less criticism for their occasional indiscretions. Indeed, can we wonder at the lack of trust the police must feel towards the likes of soccer hooligans and demonstrators who so freely 'put the boot in' whenever they get within striking distance of a policeman? Maybe they have come to resent some members of the public and would return to the 'gentle bobby' image as soon as respect was restored for them. Magistrates too could do their bit; with £1,000 and six months' imprisonment as their maximum sentence for assaults on the police, why do they mete out a fine of £25 on average for such an offence? Nobody would welcome a 'chop off their hands' remedy for crime, but I for one would like to see a more determined effort to get to grips with the problem of lawlessness.

Dr Sybil Eysenck

Analysis and discussion

The following questions can be answered in the form of a further comprehension and analysis exercise, and/or as part of a general class discussion of crime and punishment.

1 Discuss the conflicting views of the police presented by Bernard Levin and Sybil Eysenck.
2 To what extent do you support Sybil Eysenck's views of the treatment of hooligans like 'Bobby McTear' by social workers, sociologists and magistrates?
3 From the evidence of 'Bobby McTear's' account of himself, what do you think are the main factors which have contributed to his becoming a juvenile delinquent?
4 Is there anything that could be done – socially, educationally or punitively – to persuade the 'Bobby McTears' of the world to behave with a greater sense of social responsibility?

The punishment of young offenders

Varieties of punishment

Magistrates courts have a number of options available when sentencing juvenile delinquents. These are some of the main ones:

a Prison sentences.
b Fines, or restitution to the victims of the crimes.
c Probation. The offender is assigned a probation officer, to whom he or she must report at regular intervals – normally a half-hour session once a week – for a specified length of time. During these sessions, the probation officer tries to find out why his or her client committed the offence and whether there is anything that can be corrected. He or she also attempts to minimise the likelihood of the offender getting into trouble again.
d Intermediate Treatment (IT). Delinquents are 'sentenced' to 'treatment' intended to prevent them from reaching a stage where institutionalised care and control is needed. They are removed from

their immediate home environment for a brief period or a succession of brief periods, often in company with non–offenders from deprived backgrounds. A 1972 government circular explained the rationale behind IT: 'It will be an important aim to secure the child's acceptance of his treatment, so that he does not resent it; and this aim is unlikely to be achieved if it involves activities which appear to set him apart from his contemporaries.' In practice this means 'treatment' such as compulsory attendance at youth clubs or other centres where social workers organise discussions and leisure activities and/or outdoor activities, not normally available to these delinquents, such as rock climbing, canoeing, art and drama.

e Residential care at Community Homes with education (CH(E)s). Offenders are 'sentenced' to an extended period in a Community Home concerned with counselling, discussion and therapy, a central feature of which is education at anything from remedial to public examination level, and job training.

f Community Service Order (CSO). Introduced in the 1972 Criminal Justice Act, the CSO means that courts could 'award from 40 to 240 hours of service to the community, normally to be completed over a period of not more than 12 months. This new idea of justice grew out of the voluntary service movement . . . The offender would be brought into direct contact with a variety of social needs in the community . . . There was also the hope that some offenders, having the experience of helping others, might want to continue such service to the community after the legal obligation had been fulfilled.' (Dennie Briggs: *In Place of Prison*.)

g Juvenile Detention Centres. These have superceded the old military style 'borstals'. Young offenders spend extended periods in detention, where the focus is supposed to be on rehabilitation, rather than punishment, as was the case with 'borstal'.

h 'Short, sharp shock treatment.' Introduced in the early 1980s to provide brief periods of tough punishment, involving rigorous discipline and regular intense exercise in detention centres, with the aim of instilling a sense of self-discipline, this has been tried and dropped at various times over the past two decades.

Community Service Orders

To illustrate how one of these options can be made to work, here is an extract from the book *In Place of Prison*, by Dennie Briggs. The speaker is a young man of 22 called Dick Marshall, sentenced to a spell of Community Service.

I've spent time in borstal and in prison. I've had suspended sentences, fines and probation orders – I suppose you could say I've had all the alternatives to prison there are. In early 1973 I was due to go to court for 'theft'. Then I got into an argument with this full-time student when I was on day release to a college from the pits. I butted him and his teeth went through his tongue. I knew I had had it this time.

The probation officer told me about this new idea of CSO. I wasn't interested in helping people, but I didn't want to go to prison again. So, I said I'd like that, as a con. I just didn't want to go to the nick.

I made the right noises in court. The magistrate said this is my last chance as I had a very bad record. The probation officer said I was a good lad at heart. The magistrate finally gave me 200 hours which he saw roughly as seven months in the nick. He warned me that if I didn't do as I was told and stay out of trouble, he'd breach me and this time I'd go to prison.

The next day I went to see John Harding. He gave me this list of jobs that were available. Things like, you know, soup runs, painting and decorating, digging canals. Then there was a chance of doing youth work. I didn't fancy digging canals or painting. Maybe the youth club would have table tennis; I like that and I thought I could have a good time. I plumped for the youth club. I thought it would be an easy line. There was only one objection to this and that was that they might not want me because I had a record of violence and the animal description used by the magistrate stuck.

Next day I went to see my youth club leader. We got on straight away. He was a young guy with radical views. He ran an easy club and was dead against prison, wanted to open things up.

So I started at the youth club the following week. I was to go there two or three times a week. The idea of CSO is not to cram the hours up but to spread them out over time. I thought it would be a right doss, but that was soon knocked out of me. This particular youth club had the most under-privileged kids in town in it. There was no disciplining the kids, they didn't have to pay fees. There were a hell of a lot of them, all between 12 and 16.

I made the first mistake of giving one kid a piggyback ride. I didn't know what else to do. Then I had to give all of them a ride. I was grabbed by the kids to do things. I was so exhausted and pissed off after the first night, I didn't fancy doing 200 hours of this.

I liked the leader and got on with him. He had a tough job, but didn't seem to get discouraged. I carried on for a couple of months and got to liking some of the kids.

Then wham! I was called to court. I had been on bail for a previous charge. John Harding and the youth club leader both went to court and spoke up for me. The judge listened but he wouldn't hear of it.

'I fought for you in World War Two,' is the way he put it to me. Besides he said, 'What would others think if I let you off?'

'Six months,' he said. Off I went to the nick again. The youth club leader came to see me while I was in prison. We had some talks and he could see I had come around slightly. I probably could have got out of my CSO seeing I was doing six months. But I decided I'd go back to the club when I got out. I didn't know when I'd get out, as another old offence came up. While I was being arrested, a police officer hit me and broke my nose. I got mad and hit him. So I was called to trial and given another three months. I appealed and luckily won. Altogether I did five months.

When I went back to the youth club, things had changed, and I decided I needed a more definite role rather than just walking around and being grabbed to do any old thing. The most incredible thing happened, you wouldn't believe this. You see, there was another bloke who had got a CSO. While I was in prison the leader got another job. There was no one to run the club so they put this guy in charge. He was there when I got out. So I guess technically I reported to him. How about that – one ex-con in charge of another? We never worried about things like that, just got on with the job.

I organised a table-tennis team, and this gave me a role in the kids' eyes. The team started doing well and this gave me a sense of achieving something. After I came back, the kids knew I was an offender. When they realised this, we got on even better. I became a regular with them and they were less wary of me. They could identify more with me now as they didn't see me as someone coming in to supervise them. I was the one being supervised you might say.

Most of the kids in that club had been in trouble, or were at the time. So were some of their families. Some of the 16-year-olds were in fact on bail. They began to talk to me about it and ask my advice. At first it was legal questions, how to talk in court and how to beat their cases. Then they wanted to know what it was like inside and what to expect if they got locked up. I began to feel more a part of the place, more like a counsellor, and didn't think of it as serving an order or sentence.

You know a funny thing happened. Somewhere along the line, I lost my card that had to be signed each night I went to the club and the number of hours recorded. Never thought about it. Then my year was up and only 177 hours had been recorded. I had done many times that amount but no one had kept track. So John Harding had to go back to court and get the order extended for another twelve months to make up the lost time. I didn't resent this, I was going to go on working there anyway.

I was lucky to get a youth club and that particular one. If I'd ended up digging a canal, I'd have been even more resentful and probably never finished it out. This youth club wasn't regulated. And John Harding said he didn't want me clocking-in like at a Detention Centre, but to get involved and perhaps continue on after my time was up.

Most of all it gave me a chance to prove to myself that I wasn't all what people had said I was: a thief, violent, couldn't stick with a job. 'You're a right bastard,' was the exact words one judge said to me in court. But just as bad, were the professionals who talk nice to you – you know underneath they really think the same.

Dennie Briggs

Discussion/role play

1 Here is an imaginary situation:

Three youths are travelling on a bus at night, after an evening at the pub. A girl is also on the bus, alone. When she gets up, they do also; she panics, and they chase her down the stairs. The bus driver intercedes and the youths turn on him. Another passenger comes to his assistance. Both are injured, and the boys run away. The result of the incident is that the driver, after a brief spell in hospital, is traumatised by the incident, and is afraid to return to work; the passenger suffers from an eye injury which requires a series of operations over many months, and which leaves his eyesight permanently impaired, and the boys are arrested and appear at a magistrates' court, having been recognised by witnesses. During their trial, it emerges that one of them has several previous convictions for violence, vandalism and theft, the second has a single suspended sentence for theft, and the third has no previous convictions.

Which of the methods of punishment summarised on pages 118–119 would be most suitable for each of the three youths?

Do you know of any incidents of hooliganism in which the culprits were taken to court? What happened to them? What do you think caused the individuals concerned to become hooligans?

You might wish to analyse this case through role play. The situation will be a magistrates' court, with students playing the roles of the three defendants, the defence and prosecution lawyers, and the magistrates who discuss the most suitable punishment for each of the three offenders. Alternatively, you may wish to concentrate just on the magistrates' deliberations.

2 'Bobby McTear' has been arrested again for 'assault and breach of the peace' after a football match. A group of between four and six students should discuss the most suitable punishment for him, adopting the roles of magistrates, and assuming that all the information contained on pages 116–117 has been placed before them in court.

3 What is needed to stem the tide of juvenile delinquency: stricter punishment and stronger 'law and order', or more enlightened social policies to prevent delinquency from occurring in the first place?

The morality of punishment

The biblical viewpoint

The 'lex talionis' concept of retributive punishment ('an eye for an eye') goes back thousands of years. Two thousand years ago this ancient law was repudiated, and a very different view of punishment was expressed. Consider the following extracts from the Old and New Testaments (Authorised Version):

And he that killeth any man shall surely be put to death.
And he that killeth a beast shall make it good, beast for beast.
And if a man cause a blemish in his neighbour; as he hath done, so shall it be done to him;
Breach for breach, eye for eye, tooth for tooth: as he hath caused a blemish in a man, so shall it be done to him again.

(Leviticus 24 v 17–20)

Ye have heard that it hath been said, An eye for an eye, and a tooth for a tooth:
But I say unto you, That ye resist not evil: but whosoever shall smite thee on thy right cheek, turn to him the other also.
And if any man will sue thee at the law, and take away thy coat, let him have thy cloak also.

(St Matthew 5 v 38–40)

Jesus went unto the Mount of Olives.
And in the early morning he came again into the temple, and all the people came unto him; and he sat down, and taught them.
And the scribes and Pharisees brought unto him a woman taken in adultery; and when they had set her in the midst,
They say unto him, Master, this woman was taken in adultery, in the very act.
Now Moses in the law commanded us, that such should be stoned: but what sayest thou?
This they said, tempting him, that they might have to accuse him. But Jesus stooped down, and with his finger wrote on the ground, as though he heard them not.

So when they continued asking him, he lifted up himself, and said unto them, He that is without sin among you, let him first cast a stone at her.
And again he stooped down, and wrote on the ground.
And they which heard it, being convicted by their own conscience, went out one by one, beginning at the eldest, even unto the last: and Jesus was left alone, and the woman standing in the midst.
When Jesus had lifted up himself, and saw none but the woman, he said unto her,

Woman, where are those thine accusers? Hath no man condemned thee?
She said, No man, lord. And Jesus said unto her, Neither do I condemn thee: go, and
sin no more.

(St John 8 v 1–11)

No large-scale society has ever adopted the view of punishment here ascribed to Jesus Christ in the gospels of Matthew and John, though some serious writers, like Leo Tolstoy, in his late work *What I Believe*, have argued, on the basis of such New Testament passages, that society has no right to stand in judgement on individuals.

Discussion points

Do you think that Christ really meant his words to be taken as a disavowal of all forms of punishment, as Tolstoy understood them?

What do you think would happen if they were treated that way, and societies acted upon them?

The prison system

Imprisonment has for centuries been the main means by which society deals with adult criminals. For at least the past 200 years, however, questions have been raised as to the purpose of prisons, and suggestions for prison reform have been offered. In this section we will consider these issues.

Imprisonment: the issues

The key facts, figures and issues relating to imprisonment in Britain in the mid-1990s are presented in an article by Rod Morgan, entitled 'Imprisonment', which appears in *The Oxford Handbook of Criminology*, published in 1994.

In the 1980s there began the largest prison building programme since the mid-19th century. By 1994, 19,500 places will have been added to the system since 1979. Yet the hopes of the government that this expansion would see an end to overcrowding have not yet been fulfilled and still look precarious.

Nor are prisons now as orderly as they were in the past. Concerted acts of prisoner indiscipline were rare half a century ago and staff industrial action unheard of. Today prison disturbances are commonplace, and controlling officers almost as difficult a task for prison managers as controlling prisoners. The 1970s and 1980s saw a litany of serious industrial disputes and prisoner disorders.

One of the reasons for this transformation in the prisons climate is the dramatic change in the character of the prison population. In the 1940s the vast majority of prisoners – almost 90 per cent – were convicted of property, not violent, offences. Of the daily average prison population, fewer than 20 per cent of sentenced prisoners were serving 18 months or more.

The picture today is very different. Fewer than 40 per cent of offenders sentenced to custody serve sentences of six months or less.

The majority of custodial sentences are still for property rather than violent offences, but more than two-fifths of the average daily sentenced population is in prison for an offence involving violence. Prisons are undoubtedly more difficult to manage today than they were in the past. The result is that prisons are seldom out of the news. Prisons tend, as successive Home Secretaries have testified, to dominate

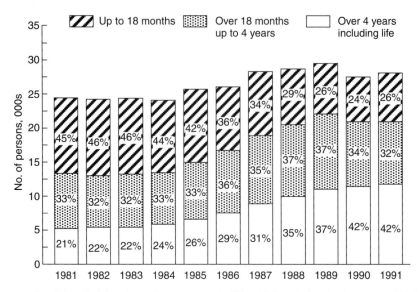

Population of adult males under sentence in the UK on 30 June, by length of sentence, 1981–1991

ministerial in-trays. The fact that prisons remain overcrowded in spite of the enormous cost of the recent prison-building programme, are a constant management headache, are a conspicuous failure in terms of the subsequent behaviour of those committed to them (approximately two-thirds of all young offenders and almost a half of all adults are reconvicted at least once within two years of release (Home Office, 1990)) and are of questionable value in terms of public protection (because so small a proportion of those responsible for offences are caught, convicted and imprisoned) has meant that there is perennial debate about the purpose of imprisonment. And once the purpose of imprisonment is called into question, there is inevitably debate about what constitutes a sensible rate of imprisonment. Though international comparisons are fraught with difficulties, British jurisdiction relies on the use of imprisonment more than almost any other Council of Europe member state. In 1988, 97 persons were incarcerated per 100,000 population in England, compared to 85 in Germany, 81 in France, 65 in Belgium, and 40 in the Netherlands (Council of Europe, 1990).

Should we, as some politicians and judges argue, be relatively unconcerned about the size of our prison population and focus rather on the rising tide of serious crime against which the courts have a duty to protect the public by locking up more offenders for longer? And if locking up more offenders means that conditions in prisons are less than ideal, should we conclude that this is no more than prisoners deserve? Or does the prison, as others argue, reflect a punitively British obsession, an expensive anachronism, and a largely chimerical crime control device, the use of which we could significantly reduce without risk to anyone? Should we regard poor prison conditions as a bar to our claims to be civilized and a misuse of state power against vulnerable and disadvantaged minorities? What after all should prisons be like: dark deterrent statements of the consequences of committing crime; training camps in citizenship; or therapeutic communities for damaged and sometimes dangerous offenders?

Rod Morgan

The views of prisoners

So what actually *does* it feel like to be in prison? Here are some extracts from *The Man Inside*, a selection of interviews with prisoners and warders in traditional British 'closed' prisons, compiled by Tony Parker and published in 1973.

If you take the majority of the prison population, basically it's made up of only two kinds of prisoner – those who've got no skills whatsoever and are virtually unemployable, and those who could work if they wanted to, but prefer to live by crime. They've no intention of going straight, when they get out, and all they think about while they're in is how to get away with it next time.

Principal Prison Officer (50)
20 years service

You can't be a person who works in a prison for long without realising what a terrible waste of time it all is, how men with brains and feelings and hearts are being ruined simply by the struggle to stay alive in the face of the stupid restrictions and regulations they're surrounded with. If only half the energy they had to devote to battling in their minds against that sort of thing could be put to some constructive use, I'd say you might even get something worthwhile out of prisons. But under the present system there's not a hope: the important things are ignored and the petty things are all-important.

Prison Welfare Officer (32)
Seconded from Probation Service

No one learns anything that will be any help to them when they go out. I'm not aware, for instance, that there's an insatiable demand at good rates of pay for men who can scrub and clean and polish, or make roughly-fitting shoes or brushes, or boil hundredweights of cabbage and potatoes. Really it's beyond me why they don't do things like buying-up old motor cars and teaching men the rudiments of being garage mechanics, show them how to rewire a house, repair television sets, or make tables and chairs – anything that's got at least some connection with some sort of job they might get outside. Or it could be clerical work, book-keeping, filing, indexing, store-keeping. The ridiculous thing is it'd hardly cost them anything; there are plenty of men serving sentences themselves who could be put to teaching things like that, which they already know about, to others. So as well as passing on their knowledge they'd be usefully employed themselves while they were in, instead of being kept pointlessly occupied at the tax-payers' expense.

Walter C (54)
Offence: embezzlement
Sentence: 6 years

You're allowed to write one letter a week, but what the hell is there to write about? 'We scrubbed the corridor yesterday, it looks terrific. We had a great time in the tailoring shop last Tuesday, we made our one-millionth pair of prison-uniform trousers. I was walking round the yard on exercise today and I completed 17 circuits before it started to rain and we were brought inside.' You couldn't say it was exactly compulsive reading for someone who got it, could you? If you were honest all you'd write would be, 'Dear Blank, I hope you are well. I'm dead. Yours sincerely'. They could have a printed form to save you writing it, then everyone'd be saved a lot of time.

Ron G (26)
Offence: possession of drugs
Sentence: 4 years

I can't help it, I hate visits. I can't tell her not to come, I suppose she wants to, but I get choked. I mean I've got another eight years still to do, I don't want to hear about what's going on outside, what she said, what someone else said, how so-and-so is. It doesn't concern me, how can it possibly concern me? When she came today what she was talking about was the present, and that means nothing at all. She was saying things about what happened last week, what's going to happen next week: to her, and to people she knows. But nothing happened to me last week and nothing's going to happen next week, so what else could it be but a completely ridiculous one-sided conversation? The most I wanted was just to look at her, remind myself what she looked like, not to talk or to listen. Now it's what, three hours later, I haven't the remotest idea of a single word she said.

> Danny A (35)
> Offence: armed robbery
> Sentence: 14 years

The incredible way time seems to stop moving altogether, that was the thing I was least prepared for and haven't got used to even now. I'll be in the workshop and my mind'll be far away, thinking of the end of my sentence next year and all the things I'm going to do and the places I'm going to go, and then I suddenly come back with a jerk to where I am. I say to myself, 'Oh well, all that helped to pass a bit of time'. Then I look up at the clock, and I see the hand's moved on exactly one minute since I looked at it before.

> Stuart H (24)
> Offence: arson
> Sentence: 4 years

All these places do for me is make me determined to hit back harder than ever when I get out. I've a chip on my shoulder, yes, but I don't think I had it so much when I first started being sent to prison. In those days I used to feel I probably deserved it. That's all gone long-since now though. All I've got is this big hatred for what's called straight society, and it's been going into prison such a lot that has turned me like that.

> Les M (34)
> Offence: housebreaking
> Sentence: 6 years

The only sort of way I could tell you about myself, how I am doing this length of time, I suppose it would be to get a cup of water and float a burnt-out match on it and say sit and watch it, see how it got water-logged and gradually got lower and lower sinking under the surface, that'd be about it, how it is, that'd be me.

> Len B (45)
> Offence: manslaughter
> Sentence: life

The reformative view of imprisonment

Over the past few decades there have been attempts to make prison regimes reformative rather than merely deterrent. The rationale behind these attempts is suggested in *The Growth of Crime* by Sir Leon Radzinovicz and Joan King, published in 1977.

Since a prisoner has to do time, cannot that time be used constructively to get him to face and change the attitudes that lead him to commit crime? Why should not the various aspects of his life in prison – work, leisure, education, contacts with prison staff, contacts with family or friends outside, contacts with other prisoners, the social environment of the institution itself – be deliberately directed towards his reformation? Surely so much control over every aspect of life should be turned to good account?

Leon Radzinovicz and Joan King

Here are a few of the major 'reformative' ideas:

Vocational and industrial training
Prisoners are given instruction in work and life skills, in the form, for example, of factory units, where they are paid wages while in prison and where they learn trades which they could use to earn an honest living on release.

Individual welfare and 'treatment'
Psychologists, psychiatrists and social workers concentrate on the individual needs of prisoners as a means of reform and rehabilitation, offering psychotherapy, or counselling to individuals, or group therapy, or regular contacts with prisoners' families.

Conjugal visits
Prisoners are allowed regular visits from partners in privacy, or periodic 'home leaves'.

While most prisons in Britain continue to be 'closed', with prisoners locked up and closely guarded, there are a number of 'open prisons', where there is a strong emphasis on 'reformative' measures. The aim of such prisons is to increase informality and opportunities for responsibility and self-determination. Typical features of such prisons are as follows:

Minimal security, in the traditional sense. Roll calls are reduced to a minimum and prisoners are often allowed to go for long, unsupervised walks in the prison estates, where they may be engaged in market gardening.

Accommodation is likely to be in single rooms, or dormitories divided into cubicles, with unbarred windows. Prisoners may be allowed to decorate their rooms, or to have pictures, ornaments and radios.

Recreation is much more varied than the traditional exercise round the prison yard. There may be television rooms, snooker and table-tennis tables, a large, unsupervised common room, music rooms, a gymnasium, with squash and badminton courts and weight-training facilities.

Education programmes are provided, encouraging prisoners to develop hobbies and skills.

Resettlement programmes may be provided with prisoners allowed out to do voluntary work in the community prior to release.

Studies of the actual results of such regimes in terms of the likelihood of prisoners 'going straight' after release from 'open prisons' have tended to be disappointing. Studies undertaken in Holland and Finland, where such prisons have been in operation over a long period, are summarised in *Open Prisons* by Howard Jones and Paul Cornes, published in 1977: 'treatment in an open institution hardly matters as regards later recidivism'.

On the following page is a newspaper report about the prison conditions of a particularly notorious murderer.

Fury over five-star luxury for Moors murderer

Brady's Xmas Feast

Salmon, turkey, scampi and a Christmas pud

EXCLUSIVE

by Frank Corless

Moors murderer Ian Brady will be eating better this Christmas than thousands of decent Britons.

On his menu over Christmas and the New Year will be scampi, roast turkey, gamekeeper's pie, fresh salmon, sherry trifle, Christmas pudding and gateau.

He may even have his first glass of beer since he was jailed 19 years ago.

But the staff who serve him will only have sandwiches.

Brady is in Liverpool's maximum security Park Lane Hospital – the Broadmoor of the North – which has been criticised before for its five-star luxury.

Brady was transferred to the hospital from Leicester's Gartree jail three weeks ago.

Staff at Park Lane have been forbidden from speaking to the Press. But there was a storm of

Closed prison (above), open prison (below).

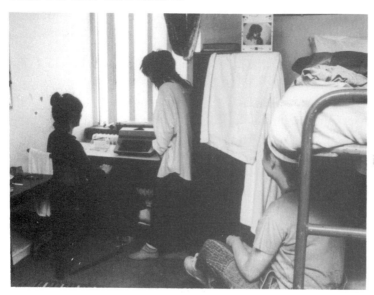

protest outside. Mrs Ann West, 56, the mother of Moors victim Lesley Ann Down, 12, who was murdered on a Boxing Day said:

'This makes me sick. Christmas is always a bad time for me – but this news will make it worse.'

Mrs Winifred Johnson, 52, whose son Keith Bennett is believed to have been a victim of Brady, said: 'I've got to work for my Christmas and he gets it all for nothing.

I don't even know what scampi tastes like because I've never had the money to pay for it.'

From the Daily Mirror

An American 'superjail'

The most extreme contrast with the 'open prison' concept is the creation of hi-tech, maximum security, so-called 'superjails', pioneered in the early 1990s in the USA, to house the country's most dangerous and violent criminals. They are described by Dinah Greek in an article in a 1996 edition of the magazine *Professional Engineering*. Oak Park Heights Prison in Minnesota is a typical example:

The earth-sheltered U-shaped prison is built into the hillside. The double perimeter fences are topped with razor ribbon–sharp, jagged, curled strips of steel virtually impossible to scale without serious injury.

Cameras and intruder detection equipment cover every angle so that blind spots are eliminated. X-ray detection and metal detectors monitor supplies coming into the prisons.

Living accommodation is also monitored by sophisticated electronic equipment. This includes closed-circuit television and alarms that can be set off by motion detection equipment. Doors are electronically controlled.

Dogs are routinely used on patrols and for drugs and contraband monitoring and detection.

And all the guards are armed.

Prisoners typically spend at least the first three years totally segregated from other inmates. They are locked up for 23 hours a day. Only one hour a day is allowed for exercise in a totally enclosed, fenced area.

The layout of the single cells precludes any contact between prisoners. Behind the electronic double door constructed from a thick-gauge steel, each contains a toilet, sink, steel-reinforced concrete desk, bed, shelves and chair. It is said to be impossible for an inmate to destroy any of these or to make a weapon or artefact from them.

After a time, provided they have not breached regulations, prisoners are allowed more freedom and can go into the work area where they have social contact.

Dinah Greek

Themes for discussion

Do you think that more prisons should be built to deal with the overcrowding in Britain's prisons, or do you think that more use should be made of non-custodial sentences for convicted criminals?

Do you think that an experimental American scheme, whereby first offenders, on probation, are taken into prisons to be lectured by 'lifers' about the reality of prison life, should be adopted in Britain?

Do you think first offenders should be kept separate from more experienced prisoners?

What are your thoughts about the *Daily Mirror* report on Ian Brady?

Which, if any, of the reformative measures outlined above do you consider valuable? What difficulties are likely to arise in the implementation of each?

Why do you think vocational training and work-experience schemes in prison have had comparatively little effect on recidivism and employment prospects amongst prisoners?

Do you think that hi-tech 'superjails' for especially violent offenders, on the American model, should be introduced into Britain?

Why, do you think, do most prisoners return to crime after being released from prison?

Research topics

1 Find out about conditions in two or three large prisons in Britain. Write a report to present to the group.

2 Find out about and write reports on countries where prison conditions are:
   a more pleasant
   b more unpleasant
   c simply different
   in comparison with the normal conditions in British prisons.

The capital punishment debate

Capital punishment for murder was abolished in Great Britain by Act of Parliament in 1964. Arguments about the morality of capital punishment and its value as a deterrent to murder have continued ever since, culminating in a parliamentary debate and a free vote, in 1983, on amendments to the law which would enable judges to sentence people found guilty of certain categories of murder to death. The amendments were defeated and the law stood. A further free vote took place in 1994 with the same result. The debate in society goes on.

Here are extracts from speeches by MPs, made in the House of Commons on 13 July 1983, presenting opposing viewpoints on the issue:

. . . I want the House to understand my position clearly, that even were there evidence to demonstrate that capital punishment was a deterrent – such evidence does not exist – I shall still believe hanging to be wrong. I know that some people will argue . . . that hanging as retribution is right in itself and that in our society one can justify, shall I say as a matter of principle, the taking of the life of a man or woman who has himself or herself taken a life . . . There is no moral or philosophical justification for that view. It is a cry for vengeance, and nothing except vengeance . . .

Even if the deterrent claim can be justified, its effect on the murder rate in Britain will be negligible . . . Time after time the hanging lobby repeats the old remedies and the venerable prejudices that capital punishment deters. I tell the hanging lobby what every informed person knows – that there is absolutely no evidence to support the view that capital punishment is in itself a deterrent.

If we compare abolitionist and retentionist countries and countries before and after abolition, we find that there is no evidence to prove that execution reduces the murder rate or reduces crimes of violence . . .

If the deterrent case is to be accepted, if we are to vote for capital punishment as a deterrent, we ought at least to be sure that it deters. If we are to hang men and women by the neck until they are dead, we ought to do it on more than a hunch, a superstition, a vague impression ... Unless there is some positive proof that hanging deters, the case for hanging cannot be made even by its most sophisticated proponents.

They cannot provide that case. I must provide for them the other statistic, of which we are certain. Had hanging not been abolished in 1964, at least five innocent men would be dead today. That seems to me . . . the only statistic about which we can be sure in this entire debate . . .

I conclude as I began. Were all the practical or pragmatic arguments against capital punishment not to apply, I should still resist its introduction. Supporters of capital punishment insist on comparing crime rates before and after abolition, as though abolition itself had created a more violent society. The truth is something different. Violence has grown within our society during the past 25 years for many reasons. To legalise violence in the way proposed would make Britain not a more peaceful nation, but one in which violence had become accepted and institutionalised . . . By killing murderers we become like the murderers themselves. The whole community is lowered to their standards. For that reason I shall vote against the motion.

Roy Hattersley
(MP for Birmingham, Sparkbrook)

The first duty of this House is not simply to debate what punishment we can place upon criminals. It is also to protect the lives of our people and to safeguard the innocent . . .

I was in the House when we abolished the capital sentence. We did so largely in the belief that life imprisonment would be an effective deterrent in its place. It has not worked out that way. On the contrary, violence and murder have increased rapidly . . .

When the capital sentence was abolished, the Police Federation warned the House that it would lead to a dramatic increase in the carrying and using of firearms. That is exactly what has happened. In the year before abolition, the number of guns used in crimes in London was 43; last year the number was close to 2,000. That is a 25-fold increase. Before abolition, when a professional gang planned a job, the elder members frisked the younger members to ensure that they were not carrying guns. They did so because they knew, to put it in the vernacular, 'if you kill a cop we all get topped'. It is no longer that way. Today, it is the norm and not the exception for criminals to carry guns when they commit robberies. They do so for the simple reason that they know that their lives are not at risk.

There is also a new balance of risk for the police officer. When a policeman confronts a criminal with a gun, the odds are tilted against him. In that split second when the armed robber must decide whether to pull the trigger and shoot the policeman, the robber knows that if he surrenders he will go to prison for, perhaps, five to seven years for armed robbery. But if he shoots the policeman, he eliminates the witness and greatly improves his chances of getting away with the loot. And even if he is caught and convicted of murder the worst that can happen to him is life imprisonment. With remission that can mean little more than ten and a half years ... I do not accept, and I doubt if the House would accept, that the difference between five to seven years for armed robbery and only ten years for murder is worth the life of a police officer ...

There is a further consequence. Whereas, before abolition, unarmed police officers would not hesitate to tackle armed criminals because they knew or they believed that they were protected by the invisible bullet-proof waistcoat of the capital sentence, today even the bravest of policemen hesitates. He often sends for a gun.

What the Police Federation and I predicted when the House abolished the capital sentence has come to pass. We have put an end to the once-proud tradition of our unarmed police force. We therefore face the risk . . . that we have not succeeded in abolishing the capital sentence. On the contrary, it will be administered more and more not by due process of law and by courts, but by armed criminals and, on occasion, by armed police officers defending themselves and the public.

Eldon Griffiths
(MP for Bury St Edmunds)

Questions for research and discussion

1 Both MPs, in the selected extracts from their speeches, concentrate on the question of whether or not capital punishment is a deterrent to murder and violent crime; both claim to draw upon the available statistical evidence, and yet they reach opposite conclusions. Who do you think is right? (To answer the question, of course, research will be necessary, possibly undertaken by a small group of students, who report back to the rest. You will need to work out exactly *what* evidence each MP is drawing on, find the relevant evidence and statistics, and present them to the class, before judgements about the viability of the opposing claims can be made.)

2 On what grounds does Roy Hattersley argue that capital punishment is morally indefensible? Do you consider that he is right when he argues that, 'even were there evidence to demonstrate that [it] was a deterrent, capital punishment would be wrong'?

3 What do you think Eldon Griffiths meant when he said, 'we have not succeeded in abolishing the capital sentence'? Do you think that there is any fundamental difference between the kinds of 'death sentence' he is talking about in the last quoted paragraph of his speech, and capital punishment carried out by legal process?

4 According to one of the speakers in the debate, Albert McQuarrie (MP for Banff and Buchan), 'an estimated 87 per cent of the total adult population have called for capital punishment to be made available to the courts again'. Yet the House of Commons voted against the restoration of capital punishment. Is this democratic?

Essay titles

a Write leading articles for both a tabloid and a broadsheet newspaper on the topic of juvenile crime and the treatment of young offenders. State which newspaper each is for, and provide appropriate headings.

b Vandalism – inevitable social evil?

c The European Court decided that birching is an offence against human rights. What is your opinion?

d Punishment should fit the crime.

e 'All punishment in itself is evil.'

f In defence of discipline and order.

g Can and should society do anything about anti-social behaviour?

Bibliography

Non-fiction

Briggs, Dennie, *In Place of Prison*, Temple Smith, 1975
Cavadino, Michael and Dignan, James, *The Penal System*, Sage, 1995
Coyle, Andrew, *The Prisons We Deserve*, Harper Collins, 1994

Gowers, Sir Ernest, *A Life for a Life: The Problem of Capital Punishment*, Chatto and Windus, 1956

Jones, Howard and Cornes, Paul, *Open Prisons*, Routledge and Kegan Paul, 1977

Lea, John and Young, Jack, *What Is To Be Done About Law and Order?*, Penguin, 1984

Longford, Lord, *Young Offenders*, Chapman, 1993

Maguire, Mike, Morgan, Rod and Reiner, Robert, *The Oxford Handbook of Criminology*, Oxford, 1994

Maurice, John and McLaughlin, Eugene, *The Problem of Crime*, Sage, 1996

Parker, Tony, *The Man Inside*, Michael Joseph, 1973

Pearson, Geoffrey, *Hooligan: A History of Respectable Fears*, Macmillan, 1988

Potter, Harry, *Hanging in Judgement: Religion and the Death Penalty in England*, SCM, 1994

Fiction

Koestler, Arthur, *Darkness at Noon*, Penguin, 1969

Malamud, Bernard, *The Fixer*, Penguin, 1966

Orwell, George, 'A Hanging' in *The Collected Essays, Journalism and Letters*, Vol. I, Penguin, 1970

Sartre, Jean-Paul, 'The Wall' in *Intimacy*, Panther, 1960

Sillitoe, Alan, *The Loneliness of the Long-Distance Runner*, Granada, 1985

Further advice on writing: note-making technique

Whether you are making notes in lessons, or from books, there are various methods which you can use to simplify and clarify your note-making.

As you can see, the points are themselves set out in note form; this is intended to illustrate an effective note-making format in itself.

❶ *Making notes in lessons/lectures*

1 Don't try to write down everything.

2 Concentrate on main points.

3 If possible, try to make sure you understand an idea before writing it down.

4 Use a system of abbreviations:
   a miss out unimportant words like 'a', 'the'
   b use abbreviations for as many words as possible:
      (i)   common abbreviations, e.g.:
            1   ∵ – because
            2   ∴ – therefore
            3   + – and
            4   c.f. – compare, remember in this context
            5   i.e. – that is

   6 N.B. – note well

  etc.

 (ii) personal abbreviations: work out as many as possible, e.g.:

   1 sim. – similar (to)

   2 diffic. – difficult

   3 diff. – different

   4 poss. – possibly

   5 prob. – probably

   6 char. – character

  etc.

 (iii) use initial letters for names of characters and titles, e.g.:

   1 L – (King) Lear

   2 M.F. – 'The Mill on the Floss'

c N.B.: never use abbreviations in writing intended to be read by someone else.

❷ Making notes from books

1 Decide first whether book is suitable:

 a skim over chapter(s)

 b concentrate on headings + 1st + last paragraphs of sections

2 Make notes by one of the following methods:

 a using a pencil:

  (i) read through a section

  (ii) re-read, underlining or marking in margin relevant points in pencil

  (iii) write out marked sections, trying to use own words

 b relying on memory:

  (i) read through a section

  (ii) re-read, pausing over each key point

  (iii) make notes from memory, as far as possible

  (iv) check back to book whenever necessary in making notes

3 Use format illustrated here in setting out notes:

 a use indentations for major and subsidiary points

 b mark points with letters and figures, if it makes notes clearer

 c use colour, underlinings, etc. to emphasise key points

 d use new page for each new set of notes

❸ Note-making as an exam exercise

1 Read through passage as many times as is necessary to understand main argument

2 Underline each main point

3 Write points in note form, but without abbreviations, a new line for each point, with sub-headings if this would be helpful

IV *Making revision notes*

1 Don't just keep re-reading your notes

2 Organise your revision:
  a Take a theme or a character in literature
  b Read through your notes, jotting down in *brief summary form*, with page references if relevant, each important detail relating to theme or character
  c Re-order your summary notes into a logical pattern
  d Learn your summarised points, looking back to original notes and/or book for amplification when necessary

3 Write out a realistic revision schedule for each day up to the exams

4 Answer exam questions in note form, as part of revision

V *Conditions for note-making*

1 Try to make notes in a quiet, well-lit and comfortable place

2 Don't start if you have something on your mind which will distract your concentration

3 Have regular breaks (but avoid watching television during them!)

4 Always have a clear end in view for each work session.

Ten Issues

9 Women

The question of women's role and identity in the modern world has become, over the past two decades, an issue which few people of either sex in the Western world are able to ignore, and it is the theme of this chapter.

The chapter begins with a comprehension passage from one of the most influential feminist works, *The Female Eunuch*, by the Australian writer and journalist Germaine Greer, first published in 1971. The chapter is then divided into sub-themes, each of which is followed by discussion questions. The themes are explored largely through extracts from books written in the 1980s and 1990s by women.

There is no particular reason to tackle the sections and questions in order; in fact, the questions themselves could well be ignored altogether, and a free-ranging discussion conducted after the chapter has been read as a whole. Alternatively, the sections can be discussed separately, without specific reference to the questions, or particular issues suggested by some of the questions can be discussed. The questions provide plenty of scope for research by students of other disciplines, ranging from history and sociology to music and art, but the only essential requirement is to read and consider the extracts themselves.

Comprehension and analysis

Read the following passage and answer the questions which follow it. You are advised to spend about one and a half hours on this exercise.

Energy is the power that drives every human being. It is not lost by exertion but maintained by it, for it is a faculty of the psyche. It is driven to perverted manifestations by curbs and checks. Like the motive force that drives the car along the highway, when it meets with an obstacle it turns to destructive force and shakes its
5   source to pieces. It is not too hard to point out to the averagely perceptive human being that women have plenty of the destructive kind of energy, but far fewer people can see that women's destructiveness is creativity turned in upon itself by constant frustration. Nervous diseases, painful menstruation, unwanted pregnancies, accidents of all kinds, are all evidence of women's energy destroying them. It extends beyond

10   them, wreaking havoc with the personalities and achievements of others, especially their husbands and their children. That is not to say that women must hate all their relatives, but that if children are presented to women as a duty and marriage as an inescapable yoke, then the more energy they have the more they will fret and chafe, tearing themselves and their dependants to pieces. When children are falsely
15   presented to women as their only significant contribution, the proper expression of their creativity and their lives' work, the children and their mothers suffer for it.

The adult woman has already established a pattern of perversity in the expression of her desires and motives which ought to fit her for the distorted version of motherhood: it will not disappear if she is allowed alternatives. Any substituted aim is
20   likely to be followed in a 'feminine' way, that is, servilely, dishonestly, inefficiently, inconsistently. In most cases women are not offered a genuine alternative to repressive duties and responsibilities: most would happily give up unskilled labour in a factory or the tedium of office work for the more 'natural' tedium of a modern household, because their energies are so thwarted by the usual kinds of female work
25   that they imagine even housework would be a preferable alternative. Women who are offered education are offered a genuine alternative, insofar as they are offered genuine education, a rare commodity in these days of universal induction. And yet, when they were offered education at first the result was not the creation of an instant race of superwomen. This is one contemporary's account of the first female undergraduates,
30   and university teachers will recognise a familiar phenomenon:

'At lectures women students are models of attention and industry; perhaps they even apply themselves too much to carrying home in black and white what they have heard. They generally occupy the front seats because they enter their names early and then because they arrive early, well before the beginning of the lectures.
35   Only this fact is noticeable, that often they merely give a superficial glance at the preparations that the professor passes round; sometimes they even pass them on to their neighbours without even looking at them; a longer examination would hinder their taking notes.'

What this rather prejudiced observer noticed is real enough: the girls were diligent,
40   even too diligent, but their efforts were expended on mistaken goals. They were anxious to please, to pick up everything that they were told, but the preparations handed around by the lecturer were the real subject of the lecture, and in that they were not interested at all. Their energy is all expended on conforming with disciplinary and other requirements, not in gratifying their own curiosity about the subject that
45   they are studying, and so most of it is misdirected into meaningless assiduity. This phenomenon is still very common among female students, who are forming a large proportion of the arts intake at universities. It is not surprising then that women seldom make the scientific advances, but rather serve men as laboratory assistants, working under direction: it is merely a continuation of the same phenomenon that we
50   observed in their undergraduate days.

By the time they have come to apply for entrance to a university the pattern of their useless deflection of energy is already set. In the very great majority of cases they have not retained enough drive to desire to qualify themselves any further; the minority who go to university do so too often as a response to guidance and pressure
55   from their mistresses at school, still not knowing what the real point is, still not interested in developing their own potential: we are not surprised to find that many of them think of even their professional life either as a stop-gap or an indirect qualification for marriage.

All the blanket objections to women in professions may be understood as ways of
60   stating this basic situation. They may appear to be the judgements of prejudice and, insofar as they adduce no other case than sex, we must admit that they are. However,

unless feminists admit that the phenomena described by critics of women's performance in industry, offices, schoolrooms, trade unions and in the arts and sciences are real, they must fail to identify the problem, and therefore to solve it. It is 65 true that opportunities have been made available to women far beyond their desires to use them. It is also true that the women who avail themselves of opportunities too often do so in a feminine, filial, servile fashion. It must be understood that it will not suffice to encourage women to use an initiative that they have not got, just as it is useless to revile them for not having it. We must endeavour to understand how it is 70 that women's energy is systematically deflected from birth to puberty, so that when they come to maturity they have only fitful resource and creativity.

Germaine Greer

a Explain the point of the simile of the car. (lines 3–5)   *(3 marks)*
b Why is the word 'feminine' in inverted commas? (line 20)   *(3 marks)*
c What is the writer's purpose in quoting the 'account of the first female undergraduates'? (line 29)   *(4 marks)*
d Why is it 'not surprising that women seldom make the scientific advances' (lines 47–48), according to the writer?   *(4 marks)*
e Explain the writer's attitude to 'the blanket objections to women in the professions'. (line 59)   *(4 marks)*
f Explain in your own words what the writer means by the final sentence. Who or what does she blame for the situation she is describing in this sentence?   *(8 marks)*
g Comment on the tone of the passage.   *(7 marks)*
h Do you consider the passage 'well written'? You should make clear your criteria of assessment.   *(9 marks)*
i To what extent do you agree and/or disagree with the overall view of women presented in this passage?   *(8 marks)*

(50 marks total)

Background to feminism

The modern 'feminist' or 'women's liberation' movement has its origins in 19th-century women's rights organisations. First sketched out by Mary Wollstonecraft in her book, *Vindication of the Rights of Women*, published in 1792, the feminist cause was taken up more concretely in Europe and America in the late 1840s and early 1850s, as British sociologist Ann Oakley explains in *Subject Women*:

The 'Declaration of Sentiments' and 'Resolutions' adopted by the first American women's suffrage convention in 1848 summarised the outlines of women's position in many countries of the world at that time. It stated the feminist grievance in no uncertain terms:

The history of mankind is a history of repeated injuries and usurpations on the part of man toward woman, having in direct object the establishment of an absolute tyranny over her . . .
He has never permitted her to exercise her inalienable right to the elective franchise . . .
He has made her, if married, in the eyes of the law, civilly dead.
He has taken from her all right in property, even to the wages she earns . . .
He has so framed the laws of divorce, as to what shall be the proper causes and, in

cases of separation, to whom the guardianship of the children shall be given, as to be wholly regardless of the happiness of women – the law, in all cases, going upon false supposition of the supremacy of man, and giving all power into his hands . . .

He has monopolised nearly all the profitable employments, and from those she is permitted to follow, she receives but a scanty remuneration.

He closes against her all the avenues to wealth and distinction which he considers most honourable to himself. As a teacher of theology, medicine or law she is not known.

He has denied her the facilities for obtaining a thorough education, all colleges being closed against her . . .

He has endeavoured, in every way that he could, to destroy her confidence in her own powers, to lessen her self-respect, and to make her willing to lead a dependent and abject life . . .

Ann Oakley

The first women's suffrage society in Britain was formed in 1865, and by the end of the century the suffragette movement was intensely active, under the forceful leadership of such women as Emmeline Pankhurst, becoming organised in 1903 in the Women's Social and Political Union. During the First World War, women were encouraged to undertake a whole range of jobs and skills for which they had previously been considered incapable or unsuitable, and, as a result of this as well as the fierce and persistent suffragette activity, women were at last given limited access to the franchise in Britain in 1918.

After that, for over 40 years, the feminist movement fell into abeyance, to be revived in the early 1960s by women's liberation organisations in Britain and America, coming to the forefront of public consciousness once more in 1968.

The significance of the arrangements for men and women in Western society before their recent modifications is suggested by the British philosopher Janet Radcliffe Richards in *The Sceptical Feminist*:

The facts are stark, but beyond any question. All social arrangements, institutions and customs which defined the relative position of the sexes were designed *to ensure that women should be in the power and service of men*.

This no doubt sounds like pure feminist rant, but it is not. It is proved by many quite incontrovertible facts about the formal devices which, for most of history, were employed by men to make sure that women were kept in their power, and involves no recourse to extravagant assertions about the general moral turpitude of men . . .

To see the position of women in this way is to see clearly what femininity traditionally was. Feminine characteristics were the ones needed for making a success of the position into which women were forced, and roughly, therefore, to be feminine was to be pleasing to men. The whole essence of femininity is, or at least traditionally was, the limiting of all endeavour and activity to a confined end. Ideal femininity has never consisted in weakness and incompetence (contrary to much popular opinion, which seems to confuse descriptive and prescriptive femininity at this point as at many others); no man ever wanted a total loss of a woman. The idea was only to direct all abilities to being useful to men and their offspring, using a great deal of skill (the more the better) but always carefully directing it so that it presented no threat to men's position. It was unfeminine of women to want to study at universities or have the vote because in doing so they were showing that they had ideas about stepping beyond their allotted sphere: higher education and political power were not among the requirements for being a devoted wife and mother, and to seek them was to want to compete with men and become independent of them, rather than to remain in service to them.

Janet Radcliffe Richards

The advances made by women in the 20th century away from this enforced domesticity and subservience owe much to advances in contraception, offering a control over reproduction which was never previously possible. As the French philosopher and novelist Simone de Beauvoir points out in her classic study of women, *The Second Sex*:

One of the basic problems of woman . . . is the reconciliation of her reproductive role and her part in productive labour. The fundamental fact that, from the beginning of history, doomed woman to domestic work and prevented her taking part in the shaping of the world was her enslavement to the generative function. In female animals there is a physiological and seasonal rhythm that assures the economising of their strength; in woman, on the contrary, between puberty and menopause nature sets no limits to the number of her pregnancies . . . Contraceptives have been in existence since antiquity . . . but [they] were practically unknown to the Middle Ages in Europe; scarcely a trace of them is to be found up to the 18th century. For many women in those times life was an uninterrupted succession of pregnancies . . .

[Birth control and abortion] are of tremendous importance for women in particular; she can reduce the number of her pregnancies and make them a rationally integral part of her life, instead of being their slave.

Simone de Beauvoir

Discussion points

Why do you think the situation of women in Europe and America summarised in the 1848 American women's suffrage convention was as it was?

What were the original conditions for female suffrage in the 1918 act? Why do you think these restrictions were imposed? When were they removed?

What happened to most of the women who were employed in 'men's jobs' at the end of the First World War? Why?

Why do you think the women's movement died down after 1918? Why did it revive in the 1960s?

Women's inferiority in the arts and sciences

Compared with now, there have been few women of recognised genius. A common explanation of this is the belief that women as a sex are generally intrinsically less capable of inspiration and more narrow in their range of feeling and thinking than men.

Simone de Beauvoir takes up this point:

The anti-feminists obtain from the study of history two contradictory arguments:
1 women have never created anything great; and

2   the situation of women has never prevented the flowering of great feminine
    personalities . . .

The women who have accomplished works comparable to those of men are those
exalted by the power of social institutions above all sexual differentiation. Queen
Isabella, Queen Elizabeth, Catherine the Great were neither male nor female – they
were sovereigns. It is remarkable that their femininity, when socially abolished, should
have no longer meant inferiority: the proportion of queens who had great reigns is
infinitely above that of great kings. Religion works the same transformation: Catherine
of Siena, St Theresa, quite beyond any physiological consideration, were sainted
souls; the life they led, secular and mystic, their acts, and their writings rose to
heights that few men have ever reached.

   It is quite conceivable that if other women fail to make a deep impression upon the
world, it is because they are tied down in their situation. They can hardly take a hand
in affairs in other than a negative and oblique manner.

Simone de Beauvoir

The British writer Bryan Magee takes a different viewpoint in this extract
from an article which appeared in *The Guardian* in November 1989. He
challenges the feminist claim that women 'haven't had a chance' to
achieve greatness in the Arts, and offers his own explanation for the
absence of any women painters, playwrights and classical composers of the
first rank.

To put it crudely, I think women are more people-oriented than men, and men more inclined to look at things in other ways, including abstractions and generalities (which, be it said, are not at all subtle or refined for the most part, but rough and ready, and nearly always self-serving). Thus if a man and a woman form a passionate attachment to each other, it usually becomes the central preoccupation of the woman's life; and if she then discovers that it is not the central preoccupation of the man's, she is uncomprehending and resentful.

I think this general difference between the sexes is one of the things that helps to explain why their most gifted members tend to shine in different spheres, and it is salutary to remember now that we are talking about one in a billion of either sex, at a level of accomplishment that excludes nearly all of us.

The creative art in which women have conspicuously excelled is the one the very stuff and substance of whose subject matter is personal relationships; namely the novel (as against drama whose stuff and substance is conflict). It explains why several women are to be found at the top level in the social sciences and the life sciences, but not in mathematics or physics; though even there we have had Marie Curie, the joint discoverer of radium who, having won a Nobel prize for physics, then won another for chemistry.

Bryan Magee,
The Guardian,
November 1989

In her book *A Room of One's Own* (1929), the novelist Virginia Woolf
discusses issues relating to women's writing. At one point she considers
the question of whether it would have been possible for a woman to
have the genius of Shakespeare. She then invents a sister for
Shakespeare, named Judith, and imagines her following in her brother's
footsteps.

She was as adventurous, as imaginative, as agog to see the world as he was. But she
was not sent to school. She had no chance of learning grammar and logic, let alone of
reading Horace and Virgil. She picked up a book now and then, one of her brother's
perhaps, and read a few pages. But then her parents came in and told her to mend the
stocking or mind the stew and not moon about with books and papers. They would

have spoken sharply but kindly, for they were substantial people who know the conditions of life for a woman and loved their daughter – indeed, more likely than not she was the apple of her father's eye. Perhaps she scribbled some pages up in an apple loft on the sly, but was careful to hide them or set fire to them. Soon, however, before she was out of her teens, she was betrothed to the son of a neighbouring wood stapler. She cried out that marriage was hateful to her, and for that she was severely beaten by her father. Then he ceased to scold her. He begged her instead not to hurt him, not shame him in this matter of her marriage. He would give her a chain of beads or a fine petticoat, he said; and there were tears in his eyes. How could she disobey him? How could she break his heart? The force of her own gift alone drove her to it. She made up a small parcel of her belongings, let herself down by a rope one summer's night and took the road to London. She was not 17. The birds that sang in the hedge were not more musical than she was. She had the quickest fancy, a gift like her brother's, for the tune of words. Like him, she had a taste for the theatre. She stood at the stage door, she wanted to act, she said. Men laughed in her face. The manager – a fat, loose-lipped man – guffawed. He bellowed something about poodles dancing and women acting – no woman, he said, could possibly be an actress. He hinted – you can imagine what. She could get no training for her craft. Could she even seek dinner in a tavern or roam the street at midnight? Yet her genius was for fiction and lusted to feed abundantly upon the lives of men and women and the study of their ways.

At last – for she was very young, oddly like Shakespeare the poet in her face, with the same grey eyes and rounded brows – at last Nick Greene the actor-manager took pity on her, she found herself with child by that gentleman and so – who shall measure the heat and violence of the poet's heart when caught and tangled in a woman's body? – killed herself one winter's night and lies buried at some cross-roads where the omnibuses now stop outside the Elephant and Castle.

That, more or less, is how the story would run, I think, if a woman in Shakespeare's day had had Shakespeare's genius.

Virginia Woolf

Themes for discussion

How were musicians and painters generally financed in Europe, up to the 19th century? Does this have any bearing on the lack of notable women musicians and painters in earlier times?

Why was George Eliot so called? What does this show about the problems of aspiring women writers in the 19th century?

How many great 19th-century British writers were women? How many of them were married, with children?

In what fields have women generally achieved fame and distinction in the 20th century? Why these, rather than others?

Does the comprehension passage from Germaine Greer's book help to shed any light on the reasons why women continue to be outshone by men in the arts and sciences? What other reasons are there to explain this phenomenon?

Do you agree that women are 'more people-oriented than men', as Magee says? If so, would you agree with Magee's conclusions about the spheres of human endeavour in which women have excelled?

How do you respond to Virginia Woolf's portrait of Shakespeare's 'sister'?

Biology or conditioning?

The most intense controversy between feminists and anti-feminists concerns *the nature of women*. Most men, and some women, tend still to argue that the sexes are by nature psychologically different because of their biological make-up. Post-war feminist writers, on the other hand, have generally contended that these differences are simply or largely the result of conditioning and that there are no fundamental differences between the sexes, beyond the obvious physical ones. Girls, it is argued, are conditioned to think of the future pre-eminently in terms of wife and motherhood, by being given dolls to play with and being expected to stay in the home to help with household chores, and by being taught such subjects in school as cookery and needlework, whilst boys are prepared for their future role as breadwinners and decision-makers by being given toys like guns, being encouraged to be aggressive and independent, and being taught technical subjects from an early age.

Janet Radcliffe Richards attempts to shed some light on this endlessly contentious issue:

Common beliefs about the differences between the sexes are still usually based only on differences between men and women as they appear. Men are seen to be interested in politics or business while women tend to talk about homes and men and babies; men are seen to have mechanical or business abilities while women are baffled when confronted with the engine of a car and don't know what to make of bank statements and so on. But even to the extent that propositions such as these stem from impartial observation (which is true of by no means all of them), they are still not enough to show that women and men really are different by nature. You cannot tell the nature of anything just by looking in a casual and unsystematic way at how it appears, because whenever something is observed, it is in some environment or other, and the total phenomenon results not only from the nature of the thing under observation, but also from the environment it is in. If, therefore, two things appear different, they may not be different in nature at all: they may simply be in different environments. And this, of course, is what most feminists claim about many of the alleged differences in nature between men and women . . .

The feminist argument is that there are all kinds of systematic differences in the environment of men and women which are so subtle, or so universally taken for granted, that they have gone completely unnoticed or are underestimated. It is only relatively recently, for instance, that we have noticed that boy and girl children are treated differently almost from birth, or understood how radically people's performances are influenced by what is expected of them . . .

Recent discoveries of the extent and significance of systematic differences in environment between men and women are indeed enough to prove that most of the evidence people thought they had about the natures of men and women is totally inadequate to support the usual conclusions. However, it is important to realise that that is all they do. We may know that traditional views are almost certainly wrong, but it does not follow that we know which views are right.

When we find the environmental differences between two things are probably enough to account for their appearing to be different from each other, it certainly follows that they may be intrinsically alike in nature, but not that they certainly are. For instance, the difference in social expectations of the behaviour of men and women is enough to account for the fact that women show emotion far more readily than men do; even if they were precisely the same by nature this would account for different behaviour. It does not, however, prove that they are the same by nature. Perhaps women really are, by nature, more inclined to show emotion, as well as being socially encouraged to do so. Or again, the fact that women have, during most of their history, been forced by their biology (and men) to spend nearly all their time in the care of small children is a perfectly sufficient condition of their having made relatively little impact on the history of the world; if men had had to do the same they would not have had time for other things either. However, it does not follow that men and women have the same inherent capacities.

Perhaps women are inherently different; perhaps nature made them less interested in other things to ensure that they would be sufficiently inclined to care for their children.

Of course, our ignorance is lessening. In several areas we have made a great deal of progress, and have certainly shown that women are capable of acquiring skills traditionally thought beyond them, as soon as they are given the opportunity. In the most complicated areas, however, dealing with innate desires, temperament and so on, it is very difficult to find out how different men and women are. In the first place, social customs are so deeply entrenched that there are relatively few natural variations in environment we can watch, and manipulating society for the purpose of experiment is difficult . . .

The reason why it is important for feminists to study history and anthropology is that knowing how women acted in different times and under different circumstances gives us a greater understanding of their natures than seeing them only here and now.

This is a kind of work which must be carried forward with care and perseverance if we are to find out about the raw material we have to work with in planning our ideal society. And in the meantime we can certainly argue strenuously that traditional ideas about women and their differences from men are founded on totally inadequate evidence, and ought to be abandoned forthwith.

Janet Radcliffe Richards

Themes for discussion

Do you think that there are any differences between men and women which we can be *fairly certain* are biological differences in the nature of the sexes?

Is the possibility that most of the apparently natural differences between the sexes may be produced by conditioning sufficient reason to treat the sexes equally, since differences *do* exist, whatever the cause?

What areas of employment have recently ceased to be exclusively male preserves? Is there any good reason why any of them should have always been reserved for men before?

Should positive discrimination in favour of women be introduced, to help women to overcome their traditional disadvantages? If so, in what areas?

What anthropological evidence has come to light about 'primitive' societies in which men and women do not behave according to their traditional sex roles? Is it of any significance?

Should parents try to avoid guiding their children into conventional sex roles? Would social and peer group influence have the effect of conventional gender differentiation anyway?

Should schools treat boys and girls equally in the choice of school subjects?

Men's attitudes to women

There can be little real doubt that throughout history men have treated women as their inferiors, and regarded feminine traits with contempt. In the late 1960s the phrase 'male chauvinist pig' was coined to describe men who allowed their prejudice to show, and masculine assumptions of superiority led some of the more radical women's groups to advocate avoidance of all dealings with men. This attitude can be seen, for instance, in the women's peace camp at Greenham Common in the 1980s, from which men were discouraged on the grounds that as soon as men take part in activities with women they attempt to take over.

Let us look at what some modern women writers have to say about sexual attitudes and their implications. First, another extract from *The Sceptical Feminist*:

It must be said on behalf of feminists who are inclined to resist any differences in function, convention and expectation between the sexes that they have one very strong argument on their side in men's quite astonishing record of downgrading whatever is associated with women. Margaret Mead commented that in every known society, men's activities were regarded as more important than women's, quite irrespective of what those activities were. 'Men may cook or weave or dress dolls or hunt humming birds, but if such activities are appropriate occupations of men, then the whole society, men and women alike, vote them as important. When the same occupations are performed by women, they are regarded as less important.'

That is very striking, but even without any special knowledge of all known societies we have a pretty good idea of what an uphill struggle we should have, even within our own, if we tried to establish respect for what has traditionally been associated with women. The average woman is very pleased if she has any understanding of any such male terrain as the engine of a car, but there are still a good many men around whose claim not to know where to find anything in the kitchen is really a boast about their never demeaning themselves with women's work. Women on the tube are happy to be seen reading city newspapers, but no man would dream of knitting in public as some women do. It is quite unthinkable that the general relaxation of conventions of dress which has led to women's wearing trousers might have resulted in men's taking to skirts, for reasons having nothing at all to do with the relative comfort of the two. Girls in schools are doing more science and metal work, but most people are still slightly shocked at the thought that boys might learn to sew. And as Michael Korda in his book on male chauvinism quotes Jules Feiffer as saying: 'Whatever ground woman manages to establish for herself man abandons, denying its importance.' It is not at all difficult to understand the point of view of feminists who see that in any difference there lies potential inequality, and who suspect that wherever there is potential inequality men will contrive to make it actual.

However, not all women are willing to give up the struggle just because they are not very optimistic about the moral improvement of men. There are feminists who think that to abandon feminine things just because men are determined to downgrade them is to give in altogether, and what we should be doing is demanding respect for whatever deserves respect, feminine or not.

Janet Radcliffe Richards

The alternative to ignoring male prejudice for women with ambitions in male-dominated areas of work – aping men – is discussed by the American writer Betty Friedan in a magazine interview from *The Sunday Times*, with Rosemary Wittman Lamb:

'I had lunch with a group of women executives, and I was horrified,' she told me. 'They were so grim, so dressed-for-success. And they told me: 'We have to be hard-headed, like the men, and get rid of all vestiges of femininity.'

In the area of love and marriage, many feminists argue that only a genuine feeling of equality between the partners can engender mutual respect which is necessary if love is to last. Here is a fairly radical view of love and marriage by the British journalist and writer, Jill Tweedie, from her book *In the Name of Love*:

It is a bitter irony for men that their insistence on women's inferiority, their refusal to grant her a place in the sun, has robbed them of the only chance they have to be loved properly. They cannot love women because they have made women unequal and forced them into all the unloving patterns of inequality. And women cannot love them because the inferior do not properly love their masters, they only prostrate themselves or live vicariously through them. Contrary to the old wives' tales, the real joy of love lies in the knowledge that your lover could manage without you, that he or she has no *need* of you but simply feels a great deal happier that you are there.

With unequals you must always lie a little, if only to save them pain. Equals know that pain is part of growing and believe each other strong enough to stand what is necessary for growth. This applies as much to the minefield of outside sexual encounters as anything else. True love accepts that one person cannot provide everything for another – indeed there is a kind of obscenity in the very notion. Besides, what have you gained if you force anything, even faithfulness, on another person? Their presence, perhaps, but who wants a body with a mind elsewhere? What is the point of trying to coerce what cannot be coerced? Love does not 'allow', 'permit' or 'forbid' or it is not love.

Jill Tweedie

Discussion points

Why do you think that women have tended to accept the idea that their activities, whatever they may be, are less important than those of men?

Should women try to develop the kind of toughness and aggressiveness normally associated with men in order to compete with them in the job market? What is the alternative?

Do you agree that a feeling of equality between partners is the strongest basis for marriage? How possible is it to achieve?

Do you think it is right for married partners to separate if they no longer feel in love?

The beauty question

For centuries it has been the convention for women to adorn themselves with make-up and ornaments of various kinds. This reflects the age-old conception of women as the 'beautiful' sex, and women's enhancement of their beauty as a source of pleasure and enjoyment for both sexes.

Recently, however, many women have come to regard the concern of both sexes with women's 'beauty' as an unhealthy obsession, with serious and even destructive consequences for women. This view is taken by the American writer Naomi Wolf in her book, *The Beauty Myth*.

Wolf sees the root of the problem in the constant pressure on women to think of themselves in terms of their appearance, in a way that is not expected of men. She sees this pressure reflected in women's magazines:

In providing a dream language of meritocracy ('get the body you deserve': 'a gorgeous figure doesn't come without effort'), entrepreneurial spirit ('make the most of your natural assets'), absolute personal liability for body size and ageing ('you *can* totally reshape your body'; 'your facial lines are now within your control') and even open admissions ('at last you too can know the secret beautiful women have kept for years') they keep women consuming their advertisers' products in pursuit of the total personal transformation in status that the consumer society offers men in the form of money.

She sees one of the results of this as an unhealthy competitiveness in terms of appearance:

'Men look at women. Women watch themselves being looked at. This determines not only the relations of men to women, but the relation of women to themselves.' Critic John Berger's well-known quote has been true throughout the history of Western culture, and it is more true now than ever.

Many women tend to resent each other if they look too good and dismiss one another if they look too bad. Ironically, the myth that drives women apart also binds

Andrea Dworkin, radical feminist writer (top left); Sinead O'Connor, Irish singer/songwriter (above);
Naomi Wolf (left)

them together. A wry smile about calories, a complaint about one's hair, can evaporate the sullen examination of a rival in the fluorescent light of the ladies' room.

Wolf sees another result in women's increasing obsession with their weight, seen at its most disastrous in the growing number of women suffering from the so-called 'slimmers' diseases', anorexia and bulimia:

The hunger cult has won a major victory against women's fight for equality if the evidence of a 1984 *Glamour* survey of 33,000 women is representative: 75 per cent of those aged 18–35 believed they were fat, while only 25 per cent were medically overweight; 45 per cent of the underweight women thought they were too fat. But more heartbreaking in terms of the way in which the myth is running to ground hopes for women's advancement and gratification, the *Glamour* respondents chose losing 10–15 lb above success in work or in love.

Wolf's conclusion is that when women regard their personal appearance as a source of anxiety rather than pleasure, then their beauty is imprisoning; it is from this that they must escape:

The real problem isn't whether women wear make-up or don't, gain weight or lose it, have surgery or shun it, dress up or down, make their clothing and faces and bodies into works of art or ignore adornment altogether. The problem is their lack of choice.
   The problem with cosmetics exists if women feel they are invisible without them.
   Whenever we ignore a woman on television before we hear what she is saying, simply because we don't like her make-up or hairstyle, the beauty myth is working.
                                                                                  Naomi Wolf

Discussion points

Are women inclined to think about their appearance significantly more than men? In what ways?

What pressures are women under to worry about their appearance?

Why are an increasing number of women suffering from the 'slimmers' diseases'?

Do you think that it is true that women have limited choice about spending more time and money on their appearance than men?

Look at the photographs on page 147. Write down your instinctive reactions to each of these three pictures, and then discuss them. Do your responses have any bearing on the points made by Naomi Wolf?

A woman's place: at home, at work, or both?

Arguments have raged, since the renaissance of the feminist movement in the 1960s, about the extent to which home and family should dominate a woman's life. At the one extreme is the traditional view that a woman fulfils her biological destiny as a mother and housewife, and that no other role can fulfil her as a *woman*. At the other extreme is the radical feminist rejection of the family, which is seen as a means of repressing women and keeping them in subjection, and preventing them from achieving their fulfilment as *people*, which can only come through the pursuit of an independent career. Housework, according to this view, is seen as a dreary and endless routine, as was colourfully expressed by Simone de Beauvoir in 1949: 'Washing, ironing, sweeping, ferreting out fluff from under wardrobes – all this halting of decay is also the denial of life; for time simultaneously creates and destroys, and only its negative aspect concerns the housekeeper'.

Writers in the 1940s and 1950s developed the image of the happy housewife, competent in a wide range of domestic skills, providing sympathy and support for her breadwinner husband, and creatively bringing up her children in a loving home environment.

The first English-speaking writer to emphasise the discontent felt by many women with this role, evidenced by the large number of housewives dependent on tranquillisers, was Betty Friedan, in her book *The Feminine Mystique*, published in 1963. She called it, 'the problem without a name', and characterised it thus:

It was a strange stirring, a sense of dissatisfaction, a yearning that women suffered in the middle of the 20th century in the United States. Each suburban housewife struggled with it alone. As she made the beds, shopped for groceries, matched slip cover material, ate peanut butter sandwiches, chauffeured Cub Scouts and Brownies, lay beside her husband at night, she was afraid to ask even of herself the silent question: 'Is this all?'

Many feminists in the late 1970s and 1980s, Betty Friedan included, have arrived at a kind of synthesis, arguing that most women need both work and family in order to be fulfilled. In *The Second Stage*, published in 1982, Betty Friedan takes this viewpoint:

Personal choices and political strategies of women today are distorted when they deny the reality of both sets of needs: woman's need for power, identity, status and security through her own work or action in society, which the reactionary enemies of feminism deny; and the need for love and identity, status, security and generation through marriage, children, home, the family, which those feminists still locked in their own extreme reaction deny. Both sets of needs are essential to women, and to the evolving human condition . . .

The enemies of feminism insist that woman's move to equality, self-realisation and her own power in society is destroying the family, which they feel is woman's real focus of power. Many feminists insist that the family was, and is, the enemy, the prime obstacle to woman's self-realisation. There are pieces of the truth in these interlocking fears, shadows of conflicts that were insoluble in the past. I believe that the first stage, woman's movement to equality and her own personhood, was, in fact, necessary for the survival and economic/emotional health of the family, and that the second stage can, and must, transcend these conflicts. For I believe, from all we know of human psychology and history, that neither woman nor man lives by work, or love, alone: the absolutely powerless, the denigrated, the self-abnegating ones are too hungry for power, too lacking in self, to love and nurture; the loveless crave power because they lack both love and self. The human self defines itself and grows through love and work.

Why are some women so afraid, on either side of this conflict, to put to the test of personal reality our own needs for power in the world and for love and family?

Such a choice can, of course, cause immense practical problems, especially when childcare facilities are lacking and husbands are not supportive in the home. Betty Friedan interviewed many working mothers before writing *The Second Stage*. Here are two typical *cris de coeur*:

A young woman in her third year of Harvard Medical School tells me, 'I'm going to be a surgeon. I'll never be a trapped housewife like my mother. But I would like to get married and have children, I think. They say we can have it all. But how? I work 36 hours in the hospital, 12 off. How am I going to have a relationship, much less kids, with hours like that? I'm not sure I can be a superwoman. I'm frightened that I may be kidding myself. Maybe I can't have it all. Either I won't be able to have the kind of marriage I dream of or the kind of medical career I want.'

'The worst problem for women today is trying to juggle it all,' said a 38-year-old lawyer in Chicago, a mother of two. 'Wanting to get ahead in your career, wanting to have a perfect marriage and really be with your husband, wanting to do all the right things about your kids, and not giving up any of it. The guilt, because you can't really do all these things and do each one perfectly.'

Betty Friedan

For many women, of course, there is no dilemma. In this letter to *The Guardian*, Ann P. Heaton expresses her feeling of fulfilment in having adopted the traditional role of homemaker and mother:

I like being a housewife. It is 30 years since I left university, but I hope my mind has not been completely atrophied by staying at home to look after my family. Bringing up my family has been a joyous occupation for the most part, and far more satisfying and entertaining than any of the jobs I held before. I have always had time for them and for my husband, and have not missed any of their childhood. Now that I am older I have time for myself and the freedom to do what I choose. I certainly don't feel like a dodo, or a parasite for that matter.

Similarly, for many women who *do* seek outlets for their creativity beyond their traditional role, the experience of bringing up children remains their greatest source of satisfaction and achievement. The Nigerian novelist, poet and television playwright, Buchi Emecheta, expressed this view in an article in *New Internationalist* in 1985:

I had my photograph taken once in my 'office' where I do my writing. The photo-journalist was a staunch feminist, and was so angry that my 'office' was my kitchen and that packets of breakfast cereals were in the background. I was letting the women's movement down by allowing such a photograph to be taken.

But that was where I worked, because it was warmer, because it was convenient for me to be able to see my family when I put my typewriter to one side. I tried in vain to tell her that, in my kitchen, I felt I was doing more for the peace of the world than the nuclear scientist: in our kitchens we raise all the future Reagans, or the future Jesuses. In our kitchens we wash for them and cook for them. In our kitchens they learn to love and to hate. And we send them out from our kitchens to be grown men and women.

What greater work is there than that? I do not think it low. A mother with a family is an economist, a nurse, a painter, a diplomat and more. Those who wish to control and influence the future generation by giving birth and nurturing the young should not be looked down upon. If I had my way it would be the highest-paid job in the world.

Buchi Emecheta

Despite two decades of women's liberation, many people continue to take the stereotyped sex roles for granted. Here are some instances:

A son to carry on the family name, and share in all the excitement of cheering on his dad's favourite football team, or a daughter who will dress in pretty frocks, borrow mum's make-up and raise the next generation? That's what every parent wonders about when a baby's on the way. And it's the biggest mystery in the world.

from *Sunday* magazine, 1985

He's earned the sort of millions that could provide a life of super luxury. Yet Paul McCartney has not forgotten his working-class roots, insisting that his wife Linda does the laundry, washes the dishes and rises at seven to cook the family breakfast

from *Woman* magazine, 1984

If the good Lord had intended us to have equal rights to go out to work, he would not have created man and woman.

Patrick Jenkin, MP

Discussion points

Do you think it is better if women stay at home while their children are young?

Do you think that most women with children who work do so mainly in the interest of personal fulfilment or financial security?

How realistic do you think it is for a woman to attempt to pursue a demanding full-time career while bringing up young children?

Do you think that employers should be compelled by law to provide crèche facilities for the children of female employees?

Women at work

In the 1970s in Britain, two acts were passed – the Equal Pay Act of 1970 and the Sex Discrimination Act of 1975 – aimed at ending discrimination against women in employment. Further tightening up occurred in the Pensions Act of 1995, with the European Court ruling against women being forced to retire at 60, while the retirement age for men was 65.

Many fields of employment opened up for British women in the 1970s, but in terms of pay the results of anti-discriminatory legislation have not been as dramatic as might have been expected. One of the reasons for this is the continued existence of 'women's jobs', which tend to be low-paid occupations. Another major reason is the increasing trend for women to be employed in other than full-time salaried jobs. Kate Figes, in *Because of Her Sex: The Myth of Equality for Women in Britain*, published in 1994, explains:

It is now estimated that half of all working women in Britain – more than twice the number of men – are employed on untypical contracts describing them as part-time, temporary or self-employed. Without the benefits of sick and maternity pay, unemployment benefit or a full state pension, these women will draw less on the welfare state, being forced back on to a male earner for their support. Traditional male sectors of employment, by contrast, are not increasing their use of a part-time casual labour force. In most heavy manufacturing, shift work with paid overtime is more common. Likewise, though many consultants, doctors, MPs and chief executives work what could be part-time hours, in order to accommodate private practices and other concerns, their pay and conditions are not docked accordingly.

Kate Figes

The country which has gone furthest in legislating for equality between men and women in employment is Sweden. Here is a report by Anuradha Vittachi on the Swedish system and its effects at the beginning of the 1980s:

In every country, rich and poor, the biggest barrier to equality for a woman is her burden of 'bearing and caring' for children. That is why you cannot travel in Stockholm now by bus or train without being confronted by government-sponsored posters promoting the idea that men should share fully in the task of bringing up their children. 'Father's freedom to be with children', reads the caption, 'it's natural. Make the most of your rights'.

Now under Swedish law men can take as much as six months' 'paternity leave' when a child is born, without loss of pay or job security. Or men and women can decide to share 'parenthood leave'.

Men and women can also take up to three months' leave at any time before the child's eighth birthday if they feel the need to spend time with a son or daughter – for example during the settling-in period at the start of school.

Men as well as women can take up to 12 days a year leave when their children are sick – and they do. On several occasions in Stockholm I found my appointments postponed because the men concerned had to go home to look after an ailing child.

Swedish law also gives couples the right to share one job so they can be free to look after their children equally. Nor can a father of a young child be legally refused his right to work a six-hour day. And there is mounting pressure to pay him for the two hours he spends at home. All these changes mean men have more time for sharing family duties.

To back up these changes there have been other reforms to help equalise the sexes. The retirement age is the same for men as for women. Free abortions are available up to the 18th week of pregnancy. Free contraception counselling services are available to all. Husbands and wives are taxed separately. Wives are no longer classified as 'dependents'. Marriage is seen now as just one form of 'voluntary cohabitation between individuals.' Custody of children following a divorce may be shared between parents and is not automatically awarded to the mother.

So the foundations seem to have been laid for achieving equality between the sexes in Sweden. But there is still a long way to go. Cooking and childcare classes for boys and metalwork for girls may be compulsory at school, but 86 per cent of students in technical courses are still boys, and girls still flock to nursing and pre-school training colleges. And although men have been entitled to parenthood leave since 1974, less than 10 per cent of fathers have been taking advantage of their rights.

Women may earn equal pay, but their access to equal work is only theoretical. The labour market is split between 'men's jobs' in heavy industry and 'women's jobs' in the service sector. Three-quarters of all gainfully employed women work at only 25 different jobs – and it can be no coincidence that these jobs are badly paid. Even in female-dominated professions, the top jobs usually go to men. For instance, teachers tend to be women, but headteachers tend to be men. The management of the hotel I stayed in was almost exclusively male, but invariably my bed was made and my room cleaned by women.

Sweden's radical idea whereby the 'time-cake' of men and women would be carved into four equal portions – one for paid work, one for family, one for community service, and the last for leisure – is still a dream. But things are on the move. Where else in the world could a woman feel within her rights to complain that her husband 'only' took two months leave to look after the baby?

Anuradha Vittachi, *New Internationalist*, 1980

*Discussion
points*

Do you think that the Equal Pay Act and the Sex Discrimination Act have succeeded in removing the discrepancies in pay between men and women in Britain?

What do you think of the various methods adopted in Sweden for promoting equality of employment prospects between the sexes?

Do you think the traditional division between men's jobs and women's jobs should or could eventually be broken down?

Do you think that day-care centres or crèches at workplaces should be available to all working mothers? Is it feasible to legislate for this?

Some final thoughts

In a magazine interview in *The Sunday Times* in November 1981, the American journalist, Nora Ephron, looked back on the women's liberation movement in the USA in the 1970s:

My point is, we started out in the 1960s with this great burst of energy, and then degenerated into *massive* divorce. In 1973, 1974, 1975 the basic feminist act was to get divorced. In 1973 it seemed to me that five million women turned around and said: 'I divorce you! I divorce you! I divorce you!'

The one thing that happened in 1972 was that all these men cleared the table. That was what everyone got their husbands to do. They all screamed and yelled about household chores and made lists about who did what and the men said: 'OK, I'll clear the table', and then looked round as though they deserved a medal. And they hoped it would all go away. And it did. It all went away. Their wives went away, everything went away. And they found someone else and they went back to being princes.

So many of us in that period were trying to smash feminism into our marriages. We ended up absolutely drained.

Nora Ephron

A magazine article in *The Sunday Times* in November 1978, written by Anna Coote, ended thus:

Will men's liberation be the movement of the 1980s, a natural successor to women's liberation? I doubt it. I am sure men are ultimately oppressed by their own machismo; but that is the price of power and most men are willing to pay it. Rarely, if ever, has any power group willingly surrendered power.

Anna Coote

*Discussion
points*

Has the women's liberation movement been essentially beneficial or damaging in its effects on the lives of men, women and children?

Do you think that a 'men's liberation movement' is needed? What might its goals be? Are there any signs of men's attitudes to their position in the world radically changing?

Do you think the 1990s has really seen the emergence of the 'new man', sharing the work in the home?

Women in the Third World

The whole of this chapter so far has been concerned with the situation of women in the developed world. In large parts of the developing world, the very idea of women's liberation is meaningless, as women continue to cope in the same ways as they have for centuries with the effects of male assumptions of women's inferiority and subservience.

In many areas of the Third World, women are forced to play a major role in agriculture as well as child-rearing and home-making, and often gain little or no recognition for their contribution to the economic and domestic life of the family. The situation of women in developing countries is, however, far too varied for brief analysis. Instead, we will take a glimpse into the life of just one woman in Latin America, whose story has been repeated across the world countless millions of times over numberless centuries. She comes from the state of Rio Grande do Norte, in north-east Brazil, where rural mothers have an average of more than seven living children. She was met by Paul Harrison while he was researching for his book *Inside the Third World*, from which the extract is taken:

You often meet women like Luisa Gomez, a slight, small 39-year-old. She married at 14. Since then she has been pregnant 16 times, once every 18 months. For half of her adult life she has been pregnant, and for the other half breast-feeding the most recent addition. Only six of those 16 are still alive. There were three stillbirths and seven died in their first year. Ten wasted pregnancies. Seven and a half years of drain on an already weak organism, for nothing. Worse than nothing, for all the anxiety, all the care, all the concern, and then the grief.

Life goes on like that. Before the first one is even on its feet, the next is on the way. Housework becomes a crushing burden with no labour-saving devices to help out. Feeding the family is like cooking for a works canteen. And with each successive birth the figure collapses a little further, the breasts sag and a paunch develops, making the women look pregnant even when they are not. Privacy, time to yourself, time to rest even, is an unheard-of, undreamed-of luxury. Bearing and rearing children, every girl is told, is a woman's only function. And because to believe otherwise would be to condemn herself to utter despair, the woman accepts the idea: and teaches it to her daughters.

Paul Harrison

Discussion points

Research and discuss some of the religious and cultural traditions which affect women in different countries and areas of the world.

Is it possible to envisage a time in the future when men and women all over the world will treat one another as equals at home and at work?

Essay titles

a '. . . most women nowadays expect to marry, have children and work.'
b 'Room at the top, but not for women!'
c 'Women's liberation has resulted in men's enslavement.'
d Is the status of women in our society still unsatisfactory?
e 'Marriage is still a woman's best investment!' Discuss.
f Do you think it desirable or undesirable that men and women should maintain separate and clearly differentiated roles at home and at work?

g How far have we got in equalising opportunities for the sexes, and how much further should we go?

h 'Literature is the only art form in which women have excelled.' How far do you agree?

Bibliography

de Beauvoir, Simone, *The Second Sex*, Picador, 1988

Figes, Kate, *Because of Her Sex: The Myth of Equality for Women in Britain*, Macmillan, 1994

Friedan, Betty, *The Feminine Mystique*, Penguin, 1992

Friedan, Betty, *The Second Stage*, Abacus, 1983

Greer, Germaine, *The Female Eunuch*, Flamingo, 1993

Neustatter, Angela, *Hyenas in Petticoats: A Look At Twenty Years of Feminism*, Penguin, 1990

Oakley, Ann, *Subject Women*, Fontana, 1985

Radcliffe Richards, Janet, *The Sceptical Feminist*, Penguin, 1983

Segal, Lynne, *Is the Future Female?: Troubled Thoughts on Contemporary Feminism*, Virago, 1991

Tweedie, Jill, *In the Name of Love*, Jonathan Cape, 1979

Wolf, Naomi, *The Beauty Myth*, Vintage, 1991

Wollstonecraft, Mary, *Vindication of the Rights of Women*, Penguin, 1992

Further advice on writing: using facts, figures, and sources in essays

It is perfectly possible to write a satisfactory argumentative essay with very little precise factual content, as was illustrated in Chapter 1. Facts and figures, however, give substance and conviction to an argument and it is sensible to learn a good deal of 'hard' information in preparation for an examination language essay. The degree to which this information needs to be detailed and exact is largely a matter of common sense. It may be helpful, nevertheless, to give some examples of the kinds of factual information which do and do not need to be exact.

Quoting sources of information is sometimes important, but it's obviously not necessary to give the source of every piece of information you include in an essay. If you are offering general information which is common knowledge, or is the kind of information which could be checked from a number of sources, such as details of the paternity-leave system and parenthood reforms in Sweden, there is no need to quote your source.

If you are giving precise figures, on the other hand, such as the percentage of the world's resources consumed by the USA, or the drop in the price of a commodity on the world market over a specified period, you ought to quote the source of the figures. The date when figures were issued also needs to be given sometimes, as when quoting the projected world population in the year 2000, since such projections are likely to change.

Exact figures and details should be given if doing so will clarify the point being made. In the case of historical background, for instance, precision is important. If you are mentioning acts of parliament, such as the Equal Pay Act, you should learn the date. A proper historical perspective on events can only be given if you can quote dates; the year in which women achieved the vote, for instance, or the year when Mary Wollstonecraft achieved publication of the first feminist book.

Drawing comparisons between different groups of people in some particular respect is another case where precise back-up information is helpful. For instance, if you are arguing that women often earn less than men for similar work, despite the Equal Pay Act, you need at least to specify in which areas of work this is so, even if you can't quote figures. Similarly, if you are making the case that one of the reasons for women's wages being lower than men's on average is that many jobs are still heavily female-dominated, the statistic that women outnumber men nine to one in a quarter of all occupations in which women work will add considerable strength to your argument. In this case, since the figures are not particularly well known or recognised, it would be useful to quote your source.

In general, exact facts and figures can often make an otherwise vague point precise and persuasive. A statement about Britain's prisons being seriously overcrowded is a case of point. If you could refer to the fact that prisoners are often held two or three to a cell built for one in Victorian times, you would establish the point convincingly. Here the source is less important, since the information is generally known and admitted. If you are mentioning famous people and places, you should try to make sure that you can give their names.

Very often, of course, points can be made perfectly convincingly without precise facts and figures. Common sense is ultimately the only guide in this matter.

10 Race

For centuries, Britain has been a multi-racial society. Only recently, however, has 'race' become an issue, owing largely to the influx of easily identifiable black and Asian immigrants, which began just after the Second World War. Racial tensions, simmering since the late 1950s, boiled over in the early 1980s in a series of riots which shocked the whole of Europe and the English-speaking world. This chapter will concentrate largely on the racial situation in modern Britain. It begins with an exercise for summary of an article concerning the virtual absence of black and Asian journalists in Fleet Street.

Summary skills

The article which follows, which was written by Yasmin Alibhai, appeared in *The Guardian* newspaper in September 1990.

You have been asked to prepare a report on the policy of British newspapers with regard to the employment of black and Asian journalists and you have decided to summarise this writer's comments on the subject, as part of your report. Write the summary.

Use no more than 200 words.
20 marks will be awarded for content.
20 marks will be awarded for organisation of material, fitness for purpose and accuracy of expression.

You are advised to spend about one hour on this question.

Still papering over the cracks

'Are you not just creating the problem by asking these questions?' enquired the voice of the spokeswoman (Department of Human Resources) from that vast media archipelago, News International. The problem under discussion was the employment of ethnic journalists on national newspapers and weeklies. I explained all I wanted to know was how many staff reporters were black or Asian: ('We don't know, to us they're all just reporters');

whether monitoring was done in this area ('No'); and how people were recruited for editorial jobs ('I wasn't told you wanted to ask that question. I'll have to get back to you').

Later I was told they had about 10 to 15 such journalists; that they had a very good relationship with the Race Relations Board (*sic*) and that recruitment was through contacts and approaches, although some senior posts were advertised.

Most other spokespeople were equally coy and defensive. Charles Burgess, managing editor of the *Independent*, thought there were maybe three Asian or black journalists on staff, but said they did not look at things in that way. Nor does *The Observer*, which has an all-white editorial team of 100 except for one foreign correspondent.

The newspapers show a similar dearth. The *Sunday Correspondent* has no general black or Asian reporters, but one on the City Desk; the *Independent On Sunday* has none. *The Guardian* has two black reporters, a black sub-editor and had an Asian reporter on work experience. *The Sunday Telegraph* seems to have a couple. *The Evening Standard* has one and the *Mirror*, according to Bill Berentemfel, the editorial manager, has very few, 'two to three out of 200'. Three quality weeklies – *The Listener*, *The Economist* and the *New Statesman and Society* – cannot conjure up one black staff reporter between them. Exceptionally *The Financial Times* has six – mostly sub-editors.

The Black Journalists Association (which includes Asian journalists) is currently carrying out a more comprehensive study, but its findings are unlikely to show anything but a thoroughly discouraging picture if this random survey is anything to go by.

The BJA held a meeting on Saturday with newspaper and magazine editors at the London School of Economics to air their concerns.

The situation seems to have arisen not out of conspiracy, but inertia. Traditional methods such as word-of-mouth recruitment and old-boy networks are known to militate most against those who come from under-represented groups. The Commission for Racial Equality recommends certain formal procedures to extend access and counter subjective factors. But the message remains anathema to the newspaper industry, even though the arguments for change are commonsensical. How can the papers harvest exciting new talent with diverse views and perspectives by sticking so rigidly to the safety of clones?

It is common to see rivulets of guilt and concern trickling down the powerful foreheads of television chiefs, even if it is for PR purposes. But to date no newspaper editor has been heard to speak out on the issue. In five years, television has transformed itself. On the BBC recently, Peter Kenyatta, the deputy Editor of Current Affairs, sat suitably contrite when asked why more had not been done to recruit and promote blacks and Asians in key departments. Independent companies such as LWT and Thames have pursued aggressive policies to redress the balance through open advertising and the results are striking, with talented journalists like Trevor Phillips and Zeinab Badawi fronting prestigious news and current affairs programmes.

Changes in the television industry were spurred on by the Campaign Against Racism in the Media and other black groups. The inadequate television coverage of Brixton and Southall street disturbances also exposed the need for ethnic reporters with an intimate knowledge of what was going on in the communities.

Newspapers have not displayed any such self-criticism. All describe themselves as equal-opportunity employers but have never sought to examine if the description is justified. Most editors/managing editors I spoke to felt they operated a genuine meritocracy and that they did not think in terms of special groups. No one, however, came up with any convincing explanations why there were so few ethnic staff journalists on their papers.

Berentemfel said that changing recruitment practices would be difficult. 'We employ people we know. We cannot afford to train anyone. They come to us from provincial papers, and they have to come up to scratch.'

But he agreed that change was necessary: 'It broadens the reporting spectrum. We should have not only ethnic minorities but perhaps Germans and French, too, as we go into Europe.'

This is good sense. Most white journalists do not have good contacts within black and Asian communities and have little genuine awareness of their lives, concerns and conflicts. It took over three months, for example, for papers to pick up on the abducted Southall baby – still missing – an event which came a few days after the Griffith baby abduction. Ethnics only exist when they riot, burn books, arrange marriages or dope deal. And yet many significant media events in the past few years have involved black and Asian Britons as this country tries to establish a multiracial identity.

'Consciousness raising does need to be done,' said Peter Fiddick, editor of *The Listener*. 'We need to diversify and become more sensitive. The reason why change is not taking place is apathy rather than not caring about it. Like women, ethnic minorities should speak out.

Trevor Grove, editor of *The Sunday Telegraph*, is also sympathetic. 'Members of these communities must not think that this is a closed shop. We believe in a meritocracy, and if they are good, race should not be an issue. It may be a positive plus. But what you don't want is to be a token figure, someone who is always typecast as the expert on these matters.'

But, if it is all right to have chess and wine correspondents, why not have race or community correspondents? Experts whose reports would have depth instead of being trite and superficial as they so often are at present.

Many black and Asian journalists do not want to be pushed into that particular box because they see it as an undervalued area of expertise and because they want to work in general interest areas. But most are not so choosy. As one young black journalist put it: 'I would love to be a token. Just tell them to give me a chance.'

David Walker, the Deputy Editor of *The Financial Times*, urged more journalists from under-represented groups to apply for jobs. 'When the UK Press Gazette did a similar article a few years ago, there was a flurry of applications,' he said. 'It was the only time we had any. Maybe these journalists are setting their sights too low, and their perceptions about jobs on the paper are negative.'

Shyama Perera, almost unique at present as an Asian woman journalist who has worked on major national papers, including *The Guardian*, is not convinced by the paucity argument. 'It is true that there were not enough of us initially. That's not the case now, but historical prejudices run deep. Editors are loath to try out this talent. And one barrier curiously is the desperately colourblind approach – "I am a Liberal: I have done India. I frequent Mauritian fish restaurants so I cannot be racist." '

This barrier of self-righteousness is less easy to break than overt prejudice. The *New Statesman and Society*, a paper for which I worked, had no other black journalists then and has none now. The *Daily Mail* on the other hand, not well known for its anti-racism, can boast that it has given space and high-profile positions to many black and Asian journalists such as Baz Bamigboye and Hal Austin.

Tariq Modood, principal officer at the Commission for Racial Equality, says: 'It is very disappointing to note the absence of ethnic minority people in newspaper journalism. When one looks at the way the issues of ethnic minorities are so poorly reported – usually too late and from the point of view of the outsider – one would have thought that papers would be desperate to buy in understanding and expertise.

In a recent article on these pages, John Pilger wrote of how the British media and its narrow, predictable coverage of issues has helped to insulate the status quo. He quoted the Runnymede Trust report, which says the press 'plays a very significant part in maintaining, justifying and strengthening racism at all levels of society, providing a cover for racist activity, especially racist violence.'

This is true of all the papers. You can do as much damage through exclusion and miscomprehension as you can through misrepresentations and falsehoods. How many Afro-Caribbean writers reported or commented on Broadwater Farm? And would the whole picture of that story have been different if they had done so? How long will white journalists on pilgrimage to Bradford continue to be amazed that young Muslims are not waiting to flee from the prisons of their lives? The ethics of racist reporting will only effectively be challenged when there is a core group of ethnic reporters on every paper.

Other vistas need to be opened, too. There are hardly any ethnic book, film or television reviewers, and no staff columnists.

There is a whole world out there, from cinema to commentary, waiting to be tapped.

Yasmin Alibhai,
The Guardian,
September 1990

What is 'race'?

Before we can talk sensibly about 'race', it is necessary to establish what we mean by the term. This definition of 'race' is taken from *A Dictionary of Race and Ethnic Relations* edited by E. Ellis Cashmore:

Physical anthropologists used to speak of human 'races' in the sense of sub-species, the most common scheme being the great tripartite division of mankind into Negroid, Mongoloid and Caucasoid. Over the last 40 to 50 years, however, it became increasingly clear that no meaningful taxonomy of human races was possible. Not only were numerous groups not classifiable as belonging to any of the three main groups, but physical anthropologists could not agree with each other as to where the genetic boundaries between human groups were to be drawn, or even on how many such groups there were. Humans have migrated over large distances and interbred extensively for thousands of years. Especially with the maritime expansion of Europe starting five centuries ago, this process of interbreeding has greatly accelerated, thereby blurring 'racial' boundaries, and contributing more than ever to the genetic homogenization of our species.

   A 'race' can also mean a group of people who are socially defined in a given society as belonging together because of physical markers such as skin pigmentation, hair texture, facial features, stature, and the like. To avoid the confusion, some people specify 'social race' when they use 'race' in this meaning. Nearly all social scientists only use 'race' in this sense of a social group defined by somatic visibility. It is important to stress here that any resemblance with the first usage is little more than coincidental. For example, 'blacks' in South Africa and in Australia, although they occupy somewhat similar social positions in their respective societies, are no more closely related genetically to each other than each of them is to the 'whites'.

E. Ellis Cashmore

So, when we talk about 'races' in this chapter, we will simply be talking about groups of people of different skin colour. For the sake of simplicity, the term 'black' is used to cover all dark-skinned people of Asian, African and West Indian origin.

   It should be borne in mind, of course, that tensions between groups within societies arise from factors other than simply 'race', and in some societies different factors are paramount. Antagonism between Protestants and Catholics in Northern Ireland, or Sikhs and Hindus in India, stem from cultural and religious, rather than 'racial' distinctions, while in many nations of Africa conflict arises principally from tribal divisions.

Immigration: some facts

There have been black people in Britain for centuries. It was only after the Second World War, however, that immigration from black Commonwealth countries became at all significant. The background to the influx of black Commonwealth immigrants which began in the late 1940s, and which was originally mostly from the West Indies, is explained by Peter Fryer in *Staying Power*:

Ten years after the 'Empire Windrush'[1] there were in Britain about 25,000 West Indians who had come since the end of the war.

1 The ship on which the first Commonwealth immigrants from the West Indies sailed to Britain in 1945.

British industry gladly absorbed them. In some industries, the demand for labour was so great that members of the reserve army of black workers were actively recruited in their home countries. In April 1956 London Transport began recruiting staff in Barbados, and within 12 years a total of 3,787 Barbadians had been taken on. They were lent their fares to Britain, and the loans were repaid gradually from their wages. Even this number was not enough, and in 1966 London Transport would begin to recruit in Trinidad and Jamaica too. The British Hotels and Restaurants Association recruited skilled workers in Barbados. And a Tory health minister by the name of Enoch Powell welcomed West Indian nurses to Britain. Willing black hands drove tube trains, collected bus fares, emptied hospital patients' bed-pans.

From the early 1950s, Britain's other black community – the hitherto tiny community from the Indian sub-continent – also began to grow as rural workers from India and Pakistan came to work in Britain, again with official encouragement. By the end of 1958 there were in this country about 55,000 Indians and Pakistanis.

All these West Indians and Asians were British citizens. The 1948 Nationality Act had granted United Kingdom citizenship to citizens of Britain's colonies and former colonies. Their British passports gave them the right to come to Britain and stay here for the rest of their lives.

In their own countries there were strong incentives to take advantage of their right to settle in Britain. In the Indian sub-continent, millions had found themselves adrift from homes and jobs when Pakistan and India went their separate ways after independence. Emigration to Britain offered the prospect of a new life unthreatened by flood, famine or the miserable poverty that was their countries' chief legacy from imperial rule. In the British West Indies, the cost of living had almost doubled during the war. There was large-scale unemployment, and those without work were desperate. There was no relief of any kind: no dole, no children's allowances; no social security at all. 'No one knows exactly how the jobless live', wrote Joyce Egginton in 1957. She added: 'It is not surprising that thousands have left the West Indies. The surprising thing is that so many have stayed.'

Peter Fryer

This 'open door' immigration policy for Commonwealth citizens lasted for a decade and a half, but by the early 1970s it had been entirely reversed. The following passage from *Racial Disadvantage in Britain* by David J. Smith explains how and why:

Government policy in the early stages of the immigration has been described as laissez-faire; that is, there was no policy. Bowing to increasing pressure, given further weight by racial disturbances in 1958 and 1960, the government introduced immigration control through the Commonwealth Immigrants Act of 1962. By this time about half the present minority population had already entered the country. One of the effects of control was to stimulate an enormous increase in immigration over the 18 months before the Act became operative. Another was to help switch the balance of immigration from the Caribbean to India and Pakistan, though it was not entirely clear how this came about.

Controls were tightened in 1965 within the framework of the existing legislation. The previous controls were superseded by the Immigration Act of 1971, which gives the 'right of abode' to people it defines as patrial. The definition of this term is complex, but essentially it means people who, as well as being Commonwealth citizens, or citizens of the United Kingdom and colonies, have some substantial connection with the UK; for example, they were born in the UK, or acquired UK citizenship by naturalization or registration, or one of their parents or grandparents acquired UK citizenship in one of these ways. Those who are patrial have the right of free entry. Those who are not may enter only if they are granted a special voucher.

Thus in three stages from 1962 onwards, the right of entry to Britain has been withdrawn from most of the population of the New Commonwealth countries, and a strict control of immigration has been imposed. Since 1971 most of those granted entry under the voucher scheme have been the dependents of people already living in Britain.

Further legislation was introduced in the 1980s – The British Nationality Act of 1981 and the Immigration Act of 1988 – to tighten immigration controls further. A 1986 government document, prepared for the Organisation of Economic Co-operation and Development Conference on Immigration Policy, clearly states the rationale behind these policies:

'In recent decades, the basis of policy in the United Kingdom has been the need to control primary immigration – that is, new heads of households who are most likely to enter the job market. The United Kingdom is one of the most densely populated countries in Europe. In terms of housing, education, social services and, of course, jobs, the country could not support all those who would like to come here. Firm immigration control is therefore essential in order to provide the conditions necessary for developing and maintaining good community relations.'

Discussion points

What factors do you think influenced various British governments to abandon the original post-war 'open door' immigration policy, and to tighten immigration controls?

Why do you think the distinction between Commonwealth and non-Commonwealth citizens was effectively withdrawn in the 1971 Immigration Act? Do you agree with the Act?

Do you consider the current immigration controls too severe, about right, or insufficiently severe?

Black people in Britain

An ever-increasing proportion of black Britons have spent all their lives in this country. But their experience of life in Britain depends to a large extent on their country of origin; their cultural background has an enormous bearing on their attitudes and aspirations.

In the extract which follows, from a book edited by E. Ellis Casmore and Barry Troyna entitled *Black Youth in Crisis*, the term 'black' is used to mean people of West Indian origin, as distinct from 'Asian', which refers to people of Indian, Pakistani and Bangladeshi origin.

As the 1970s drew to a close, apprehension mounted in regard to black youth in England. Maybe they were expected to exhibit docility, indifference to what was going on about them, resign themselves to social circumstances. If there was optimism about their ability, or inclination, to integrate fully into the society that had played host to their parents, it faded as the years passed by ... The futility of technical measures directed at avoiding the type of furores caused by blacks in the USA in the 1960s became apparent as unemployment grew disproportionately amongst this group, street offence and theft convictions spiralled ominously, feelings of disengagement intensified ...

Perspectives on the problematic nature of young blacks were provided by simple comparison with another major ethnic group – Asians. Studies suggested that the first wave of Asians to England were materially in the same position as West Indians; further, they housed similar expectations as to what they might get out of the new society: a relatively smooth reception, better living conditions, possibly an accumulation of wealth followed by a return to the homeland. Objectively, the position of Asians was in alignment with that of West Indians; both groups crystallised in the less salubrious regions of urban centres where housing was most available but least desirable.

Discernibly, the Asians made most inroads in the commercial sphere, establishing small businesses, retail outlets, wholesale and manufacturing services, and many grew to prosperity. West Indians, on the other hand, seemed anchored. Young Asians, highly motivated by their parents to work steadfastly at school and maximise the benefits they might receive from formal education, improved quite dramatically. The emphasis on education in Asian culture had its effect on them and, by the late 1970s, they were comfortably in range of white school-children in terms of actual achievements.

The picture was very different for black youth, very, very different. Study after study led to the depressing conclusion that young blacks were making little or no impression. Continually, they achieved less than both whites and Asians and there were utterly no grounds for expecting a change. If anything, black youths seemed to be reinforcing their own lack of achievements by consciously promoting an attitude of rejection of education. Whether the lack of achievement bred the loss of affiliation or vice versa is a chicken-and-egg conundrum; for the moment, however, we rest with the observations that young blacks did not do well at school and their orientations to education were such that they gave no cause for believing they would do better in the future. In brief, they did not want to know.

Depicted is a scene where Asian youths, supported by their parents, entertained positive orientations towards education and improved steadily in terms of actual achievements. The importance of formal education as a route to social mobility and material gain was not lost on Asians as it seemingly was on blacks. Their collective attitude towards education was captured nicely by a black youth whom one of us encountered whilst engaged in research in the late 1970s: 'Education. What good is that to the black man? Qualifications? Them mean nothing so long as you're black.'

E. Ellis Cashmore and Barry Troyna

Generalisations about human beings always distort to some extent. But some experiences and personal conflicts are extremely common to black people living in Britain.

In the extracts which follow, which appear in a book called *Race in Britain*, edited by Charles Husband, two young men, one of West Indian and the other of Indian origin, talk about their lives in this country:

A West Indian/British male

Ever since I can remember, and this is going way back, early 1960s, from being very small, I was always aware of being dark – black – and for a six-year-old it wasn't very pleasant being called 'darkie' and 'monkey'. Because if you're dark, then you're stupid – a fool – and I wasn't stupid, I wasn't a fool, but I was quiet and different. I remember wanting to be white when I grew up because being black was something bad and awful, and in all my dreams I was white and I'd go round in space from planet to planet in my spaceship doing good deeds and rescuing people. Then we moved to Leeds, and Leeds was a big frightening place . . .

I remember the first day I went to school in Leeds. I don't know why – perhaps it was because I spoke differently or looked different – but this white kid came up and

started to pick on me. All the resentment, all the fear and frustration of coming to
Leeds just came out and I found myself attacking him. I'd never done anything before
like that in my life and I haven't since, but I had to be dragged away. Since then
nobody ever picked on me, which was surprising because there were kids who were
stronger than me who got picked on and cowed. I still wanted to be white, and most of
my friends were white, I suppose, and then we moved to junior school which was just
across the playground. There I had to be much more aware of black kids because we
all seemed to be lumped together in the same class, and I suppose because we were
all black we just got on – it wasn't a question of making friendships but I still went
around with my white friends. I felt I didn't belong to either group – white or black. I
was in a sort of limbo of my own . . .

The weird thing was that, although I had this attitude in me that I wasn't going to
be a 'blackie' no matter what, the people I used to go round with used to come out
with 'nigger' jokes. It was OK because I was supposed not to mind, 'It's all right, he
doesn't take offence', I was part of their group so I had to accept it. I did mind, but I
didn't say, because it was something apart from me. I wasn't what they were talking
about – I was almost like them. It was a really strange attitude when I look back on it
now – I don't understand it – but at the same time I wasn't going to conform to what
other people wanted me to be. I wasn't going to be a 'happy nigger' or an athlete or a
footballer, I wanted to be something that everyone else was – everyone white that is.
As far as I could see, there were no black guys doing A levels and writing essays, they
were all playing football – and I wanted to be somebody . . .

Racism doesn't exactly help you feel secure as a person. I've been followed by the
police and I don't look your sort of heavy dread guy. I've had the police follow me in a
car all the way up Roundhay Road at ten o'clock at night, just cruising by the side of
me not saying a word. It was really eerie and I just carried on walking, because I knew
that if I stopped or jumped over a wall or something they'd have got me and there'd
have been no witnesses. And I've had people in the middle of the town trying to run
me over, and other people don't believe it. Patti and I have suffered abuse from people
– it happens all the time, and when we tell people they're so amazed. Drivers have
made U-turns to come back at me, shouting 'you wog, you bastard, you nigger', and
people just walk on – I just walk on, I mean I'm so hardened to it now. I've been
attacked in Safeways in Headingley and nobody did a thing – and that was when I was
out with one of the children from the home where I work. You can't go into a shop
without being the focus of attention because people expect you to steal something. If
you go into a restaurant for a meal, then you are shunted off into a corner where you
won't offend the other all-white clientele.

Being a mixed couple, we tend to move in racially mixed circles when we can,
except where we have to move in all-white ones because of work or colour reasons.
This means that for a lot of the time we are with a lot of white people and we stand
out. We have to fight continuously against people's stereotyped ideas about us as a
racially mixed couple. When you are out, you are always aware of people because they
are always aware of you. They are always staring and making comments, and you
learn to sum people up in one go, because you have to for your own survival,
otherwise you could be walking straight into trouble. You learn to read body language
– you immediately know if someone is being friendly or not, then you have to decide
how to deal with it . . .

Younger generation blacks who don't know us would feel that it was a promotion
of the sexual stereotype – perhaps some of those who do know us as well – but most
of them accept us for what we are. The same with our white friends, but for the
majority of white people who see us in the streets, we just fulfil their idea of the sexual
stereotype – white girls who go with black men must be of 'loose morals', just looking
for sexual excitement.

I'm a lot more secure now in my black identity than I have ever been, but it took a long time getting there, through a lot of stages. I didn't go through what some would term the 'ethnic road' of, say, youth cult groups. For white kids there's always been teds, skins, mods, rockers, punks, but for black kids there's never been anything they could really identify with, that was really culturally theirs, until Rasta came along. Like, it was embarrassing to be black – for me anyway – I didn't even speak patois, I didn't want to sound like an ignorant 'wog'. It was easier to get along without any hassle by conforming to a stereotype because you were being what people expected of you, whereas it was harder and more threatening if you were something that was close to them. If you acted like the jolly buffoon or the thicko who was good at sports you were then conforming to all the stereotyped attitudes that are around, of black people being musical, good dancers, etc., but not very intelligent. If you wear a woolly hat and spend your time building a sound system, then you also conform to the stereotype, but if you aspire to be something else, a substitute white, an imitation white as they see it, wanting to study and do well, then you are threatening because you have the ability to take people's jobs away and be in a position of telling other people – especially white people – what to do. But in doing that you don't feel comfortable on either side of the fence because you're not black and you're not white . . .

Black people tend to be more accepting than white people, and Patti often feels a lot easier in all-black gatherings than I do in all-white ones. White people often forget that black people have to face this every day of their lives, yet if the situation was reversed, they would feel a lot less confident. A white friend of mine is a good example of this – he says he feels uncomfortable if there are a lot of black people and he is the only white, yet he never expects me to mind being in all-white situations . . .

Most of the things I've been talking about are psychological – how people see themselves and how they see other people. Black people in Britain in my opinion are still slaves, but the chains are not on their bodies but on their minds, and black kids especially need someone to help them break out of these chains, because otherwise they've got no future, they've got nothing. They've got to learn, but more important, white people have got to learn to accept them for themselves, then perhaps we can learn to accept each other.

A young Gujerati/British male

Being about five years old when I came to England, I had few memories of India – I had not formed my Indian identity. Having emigrated to England, I was to form two identities alongside each other: that which my family and community socialised me into, and that which the white society wanted.

My first real encounters of racial violence were when I moved into secondary school. Gangs of white youths used to go around 'Paki-bashing'. Only when this persisted did Indians form gangs and retaliate. However, by now I had some idea of the British class structure and knew that these 'troublemakers' were from the lowest rungs. I was convinced and knew that the 'others' were not like them. Though objectively I was from the same class as they were, I differentiated myself from them and identified myself with those above me. I aspired to their good, commonsense way of life, values, attitudes, etc.

By now I was about 15 years old and I was becoming well integrated into the white culture. It was about at this age that I realised that I was leading two lives, that of an Indian at home, and the black man with a white mask outside. I realised that I was experiencing culture conflict and had difficulty in identifying with either and coming to a compromise. I now realise that in the few years before the age of 15, when I thought I was going through the normal phase of being a rebellious teenager, that they were really acts which manifested the internal cultural and identity crises that I was going through.

Difficulties arose when, for example, the norm in the white society was in the belief of 'individualism'. Youths were expected to drink, smoke, have girlfriends, etc. This was not the case in the Indian culture. The family was a tightly knit and integrated unit with the Indian community. The belief was that of 'collectivism': life was with the people.

This presented real problems to me because on the one hand I was expected to conform with my white friends and their culture, and on the other hand, with my family and the Indian community culture . . .

There were frequent periods of confrontation with my family when it became apparent to them, from my behaviour, that I was slipping away from them, rejecting the Indian culture and becoming totally immersed in the white culture. These confrontations often served to bring me into a state of equilibrium. From there, I would again try the futile pursuit of trying to find a compromise between the two cultures, for this seemed the only logical way ahead. It seemed to me that my parents wanted me to succeed in the white society, yet retain my identity as an Indian; and the white society was making demands upon me to fully incorporate myself into their culture and only then would I be accepted. In a sense, they were ready and waiting with their arms to embrace me.

It was when I started to date white girls and generally go out with them that I realised that this was not so. The malicious and contemptuous looks and abuse that were received made me realise that, although I wanted to be fully integrated into the white society, the white society would only let me in at a superficial level. Thus, underneath the surface the divisions were to be maintained and reinforced. The purity of the Indian culture and race was insisted upon by my parents. Whereas before I felt that this was not the case for the white man, (for he could 'understand' the culture conflict and be more 'liberal' minded), I was to change my mind. Any notion that I had of being fully integrated, finding a compromise, or marrying a white girl in society, had to be rejected. I was in a situation where, should I marry a white girl, I would be excommunicated from my Indian community and be virtually in the same situation with the white society. Thus, the cost outweighs the benefits . . .

So I set out positively to form a white identity. This resulted in a conflict and a period where I was in search for a compromise. This leaves one in a precarious and difficult situation. This leaves the vast majority of Indians (including myself) being forced to go back and identify with their Indian culture. For I am in a situation where I cannot integrate fully into the white society, and, not wanting to be rejected by both, opt for the safest and surest way of identifying with my Indian culture more.

Perhaps the majority of my generation will take this route, because to some extent we are still able to identify with the poor social and economic conditions with which they started when arriving as immigrants. So, we also suffer from a guilt complex in that we feel our parents have given their lives and suffered so that we would be better off, and yet here we are repaying them by denouncing everything they believe in and have worked for. Their blood, sweat and tears have been worthless.

However, the children of my generation will hopefully not suffer too much from the cultural and identity crises. At least my generation will have a better understanding of the acculturation processes that their children will be going through and the crises that will confront them. Thus I hope the assimilation processes will be a little easier for them, for the pressure from Indian parents will ease a little. But I doubt very much if the same will happen with regards to the white man's view on integration.

Themes for discussion

What factors do you think might have influenced the differing general responses of people of West Indian and Asian origin to life in Britain?

What do you think of the idea of 'positive discrimination' in employment, such as legislation demanding that a certain proportion of vacancies in factories must be filled by people of ethnic minority background?

Do you think that more should be done in schools in Britain to make education genuinely multi-cultural, so that children of different ethnic backgrounds can be helped to understand and appreciate one another's cultures better? Alternatively, do you think special schools should be set up for children of ethnic minority ancestry, paying more attention to their cultural and linguistic background?

What is your attitude to 'mixed marriages' between people of different racial origins?

Do you think that black and white people will ever 'learn to accept each other'?

Racial prejudice

Though support for the overtly racist political parties like the National Front has waned slightly since its zenith in the late 1970s, prejudice and violence against black people has remained a constant feature of life in racially mixed areas of Britain. Its growth over the quarter century up to 1990 is traced in *Sociology* by Anthony Giddens.

In 1968, while Parliament was discussing race relations, Enoch Powell (then Conservative front-bench spokesman for defence) delivered a speech in Birmingham in which he envisaged an extraordinary growth of the non-white population: 'like the

Romans, I seem to see "the River Tiber flowing with much blood".' A Gallup poll showed that 75 per cent of the population were broadly sympathetic to Powell's views.

The end of the 1970s and early 1980s witnessed increasing unemployment in Britain concentrated particularly among the ethnic minorities. There were waves of unrest, with racial clashes in Brixton, Handsworth and Tottenham in London, Toxteth in Liverpool and St Paul's in Bristol.

In a 1985 survey, nine out of ten British whites said that they believed there is prejudice against Asians and blacks. The survey also revealed that over a third of whites openly admit to being racially prejudiced themselves (a far higher proportion than in similar surveys in the United States). Men are more likely than women to admit to prejudice, as are older people and those in working-class jobs or the unemployed. Although the whites surveyed were sceptical of the claim that the level of racial prejudice had increased over the past five years (it had), they were generally quite ready to believe that racial prejudice in Britain is likely to grow rather than diminish.

Anthony Giddens

Racial prejudice is born largely of ignorance and insecurity. In his book *Black Testimony: The Voices of Britain's West Indians*, Thomas J. Cottle explains some of the most widespread misconceptions concerning black people in Britain:

During the last few years, I have spoken with people in Great Britain who, never having met families from the West Indies, were in doubt of the languages spoken by West Indians . . . I have heard estimates of the number of blacks in Great Britain reach as high as 25 per cent of the population. It was not uncommon for people to believe that fewer than 5 per cent of England's black citizens were English born.

In point of fact, some 2,000,000 blacks live in England, 40 per cent of whom were born in this country.[2]

Thomas J. Cottle

Here are some of the most commonly heard complaints of white Britons against blacks and vice-versa, taken from *Learning to be Prejudiced* by Alfred Davey:

'They don't fit in.'
'They take the houses needed by the whites.'
'They won't learn the language.'
'They don't like us, they just tolerate us because they have to live here; they should ship them back.'
'They don't mix; they pretend to be tolerant but they're not.'
'There's too many of them.'
'They do their toilet in the street; they take houses and turn them into slums.'

'Blacks seem to be synonymous with barbarians.'
'Too many black kids are relegated to ESN schools; they see us as inferior.'
'Parliament pays lip-service to equality; we are dominated by whites; they treat us like second-class people.'
'They say we take their jobs; they think only of themselves.'
'We're picked on by the police.'

Prejudice can take horrifying forms, as was illustrated in a BBC radio *File on 4* programme, in which Janet Cohen interviewed residents of the East End of London:

2 At the end of the 1980s, 6 per cent of the population were officially classified as non-white; approximately half of these were born in the UK. (Giddens, *Sociology*, 1990)

Cohen:	Teachers, too, complain of growing racial hostility in the classrooms. J., a teacher, who is considering joining a vigilante group, says he faces a daily tide of abuse from his pupils.
J:	Oh, it affects me all the time.
Cohen:	How?
J:	Because they call me, you know, 'Paki' and 'Paki out', and they scrawl on the door of my teaching room. I mean, I've been in the school for seven years but now things are deteriorating. They may say, well, we're doing it for a laugh or something like that, but then they are influenced by the older people, you see, because in that area where I live there are, you know, lots of demonstrations organized by the British Movement.
Cohen:	You know it's the British Movement, do you?
J:	They write on my blackboard, they write BM, and then they have these Nazi signs, you know, under their lapel and they show it to me and they ask me to read their leaflets, they carry them around. Oh yes, I know – the leaflets from these various movements, the New National Front, the National Front, the British Movement, kids now start saying to me, oh, you have taken our job; suddenly they have found that I have taken their job, so why don't I go back, you Paki, you see, they shout.
Cohen:	Many black families don't even feel safe at home; in the heart of the East End one family claims their house has been attacked 35 times. White gangs, they say, have aimed bricks, bottles and airgun pellets through their front windows. The glass is now protected by two layers of metal grilles, sheets of plywood, and then shutters. The police have advised the three adults and ten children to move into the two back rooms of the house. But the attacks continue and they aren't limited to the home. This man, who's too frightened to broadcast his name, fears for his and his brother's children; all of them have been threatened and assaulted on the streets . . . Today's violence takes place against a background of rising unemployment. In some boroughs, one person in seven is out of a job. A report published today claims that blacks are more likely than whites to lose their jobs in the economic recession, but skinheads on the streets don't see it this way. Their heads shaved, their trousers cropped six inches above their ankle, their faces pinched in the cold, they feel the blacks are stealing their jobs. As for violence against the ethnic communities:
1st skinhead:	Do I condone it? Yes. They've got no right to be here.
Cohen:	That families should have bricks thrown through the window, airgun pellets, that kind of thing?
1st skinhead:	Well, only blacks like, and Jews, yeh. White European race, right, is the superior race and always will be.
Cohen:	Is it really fair that families should be intimidated; after all, they are people?
2nd skinhead:	Yes, course it is. They're not people, they're parasites, they're just poncing off us . . .
3rd skinhead:	The fact is, right, ordinary people don't like 'em moving in round the East London environment round there, right, and they want 'em out.
Cohen:	But is it fair to attack these families?
All skinheads:	Yes, it is.

3rd skinhead:	It's the only way, isn't it, I mean the government ain't doing nothing are they, nobody's doing anything, are they?
1st skinhead:	It takes ten years for a bill to get through Parliament, right, and nothing happens, right, so if you give them like a good dig and all that like, it might just send a couple of them home; you know what I mean. They might think, oh, you know like, we've had enough like, we're going to get home. So we're doing our little bit.
4th skinhead:	We believe that the blacks are taking over our country, the Yids are taking over our country.
Cohen:	So how much violence do you think there is around here, then, towards . . .
All skinheads:	There's a lot more, there's a lot more, there should be a lot anyway. There is, there's a lot going around.
Cohen:	It's gangs of youths like those who are blamed for the growing number of racial assaults, but where in some boroughs immigrants make up 14 per cent of the population, members of the older generation, too, say they understand the powerful feelings of the young, even if they don't support the violence.
1st man:	Well, it's out of order, isn't it? Everyone's entitled to live, you know, you know, there's a little bit of racial in everyone, but there you go. Especially if we're sort of, we're inundated with them, ain't we, it's getting overcrowded. I mean you've got to admit, even though the housing problem's enough, isn't it?
2nd man:	I think, quite honestly, the economic situation today forces them into this: you get kids who are left on the streets, they haven't got any work or anything like that; they've got to take their anger out on somebody, so they take it out on the unknown. It'll certainly take years before we sort the problem out, we'll probably have to go through the sort of problems that America has suffered before we can really sort it out.

Themes for discussion

Why do you think that white people have stereotyped views of what black people are like? Do you think other minority groups are stereotyped in a similar way?

Consider the list of complaints by whites against blacks and blacks against whites, and discuss the reasons for them.

How do you explain the degree of hatred of black people expressed by the skinheads in the *File on 4* interviews?

Do you think that racial tension in Britain is increasing or decreasing? Do you think that the government could or should do more to promote racial harmony?

Research suggestion

Write a brief report on British government legislation to combat racial discrimination, and its effectiveness.

Racial tension in America

In his novel, *Go Tell it on the Mountain*, the black American writer, James Baldwin, explores the feelings of black people in the 1960s living in a society in which racial prejudice is deep rooted and often intense. Here is an extract from the novel, which forms, in effect, a short story:

Go Tell it on the Mountain

She lived quite a long way from Richard – four subway stops; and when it was time for her to go home, he always took the subway uptown with her and walked her to the door. On a Saturday when they had forgotten the time and stayed together later than usual, he left her at her door at two o'clock in the morning. They said goodnight hurriedly, for she was afraid of trouble when she got upstairs – though, in fact, Madame Williams seemed astonishingly indifferent to the hours Elizabeth kept – and he wanted to hurry back home and go to bed. Yet, as he hurried off down the dark, murmuring street, she had a sudden impulse to call him back, to ask him to take her with him and never let her go again. She hurried up the steps, smiling a little at this fancy: it was because he looked so young and defenceless as he walked away, and yet so jaunty and strong.

He was to come the next evening at suppertime, to make at last, at Elizabeth's urging, the acquaintance of Madame Williams. But he did not come. She drove Madame Williams wild with her sudden sensitivity to footsteps on the stairs. Having told Madame Williams that a gentleman was coming to visit her, she did not dare, of course, to leave the house and go out looking for him, thus giving Madame Williams the impression that she dragged men in off the streets. At ten o'clock, having eaten no supper, a detail unnoticed by her hostess, she went to bed, her head aching and her heart sick with fear; fear over what had happened to Richard, who had never kept her waiting before, and fear involving all that was beginning to happen in her body.

And on Monday morning he was not at work. She left during the lunch hour to go to his room. He was not there. His landlady said that he had not been there all weekend. While Elizabeth stood trembling and indecisive in the hall, two white policemen entered.

She knew the moment she saw them, and before they mentioned his name, that something terrible had happened to Richard. Her heart, as on that bright summer day when he had first spoken to her, gave a terrible bound and then was still, with an awful, wounded stillness. She put out one hand to touch the wall in order to keep standing.

'This here young lady was looking for him,' she heard the landlady say.

They all looked at her.

'You his girl?' one of the policemen asked.

She looked up at his sweating face, on which a lascivious smile had immediately appeared, and straightened, trying to control her trembling.

'Yes,' she said. 'Where is he?'

'He's in jail, honey,' the other policeman said.

'What for?'

'For robbing a white man's store, black girl. That's what for.'

She found, and thanked Heaven for it, that a cold stony rage had entered her. She would, otherwise, certainly have fallen down, or begun to weep. She looked at the smiling policeman.

'Richard ain't robbed no store,' she said. 'Tell me where he is.'

'And *I* tell you,' he said, not smiling, 'that your boyfriend robbed a store and he's in jail for it. He's going to stay there, too – now, what you got to say to that?'

'And he probably did it for you, too,' the other policeman said. 'You look like a girl a man could rob a store for.'

She said nothing; she was thinking how to get to see him, how to get him out. One of them, the smiler, turned now to the landlady and said: 'Let's have the key to his room. How long's he been living here?'

'About a year,' the landlady said. She looked unhappily at Elizabeth. 'He seemed like a real nice boy.'

'Ah, yes,' he said, mounting the steps, 'they all seem like real nice boys when they pay their rent.'

'You going to take me to see him?' she asked of the remaining policeman. She found herself fascinated by the gun in his holster, the club at his side. She wanted to take that pistol and empty it into his round, red face; to take that club and strike with all her strength against the base of his skull where his cap ended, until the ugly, silky, white man's hair was matted with blood and brains.

'Sure, girl,' he said, 'you're coming right along with us. The man at the station house wants to ask you some questions.'

The smiling policeman came down again. 'Ain't nothing up there,' he said. 'Let's go.'

She moved between them, out into the sun. She knew that there was nothing to be gained by talking to them any more. She was entirely in their power, she would have to think faster than they could think; she would have to contain her fear and her hatred, and find out what could be done. Not for anything short of Richard's life, and not, possibly, even for that, would she have wept before them, or asked of them a kindness.

A small crowd, children and curious passers-by, followed them as they walked the long, dusty, sunlit street. She hoped only that they would not pass anyone she knew; she kept her head high, looking straight ahead, and felt the skin settle over her bones as though she were wearing a mask.

And at the station she somehow got past their brutal laughter. (*What was he doing with you, girl, until two o'clock in the morning? – Next time you feel like that girl, you come by here and talk to me.*) She felt that she was about to burst, or vomit, or die. Though the sweat stood out cruelly, like needles on her brow, and she felt herself, from every side, being covered with a stink and filth, she found out, in their own good time, what she wanted to know: he was being held in a prison downtown called the Tombs (the name made her heart turn over), and she could see him tomorrow. The state, or the prison, or someone, had already assigned him a lawyer; he would be brought to trial next week.

But the next day, when she saw him, she wept. He had been beaten, he whispered to her, and he could hardly walk. His body, she later discovered, bore almost no bruises, but was full of strange, painful swellings, and there was a welt above one eye.

He had not, of course, robbed the store, but, when he left her that Saturday night, had gone down into the subway station to wait for his train. It was late, and trains were slow; he was all alone on the platform, only half awake, thinking, he said, of her.

Then, from the far end of the platform, he heard a sound of running; and, looking up, he saw two coloured boys come running down the steps. Their clothes were torn, and they were frightened; they came up the platform and stood near him, breathing hard. He was about to ask them what the trouble was when, running across the tracks toward them, and followed by a white man, he saw another coloured boy; and at the same instant another white man came running down the subway steps.

Then he came full awake, in panic; he knew that whatever the trouble was, it was now his trouble also; for these white men would make no distinction between him and the three boys they were after. They were all coloured, they were about the same age, and here they stood together on the subway platform. And they were all, with no questions asked, herded upstairs, and into the wagon and to the station house.

At the station Richard gave his name and address and age and occupation. Then for the first time he stated that he was not involved, and asked one of the other boys to corroborate his testimony. This they rather despairingly did. They might, Elizabeth felt, have done it sooner, but they probably also felt that it would be useless to speak. And they were not believed; the owner of the store was being brought there to make the identification. And Richard tried to relax: the man *could* not say that he had been there if he had never seen him before.

But when the owner came, a short man with a bloody shirt – for they had knifed him – in the company of yet another policeman, he looked at the four boys before him and said: 'Yeah, that's them, all right.'

Then Richard shouted: 'But *I* wasn't there! Look at me, goddammit – I wasn't *there*!'

'You black bastards,' the man said, looking at him, 'you're all the same.'

Then there was silence in the station, the eyes of the white men all watching. And Richard said, but quietly, knowing that he was lost: 'But all the same, mister, I wasn't there.' And he looked at the white man's bloody shirt and thought, he told Elizabeth, at the bottom of his heart: 'I wish to God they'd killed you.'

Then the questioning began. The three boys signed a confession at once, but Richard would not sign. He said at last that he would die before he signed a confession to something he hadn't done.

'Well then,' said one of them, hitting him suddenly across the head, 'maybe you *will* die, you black son-of-a-bitch.' And the beating began. He would not, then, talk to her about it; she found that, before the dread and the hatred that filled her mind, her imagination faltered and held its peace.

'What we going to do?' she asked at last. He smiled a vicious smile – she had never seen such a smile on his face before.

'Maybe you ought to pray to that Jesus of yours and get Him to come down and tell these white men something.' He looked at her a long, dying moment. 'Because I don't know nothing *else* to do,' he said.

She suggested: 'Richard, what about another lawyer?'

And he smiled again. 'I declare,' he said, 'Little-bit's been holding out on me. She got a fortune tied up in a sock, and she ain't never told me nothing about it.'

She had been trying to save money for a whole year, but she had only thirty dollars. She sat before him, going over in her mind all the things she might do to raise money, even to going on the streets. Then, for very helplessness, she began to shake with sobbing. At this, his face became Richard's face again. He said in a shaking voice: 'Now, look here, Little-bit, don't you be like that. We going to work this out all right.' But she could not stop sobbing. 'Elizabeth,' he whispered. 'Elizabeth, Elizabeth.' Then the man came and said it was time for her to go. And she rose. She had brought two packs of cigarettes for him, and they were still in her bag. Wholly ignorant of prison regulations, she did not dare to give them to him under the man's eyes. And, somehow, her failure to remember to give him the cigarettes, when she knew how much he smoked, made her weep the harder. She tried – and failed – to smile at him, and she was slowly led to the door. The sun nearly blinded her, and she heard him whisper behind her: 'So long, baby. Be good.'

In the streets she did not know what to do. She stood awhile before the dreadful gates, and then she walked and walked until she came to a coffee shop where taxi drivers and the people who worked in nearby offices hurried in and out all day. Usually she was afraid to go into downtown establishments, where only white people were, but today she did not care. She felt that if anyone said anything to her she would turn and curse him like the lowest bitch on the streets. If anyone touched her, she would do her best to send his soul to Hell.

But no one touched her; no one spoke. She drank her coffee, sitting in the strong sun that fell through the window. Now it came to her how alone, how frightened she was; she had never been so frightened in her life before. She knew that she was pregnant – knew it, as the old folks said, in her bones; and if Richard should be sent away, what, under Heaven, could she do? Two years, three years – she had no idea how long he might be sent away for – what would she do? And how could she keep her aunt from knowing? And if her aunt should find out, then her father would know, too. The tears welled up, and she drank her cold, tasteless coffee. And what would they do with Richard? And if they sent him away, what would he be like, then, when he returned? She looked into the quiet, sunny streets, and for the first time in her life, she hated it all – the white city, the white world. She could not, that day, think of one decent white person in the whole world. She sat there, and she hoped that one day God, with tortures inconceivable, would grind them utterly into humility, and make them know that black boys and black girls, whom they treated with such condescension, such disdain, and such good humour, had hearts like human beings, too, more human hearts than theirs.

But Richard was not sent away. Against the testimony of the three robbers, and her own testimony, and, under oath, the storekeeper's indecision, there was no evidence on which to convict him. The courtroom seemed to feel, with some complacency and some disappointment, that it was his great good luck to be let off so easily. They went immediately to his room. And there – she was never all her life long to forget it – he threw himself, face downward, on his bed and wept.

She had only seen one other man weep before – her father – and it had not been like this. She touched him, but he did not stop. Her own tears fell on his dirty, uncombed hair. She tried to hold him, but for a long time he would not be held. His body was like iron; she could find no softness in it. She sat curled like a frightened child on the edge of the bed, her hand on his back, waiting for the storm to pass over. It was then that she decided not to tell him yet about the child.

By and by he called her name. And then he turned, and she held him against her breast, while he sighed and shook. He fell asleep at last, clinging to her as though he were going down into the water for the last time.

And it was the last time. That night he cut his wrists with his razor and he was found in the morning by his landlady, his eyes staring upward with no light, dead among the scarlet sheets.

James Baldwin

Discussion points

Why do you think Richard committed suicide in the story?

Do you think Elizabeth's attitude to white people is racist?

Suggestion for writing

Write two newspaper articles about the arrest, acquittal and suicide of Richard. In the first one, tell the story from a position sympathetic to the attitudes of the policeman and the shopkeeper. In the second, make your report and comments those of a reporter in sympathy with Richard and Elizabeth. The articles should include details of the court case, interviews with the people involved, and, possibly, conclusions and recommendations for action.

Research suggestions

Write a brief report to present to the class on the history of relations between American Indians, whites and blacks in the USA.

Write a brief general report on relations between American Indians, 'mestizo' (people of mixed racial origin) and white people in Latin America.

Essay titles

a Colour
b 'Race relations have little to do with race itself.'
c Problems and opportunities in a multiracial society.
d How do you think racial harmony can best be achieved in Britain?
e The blasphemy laws in Britain have their basis in Christianity and Judaism. Do you consider that their amendment to include additional religions would be beneficial to race relations in Britain?

Bibliography

Non-fiction

Cashmore, E. Ellis (ed.), *A Dictionary of Race and Ethnic Relations*, Routledge and Kegan Paul, 1994

Cashmore, E. Ellis and Troyna, Barry (eds), *Black Youth in Crisis*, Allen and Unwin, 1982

Claire, Alexander, *The Art of Being Black: The Creation of Black British Youth Identities*, Clarendon, 1996

Cottle, Thomas J., *Black Testimony: The Voices of Britain's West Indians*, Wildwood House, 1978

Davey, Alfred, *Learning to be Prejudiced: Growing up in Multi-Ethnic Britain*, Edward Arnold, 1983

Fryer, Peter, *Staying Power: The History of Black People in Britain*, Pluto Press, 1984

Giddens, Anthony, *Sociology*, Polity Press, 1993

Hiro, Dilip, *Black British, White British: A History of Race Relations in Britain*, Grafton, 1991

Husband, Charles (ed.), *Race in Britain: Continuity and Change*, Hutchinson, 1987

Osler, Audrey, *Speaking Out: Black Girls in Britain*, Virago, 1989

Smith, David J., *Racial Disadvantage in Britain*, Penguin, 1977

Solomos, John, *Race and Racism in Britain*, Macmillan, 1993

Fiction

Baldwin, James, *Go Tell it on the Mountain*, Corgi, 1984

Ellison, Ralph, *The Invisible Man*, Penguin, 1965

Icaza, Jorge, *Huasipungo*, Dennis Dobson, 1962

Wright, Richard, *Uncle Tom's Children*, Harper and Row, 1965

Wright, Richard, *Native Son*, Penguin, 1972

Further advice on writing: illogical argument in essays

Logicality of argument is obviously one of the absolute essentials of language-essay writing. A basic logical flaw can invalidate a whole line of argument, with disastrous results. Here are some of the most common ones.

❶ Irrelevance

One of the most damaging errors of logic in essay writing is to stray from the point at issue into a discussion of something which has no direct relevance to the essay title. An absolutely cardinal rule of essay writing is to keep the point at issue constantly in mind, and the simplest way to do that is to glance back at the title frequently, and check whether the argument which is being developed is relevant to it. All manner of irrelevancies can creep into essay writing. Here are a couple of typical examples.

- You are writing an essay on crime and punishment, the title of which reads: 'The only way to reduce the crime rate is to make punishment more severe.' If you have strong feelings about capital punishment, it would be easy, if you were not careful, to enter into a discussion of the morality of capital punishment, making a case for its restoration on the 'eye-for-an-eye' principle. This is a different issue altogether from the question of whether or not the restoration of capital punishment would reduce the crime rate, which would be the only valid reason for mentioning it.
- You are writing an essay on education with the title: 'What changes would you like to see in the educational system of this country?' If you were to write a paragraph on the relative merits of the comprehensive and selective school systems, it would be irrelevant *unless* you concluded the discussion by relating it precisely to the question; by arguing, for instance, that you would like to see selective schools abolished entirely.

❷ Failure to define your terms

This is another error which can have a damaging effect on the validity of an argument. This is particularly the case when you are dealing with abstractions such as 'freedom' or 'democracy' or 'socialism' or 'equality', which can have different meanings for different people in different contexts. Many words are simply ambiguous, and it is impossible to argue sensibly about them without defining what you understand by them. When a term about which you are writing has a straightforward, generally recognised meaning, on the other hand, there is no point in wasting time and effort on defining it.

❸ Interpreting an issue too narrowly

A further problem can arise when you *do* attempt to define the terms you are using. If you define a term or an issue too *narrowly*, then the subject becomes oversimplified. For example, if you are answering the question: 'Is educational equality a myth?' you should consider a variety of possible ramifications of the term 'equality'. If you see the issue simply in terms of the debate over comprehensive and selective school systems, and/or over the abolition of private education, and concentrate exclusively on inequality of access to a 'good' education, higher education and top jobs, you are limiting the range of the question unduly. Aspects of 'equality' such as natural aptitudes for and parental attitudes towards education, ethnic factors and so on, should also be considered. Oversimplification is a particular danger when discussing politics, especially since political propaganda relies on gross oversimplification. If politicians sometimes use terms like 'totalitarian' to mean states which are ruled by a 'communist' system, and 'the free world' to mean all the states which are not, you should avoid falling into the same error.

④ *Generalis-ation*

This is another pitfall to be wary of in essay writing. However common a particular phenomenon may be in a particular human group, there are virtually always exceptions which invalidate a sweeping generalisation. Some quite frequently repeated generalisations, such as the assertion that 'women are illogical' are themselves patently illogical. Generalisations about foreigners are particularly common. Many West Indians, for instance, are good dancers, but it would be absurd to state baldly: 'West Indians are good dancers'. Generalisations are often introduced by phrases such as 'It is a known fact that . . .' and 'History proves that . . .' Such expressions do not make dubious statements any more convincing, and should always be avoided.

A particularly common and dangerous variety of false generalisation is the error of arguing from the particular to the general. This commonly takes the form of drawing general conclusions from personal experience. Here are a couple of examples.

- The essay title is 'Do schools try hard enough to develop pupils' creativity?' You claim that your own education was lacking in creativity, and draw from this the unwarrantable conclusion that British education generally is insufficiently creative.
- You are writing an essay about the prison system in Britain. You have read a report of a prison where the inmates are allowed to watch television and wander in the extensive grounds, and you conclude from this that prisons in Britain generally resemble 'holiday camps'.

⑤ *Biased use of evidence*

A similar error of logic is that of drawing conclusions from selected evidence, and ignoring the evidence which tends to point in the opposite direction. A classic illustration of this is in the popularity of newspaper horoscopes, which depend to some extent on people's willingness to ignore predictions which are *not* fulfilled and take notice only of the ones which *are*. Literary criticism, at its worst, is prone to this error, when critics select quotations from a text to support their theses, and conveniently ignore quotations which tend to refute them.

⑥ *False analogy*

The most popular form of this logical flaw is in drawing irrelevant conclusions about human behaviour based on observation of other species. Darwin's theory of 'the survival of the fittest', for example, is used as 'proof' that human affairs are most effectively conducted on a competitive, 'dog-eat-dog' principle, taking no account of the complexity of human social evolution.

7 *Agreeing with both sides of an argument*

Essays which specifically ask for arguments for and against some premise can easily lead to another error. Students sometimes argue an apparently personal case for the proposition, and then present the opposite case in such a way as to suggest that they agree also with the arguments *against* it. Care must be taken to avoid appearing to agree with incompatible viewpoints.

8 *Presenting opinions as facts*

Care must also be taken to distinguish between opinions and facts. The former should never be presented as the latter. You should never make statements, for example, like this: 'The fact that the government has allowed in too many coloured immigrants is one of the major causes of racial tension in this country'. This is a value judgement, not a fact.

9 *Misuse of statistics*

Finally, care should be taken over the use of statistics. It has become an axiom that statistics can be used to prove anything, and assessing the validity or otherwise of published statistics requires some understanding of the complexities of statistical method. Probably the best advice that can be offered with regard to statistics is that they should be used with caution, and should never be offered as proof of any contention.

Statistics showing that crimes of violence have increased dramatically since capital punishment was abolished, for instance, should not be treated as a proof that abolition was a mistake, since the increase could equally be attributed to other factors. Likewise, statistics showing that world population and deaths from starvation have both increased alarmingly over the past 30 years do not prove that the population explosion is the cause of starvation. Other factors may in fact be more significant.

Many other types of false reasoning could be mentioned, but if you can succeed in avoiding all of the ones discussed here, you're unlikely to lose marks in an essay because of invalid argument.

Ten Issues

11 The Mass Media

In the Western world, in the late 20th century, you would have to be completely sealed off from society to avoid daily contact with the mass media. In Britain, over 90 per cent of households own a television set, and it is watched, on average, for 25 hours a week. Few homes are without daily or Sunday newspapers, and the most popular British Sunday paper has a circulation which is topped only by *Pravda*. The rise of television since the Second World War has brought about a steady decline in the importance of film and radio: the latter, in fact, has become, for most young people, merely an endless supplier of 'rock' music, which is now, in itself, a major mass medium. It is a feature of the media that they feed off one another. Tabloid newspapers constantly report the peccadilloes of 'rock', film and television stars, and for many readers such tittle-tattle provides the primary interest in the papers they buy.

This chapter is concerned with exploring and analysing different mass media. It begins with a comprehension exercise on a passage, written by a celebrated journalist and novelist, about the language and style of popular journalism in Britain, and in particular of tabloid journalism. As well as providing comprehension and analysis practice, you may find Keith Waterhouse's critique and illustrations of 'tabloidese' useful when you are preparing for summary skills and continuous writing exercises in which you are required to summarise or write a piece in the style of a tabloid newspaper. You will also find a summary skills exercise on the theme of violence on television in Chapter 3, on pages 35–37.

Comprehension and analysis

Read *The Sunday Times* article on the next two pages, called 'I'm Sorry I'll Write That Again', and answer the questions which follow it (page 182).

Journalese is an exercise in stringing together words and phrases used nowhere else but in journalism.

In an unprecedented move signalling a ferocious new crackdown... The urgent prose conjures up a dashing image of an intrepid foreign correspondent phoning down a crackly line from the only hotel bar left standing in some far-off trouble spot.

A gold dealer who fleeced his clients to finance a lavish lifestyle of champagne and fast cars... Here one visualises the stereotype reporter in belted raincoat, frantically tapping away against a deadline on a battered Remington between mouthfuls of cheese sandwich.

Reporting, unless it is of the personalised James Cameron or John Pilger variety, should not summon up even a vague picture of the reporter. The words should not intrude on the message they are conveying. The reason they do is that they are selected for their pushiness. Except in urgent telegrams, no one else writes like this:

Mrs Thatcher is *backing* Prince Charles in his *bid* to *curb* sex and violence on television, it was *revealed* last night.

She has *given the go-ahead* for a *battery* of *new controls* to ensure programmes are fit for family viewing when a broadcasting *free-for-all* is *unveiled* next month.

The *curbs* will be far more stringent than TV *chiefs* expected, and the government is *braced* for protests that they are being *shackled* and censored...

In journalese, *shock*

reports forever *call* on the government, which in turn is *set* to make *sweeping changes.* Plans are *under attack* or *facing broadsides*, commitments are *spelled out*, remarks are *certain to spark off a new political storm*, steps are *urged to curb*

growing menaces, ministers *sound clear warnings*, new crises *loom*, new crazes *reach epidemic proportions...* There are so many *dramas* in the dramatic world of journalese that when one reads a headline in The Independent, CHANNEL 4 EXPANDS DRAMA, one reads on in expectation of a drama involving Channel 4's territorial ambitions rather than an account of how Channel 4 proposes to expand its drama output.

Like tabloidese (see below), journalese is not

the most reliable conveyor of the English language:

Margaret Thatcher is actively contemplating a fundamental restructuring of Whitehall departments which could lead to a crucial new role for Cecil Parkinson...

Thus, breathlessly, The Sunday Times, incidentally dressing its journalistic mutton as lamb by the use of expensive words like *contemplating* and *fundamental restructuring* rather than *rethinking* and *radical change.* But The Sunday Times could not resist *crucial* from the lexicon of journalese. Crucial, however, does not mean important in the straightforward sense, but essential to the resolving of a crisis, significant. The word has been selected for its souped-up quality of being more dramatic than

the proper one. If *important* wasn't important enough for the story, then the selection of *key* from the journalese vocabulary would at least have had the merit of being less misleading.

Journalese, expertly and sparingly used, helps give a newspaper its flavour, its character of being a newspaper rather than a copy of Hansard or a court transcript. In large doses it can be clammy and claustrophobic as the reader struggles to extricate himself from a morass of *moves, clampdowns, crackdowns, pledges, clashes* and *stalemates.*

No story ever lost impact by being told in plain English.

ONE specialised form of journalese is tabloidese, that tough-guy, hat-on-the-back-of-the-head talk that makes newspapers sound like James Cagney (*trap, probe, bid, swoop, axe*). It was devised to accommodate the largest type to the smallest page. Partly inspired by the back numbers department of the New York Daily News (a newspaper which still uses a logo of a squeeze-bulb plate camera on its masthead) and by old Death Row movies, it is essentially a made-up language, a kind of primitive Esperanto where nouns, verbs and adjectives are interchangeable.

So long as readers are well versed in this Esperanto, it is a useful – indeed an essential – headline aid. But is it always comprehensible? Do those hard-boiled newspaper cynics who habitually ask, 'Will our readers in Wigan understand this?' ever ask themselves if the reader from Wigan (or the Bronx) can follow, for instance, TORCH BOY SET ABLAZE BY GANG?

● Keith Waterhouse slams hacks in the war of words

I'M SORRY I'LL WRITE THAT AGAIN

The novelist and veteran Fleet Street columnist offers an entertaining critique of the journalist's art in an extract from his new book, Waterhouse on Newspaper Style

Set ablaze by gang is clear enough, but what is a *torch boy*? It can only be, (as the copy confirms) a boy who has been set ablaze. So if the Esperanto headline were translated into something approaching English, it would read ABLAZE BOY SET ABLAZE BY GANG.

Is the headline TRIPLE LOVE-SNATCH BOY IS HUNTED any relation to TORMENT OF A LOVE-TUG MUM? Do we all understand, without reference to the accompanying text, that a *triple love-snatch boy* is one who has been seized by his father, from his mother, for the third time? Do we have some idea what a *love-tug mum* is? If so, does it confuse us or enlighten us when in the first paragraph of the love-tug mum's story she becomes a *love-tug wife*?

Perhaps further discussion of the uses and abuses of this peculiar language could be helped by a 'Concise Dictionary of Tabloidese' (see box).

It will be noticed from the Dictionary that in nearly every case (the most notable exception being *sex romps* for sex), the tabloid word is shorter than its definition, which is as it should be. It is also usually harder – in many cases (*slam*, *hit back*, *clash*, *war*) to the point of downright belligerence. This is often where reality leaves off and something approaching Ramboism takes over. The great danger of tabloidese is that its macho approach combined with a highly developed sense of the melodramatic can lead it to exaggerate.

In tabloid terms an attempt may always be a *bid*, a connection a *link* and a fatal fall a *death plunge*, but is an argument invariable a *storm*, a contest a *battle*, a surprise a *shock* – and indeed is a drama always a drama?

CHARLES IN FILM SNUB DRAMA promises much but delivers little. It turns out that in initially refusing to boycott a film (the headline, incidentally, suggests the opposite), Prince Charles has incurred the displeasure of one or two people whose mildly reproving quotes form the burden of the story – a controversy, perhaps, but hardly the stuff of drama, and certainly not one that places him *at the centre of a bitter row*, as the introductory paragraph, in an attempt to support its own headline, would have it.

There will always be a demand for short bold words to fit big bold headlines. There is no reason why these should not be 'label' words, often found nowhere else in the language – a label, after all, is precisely what the headline is. But as any reputable patent medicine manufacturer would agree, a label must tell the consumer clearly what is in the bottle. If it doesn't, it is a case of quackery, flimflam or incompetence.

But what of tabloidese 'label' words that – seemingly with the same territorial ambitions as puns – have slunk down from the headline to the text? What are they doing there?

The average news story, after all, is not set in two-inch-high type. True, space is always a premium, but is it at such a premium that the reader must have his Tabloidese Dictionary at the ready?

Doctors and ambulancemen were *slammed* yesterday . . .

Diesel train services are to be *axed* by British Rail in a desperate *bid* to save fuel . . .

A lonely old peer lured young girls into bed for *sex romps* . . .

A *call* to end a union *civil war* was made yesterday as a *threat* to *boot* electricians out of the TUC *loomed* . . .

A *blaze* superstore has told its *till girls*, 'Dump the money and run for your lives . . .'

It could be argued that most of these expressions have been used (overused?) so often that readers know exactly what they mean. Probably so, in the headline sense. But what, outside the headlines, is a *sex romp*? What is a *blaze superstore*? Who are *till girls*? Why, if these words are so common, are they not in common use?

Why do we not hear housewives at bus-stops saying 'Our Marlene used to be a till girl at that blaze superstore' or 'Did I tell you about young Fred being rapped after he slammed his boss? He thinks he's going to be axed'?

Words that have never managed to get into the mainstream of the language are suspect as a means of popular communication.

They are, and remain, labels. They do not convey precise meanings. The reader looks at the label, opens the tin – and finds a tin of labels.

Tabloidese, furthermore, is essentially passive. In tabloid-land, *400 jobs face axe*. In real life, 400 may lose their jobs. Intended to be dramatic, tabloidese has a curiously deadening effect. *A pay war loomed last night* is not dramatic because it has all the ingredients of drama except the players – the story does not come to life until we know who is involved in it.

Sometimes it does not come to life even then. Two athletes who are *set for a head-on showdown* prove to be simply competing in the same event.

Tabloid Guide	
Anger	fury
Annoyance	outrage
Attempt	bid
Avoid	shun
Cancel	axe, scrap
Confiscate	grab
Control	crackdown
Controversy	row, turmoil
Criticise	slam, blast
Difficulty	snag, hurdle
Disagreement	clash
Dismissed	dumped, axed
Division	split
Encourage	boost
Exclude	bar, ban
Fail to attend	snub
Fatal fall	death plunge
Happening	drama
Mystery	riddle
Possibility	threat
Promise	vow, pledge
Proposal	plan
Question	quiz
Quarrel	feud
Raid	swoop
Reform	shake-up
Replace	oust
Reprove	rap
Request	call
Resign	quit, storm out
Restrict	curb
Rise	soar
Rivalry	war
Setback	blow
Sex	sex romps
Vital	key

Keith Waterhouse

a Present clearly and concisely the different objections Waterhouse has to journalese.   (*8 marks*)

b List in note form the different characteristics of 'tabloidese'.   (*6 marks*)

c In what ways can journalese be effective, according to Waterhouse?
                                                                            (*4 marks*)

d Examine the page as a whole and comment on each of the following, giving supporting evidence:
  (i)   the impact of the layout of the whole page;
  (ii) the relationship of the captions and the cartoon to the written article;
  (iii) the reasons for including the Tabloid Guide;
  (iv) the nature of the audience the article is aimed at.   (*20 marks*)

e Identify the characteristics of Waterhouse's own style. How far has he succeeded in avoiding excesses of journalese? Give details to support your views.   (*12 marks*)

Newspaper organisation

Newspapers

Over the past 60 years, newspapers in Britain have come to be divided into two broad categories: popular (or tabloid) and serious (or broadsheet). Control of the press has altered during the same period. Between the wars, the newspapers were owned and controlled by wealthy individuals, frequently referred to as 'press barons', like Lords Beaverbrook, Northcliffe and, more recently, Thompson; now they have generally been swallowed up into large corporations, whose primary interests lie outside the press.

In the same period the diversity of political affiliations of the press has largely disappeared, until now there are only two national daily newspapers which are consistently left of centre (the *Guardian* and the *Mirror*); the others, with the exception of the *Independent* are right of centre. All British newspapers maintain a fairly rigid editorial line, establishing limits beyond which their journalists cannot step.

The structure within which journalists work is discussed by the journalist Eamonn McCann in an article entitled 'The British Press and Northern Ireland', included in *The Manufacture of News*, edited by Cohen and Young:

Those who have ultimate control over what is printed and what is not are drawn from a relatively tiny segment of society – the owners of big business. Generally speaking, what is printed tends to support their interests.

One of the qualifications for editorship is, naturally, a general acceptance of the owners' attitudes. This is reflected in the editorial 'line' of every paper and it filters through to reporters, sub-editors, etc. A journalist who has covered Northern Ireland for a British daily paper explains:

'You must remember that every journalist wants what he writes to appear, and in practice all journalists know pretty well what their paper's line is, what is expected of them. There is a fair amount of self-censorship. This happens without thinking. No journalist I have met writes what he knows will be cut. What would be the point? If he has a story which he knows will cause controversy back at the newsdesk he will water it down to make it acceptable.'

Most journalists rely heavily on 'official' sources. This explains the sometimes striking similarity of coverage. Stories from 'official' sources will, of course, be eminently acceptable. Moreover, as a former *Mirror* employee writes:

> 'In a situation like Northern Ireland, our people would have to keep in close touch with the Army Press Office. It would be more or less part of their job to get to know the army press officer as well as possible, and that in itself would affect their judgement a bit. Then one of their bigger preoccupations is not be scooped by a competitor. No one on the *Mirror* would be sacked because he didn't come up with a carefully authenticated and researched piece, written from local hard work. You do get sacked if the rival has a sensation about the IRA.'

Even if a reporter does send through copy which is critical of the establishment and its representatives (e.g. the army), it is at the mercy of the news editor and the sub-editors. These are likely to be the most conservative of all the journalistic staff, with years of grinding practice in what is acceptable to the editor and the management. The average senior sub-editor will, as a reflex action, strike out any sentence which jars his sense of propriety.

Eamonn McCann

The influence of newspapers

How influential is the press in affecting the attitudes of its readers? To what extent does a newspaper merely respond to the expectations of the readership at which it is aimed? Contrasting views on the question of newspaper influence are represented in the following two extracts.

The first offers a general view of the British press, arguing that the content of newspapers is dictated largely by the nature and attitudes of their readers. It is taken from a book called *The Politics of the Media* by John Whale.

The tastes of a body of readers may alter over the years. They change as the prevailing climate of ideas changes. They change as a result of what they discover to be appearing in rival newspapers. The *Daily Mirror* would never have begun (in the 1970s) to show photographs of naked women, or to lead the paper with stories like 'I married the monster who raped Miss X', if *The Sun* had not led the way after its change of ownership in 1969. Once *The Sun* had demonstrated that its readers liked that kind of approach, the *Mirror* adopted it too, and the decline in the *Mirror*'s circulation was at least checked. Yet it was not an expedient which was open to *The Times*, struggling for new readers at much the same time. Existing readers of *The Times* would have been outraged at being addressed in that way. The loss would have far outweighed the gain.

It is readers who determine the character of newspapers. *The Sun* illustrates the point in its simplest and saddest form. Until 1964, the *Daily Herald*, and between 1964 and 1969 the broadsheet *Sun*, had struggled to interest working people principally through their intellect. The paper had declined inexorably. Murdoch gave up the attempt and went for the baser instincts. Sales soared. It was an owner's decision, certainly; but it would have meant nothing without the enthusiastic ratification of the readers.

That, in the end, is the answer to the riddle of proprietorial influence. Where it survives at all, it must still defer to the influence of readers. The policy of *The Daily Telegraph*, its selection and opinion of the news it reports, is decided by the editor and his senior colleagues. But there is a regulatory force which keeps the paper's policy from straying too widely or suddenly from pre-ordained paths; and that force is not the proprietor but the readers. They choose the paper for qualities they expect to see continued.

The press is thus predominantly conservative in tone because its readers are. If any substantial number of people seriously wanted the structure of society rebuilt from the bottom, the *Morning Star* would sell more copies than it does. The reason why national newspapers fall tidily into two bundles – popular and posh, with the popular ones all physically smaller than the posh (since the *Daily Express* joined the other tabloids in January 1977) but selling five times as many copies – is that British life remains similarly and obstinately divided. The steady lessening of the economic differences between classes has done nothing to narrow the cultural gap. Certainly there are people who read both a posh and a popular paper, just as there are gradations between the popular papers; both the *Mirror* and *The Sun* aim at readers who are more squarely working-class than the *Express* and the *Mail* do. These things show the complexity of the class pattern, without denying its general lines. The broad shape and nature of the press is ultimately determined by no one but its readers.

John Whale

The second extract argues a more positive influence by newspapers on readers' attitudes. It is taken from a book called *News Limited* by the journalist, Brian Whitaker.

There are numerous examples of strange effects induced by the media. Probably the most famous was the panic caused by an American radio dramatisation of H.G. Wells' *The War of the Worlds* in 1938. But that was the result of people mistaking the play for reality. On another occasion, as an experiment, British astronomer Patrick Moore pretended to have seen an Unidentified Flying Object near his home. The story he told to his local paper was entirely fictitious, but when it was published several 'witnesses' came forward to confirm the 'sighting'. At a more down-to-earth level, a British newspaper once warned of the possibility of a salt shortage within a few months. The prophecy was fulfilled immediately as people rushed to the shops to stock up.

No self-respecting person admits to being easily influenced. If you were asked: 'Do you believe everything you read in the newspapers?' the only sensible answer would be 'No'. And yet what alternative have we but to believe? We all rely very heavily on newspapers and television for our knowledge of what is going on in the world. So how do we decide what to believe and what not to believe? Partly, it is a question of credibility: does it seem likely that an event has actually happened in the way it is reported? Also, it is a question of reputation: we regard some sources as more reliable than others – often without any good reason. A survey in 1973 showed that only 27 per cent of people who said newspapers were their main source of news also believed newspapers were the most accurate and trustworthy source of news.

Also – rather illogically – we tend to become less sceptical about news reports the further they are removed from our personal experience. So factory workers may dismiss newspaper reports of a dispute in their own factory as a load of rubbish, but not question stories in the same paper that say the social security provides a life of luxury for immigrants.

Stories about 'scroungers' and social-security fiddlers, for example, are common in the popular press. These papers are read by vast numbers of ordinary people, and they influence ordinary people. Stories about 'scroungers' can be effective in several ways. They can:

a make people more willing to accept work for low wages rather than stay on the dole;

b get popular support for keeping state benefits at a low level;

c create divisions between the employed 'taxpayers' and the unemployed;

d encourage people to inform on fiddlers.

And by the simple repetition of such stories, the public begin to accept that 'scroungers' are a major drain on public resources. But if the papers' real purpose was to save money, they would concentrate on the much more serious problem of tax evasion.

Brian Whitaker

Tabloid journalism

The 'tabloid revolution' was begun by the *Daily Mirror* in the mid-1930s. A formula was established then which has been broadly followed by tabloid newspapers ever since: huge headlines, short paragraphs, a focus on 'human interest' stories, especially sex and crime, and constant personalisation of all world figures and news stories.

It would be wrong to view all contemporary tabloid newspapers as following exactly the same pattern, however. One tabloid, the *Daily/Sunday Sport* is *not* a newspaper, in the sense of presenting national and international news, at all. Of the others, the *Mirror*, the *Star*, *The Sun*, *The People* and the *News of the World* carry so little serious news that they also can hardly be regarded as newspapers in the traditional sense, and they are commonly referred to by the derisory term 'the gutter press'. The remaining two tabloids, the *Express* and the *Mail*, tend to be more middle-brow, and to regard themselves as more serious purveyors of news.

When a tabloid like *The Sun* takes up an issue of national/international importance, its treatment of it is generally very different from that of a broadsheet. The political stance taken by tabloids may also differ sharply from one another. The Falklands crisis in 1982 was an issue on which all newspapers were forced to take sides. The *Daily Mirror* was initially opposed to armed conflict, whilst *The Sun* took the opposite line with a vengeance! The following extract from *Gotcha! The Media, the Government and the Falklands Crisis* by Robert Harris traces *The Sun*'s handling of the Falklands Crisis, and draws some conclusions about the nature of the popular press, and its significance as a vehicle for news in the late 20th century.

When three national newspapers opposed the Government's handling of the Suez Crisis in 1956, they lost readers heavily. *The Guardian* lost 30,000 in a matter of days, though it later recouped them. *The Observer* lost 30,000 in a week, fell behind *The Sunday Times* for the first time and never caught up again. It was the *Daily Mirror* itself which fared worst, losing 70,000 readers. The lesson appeared clear. Supported by Rupert Murdoch, *The Sun* moved swiftly to corner the market in patriotism and to label its rival firmly as a disloyal defeatist.

The Sun had already attacked 'the sinking *Daily Mirror*' as a 'paper warrior' on 2 April, the day of the invasion. On 6 April it struck again. 'At home the worms are already coming out of the woodwork,' taunted *The Sun*.

> 'The ailing *Daily Mirror*, which tried to pretend that there was no threat to the Falklands until the invaders had actually landed, now whines that we should give in to force and obligingly settle the islanders. But our whole experience with dictators has taught us that if you appease them, in the end you have to pay a far greater price.'

'Youths demonstrated outside the Argentinian Embassy in London last night,' reported *The Sun* on 3 April. 'They sang "Rule Britannia", ending with "Don't Cry for me, Argentina, We're going to Nuke you".' 'Sack the guilty men!' ran the paper's editorial on the same day. 'What the hell is going on at Britain's Foreign Office and Ministry of Defence?' To oppose sending the task force was to be 'running scared'; on 7 April '*The Sun* Says' fired this salvo:

> 'Out of the woodwork, like the political termite he is, crawls No 1 Left-winger Tony Benn to demand the evacuation of the Falkland islanders ...
> And of course, he immediately wins backing from the whining namby-pamby ultra-Left, who always run scared at the first sign of a crisis.'

The following day, *The Sun* printed a two-page spread of photographs of British marines surrendering on the Falklands. 'LEST WE FORGET' was the headline. 'This is why our lads are going to war.'

> 'These were the first moments of humiliating defeat for our brave Falklands few. It was a black moment in our history ... a wound we cannot forget. But now our troops are on their way ... to wipe out the memory and free our loyal friends.'

The Sun's attitude to a negotiated settlement was summed up in a five-word headline on 20 April: 'STICK IT UP YOUR JUNTA'. 'We urge every housewife NOT to buy corned beef produced in the Argentine' was the theme of an early campaign. Two days later, *The Sun* reported that 'all over the country, families blacked the "bully" beef to show the South American bully boys what they thought.' 'Angry Sonia Lewis of Hockliffe, Beds', was reported as saying: 'Refusing to buy corned beef is one way we Brits can show the flag.'

Argentinians were 'Argies', a good target for humour. A daily series of 'Argy-Bargie' jokes was instituted, and soon *The Sun* was able to tell its readers, 'Your very own gags have been pouring in'. 'They are so funny that we have decided to give £5 for every reader's Argy-Bargie joke published. Plus a can of Fray Bentos "non-Argentinian" corned beef. Today's joke was told to us by Titus Rowlandson, 9, from Brighton ...' (Titus earned £5 for a joke about two British soldiers wiping out hundreds of 'Argy' soldiers.)

The Sun's promotions department was equally busy. On 7 April, 'to give the lads a big morale-booster', the paper began distributing free badges bearing the legend: '*The Sun* says Good Luck Lads'.

'THE SUN SAYS KNICKERS TO ARGENTINA!' was the banner headline on 16 April. 'Britain's secret weapon in the Falklands dispute was revealed last night ... it's undie-cover warfare.' The article revealed that 'thousands of women' were 'sporting specially made underwear embroidered across the front with the proud name of the ship on which a husband or boyfriend is serving.' Even Prince Andrew had 'bought several pairs of battle-briefs ... But Palace officials are keeping mum about who will get them as a Royal gift.' Alongside the story was the inevitable picture of 'delightful Debbie Boyland ... all shipshape and Bristol fashion' in her 'nautical naughties' embroidered with the name of 'HMS *Invincible*.'

From 11 May every front page bore the slogan 'THE PAPER THAT SUPPORTS OUR BOYS'. The comic-strip headlines continued: 'ARGY JETS SHOT DOWN' (13 May), 'OUR PLANES BLITZ ARGY SHIPS, HOW OUR TOUGH GUYS HIT PEBBLE ISLAND' (17 May), 'ARGIES BLOWN OUT OF THE SKY' (24 May), 'PANICKY ARGIES FLEE BAREFOOT' (3 June), 'HERO BAYONET TROOPS KILL FIFTY' (14 June). Following their peace initiative, the 'contemptible, treacherous Irish' joined *The Sun*'s gallery of hate-figures: 'Don't buy Irish golden butter ... Don't holiday there this summer. It's not much, but it's better than giving succour to our new enemy.' The names of all 33

Labour MPs who voted against the Government on 20 May were printed as a 'Roll of Shame'. 'Enemy quail at the touch of cold steel', reported *The Sun* on 14 June. 'The Argies had no stomach for close-quarters combat and crumbled before the Task Force's full-blooded assaults.' The level of abuse was kept up to the end, even spilling over on to the sports pages during the coverage of the World Cup. 'ARGIES SMASHED . . . They strutted, they cheated and afterwards they bleated. That was the arrogant Argentinians last night. They swaggered on as world champions, and crawled off, humiliated by little Belgium . . .'

Yet, if *The Sun* hoped by such coverage to improve circulation, there was no evidence of that by the end of the war. Throughout the country as a whole there was only a tiny rise in the total circulation of all Fleet Street papers: from 14.9 million per day in March to 15.2 million in May (when fighting was at its height), falling back to 15 million in June – an overall increase of less than 1 per cent. In the same period, *The Sun* actually lost sales of 40,000 a day, while the *Mirror* added 95,000. 'We put on 100,000 thanks to a promotional campaign just before the war started,' says Molloy, 'and we managed to keep most of them.' Peter Stephens agrees: 'I don't think anyone prospered or suffered as a result of the war.'

Bearing in mind the precedent of Suez, this was, from the *Mirror*'s point of view, an impressive performance. Why was this? The Falklands war was, after all, a much more popular venture than Suez. If papers opposed to military action lost readers in 1956, surely they should have done even worse in 1982?

It seems almost certain that the explanation lies in the expansion of television over the past 25 years. At the time of Suez there were less than six million television licence holders in the United Kingdom; today there are around 18 million. By 1971, a BBC Audience Research Unit report found that 86 per cent of the population found television a 'trustworthy' source of news; only 30 per cent 'trusted' newspapers.

The Falklands crisis rammed home the lesson of how powerful a means of communication television has become. When the Ministry of Defence spokesman appeared 'live' on television to announce the latest news from the South Atlantic, the night editor in Fleet Street was receiving the information no more swiftly and in no different a manner from his readers sitting at home. Voice reports from the television correspondents with the task force were arriving back hours, sometimes days, ahead of written dispatches. Throughout the war, as the *Daily Mail* pointed out in its evidence to the Commons Defence Committee, 'most of Britain's national newspapers were largely dependent on taking notes from Brian Hanrahan and Michael Nicholson.'

Given this immediacy, fewer people care any more what *The Sun* or the *Mirror* says. With bingo, the mass-circulation papers of Fleet Street are ceasing to be 'newspapers' in the traditional sense. As bingo can apparently lead half a million readers to change their newspaper in a matter of weeks, it is scarcely surprising that the editorial pages are fast turning into wrapping paper for the day's lucky numbers. Add to this the fact that in recent weeks *The Sun* has sometimes had seven pages of sport and a further five of advertising in a 28-page paper, and the reason why the Falklands war hardly touched circulation may well stand explained.

Robert Harris

Suggestion for analysis | Identify and analyse the various features of the style, presentation and approach to news in the *Sun* extracts above, giving illustrative examples.

Themes for discussion

What is the political affiliation of each of the British daily and Sunday national newspapers? Do you think it would be better if there was greater political diversity in the British press?

Why do you think people choose the particular newspaper they read?

How far do you think newspapers set out to influence their readers' attitudes? How far do you think they succeed?

What do you think is the appeal of the type of 'human interest' stories favoured by 'tabloid' newspapers?

Why do you think *The Sun* treated the Falklands Crisis in the way illustrated by the extracts above? What is your view of this kind of journalism?

Do you think many people are likely to have been influenced by *The Sun*'s Falklands coverage?

Why do you think broadsheet newspapers never adopted the sensationalising and personalising approach to news taken by tabloid newspapers?

Why do you think *The Sun* is Britain's largest-selling daily newspaper?

What is your opinion of the general standard of the press in Britain?

Research suggestions

Write a report on the work of each of the following:
a staff reporters;
b correspondents;
c news agencies.

Write a report on the ways in which (a) national and (b) local newspapers are financed.

Group assignments

The best way to carry out group research on newspapers is probably to have available a full range of a particular day's papers to work on, individually or in small groups, one paper per person or group. Here are a few suggestions for analytical work on newspapers:

1 Compare the main front-page headlines in each paper, and consider what they reveal about the paper's priorities. Then compare the other front-page headlines. This is best done over a number of days, if a significant picture is to emerge.

2 Look at the main front-page story in each paper. Estimate the proportion of the page devoted to each of the following: the total item; the headline; the photograph; the story itself. Then work these out as a proportion of the total number of column inches of the page. Discuss the differences between the papers in this respect, and their significance.

3 Compare the main front-page stories in each of the papers. Decide which has the greatest national or international importance. Look for this story in each of the other papers, and discuss its position and the amount of space devoted to it, and the significance of your findings.

4   Work through the paper, marking each *news* story **H** or **S**, according to whether it deals with 'hard' or 'soft' news. ('Hard' news is that which is concerned with political or economic affairs or social welfare, or which affects a large number of people; 'soft' news is that which deals with events which have no broad significance, such as revelations about the private lives of celebrities, or crime stories.) Work out the percentage of the paper devoted to 'hard' news. Compare the papers.

5   Look at an editorial (or leader). Draw what conclusions you can about the political line taken by the paper, the use of biased language and the depth of analysis it contains. Pick out illustrative quotations. Compare the papers. Do the same for a political news story.

6   Look at a lengthy news story and make brief notes, with illustrations, on the following: length of words, length of sentences, length of paragraphs, general style and tone. Compare the papers.

7   Read through your paper and write down examples of emotive language, clichés, alliteration, puns, 'tabloidese' (see the 'Tabloid Guide', on page 181). Compare the papers.

Some of these assignments could be extended to take in foreign newspapers as well, if the class contains linguists.

Individual newspaper analysis

The exercises which follow include detailed written work, which is best done individually rather than in groups.

1   Look at the reproductions of the front pages of some of the English Sunday newspapers on page 189. What conclusions can you draw from this collection? Write a detailed statement about the nature of the press in Britain, based on these conclusions.

2   Collect as many copies as possible of *either The Sun*, the *Star* or the *News of the World*. Make a study of several national or international news stories in the copies you have collected. You should attempt to analyse, with illustrative examples, all of the following: the type and complexity of vocabulary employed; the use of slang, cliché, emotive phrases and alliteration; the syntax; the paragraph lengths; evidence of political bias.

3   Read the following editorials from British daily newspapers in October 1988, and answer the questions which follow. The editorials deal with issues raised by the Appeal Court's decision to lift the ban on the publication of Peter Wright's book *Spycatcher*, which revealed secrets he had discovered while working for the British Intelligence agency MI5.

a   Comment briefly on the style of each passage.

b   Compare the attitudes taken by the two leader writers towards the government's attempts to ban the publication of *Spycatcher*.

c   From which newspaper would you imagine each editorial might have been taken? Briefly explain why?

This could be treated as a comprehension exercise, with a 45–minute time limit and a mark out of 25 (10 marks each for questions **a** and **b** and 5 for question **c**.)

At last, the balance is struck

The tide finally turned yesterday. You do not, normally, expect to find impeccable definitions of press freedom falling from the lips of the Master of the Rolls. Nor do you expect to find a Lord Justice of Appeal describing a Government's argument as 'futile and plainly silly'. But these, and other magical events, came to seem almost commonplace as the Court of Appeal gave judgement on *Spycatcher*. 'Most of the great works of the French Enlightenment were, for good reason, published outside France,' remarked Lord Justice Bingham. 'But the Bastille still fell.'

The key word, yesterday, was balance; the balance between public interest and executive secrecy. And the clear conclusion was that balance had been pushed out of true through the long months of *Spycatcher* litigation. No one needs to hail Mr Peter Wright as a good and fragrant egg to see that a world outside Britain which buys over a million copies of his book but forbids newspapers in Britain to detail and investigate his serious allegations is a world that has slewed off its axis. Now, said the three lords a'chiming, the stories should be written, and booksellers should be able to carry stocks without fear. More, for the future (a majority view) the reasonable supposition of iniquity in high and secret places was a public interest, there for investigation and publication. No need to assume that, because the great and good of government claimed all was well, that that was the end of every affair.

Talking of the end of anything in relation to *Spycatcher* is a dodgy business. The House of Lords may still await. Whitehall's legal coffers never close. But while there is balance, let us stick to it. The free press, said Sir John Donaldson yesterday, 'is an essential element in maintaining parliamentary democracy and the British way of life as we know it.' It is essential not because of any special wisdom or status – but because it is 'the eyes and ears' of the general public. 'The media's right to know and their right to publish is neither more nor less than that of the general public. Indeed, it is that of the general public.' Just (however poorly we sometimes interpret it) so. The judiciary, perhaps, is growing tired and alarmed by the way the Government loses sight of ordinary freedoms, basic public interests. Here, on all sides, is a fundamental moment to pause and take stock.

Dangerous obsession

The Government appears to be dangerously obsessed with the *Spycatcher* affair.

It has now lost its bid to have the book banned from publication in both the High Court and the Court of Appeal. But it is nevertheless pursuing its case all the way to the House of Lords.

Government motives are perfectly understandable. It is determined to stop the ex-MI5 officer Peter Wright profiting from the sale of secrets he learned in the Government service and so setting an evil example to other ex-spies on the make.

But enough is enough. Mr Wright's secrets are now available to every rival spy firm in the world. The Government cannot hope to shut this particular door so long after the horse has well and truly bolted.

In the nature of the case, a Government backdown will be no great triumph for press freedom.

Being able to publish Mr Wright's tales out of school does not serve any true public interest.

When you boil it down, Mr Wright is no better than a traitorous turncoat who peddles his charges and innuendoes about his former bosses from the safety of a far country.

Publishing his tittle-tattle is no hard won feat of deeply researched investigative reporting either. It is simply a question of buying and repeating Mr Wright's unsubstantiated allegations.

In fact, by making a major issue out of Mr Wright, newspapers may have unwittingly set back their own cause.

They have antagonised a further section of political opinion in Britain which is becoming significantly critical of press behaviour.

Last week one Bill was put before Parliament demanding a right of reply to newspapers and this week another Bill on privacy is due to be debated.

Press freedom is too important to be hobbled by measures like these. But newspapers need to find better ground than *Spycatcher* from which to fight their corner.

Television

Television in Britain

Television as a medium is a phenomenon of the post-Second-World-War era. Its importance can hardly be overestimated. It has penetrated all but the remotest areas of the globe, and has been largely responsible for the present American cultural domination over much of the world. The saddest effect of this has been to open the eyes of millions of the Third World's poor to a lifestyle and level of affluence to which they can never aspire.

Yet television has developed in different ways in different countries. In countries ruled by totalitarian regimes, the mass media are substantially propaganda tools, so that television is controlled and manipulated by the ruling élites. In the USA, the main emphasis has always been on the commercial use of the media, with advertisers sponsoring TV programmes, and constant commercial breaks.

In Britain, the concept of public-service broadcasting was pioneered, in the mid-1920s, through the creation of the BBC, funded by licence fees rather than by advertising. Despite the coming of commercial television in Britain in 1954, and the resultant competition with the BBC over audience ratings, the tradition of providing more experimental programmes and catering for a minority audience was expanded with the creation of BBC 2 (1964) and Channel 4 (1982), which were not expected to compete so strenuously for a share of the television audience.

The coming of satellite and cable television in the 1990s has vastly broadened the range of viewing possibilities, though whether or not the effects are generally beneficial is very much open to question.

Television: boon or bane?

If it is used with intelligence and discrimination by producers and public, television is uniquely equipped, in the immediacy and vividness of its sensory appeal, to help break down the barriers of misunderstanding between peoples. In Marshall McLuhan's much-quoted phrase, it has turned the world into a 'global village'. It can even have a significant impact on the course of world events. The day-by-day American television coverage of the Vietnam War, in the 1960s and 1970s, exposed the carnage and horror of that war with such stark vividness that the war became unacceptable to a large body of the American people.

Used without intelligence, however, television tends to produce inertia or worse. It enslaves millions of undiscriminating addicts. It can even, at its most insidious, blur the line between reality and fantasy. These negative aspects of television are discussed in the following extracts from Peter Conrad's book, *Television: The Medium and its Manners*:

Commercials

As well as enticing us to lust for hardware instead of human bodies, consumerism boasts of its victory over economic necessity by striving to make us hungry when we don't need to eat. This is why television has so charmed a generation with the junk food it advertises. We watch television between meals, when we oughtn't to be thinking about food, but the medium exploits our suggestibility by encouraging us to slaver at the chocolate bars, potato crisps and popcorn it's selling. Consuming these unnutritious victuals isn't eating so much as the repletion of a bored and querulous vacancy, as indeed is watching television. One of the mixtures of toffee and chocolate advertised on British television presents as its chief virtue the time it takes to chew. Disconsolate queuers at a bus stop snap at their chocolate bars and gobble them up at once. The chap armed with the correct brand is still contentedly toiling over his when – presumably hours later – the bus arrives. This is a kind of eating which, like gaping at television, is a substitute for doing anything, a condition of inane passivity. The original technological revolution was about saving time, shortcutting labour; the consumerism which is the latest instalment of that revolution is about wasting the time we've saved, and the institution it deputes to serve that purpose is television. The ads are always admonishing us to stop working. A dishwasher volunteers to relieve us of our chores, saying, 'Sit, America – we'll do the washing up'. But what do we do while we're not washing up? Television's answer is smugly self-referring: we watch television, and on it we see the dishwasher uncomplainingly toiling on our behalf.

Soap operas

Stardom on television is experienced by its beneficiaries as a limitation and an ignominy not, as in the movies, an access of monarchical power or an ascension to the company of divinity. The television star is someone who has been made the victim of a stereotype, and who feels cramped and depreciated by its strictures. He longs to shed the image which has supererogated his own reality, and battles frantically to break out of the box. Henry Winkler, donating the Fonz's scuffed leathers to the Smithsonian, resents the programme to which he owes his celebrity and irritably corrects infants who yell, 'Hi Fonzie!' at him, explaining that his name is Winkler.

The type may, as in the case of *Dempsey and Makepeace*, seem benign, but the stereotype is malignant, and its most pathetic victims are the actors on the soap operas. They're required by their contracts to conduct their private lives as extensions of the fiction: morality clauses empower the producers to dismiss a performer if he or she violates the sudsy probity which the serials defend. Yet at the same time they're punished in their own persons for the malfeasances of the characters they play. The soap actors have a sorry history of bruises and buffetings, administered by a censorious public. Margaret Mason, when playing Linda in *Days of Our Lives*, had a carton of milk poured over her in a supermarket by a consumer outraged at the character's perfidy; Eileen Fulton, playing the bitchy Lisa in *As The World Turns*, was clubbed with a handbag by another viewer who shrieked while beating her, 'I hate you!' Paranoia is an occupational ailment for these people. When Rachel Ames as Audrey was flirting extra-maritally in *General Hospital*, she was accosted and abused by a man who claimed that his wife had been so upset by her vicious goings-on that she'd almost suffered a heart attack. When her character was on trial for murder, Rachel Ames was convinced that shop assistants were punishing her by refusing to wait on her. In spite of their protests, these actors have been subsumed by their roles.

News

Television's deftest alteration of content to match its hermetic, transistorised form occurs with the news. As we watch, reality is remade as televisual fiction. For, rather than reporting the news, television's presumption is to invent it. The news on television isn't hearsay, relayed to us by an impartial messenger. It happens at the medium's instigation, for the cameras are no longer obsequious witnesses but agents of provocation. The demonstrators raise their voices and their clenched fists when the cameras arrive. The newsman won't scruple to incite a media event if it seems reluctant to occur. Gary Paul Gates – in his account of CBS television news, *Air Time* – described an adventurer who, hastening to New Jersey to film what he hoped would be a prison riot, found only a mild ruckus, which had already been pacified. The prison authorities at first refused to admit the cameras, knowing they could easily reignite the protest. Eventually they relented, but still would not allow the crew direct access to the prisoners. The news team therefore went sedately about its business, preparing to film some indifferent and inactive convicts. Then, when all was ready, the reporter in charge signalled to the prisoners with a raised arm and a single extended finger in a gesture of scabrous disdain. They of course co-operated by staging a noisy riot for the cameras.

Peter Conrad

Hidden bias

Whilst a 'tabloid' newspaper can present a trivial but titillating discovery about the private life of a popular entertainer as its main front–page feature, national television news generally concentrates on events of genuine significance.

Since its foundation, the BBC has maintained a reputation for providing an exceptionally unbiased news service. However, selection is an essential part of television news presentation, since only half a dozen or so items can be dealt with in any single news bulletin. In its selection of which items to include in a news broadcast, hidden bias is manifested. In her essay 'Fourth Channel: Third World', from which the following extract is taken, J. Ann Kammit analyses this hidden bias in British television news coverage of Third World affairs.[1]

Television tends to be interested in the stories, not the issue. Therefore most programmes and reports on the developing world are eye-catchers focusing on the drama of disasters – floods, famine, earthquakes and disturbances such as wars and coups. This is further accentuated by the news, which normally only refers to the Third World when there are catastrophes or political conflicts. This gives an extremely negative impression of developing countries and their populations.

The real drama affecting Third World countries is the drastic poverty and exploitation which forms the permanent economic and social context for the mass of the population, who are only occasionally affected, if at all, by the more newsworthy hurricanes. But the many programmes which deal with the immediate effects of such disasters naturally concentrate on those most affected – the poor – helping to establish the overall impression that all Third World people are desperately poor. Those of us who have benefited from travel or study know this not to be the case. As in our own society, most underdeveloped countries do have wealthy, sometimes very wealthy, élites and often a sizeable middle class. This is not to argue of course that we should not be concerned most with the poor and oppressed, but that we should see their poverty in context.

---

1 Included in *What's This Channel Four? An Alternative Report*, edited by Simon Blanchard and David Morley (Comedia Publishing Group, 1982).

However, media treatment, like many development policy documents, tends to make frequent reference to Third-World countries or nations rather than particular social groups. This is an effective means of depoliticising issues, leaving aside crucial questions about the simultaneous existence of extreme poverty and substantial wealth, and the social, political and economic structure which explains that poverty.

The view of 'the Third-World problem' which underpins the perceptions and analyses of most programme makers, and particularly news reporters, reflects the ideological structures of our own society. Thus TV programmes are informed by the dominant model of so-called development theory, which still holds sway in most of academia and schools education. This model of the causes (ignorance, ill health) of Third-World poverty, and of the remedies (modernisation, increased aid) has been persistently challenged within development studies over the last decade.

J. Ann Kammit

Sex and violence on film and video

The question as to whether or not lurid scenes of sex and violence on television, film and video have a corrupting influence has been argued over by psychologists and sociologists for decades. The summary skills passage on pages 36–37 deals with this theme.

In the extracts which follow, from an interview with Beverley Brown in a 1982 issue of *Screen* magazine, the Secretary of the British Board of Film Censors, James Ferman, took up the issue of whether it can be said that some films 'have a tendency to deprave and corrupt', in the terms of the Obscene Publications Act:

I think it's fair to say that no film made before 1970 had a serious tendency to deprave and corrupt by today's standards. But since then there has been a tendency to indulge in an exploitation of evil for its own sake: 'We are now going to show you the nastiest, most unpleasant thing you've ever seen – and if this isn't strong enough for you, next week we'll show you something even stronger,' putting the idea into people's minds, that is, actually inciting them to find evil attractive, saying, 'We want to put you in the position of the rapist, we want you to watch this from the standpoint of a man who is enjoying participating in it.'

The problem is that the way the films work is not necessarily a direct incitement. The law talks of a tendency to deprave and corrupt, which is exactly what it is. There's very little evidence that if you see one rape film, it will incite you to rape, but if you see two, six, ten? I think it's a tendency, the cumulative impact of a whole genre of film . . .

In a *Newsweek* programme on pornography, Gene Abel, the New York researcher, found that in showing rape images to normal men, measuring their physiological sexual response, the erotic content was the main factor and the physical response decreased when the violence factor was increased. With convicted rapists, on the other hand, it was the other way around; and this is the problem with these recent 'slasher' films – which are in fact all heavily censored in Britain, more than the critics notice – that violence and rape itself is presented as a 'turn on'.

And, again, I think we must remember that films are not isolated experiences, people go to the cinema repeatedly. The generation 16 to 25 used to go a couple of times a month, or used to when they had money. Now they're hiring video, and seeing far worse things, with the added factor that they don't even have to see the 'film as a whole' – they can just skip the boring dialogue and spool through to the rape or the brutality, and see it again and again.

James Ferman

Themes for discussion

The Television Act (1964) requires 'that nothing is included in the programmes which offends against good taste or decency or is likely to encourage or incite to crime or to lead to disorder or to be offensive to public feeling'. Do you think there is too much sex and/or violence on British television? Can you think of any programmes which you have seen recently which infringe any of the prohibitions in the Act?

Do you think the distinction between the behaviour of heroes and villains in crime series is clear enough? Does it matter?

Do you think British television is sufficiently broad and enterprising in its scope? What kinds of programmes would you like to see more, and less, of?

Do you see any advantages in the British system of financing television programmes partly through licence fees rather than wholly by advertising? How would you feel about the BBC introducing advertising?

The avowed purpose of television in Britain is 'information, education and entertainment' (Television Act). How much of each is reflected in a typical evening's viewing? How much of each do you think the typical viewer watches? Do you think most people discriminate sufficiently in their television viewing?

To what extent do you think television increases passivity and unsociability?

Are there any television programmes that you try never to miss? What are they?

What is the appeal of 'soap operas'? Do you consider any of them to be successful artistically? Why do you think some people become involved in the lives of 'soap opera' characters to the extent illustrated by Peter Conrad?

Do you think British television presents the news in an unbiased way? Do you think it is too parochial in its choice of news items?

Do you think news bulletins should be more positive, and concentrate more on success stories (e.g. good industrial relations) and less on conflict (e.g. strikes)?

Why do you think television (and the mass media generally) fails to follow up situations once their initial news value has waned? Do you think it ought to produce more follow up items?

In what ways do you think poor people in the Third World are influenced by seeing television programmes showing life in the West?

Do you think cable television is a welcome development?

Why do you think people watch 'video nasties'? Do you see them as a reflection of any trends in our society? What do you think is the probable effect of films which present rape and other forms of sadistic cruelty as a 'turn on'?

Questionnaire

After reading the guidelines for preparing and presenting a questionnaire on pages 111–112, it could be of value to produce a questionnaire on television viewing habits. Here are some specimen subjects on which questions might be set:

- the number of hours of television watched each week on average;
- whether a television programme or a book is preferred on a particular theme, such as an adventure story;
- whether TV is watched mainly for amusement, relaxation or education, or for no special reason;
- if radio is ever preferred to TV in the evenings, and the sort of radio programmes listened to;
- if there are any TV programmes which the interviewees try never to miss, and what they are.

(Some of the questions could be correlated, to work out, for example, if people who watch large amounts of television discriminate as much as those who watch less.)

Assignments

1 With the help of a copy of a listings magazine, such as *Radio Times* or *TV Times* for a particular week, work out the proportion of broadcasting time in the evenings devoted to 'serious' and 'light' programmes, following discussion to establish the distinction. This could be undertaken in groups, working on different channels and blocks of time. The findings can be correlated, and percentages worked out.

2 Using your listings magazines, draw up a chart of the number of hours per day or evening, over the period of a week, which each channel devotes to each of the ten following categories of programme:

news and news magazines   'soap operas'
current affairs   comedy
documentaries   quiz shows and other light
film   entertainment
drama   sport
music

Work out percentages for each channel and draw conclusions.

3 Watch an instalment of a 'soap opera' or an episode of a weekly crime or drama series, and make notes on each of these features:

The characters: Were they convincingly drawn, or merely stereotypes?
Were their reactions to situations realistic on the whole?
Were you able to get involved with the characters and situations?

The dialogue: Was it convincing?

The story: Was it realistic, amusing or exaggerated?

Did it contain any interesting insights into life?

You should note down any episodes or incidents which particularly illustrated any of these features, positively or negatively.

4 Make a study of fictionalised violence on television, over several days, noting the number and instances and the types of violence portrayed. The best way to organise this work would be for students to volunteer to watch particular programmes advertised in a listings magazine, so that the entire range of programmes in which fictionalised violence is likely to feature is covered.

5 Watch the evening news bulletin on each channel, over a period of three or four days. List each item, and work out the proportion of domestic and international news on each channel. Work out the proportion of items involving conflict, and involving violence. Compare the selection of items on the different channels. Were you aware of bias in any of the news coverage?

Advertising

Social effects of advertising

Advertising is massively big business, and is the only mass medium from which no one in the Western world can escape. A whole new pseudo-science of 'motivational analysis' has grown up over the past few decades, seeking ways of persuading us to buy one company's product rather than another's. Since, for all practical purposes, there is nothing to choose between different brands of toothpaste, soap powder, petrol and thousands of other consumer items, advertising is inevitably concerned largely with the creation of imaginary differences between brands, which in turn leads to all kinds of distortion and deception on the part of the advertisers. As J.A.C. Brown put it: 'It is obviously impossible to appeal to common sense by truthful advertising which relies on giving factual data if the brands from which the customer is expected to choose are alike in all essential qualities.'[2] What are the implications of this?

The psychological and social effects of advertising in Western society are discussed by Frank Whitehead in a chapter of the book, *Discrimination and Popular Culture*, edited by Denis Thompson.

In recent years the advertising world has turned increasingly to the twin techniques of market research and motivational research, in order to make more efficient its empirically-gained knowledge of how best to work upon human frailty.

It can be argued that the constant appeal to discreditable impulses is unlikely to have much effect except on those who are already abnormally susceptible. We may agree that it is the self-indulgent who will respond with most alacrity to slogans about chocolates with 'less-fattening centres', or to the stomach-powder manufacturer's encouragement to 'Eat what you like – without suffering for it'. On the other hand, advertising agents are united in their conviction that sheer weight of repetition can be

---

2 J.A.C. Brown, *Techniques of Persuasion* (Penguin, 1963).

amazingly effective (hence the remarkably long life meted out to such slogans as 'Players Please' or 'Guinness is Good for You'); and it should be remembered that what we are exposed to is a combined assault by many different advertisers, all converging to direct their appeal to a small number of well-proved human weaknesses. Thus although it may be only the exceptional motorist who falls in at all fully with the implications of the invitation to 'Put a Tiger in your Tank', nevertheless this particular extreme example works in consort with a host of other advertisements for petrols, cars and motoring accessories to establish an unquestioned assumption that what every motorist longs for above all (on our overcrowded roads) is speed, engine-power and acceleration. Road safety is not apparently considered a strong selling-point for motor-cars.

For the most part, advertising acts (and is content to act) as a reinforcement of already existing tendencies, but even so it seems likely that the multiplicity of small pressures work together to effect significant shifts in the total pattern of socially accepted values. In countless ways often unnoticed we are led to accept as common ground a world in which the key to happiness is the possession of the newest model of car, dining-room suite, refrigerator and television set, in which any malaise can be neutralised by recourse to a branded anodyne or laxative, and in which the chosen reward for a hard day's work is to 'treat yourself' to a luxury you can't afford because you feel you 'deserve it' – or even 'owe it to yourself'.

The tendency to reinforce impulses which are socially undesirable is only part of the problem. Even more insidious may be the advertiser's growing ingenuity in linking his product with ideas and images which are in themselves innocuous, pleasurable, even commendable. In consequence of this the concepts of sexual love, manliness, femininity, maternal feeling are steadily devalued for us by their mercenary association with a brand name – as though the real human values they represent can be purchased by rushing out and buying a new shaving lotion, a new deodorant, even a new washing machine. Mother-love seems to be the target most favoured by practitioners of this tactic, and the following example is only a little more nauseating than most of its kind:

'When there's love at home, it shows. It shows in the smile of the mother who gives it. It shows in the happiness of her family who are secure in it . . . It shows in the fact that she chooses Persil for their clothes.'

Frank Whitehead

The rationale of advertisers

Advertising costs large companies millions of pounds. How can the expense be justified? In an essay entitled 'Understanding Advertisers'[3] Kathy Myers reveals some of the underlying assumptions, approaches and justifications of the advertising industry:

For a product to become a brand it needs to establish and maintain a position in the market over a defined period of time. Market stability ultimately depends upon repeat purchases.

Ralph Horowitz put the case for manufacturer's investment in advertising as follows: 'The role of advertising is to diminish uncertainty. Advertising sets out to secure a predetermined level of demand for a given future and to diminish fluctuations

3 Included in *Language, Image, Media*, edited by Howard Davis and Paul Walton (Basil Blackwell, 1983).

around that predetermined level.' The ability to predict total revenue from advertised products is crucial if manufacturers are to accurately plan future output, product development and capital investment.

It is therefore the need to take the trial and error out of selling that motivates advertisers to create a clear picture of the audience they are selling to and what role or function the product could play in people's lives.

Attention to the 'needs' and 'desires' of the consumer informs every level of marketing strategy: the design of the campaign, the kind of media exposure given, the amount of exposure, the choice of packaging, distribution, etc. The advert which we see is only one part of this highly co-ordinated marketing offensive.

From the advertiser's point of view, women's magazines are a highly reliable way of reaching the female consumer. Readership profiles are available for each magazine on the market.

One unquantifiable benefit to advertisers is that magazines provide a 'hospitable environment' for the digestion and assimilation of advertised information. Glossy, colourful and eye-catching, women's magazines are reputed to have a 'keep' value. They may be read at leisure, used for reference, shown to friends or left about the house. Publishers and advertisers believe that these magazines provide a source of information, advice, solidarity and companionship, and that women have grown to trust the opinions voiced. It is a credibility jealously guarded by editors and highly valued by advertisers, for both groups feel that some of the journalistic credibility is carried over into the advertisements. The magazine environment as an essential ingredient of advertising success was the message of an IPC advert for their Women's Group of magazines. The copy quoted a Saatchi and Saatchi spokesman on the subject of Anchor Butter:

> 'While our TV advertising is promoting the use of Anchor Butter in the family, we are looking to posters and women's magazines to reinforce our branding for us. We want the housewife to be absolutely certain that Anchor is the name she can rely on for real butter goodness, and we are confident that in the relaxed, intimate environment of women's magazines our message carries complete conviction.'

Conflicts within agency strategy are reflected in the system of beliefs which validate the industry as a whole. On the one hand, members of the advertising profession see advertising mythically as consistent with the needs of a democratic egalitarian society: it helps to make the consumer aware of available market 'choices'; it 'educates' the consumer into 'product benefit' and so on. But the vision of advertising as a democratic information service is distorted by the fact that it is the job of each individual agency to promote one product at the expense of competing products. The apparent contradiction between these two aspects of commercial philosophy is rationalised in terms of the 'Darwinian' survival of the fittest product. In the Western economy, where 95 per cent of the new products introduced onto the market each year fail to maintain a market position, successful marketing and advertising is felt to be essential to give products a competitive chance.

Kathy Myers

Themes for discussion

Why do companies spend so much money on advertising?

How do you think people in general are influenced by advertising?

Can you think of any ways in which you personally have been influenced by advertising?

What influence do you think advertising has on people's lifestyles, attitudes and aspirations? How important a part does it play in Western culture?

Do you think that advertising has a tendency to cheapen and debase language?

Are there any aspects of advertising which you feel should be legislated against?

Research topic

Write a brief report on the advertising code of practice in Britain.

Assignments

1 Collect a range of newspaper and magazine advertisements and analyse the appeal of each. Try to find an example of an advertisement appealing to each of the following basic urges and anxieties:

greed;	ease and comfort;	health fears;
security;	maternal feelings;	sex appeal;
identification with famous people;		snob appeal;
fear of nonconformity and urge for acceptance.		

2 Analyse some of the advertisements in more detail. Consider:

The picture: Is it appropriate to the product? If not, what urge is it appealing to?

The slogan: Is it a logical, verifiable statement?

The copy: Does it concentrate on presenting facts which will help the reader make an informed decision? Does it make any claims or statements which cannot be verified? Does it use inappropriate pseudo-scientific language? Does it use an inappropriate or exaggerated style?

Does the advertisement as a whole link the product with irrelevant drives, and make questionable statements?

3 Decide what kind of people the advertisement is appealing to, on the basis of your analysis.

4 Look at a selection of recorded television commercials. Analyse the appeal of each, in similar terms to those suggested above.

5 List the commercials in order of effectiveness, and discuss what makes an effective television commercial.

6 Make a collection of advertisements from each of the following: a 'quality' Sunday newspaper colour supplement; a 'tabloid' newspaper; a women's magazine. Look at some of the advertisements in each, and try to draw some conclusions about the kinds of appeals and audience each is aimed at.

7 Look at a range of advertisements for the same type of product, e.g. cosmetics, cars, beer, chocolates, shampoo. Decide whether the basic appeal is similar in each, and if not, why not.

8 Collect some advertisements which link products with irrelevant urges.

9 Make a collection of meaningless slogans and statements used in advertisements.

10 Make a collection of inflated, inappropriate phrases used in advertisements.

Essay titles

a What do you think makes an effective advertisement?

b Should the press be prevented from exposing the follies of the famous? If so, what limitations should there be to the freedom of journalists to pursue stories, and newspaper publishers to print them? If not, why not?

c Write a letter to a broadsheet newspaper outlining proposals for improving leisure facilities for young people living on under-resourced housing estates. Then write a short article for a tabloid newspaper exposing some aspect of the deprivation of those living in such areas.

d Do British newspapers have anything to do with 'news'?

e How far do newspapers influence views in society and how far do they merely reflect them?

f In what respects do you think standards in television may be in decline?

g Consider the treatment by the mass media of any *one* important recent issue.

h What is the appeal of soap operas, and how do you react to them?

i 'A good newspaper is a nation talking to itself.' What are your views on what constitutes a good newspaper?

j 'Television dulls the senses and prevents rebellion.' Do you agree?

Bibliography

Cohen, Stanley and Young, Jock, *The Manufacture of News: Deviance, Social Problems and the Mass Media*, Constable, 1976

Conrad, Peter, *Television: The Medium and its Manners*, Routledge and Kegan Paul, 1982

Curran, James and Seaton, Jean, *Power without Responsibility, the Press and Broadcasting in Britain*, Methuen, 1991

Glasgow Media Group, *Bad News*, Routledge and Kegan Paul, 1976. *More Bad News*, Routledge and Kegan Paul, 1980

Goodwin, Andrew and Whannel, Garry, *Understanding Television*, Routledge, 1990

Harris, Robert, *Gotcha! The Media, the Government and the Falklands Crisis*, Faber & Faber, 1983

Price, Stuart, *Media Studies*, Pitman Publishing, 1993

Smith, Anthony, *The Newspaper: An International History*, Thames and Hudson, 1979

Thompson, Denis (ed.), *Discrimination and Popular Culture*, Penguin, 1973
Whale, John, *The Politics of the Media*, Manchester University Press, 1980
Whitaker, Brian, *News Ltd: Why You Can't Read All About It*, Minority Rights Group, 1981

12 Three Themes in Brief

In this chapter, three more themes are suggested, in addition or as alternatives to the seven already explored in depth. Written exercises and ideas for planning a discussion or debate are provided on each. The themes are: politics; science; and youth, marriage and old age.

1 Politics

With a topic as wide as politics, all that can usefully be done is to suggest a few approaches to discussion.

Reading a political article

A good way to develop political awareness is to take a political article in a newspaper and to analyse it in terms of political phraseology and ideas. The article which follows appeared in *The Times* in October 1990, and deals with the issues of German reunification, the problems facing East Germany after achieving its freedom from Soviet domination, and the implications of a single German nation for the European community.

The article and accompanying questions are designed for use in a discussion session rather than as a written comprehension, and are intended to highlight issues: the answers are not, in general, meant to be found in the article itself.

With all its might, Germany can be a power for good

On the eve of unification, **Helmut Schmidt**, former West German
chancellor, sets out his hopes – and anxieties

East Germany's craving for freedom from communist dictatorship first became clear to the world on 17 June, 1953, when Soviet troops crushed the uprising in East Berlin. Thirty-six years were to pass before the Brandenburg Gate was finally forced open, the Wall pulled down and the killing zone neutralised. Such was our joy that tomorrow's celebrations of unification can only be an echo of those momentous events of last November.

None the less, 3 October will be an important date for the future because reunification alters significant aspects of our foreign defence, and domestic and international economic policies. New opportunities present themselves, but at the same time there are grounds for concern.

There is so much to do in what was the GDR. During a visit last month, thousands of people expressed anxiety to me about the power still exercised by former members of the secret police and ex-Communist party career politicians running the factories, co-operatives and government offices. Because of the falling sales of East German goods, companies are threatened with closure, with a consequent loss of jobs. Already unemployment is approaching a million.

Who owns what is in practice unclear. The mayor of a town simply does not know how much of the land is at local government's disposal. There is a genuine cash crisis in both the public and private sectors. Local treasurers doubt whether they will be able to meet their wage bills during the next quarter. Much of the money Bonn is pumping eastwards is flowing back as East Germans buy West German goods.

Although there is a danger of psychological setbacks and political disillusionment, I believe there will be an upswing during 1992 at the latest and that East Germans will reach West German productivity levels and standard of living by the turn of the century. The quality of housing will lag behind far longer, however, and the federal government needs to show greater urgency in improving roads, railways and telecommunications.

If anyone still believes that the financial aid required can be raised through the issue of government bonds, he is mistaken, particularly in view of the Gulf crisis and Bonn's huge obligations to the Soviet Union.

Despite these demands on our resources, and the competing claims of financial aid to Poland, Hungary and Czechoslovakia, many politicians and journalists abroad take for granted that Germany, with its 60 million people, will have achieved dominant economic and financial power by the end of the decade.

This assumed economic power, in turn, fuels the fear that Germany will be tempted to a new arrogance in foreign policy and an exertion of our will over the European Community and its politicians. Because of our treaty with Moscow, some fear that Germany might try to have a foot in both camps, West and East, throwing our great weight first to one side then to the other.

Such anxieties are certainly exaggerated, but they exist, in London, Paris, Warsaw and elsewhere, and Germany has to take them into account as a political fact of life. Those particularly fearful of the Moscow treaty should recognise that without it, there would have been no unification, and Soviet troops would have stayed in East Germany indefinitely.

In the past, West Germany has stood up to both the Soviet Union and the United States over nuclear weapons. In future, clashes of interest are more likely with medium-sized European powers, notably Poland, and will require delicate handling. All

German–Polish problems are, and will long remain, overshadowed by memo-
145 ries of Auschwitz and the tragic history of our bilat-eral relations stretching back for more than two centuries. Added to these
150 today are negotiations about exit visas for ethnic Germans, Polish financial demands, and recognition of the Oder-Neisse Line. In
155 dealing with any weaker country, we Germans need to show not only tact and understanding but generos-ity.
160 Relations with France, an equally important neigh-bour, are no longer as firm and co-operative as they were in the early 1960s, at
165 the time of Adenauer and de Gaulle, or during the seven years I worked with Giscard d'Estaing. Although German and French inter-
170 ests clashed at times, nei-ther side ever lost sight of the vital truth that without trust and close co-opera-tion between the two, there
175 can be no peace in Europe, no common security, no European integration and no progress in the EC, which is vital for Europe's
180 future political and eco-nomic stability. Although these truths have not been forgotten completely by Bonn or Paris since 9
185 November last year, they

have been neglected.
That brings me to rela-tions with Britain. When I first became involved in
190 politics after Hitler's war, I was an Anglophile – the result of my schooling in Hamburg, where I was born. But since the late
195 1950s, when I was disap-pointed by the way the British remained on the sidelines of the EC, I have leaned strongly towards
200 Franco–German co-opera-tion. Given the concern expressed in Britain about the economic muscle that Germany is expected to
205 exercise in future, my heart-felt wish is to make one thing clear to British read-ers. If the ecu is not intro-duced as the single common
210 currency in the EC, the mark will indeed become Europe's dominant cur-rency, which I would con-sider most undesirable.
215 So I appeal to you: see to it, along with us, that we create an independent sys-tem of European central banks with the ecu as the
220 EC's one and only cur-rency. A common market with 11 or 12 currencies is the most uncommon mar-ket that world economic
225 history has ever seen.

The constitutional and internationally recognised reunification of Germany

230 ends a long, difficult and painful phase of our post-war policy. The years ahead, however, confront us with even more difficult tasks.
235 We have to ensure that Germany stays on a foreign-policy course that does not disturb our neighbours, but strengthens and justifies
240 their trust in us.
European countries with democratic constitutions and a market economy are pinning their hopes on the
245 future influence of the EC. The British and the Germans should therefore bring all their political and economic power to bear in
250 the Community. All the other countries of Europe, even the Soviet Union, are hoping along with the EC member states that a contin-
255 uation of the Helsinki process will achieve increased co-operation.
At the end of this terrible 20th century, my people
260 have been given another great chance. We shall be able to take it if, as well as solidarity with the people of the old GDR, we remember
265 the need for solidarity with our neighbours. I pin my hopes and trust on a stead-fast continuation of the poli-cies that West Germany has
270 so far pursued.

Helmut Schmidt, *The Times*, October 1990

---

1 What does Helmut Schmidt mean by 'communist dictatorship'? (lines 3–4) What were the essential features of the Communist system in East Germany?

2 What was 'the Wall'? (line 12) What was the significance of its being 'pulled down'?

3 What was 'the GDR'? (line 31)

4 What is the reason for the fears of the people of East Germany about 'former members of the secret police and ex-Communist party career politicians'? (lines 35–8)

5 Why is unemployment rising in East Germany? (lines 46–8)

6 Why is it unclear 'who owns what in practice' (lines 49–50) in East Germany?

7 What does Schmidt mean by 'Bonn's huge obligations to the Soviet Union'? (lines 88–90)

8 Why are Poland, Hungary and Czechoslovakia competing for aid? (lines 92–5)

9 What does he mean by 'a foot in both camps'? (lines 113–4)

10 What does he mean by saying 'All German–Polish problems are . . . overshadowed by memories of Auschwitz'? (lines 141–5)

11 What is the 'ecu'? Why is its creation preferable to the mark becoming 'Europe's dominant currency'? (lines 212–3)

12 What is 'a market economy'? (line 243)

13 What is 'the EC'? (line 246)

14 Why does Schmidt say that 'even the Soviet Union' is hoping for a continuation of the process of 'increased cooperation' in Europe? (lines 252–7)

15 Why do you think Schmidt talks of 'this terrible 20th century'? (lines 258–9)

Topics for discussion

There are plainly any number of approaches to a discussion of politics. Exploring particular issues can be a valuable way of developing a political perspective, but the goal of being able to read political reports in newspapers with some degree of understanding is probably as valuable as any. The suggestions which follow have this end in view.

British politics

A debate, in which individuals or pairs present a general case for the main British political parties' current policies.

A discussion of the different parties' policies with relation to specific issues, such as law and order, education, privatisation, defence, the health service, taxation, etc., following research by individual students.

Research and/or discussion of current political vocabulary, such as: 'left' and 'right' in a party and general political sense; the 'market'; Keynesian economics; proportional representation; federalism; oligarchies, etc.

World politics

A discussion of the major world political systems: anarchism, 'laissez-faire' capitalism, centralist communism, democratic socialism, fascism.

A discussion concentrating on the different political systems in particular countries, eg: China, India and Iran, following individual research.

As a follow up or an alternative to this kind of approach, discussion could centre on more general political abstractions such as: the meaning and value of 'democracy', the concepts of 'freedom' and 'liberty', the uses and limitations of bureaucracy, etc.

Essay titles

a 'Fixed-term governments would be good for democracy.' Discuss the advantages and disadvantages of such a proposal, and suggest the length of time a government should remain in office.

b 'Power tends to corrupt, and absolute power corrupts absolutely. Great men are always bad men.'

c In pursuing higher living standards, do we overlook the quality of life?

d Discuss the case for the complete revision of the electoral system in Great Britain.

e 'As society becomes more complex, we have more government and less freedom.' Is this inevitable?

f 'Liberty must be limited in order to be possessed.'

g 'The principal concern of politics is the allocation of resources.'

h Is 'equality of opportunity' attainable or is it only an ideal?

i 'Democracy is the tyranny of the majority.' How do you respond to this assertion?

2   Science

A detailed understanding of scientific theory and its practical applications cannot be expected of arts students. However, it is not unreasonable to assume an awareness of the major scientists and inventions in layman's terms, and discussion of these, as well as a more philosophical consideration of the value and limitations of science in terms of its practical applications in human affairs, would be valuable.

A comprehension/summary exercise on a radical feminist analysis of the nature of scientific activity should serve as a useful lead-in to discussion.

Comprehension and analysis/ summary skills

The article which follows appeared in *New Internationalist* magazine in April 1988. Read it carefully and answer the questions. You are advised to spend about one and a half hours on this exercise.

a Explain and comment on the links which the writer asserts in lines 24–86 between scientific activity and masculinity.   *(8 marks)*

b Explain the parallels which the writer draws between 'the attack on nature by the scientists' and 'the rape and exploitation of women in misogynist cultures'. (lines 99–104)   *(6 marks)*

c How do you react to the final paragraph?   *(5 marks)*

d By detailed reference to the language used, and the presentation of the arguments, show the extent to which you consider the article to be biased.   *(9 marks)*

e Magazine articles generally assume a certain kind of readership. By reference to the details of the passage, and especially to its register, vocabulary, tone and political stance, deduce what kind of audience the article is aimed at.   *(12 marks)*

f Summarise the writer's theory about genius in not more than 50 words.   *(10 marks)*

(50 marks total)

Science on the couch

Why is science dominated by men? What draws them to it? Judy Gahagan argues it has more to do with virility than the creative search for knowledge.

'It's a boy!' read the telegram from nuclear physicist Edward Teller announcing his pride and joy – the successful detonation of the first hydrogen bomb. His choice of image was apposite: a telling hint of what makes mad, male science tick.

Science begins in the mind, of course, keeping company with all the fantasies, conflicts and symbols of the human psyche. When it emerges it is permanently shaped by these things. This is why much of the prestigious science produced over the last three centuries in Western Europe has been obsessed with virility and fertility.

The domains of science are themselves arranged in a prestige hierarchy according to their 'hardness'. Those subjects – such as particle physics – which are most abstract, have least contact with matter, which 'penetrate' furthest into Nature, are the 'hardest' and therefore the most prestigious. Biology and psychology, which observe living beings interacting with their natural environment, are the 'softest'. This hierarchy has nothing to do with complexity, profundity, progress, even importance. It has everything to do with virility.

Hard science has triumphed in an age of capitalism and materialism. Because it masquerades as the apotheosis of pure reason, few have been inclined to poke around inside its psyche. But as we approach the apocalypse, brought about by its proudest achievements, many reckon it's time to get this god onto the analyst's couch.

Once inside that psyche, we are confronted by three major ideas that have been around for several centuries, and underlie all scientific activity. The first is the division between mind and matter. Since the time of Francis Bacon, (male) mind has sought to penetrate (female) matter.

Related to this idea is the assumption that the scientist's purpose is to control or exploit nature, as opposed to caring for, measuring, conserving – or just simply understanding it. And rounding off the trio is the way each scientific discovery glorifies its author's ego, in a way that, say, running a nursery school could never do. And so the race to be first, to claim paternity, is on. Thus is prestigious modern science relentless, aggressive and competitive.

But before we can look at the minds of individuals, we have to explain how these three ideas came to hold such sway within science's collective psyche. Many people have suggested they arise from a fear and hostility towards feminine principles that is thought to gnaw away at the vitals of the masculine unconscious (and not so unconscious). They see the attack on nature by the scientists as parallel to the rape and exploitation of women in misogynist cultures. This hostility, they argue, is rooted in a fundamental of biology. The story runs thus: the female's role in creating life is visible and unchallengable. Motherhood cannot be disputed and makes the primary family unit a matriarchal one. The male is excluded from this primal creative process – and his resultant envy and insecurity are terrible. It can only be assuaged by creating secrets and miracles for himself or by exerting total control over women. The assuagement takes many forms. One form is the widespread and brutal enforcement of virginity to ensure biological paternity. A considerably less oppressive method is found among many indigenous peoples, where the men have secret societies and ceremonies which allow them special communion with nature, and from which women are strictly excluded. (Australian aboriginal women comment scathingly that 'men make secret ceremonies, women make babies'.) But the form we know best is men's modern quest to produce fantastic, dangerous and futile technologies in an effort to

gain control over life itself.
145 This quest has the effect of both dominating over and escaping from everything associated with femininity. Scientists have a
150 reputation for being obsessive, working 17 hours a day in conditions of mental and physical isolation. Such dedication earns our
155 approval, and we understand that it is essential for scientific progress. But is it? Why should this flight from life be seen to be the
160 real hallmark of the genuinely committed scientist? And what of the passion to be the undisputed author of a discovery, the
165 father of the brainchild, to be first? In reality there is no hurry at all. In fact, if there had been a bit less urgency about nuclear
170 research, scientists might have got around to contemplating just where the radioactive garbage was going to go. Indeed, the
175 whole course of science might have been different had all scientific papers been published anonymously, solely in the ser-
180 vice of knowledge.

The mysterious nature of scientific research, its isolation and the secrecy so often surrounding it, also
185 help feed the myth of genius. The genius is a person with a different kind of intellect, blessed with extraordinary gifts and powers.
190 Or so we've always assumed. But recently psychologist Robert Weisberg has been examining the evidence for this assumption.
195 And he has discovered that the processes needed for solving problems like the structure of DNA, the mechanism of evolution,
200 the behaviour of particles, are no different from those involved in putting a new lock on the front door or investigating which signals
205 an autistic child responds to most positively.
To qualify as genius, a scientist will indeed have above average fluency in
210 certain logical, spatial or mathematical operations. But more important than these is their fascination, or obsession, with a subject.
215 This means they often persist with a single problem for years. Using biographical

and historical documents, Weisberg demonstrated con-
220 vincingly how perfectly ordinary were the processes leading to 'great' discoveries. Only the obsession with the subject and the passion
225 to be first were distinctive to the genius. Yet both are, as we have seen, potentially lethal characteristics.
All this leads to a conclu-
230 sion: that true science must emerge from feminine and masculine qualities. Every institution that isolated men from the creative care of
235 children, that alienates them from the feminine in themselves and other people, helps to set in motion a monstrous perversion of
240 human intellect, rather than a creative search for knowledge.
Judy Gahagan is a freelance writer and former psychology lecturer based in London.

from *New Internationalist*, April 1988

Discussion and analysis

List the most significant scientific discoveries of the century. What makes each of them important?

List as many famous scientists as you can, and name their discoveries.

What was life in Britain like before the development of modern science?

What are the negative effects of scientific discoveries?

Should scientists be expected to take account of the social and moral implications of their research?

On the whole, has the development of science been a good thing for the human race or not?

3 Youth, marriage and old age

This may seem a rather artificial linking of what are, in reality, separate themes. They can of course be treated separately, but since each is in itself a relatively minor social issue in terms of a written English language examination, it may be convenient to deal with them all in a single discussion session.

A comprehension on marriage will serve as the preliminary written exercise.

Comprehension and analysis

Read the following passage, and answer the questions that follow. You are advised to spend about one and a half hours on this exercise.

The most neurotic, the most difficult marriages, those with a lot of anger and frustration, are not those that dissolve most easily. In fact, outwardly bad marriages often last till death. It is the easy marriages, those with less pathology, that often separate so smoothly they scarcely seem to have been joined.

5   In fact, marriage until death seems an absurd route to choose for an easy life. An absurd route to choose for other goals – not necessary for sex, indeed in the long term inimical to it; very difficult for equal and mutual growth; deep relationships are quite possible outside it (one of the messages of Ingmar Bergman's *Scenes from a Marriage* was that the couple could only be genuine friends once they were apart. Only

10   then did they understand each other). Indeed, one quite possible explanation of the state of marriage today is that a great many people are entering it who are quite unsuitable to something so strenuous. A hundred years ago far fewer people were able to marry, largely because of their financial situation. About one-third of women under 44, for example, were not married in the Victorian era. Today about 95 per cent of

15   males and females have been married by the time they reach 45.

         What then is the point of the monogamous marriage till death? Guygenbuhl-Craig, the Swiss Jungian psychiatrist who made all these observations, derived the facts from the married people he treated in his practice. In his book *Marriage – Dead or Alive*, he looks at the archetypal marriage, that of Hera and Zeus. To the Greeks, this

20   was marriage. It was extremely stormy – usually about Zeus's incessant infidelity (though Hera was by no means faithful herself). At one time Hera tied Zeus up so completely that helpers from Tartarus had to free him. At another, he had her hung from the rafters of heaven. She was furiously jealous and would exact appalling revenge against his lovers. When he seduced Io, Hero turned her into a cow. This

25   wasn't enough, so she loosed upon Io a gadfly, a gigantic insect whose stings drove her mad. In complete panic, raving with fear, Io as cow raced through large parts of the world. Many wives have longed for such powers.

         This myth holds a clue to what marriage is about. It is about the Jungian view of salvation.

30   Salvation is distinct from well-being. Well-being means comfort, freedom from anxiety, sexual relief, companionship. Salvation has to do with the meaning of life far beyond comfort. It is about facing up to suffering and death. Jungians have a word to describe the search for salvation – 'individuation'. Guygenbuhl-Craig says that individuation can be described exactly, in detail. This is not true. It is a mystical

35   concept which is rather fuzzy and that is its strength. It can only be described in terms of the kind of things it involves, and by reference to myth and metaphor. It means not just finding out about, but working through, the forces in our subconscious: in a man,

the powerful aspects of the feminine which are part of him; in a woman, the active
masculine aspects; dark forces of destruction and cruelty which are also part of our
40 natures. This last is particularly difficult, and all ages try and avoid it (putting it on to
the devil, for instance, or, like us, on upbringing or social forces or 'capitalism',
'communism'). This process is, in fairy stories, a journey. But individuation is both the
journey and the goal – the process of working through the self and the achieved
reconciliation. It is like the life of Christ, where the life and its end were together the
45 message.
       Marriage till death is a pathway to salvation, a process of individuation. Because there
is no avenue of escape it is an extremely unusual path. Here it resembles the strictest of
enclosed medieval orders, or the vocation of a hermit. 'In this partially uplifting, partially
tormenting evasionlessness lies the specific character of this path.' It is absurd to expect
50 that marriage should be 'happy'. It is the way of salvation, and in myth the road to
heaven leads through hell. Because it is a way of salvation, marriage is an endless series
of exalted high feelings and deep low ones, a continuous belt of ups and downs. It has
happy moments of course, many of them, but also suffering and sacrifices.
       Sacrifice always plays a major role in the myths of salvation. It is true that with
55 Abraham and Isaac, God accepted a goat, but many myths have a tendency to
comfort. The point was that Abraham had to be ready to sacrifice. In Christianity, the
central myth of the last 2,000 years, sacrifice is cardinal. In any road to salvation there
is a profound need to sacrifice oneself, a feeling one should pay the price. It goes
without saying – you have only to look – that great sacrifices are demanded by
60 marriage. The long-term confrontation of marriage is only possible if one or both
partners renounce something important. This sacrifice is necessary to the personality.
It is quite wrong for friends or therapists to say no one should have to go on giving
affection to someone cold, no one should have to make such sacrifices. That situation
is the marriage. Their sympathy is misplaced. Dante crossed hell, but he reached
65 heaven. The successful marriage, the endured marriage, leads to the deepest kind of
existential satisfaction.

                                                                        Jonathan Gathorne-Hardy

Note: Your answers should be *in your own words* as far as possible.

a Consider the meaning of the sentence 'it is the easy . . . seem to have
been joined'. (lines 3–4)   *(3 marks)*

b Explain, in your own words, what the writer means by saying
'marriage until death seems an absurd route to choose for an easy life'.
(line 5)   *(4 marks)*

c Why do you think the writer mentions the myth of Hera
and Zeus?   *(4 marks)*

d What do you understand by the term 'individuation'?   *(5 marks)*

e Consider the significance of the references to: (i) the devil and (ii) the
life of Christ.   *(6 marks)*

f What do you think that the writer means by saying that marriage
'resembles the strictest of enclosed medieval orders, or the vocation of
a hermit'? (lines 47–48)   *(5 marks)*

g Why is the 'sympathy' of 'friends or therapists' in the final paragraph
'misplaced', according to the writer?   *(5 marks)*

h Comment on the view of marriage expressed in the last
paragraphs.   *(8 marks)*

i Comment on the effectiveness of the author's prose style in this
passage, looking in detail at his language and syntax.   *(10 marks)*

                                                                 (50 marks total)

Youth

A discussion of the theme of youth may usefully take in youth culture. Here are some forms of preparation:

A history of post-war fashions and ideologies amongst young people might provide an enjoyable project to undertake.

A more time-consuming but more creative approach to youth culture would be for a group of students to present a history of rock music since the mid-50s. A cassette could be prepared, illustrating the changes in popular music, to be accompanied by an analysis of the movements and trends in fashion and philosophy which went with these musical styles. Different students might perhaps work on different eras. A strict time limit must be established at the outset, however, if this project is not to last for ever! The following books might be useful for research into the music and movements of the 1950s and 1960s:

Colin, Nic, *Awopbopalubopalopbamboom: Pop from the Beginning*, Paladin, 1970

Gillett, Charlie, *The Sound of the City: The Rise of Rock and Roll*, Souvenir Press, 1983

Melley, Goerge, *Revolt Into Style: The Pop Arts in Britain*, Penguin, 1970

More formal discussion might take in such questions as inner-city riots, the effects of unemployment on young people, or, on a more personal level, young people's experiences of the 'generation gap' and the problems of adolescence. Five books which deal with these issues through the eyes of teenagers are the following:

Cashmore, E. Ellis, *No Future: Youth and Society*, Gower, 1985

Everett, Peter, *You'll Never Be 16 Again: An Illustrated History of the British Teenager*, BBC, 1986

Fisher, Susie and Holder, Susan, *Too Much Too Young?*, Pan Books, 1981

Lawton, Anthony, *Parents and Teenagers*, Allen and Unwin, 1985

McCormack, Mary, *The Generation Gap: the view from both sides*, Constable, 1985

The family

Any discussion of the family will inevitably enable you to talk from personal experience. The theme can be considered purely on a personal level, without any prior preparation, dealing with such questions as:

- What is the best age at which to marry?
- Should marriage be a lifelong commitment?
- Under what circumstances should partners consider divorce?
- Are extra-marital affairs ever right?
- Should both husbands and wives work if they have young children?
- Should children be brought up in a strict or a liberal family environment?

Research can again be useful to back up discussion of the family. It may be interesting to look up comparative divorce statistics, and statistics of the ages at which men and women married in different eras and areas. More detailed research could be undertaken on such subjects as alternative methods of child rearing (such as the Israeli Kibbutz system) and differing concepts of marriage in different countries. The following books may be of interest:

Bernard, Jessie, *The Future of Parenthood*, Calder and Boyars, 1975

Cleese, John and Skinner, Robin, *Families and How to Survive Them*, Methuen, 1993

Gathorne-Hardy, Jonathan, *Love, Sex, Marriage and Divorce*, Jonathan Cape, 1981

Khavari, Khalid A. and Khavari, Sue Williston, *Creating a Successful Family*, One World, 1989

Old age

Old age is becoming an increasing social problem in Western society, and, once again, research will considerably aid discussion. An illuminating exercise would be to compare the numbers of people over retirement age in Europe with those under school-leaving age in Latin America or other areas of the Third World. A discussion of the significance of these statistics would provide a useful introduction to the problem.

Further research could be undertaken into such matters as the National Health Service provisions and services for old people, methods of preparing people for retirement, and the problem of senility.

A more personal response to growing old might be evoked from reading stories about old people, such as 'Uncle Ernest', in Alan Sillitoe's *The Loneliness of the Long-Distance Runner* (Granada, 1985) or listening to songs such as 'Bookends' (and the accompanying 'Voices of Old People') from Simon and Garfunkel's *Bookends* album (CBS, 1968). A collection of stories and extracts about old people is to be found in a book called *Old Age*, in the Routledge and Kegan Paul *Themes* series, published in 1972. Books of general interest on the theme are as follows:

Greengross, Sally (ed.), *Ageing, an Adventure in Living*, Condor, 1985

Hellie Huyck, Margaret, *Growing Old: Things you Need to Know About Ageing*, Prentice Hall, 1974

Hobman, David (ed.), *The Social Challenge of Ageing*, Croom Helm, 1978

Young, Michael and Schuller, Tom, *Life After Work: The Arrival of the Ageless Society*, Harper Collins, 1991

Essay titles

a   Can 'teenage culture' be properly called culture at all?

b   'Fashion dictates the way we live.'

c   Is there a 'generation gap'?

d   Do you agree that personal happiness is best found in long–term relationships?

e   Do you think that marriage will survive as a social institution in the 21st century? If it does not, will it matter?

f   It used to be said that it was a woman's business to get married as soon as possible, and a man's to keep unmarried as long as he could. Is this a fair view of marriage?

g   The duties, responsibilities and pleasures of the family.

h   In the early years of the 21st century, there will be an increasing number of old people in Europe. What problems do you think this will cause and how would you tackle them?

i We do not respect the old; they are no longer wise.

j How will we cope with the problems of living to an average age of 100 years?

Further advice on writing: preparing for the exam

Writing at Advanced level in English language ought to be a reasonably stimulating and enjoyable experience. It should combine intellectual rigour and creativity, and practice in writing should enhance the precision and accuracy of your expression. Let us end the language section of this book with a few concluding observations and suggestions about English language writing in general, and preparation for an exam in particular.

Whatever question you choose for continuous writing in exam conditions, you will be marked according to three essential criteria: content, presentation and expression. The quality of ideas, information and/or imagination which you display, in other words the content of your writing, is of absolutely prime importance. It is to be hoped that the discussion and analysis and subsequent essay practice provided in this book will help with the content of your essays. The essay you write in the examination must also be well presented, in other words clearly and effectively structured and paragraphed, as the first two chapters stress. Thirdly, it must be effectively and accurately written.

The examiner will hope to find fluency and clarity, and ideally vividness of expression, in your writing. He or she will also look for formal accuracy, which means correct spelling, a suitable register and accurate sentence structure and punctuation. Since professional writers frequently break the rules and write ungrammatically for effect, this may seem over-formal. James Joyce, after all, avoided punctuation altogether in the last 60 pages of his masterpiece, *Ulysses*, and used his own method of indicating dialogue when he *did* punctuate. The justification is, of course, that you have to prove that you can apply the rules accurately before you are allowed to break them!

You must, therefore, work at the formal accuracy of your writing. You must try to ensure that you always write grammatically accurate sentences. Every sentence you write must be a complete statement, with subject(s) (noun or pronoun) and finite verb(s) (verb(s) with a past, present or future tense). You must try to punctuate as accurately as possible. Commas are a particular problem for most people, and it might be a good idea to learn and practise the rules for the use of commas. Dialogue is notoriously difficult to punctuate accurately, and you must make sure that you always separate the actual spoken words from the verbs of saying (she said, she shouted, etc.) with punctuation marks. Apostrophes are frequently left out or misused, and you should make sure that you are confident about their use, and check, when you have finished writing, that you have put them in correctly. The semicolon is a sophistication of punctuation which it might be worth your while to master.

Spelling is a particular problem for some people. There are some words (like argument, tragedy, 'alot' for 'a lot', 'infact' for 'in fact') which are extremely commonly misspelt. If your spelling tends to be a bit shaky, it would be a good idea to write down, in a small notebook, correct versions of words you have spelt wrongly in written work, and reread the correct spellings frequently. Only by seeing how words *look* will you imprint the correct version on your memory. However, you should not allow uncertainty about the spelling of difficult words to inhibit you from using them (as long as you are certain of their meaning!). You will be penalised for misspelling common words, but not for attempting more unusual ones. The most important requirement is for you to create a sense of personal engagement in what you are writing, and attempt to write as expressively as you can.

Finally, a word about timing. In all examinations, timing is crucial. When you have two quite different exercises on the same exam paper (continuous writing and summary skills, for example), it might be best to decide the order in which you are going to tackle the questions before you go into the exam room. A case can be made, on the paper referred to above, for starting with the summary exercise, on the grounds that it is easier to wind up an essay in a hurry than a summary. In a comprehension exercise, it might be best to leave questions which carry few marks till last, unless you are confident that you can answer them quickly.

With regular practice, there is every chance that your writing will improve, as long as you learn from your mistakes.

13 Literary Style

In this chapter, we will look at the basic figures of speech which writers have been using for thousands of years to give special vividness and resonance to their writing. There is, in fact, a considerable range of literary devices used by writers for particular effects. What we are concerned with here, however, is the small number of figures of sound and meaning which almost anyone with any literary (or even, for that matter, sub-literary) pretensions is likely to draw on from time to time, to give their writing added life and sparkle.

Poets in particular tend to make frequent use of these devices, and an understanding of how the basic figures of speech work is essential for anyone who is attempting to analyse poetry. Journalists and writers of prose fiction tend to use them frequently as well, and any exam question calling for an analysis of a writer's style, or the ways in which a writer achieves his or her effects, is likely to necessitate analysing imagery and figures of sound.

In your personal writing also you may find an awareness of these devices useful. If you decide to write a short story, or a poem, or a descriptive piece, you may be able to draw on your understanding of the effectiveness of similes, metaphors, alliteration and so on, in order to make your own writing more vivid and effective. Even tabloid journalists use some of these devices (if not particularly subtly!), and in an exercise requiring you to produce a piece of writing in the style of a tabloid newspaper, you can draw on what you have learned in this chapter.

The main techniques are explained and illustrated first, and then passages from works of literature by three modern writers are offered for further exploration.

Figures of meaning (or imagery)

Simile

A comparison between two distinctly differing things indicated by the word 'like' or 'as':

> e.g.   Sometimes I might get drunk,
> Walk like a duck and smell like a skunk.

Bob Dylan (*I Shall Be Free*)

The child was like ice in her womb.

D.H. Lawrence (*Odour of Chrysanthemums*)

Comparisons are used to clarify ideas by appealing to our imagination. The similes in the Bob Dylan song appeal directly to our senses, creating a vivid momentary picture in our mind's eye. The line from the D.H. Lawrence story also creates a powerful sense impression, of extreme physical coldness, capturing the mother's emotional coldness towards the baby inside her, far more vividly than any literal explanation could.

Metaphor

A direct statement of identity between two distinctly different things, *without* using 'like' or 'as':

> e.g.   But at my back I always hear
> Time's wingèd chariot hurrying near;
> And yonder all before us lie
> Deserts of vast eternity.

Andrew Marvell (*To his Coy Mistress*)

> Life's a long song,
> But the tune
> Ends too soon
> For us all.

Ian Anderson (*Life's a Long Song*)

The pair of metaphors in the Marvell extract heighten, and make more imaginatively compelling, the contrast between the intensity and brevity of earthly life, and the infinite nothingness of death. By comparing the rapid movement of earthly time with a 'winged chariot hurrying near', a powerful sense of speed and urgency is created, and this forms a vivid contrast with the impression of everlasting barrenness captured by the metaphor of 'deserts'. The images are largely visual. The idea of the shortness of life is also suggested in the lines from the Ian Anderson song, though here the metaphorical comparison of life with a song which 'ends too soon' has a direct, non-visual appeal.

Personification

An inanimate object or an abstract concept is spoken of as though it were endowed with life or with human attributes or feelings:

> e.g.   The yellow fog that rubs its back upon the window-panes

T.S. Eliot (*The Love Song of J. Alfred Prufrock*)

> Pale flakes with fingering stealth come feeling for our faces

Wilfred Owen (*Exposure*)

In these two images, fog and snow are given the force of living presences by the use of personification. A gentle, quite benign quality is given to Eliot's 'yellow fog' by the comparison with a living creature, whereas

Owen's 'pale flakes', though also gentle, are made to seem much more sinister and malign, by the comparison with human fingers feeling for the faces of the soldiers in a First-World-War trench.

Though not strictly personification according to the conventional definition, the attribution of human qualities to non-human living creatures has much the same effect:

> e.g.   . . . the hens twitch and grieve for their tea-soaked sops
>
> Dylan Thomas (*Under Milk Wood*)

Thomas's description of the hens in terms of human beings in a state of nervous anxiety might well be considered to be an example of personification.

Symbol

A word, object, incident or situation which is both literal and which signifies something beyond itself. Some symbols are widely recognised in Western culture, for example, the peacock as a symbol of pride and vanity, the eagle as a symbol of heroic endeavour. Leonard Cohen uses the former in this symbolic sense in *Story of Isaac*, a song about the dangers of self-glorification, the final line of which is:

> The peacock spreads his fan.

Other symbols are particular to a writer and work. Charles Dickens' *Great Expectations* is considered to be rich in symbolism. The manipulative lawyer, Jaggers, for instance, is frequently described washing his hands after returning from court, or smelling of soap. He literally *does* wash his hands, but the physical action can be seen as a symbol of his need to distance himself from the corrupting effects of the criminal world and the legal system that is a part of his daily life.

Mr Jaggers in David Lean's film of
Great Expectations, 1946

Whether or not symbolism is present in a work depends on personal interpretation: sometimes it is obvious, sometimes less so.

Figures of sound

Alliteration

The repetition of consonants in a sequence of words:

> e.g. Only the stuttering *r*ifles' *r*apid *r*attle
> Can patter out their hasty orisons.

> > Wilfred Owen (*Anthem for Doomed Youth*)

Figures of sound produce sound colouring, designed to add emphasis to ideas and emotions, and to create and reinforce tone and feeling. The lines from *Anthem for Doomed Youth* capture the sound and rapidity of rifle fire in wartime, an effect which is created partly by the repeated, relatively harsh 'r' consonant. The line from *Exposure* by the same poet, quoted in the section on personification ('Pale flakes with fingering stealth come feeling for our faces') also employs alliteration. The effect here is quite the opposite. The repeated soft 'f' sounds help to capture a sense impression of the gentle, slow, unremitting, deathly penetration of snowflakes in a trench in wartime, killing the soldiers who are exposed to them more slowly, but more certainly, than bullets.

Sibilants

Alliteration using 's' sounds:

> e.g. And as he *s*lowly drew up, *s*nake-easing hi*s s*houlders

> > D.H. Lawrence (*Snake*)

The sound and motion of an uncoiling snake, lithe and leisurely and hissing, is here captured partly by the use of repeated 's' sounds.

Assonance

The repetition of vowel sounds in a sequence of words:

> e.g. H*ea*ps of entangled w*ee*ds that sl*ow*ly fl*oa*t

> > George Crabbe (*Peter Grimes*)

The sound colouring of a passage is largely dependent on the juxtaposition of vowel sounds. If a particular vowel sound is repeated, it gains special emphasis, and tends, therefore, to be the dominant sound. In Crabbe's poem *Peter Grimes*, heaps of weeds in the water impede the movement of Peter's boat, and the sense of this is enhanced, in the line quoted, by the two pairs of identical vowel sounds. Both are long vowels, helping to emphasise the impression of slow, meandering movement of the 'heaps of . . . weeds'; the repeated long 'o' sound at the end of the line creates an especially heavy, sombre effect. The sentence from the D.H. Lawrence story, quoted in the section on simile ('The child was like ice in her womb'), also employs assonance. The key word 'ice' receives great emphasis from the repetition of the long 'i' sound in the words 'child' and 'like', investing the line with an 'icy' feel. The chilling effect of the line is enhanced still further by the dark, heavy sound of the final word, 'womb'. In the lines from *Anthem for Doomed Youth*, quoted above to illustrate alliteration ('Only the stuttering rifles' rapid rattle/Can patter out their hasty orisons'), assonance is also used, in the words 'rapid rattle/Can patter', the sharp, hard, short 'a' sounds adding to the violent, mechanical impression of rapid gunfire.

A couple of further points should have emerged from this discussion. Firstly, it is important to be aware that assonance is a matter of the repetition of vowel *sounds*, not merely the vowels themselves. The phrases 'brightly lit', for instance, is not an assonantal phrase, because the first 'i' sound is long and the second is short, and therefore the vowel sound is different. Secondly, it is possible to make broad generalisations about the *quality* or *effect* of vowel sounds. Some vowel sounds tend to create a light sound impression, especially the short 'i' vowel sound (as in the word 'fin'), while the long 'i' vowel sound (as in the word 'fight') often creates an impression of intensity. The long 'e' vowel sound also sometimes creates an impression of intensity, as in the words 'fear' and 'fleet'. The longer 'o' and 'u' vowel sounds tend to create a heavier, more sombre sound impression, as in the words 'foul' and 'flow'. The short 'a' vowel sound (as in the word 'flat') often creates a rather harsh sound impression.

Onomatopoeia

A word, or sequence of words, whose sound seems to resemble the sound it denotes:

> e.g.   And *droning* shells *burst* with a *hollow bang*.
>
> Siegfried Sassoon (*The Redeemer*)

The line is intended to capture the sound of shells in flight and exploding. Onomatopoeia is also used in the lines from *Anthem for Doomed Youth*, in the word 'stuttering' and the phrase 'rapid rattle/Can patter', where the assonance, discussed earlier, together with direct onomatopoeia in the words 'rattle' and 'patter', gives the whole phrase an onomatopoeic effect.

Analysing literary style in essays on literature set texts

Without a thorough understanding of the literary techniques explored in this chapter, it is likely to be difficult to write very convincing answers on poetry and blank-verse drama texts. Questions on poetry and poetic drama sometimes explicitly ask for an analysis of literary style, with questions like 'analyse the language and imagery' of a scene from a Shakespeare play, or 'how effectively do language, structure and imagery convey feeling?' in a group of sonnets. Any question which requires analysis of 'language' in poetry is likely to be answered fully *only* if reference is made to different kinds of imagery and figures of sound. Often, even when the question is less specifically about style, for instance, if it asked you to 'explain in detail why you have enjoyed' a group of poems, or 'how are the ideas conveyed' in a poetry collection, it would be difficult to answer it properly without analysing specific literary devices.

In prose texts, also, questions are sometimes specifically asked about style, such as 'analyse the writing techniques' in a section of a novel. A satisfactory answer to such a question is likely to include the analysis of figures of sound and meaning. As with poetry, answers to prose text questions which are not specifically about style can sometimes usefully include reference to a writer's uses of imagery and figures of sound. For example, a question might be set on the different ways in which a novelist 'conveys the immediacy' of a character's 'experience' in a section of a novel, or it might ask for an assessment of 'how successful' a writer is in 'bringing her autobiographical material to life'. Your essay is likely to be more varied and effective if you include a paragraph on the use of similes or onomatopoeia or whatever the writer's favourite stylistic devices are.

Passages for literary analysis

Let us now see how these techniques can be used by a skilful writer for atmospheric and dramatic effect.

The Birds

The passages which follow are from *The Birds*, a short story by Daphne du Maurier. *The Birds* is a horror story (which was freely adapted by Alfred Hitchcock for his famous film). It explores the reactions of a Cornish farm labourer, Nat Hocken, and his family and neighbours, to regular, concerted attacks on people and their homes by birds, whose aim, as the story gradually reveals, is the destruction of the human race!

The first three passages illustrate the use of literary devices to create atmosphere: the first, of the restless movement and the abnormality of the birds' behaviour, at the beginning of the story: the second, of cold and desolation; and the third, of a more relaxed atmosphere, as normality seems to have returned. The fourth passage is both atmospheric and dramatic, as Nat watches the birds mass over the sea for an attack, and the final passage is a climactic description of birds swooping down on Nat as he rushes across the fields towards his home.

1

Black and white, jackdaw and gull, mingled in strange partnership, seeking some sort of liberation, never satisfied, never still. Flocks of starlings, rustling like silk, flew to fresh pasture, driven by the same necessity of movement, and the smaller birds, the finches and the larks, scattered from tree to hedge as if compelled. Nat watched them, and he watched the sea birds, too. Down in the bay they waited for the tide. They had more patience. Oyster-catchers, redshank, sanderling and curlew watched by the water's edge; as the slow sea sucked at the shore and then withdrew, leaving the strip of seaweed bare and the shingle churned, the sea birds raced and ran upon the beaches. Then that same impulse to flight seized upon them too. Crying, whistling, calling, they skimmed the placid sea and left the shore. Make haste, make speed, hurry and begone; yet where, and to what purpose? The restless urge of autumn, unsatisfying, sad, had put a spell upon them and they must flock, and wheel, and cry; they must spill themselves of motion before winter came.

2

The sky was hard and leaden, and the brown hills that had gleamed in the sun the day before looked dark and bare. The east wind, like a razor, stripped the trees, and the leaves, crackling and dry, shivered and scattered with the wind's blast. Nat stubbed the earth with his boot. It was frozen hard. He had never known a change so swift and sudden. Black winter had descended in a single night.

3

She said nothing of the birds. She began to push and struggle with another little girl. The bus came ambling up the hill. Nat saw her on to it, then turned and walked back towards the farm. It was not his day for work, but he wanted to satisfy himself that all was well. Jim, the cowman, was clattering in the yard.

4

He got up and went out of the back door and stood in the garden, looking down towards the sea. There had been no sun all day, and now, at barely three o'clock, a kind of darkness had already come, the sky sullen, heavy, colourless like salt. He could hear the vicious sea drumming on the rocks. He walked down the path, half way to the beach. And then he stopped. He could see the tide had turned. The rock that had shown in mid-morning was now covered, but it was not the sea that held his eyes. The gulls had risen. They were circling, hundreds of them, thousands of them, lifting their wings against the wind. It was the gulls that made the darkening of the sky. And they were silent. They made not a sound. They just went on soaring and circling, rising, falling, trying their strength against the wind.

5

As he jumped the stile he heard the whirr of wings. A black-backed gull dived down at him from the sky, missed, swerved in flight, and rose to dive again. In a moment it was joined by others, six, seven, a dozen, black-backed and herring mixed. Nat dropped his hoe. The hoe was useless. Covering his head with his arms he ran towards the cottage. They kept coming at him from the air, silent save for the beating wings. The terrible, fluttering wings. He could feel the blood on his hands, his wrists, his neck. Each stab of a swooping beak tore his flesh. If only he could keep them from his eyes. Nothing else mattered. He must keep them from his eyes. They had not learnt yet how to cling to a shoulder, how to rip clothing, how to dive in a mass upon the head, upon the body. But with each dive, with each attack, they became bolder. And they had no thought for themselves. When they dived low and missed, they crashed, bruised and broken, on the ground. As Nat ran he stumbled, kicking their spent bodies in front of him. He found the door, he hammered upon it with his bleeding hands. Because of the boarded windows no light shone. Everything was dark. 'Let me in,' he shouted, 'it's Nat. Let me in.' He shouted loud to make himself heard above the whirr of the gulls' wings. Then he saw the gannet, poised for the dive, above him in the sky. The gulls circled, retired, soared, one with another, against the wind. Only the gannet remained. One single gannet, above him in the sky. The wings folded suddenly to its body. It dropped, like a stone. Nat screamed, and the door opened. He stumbled across the threshold, and his wife threw her weight against the door. They heard the thud of the gannet as it fell.

Daphne du Maurier

Analysis of The Birds passages

Let us look in detail at passage 1, and see how Daphne du Maurier creates atmosphere in the extract through figures of meaning and sound, and through the rhythm of her prose.

The predominant consonant in the first two sentences is 's', the sibilants emphasising the restlessness and nervous energy of the birds. The simile 'rustling like silk' in the second sentence reinforces this sensation. The sibilants here, together with the simile, add to the onomatopoeic effect of 'rustling'. The sentence as a whole is broken up into a sequence of short phrases, which in itself adds to the sense of agitation. This is then followed by three short, fairly dramatic sentences, the last of which consists of only four words, which reinforces the sense of tense expectancy.

In the long sixth sentence, sibilants again feature prominently. The sound of the words is combined with the rhythm of the prose to suggest an impression of the sound and movement of the sea: the separated monosyllables of 'the slow sea sucked' create a slow rhythm which is enhanced by the 's' consonants and the long, heavy vowel sounds; but the rhythm of 'at the shore and then withdrew' is faster, and the whole effect is to suggest the movement of a wave itself, rolling in and rushing out again. Similarly, rhythm and sound combine in the last part of the sentence, the alliteration of 'raced and ran' adding emphasis to the rushing rhythm of the words.

Onomatopoeia is used again in the eighth sentence, in the word 'whistling', and the effect is enhanced by the assonance in 'whistling . . . skimmed'. The sea is here personified in the phrase 'the placid sea', and personification is used again in the final sentence, as 'autumn' is described as putting 'a spell upon' the birds, with its 'restless urge'. The last two sentences also display the technique of rhetorical repetition, in the phrases 'Make haste, make speed' and 'they must flock . . . they must spill', adding again to the intensity of the writing, and the sense of restlessness and agitation which du Maurier is trying to convey.

Some of the sound colouring and the rhythmic movement of this passage are, in fact, too subtle for simple analysis in terms of recognisable techniques to be possible. The extent to which the use of the techniques analysed is deliberate, and how much of it is instinctive is, of course, impossible to tell.

Now attempt a similar analysis of the other four passages from *The Birds*. You should comment on the syntax as well as on the figures of speech.

The Village By The Sea

In her novel *The Village By The Sea*, the Indian writer Anita Desai focuses on a small fishing village in rural India, and the struggle of a poor family to come to terms with the changes which are overtaking the ancient, settled ways of village life. Part of her purpose in writing the novel was to capture for the reader a sense of the atmosphere of a place and a lifestyle which is disappearing.

The two extracts which follow are from the first three pages of the novel. Lila, a teenage Hindu girl from the village, is described going down to the seashore in the early morning.

The writing is highly atmospheric and evocative. Try to define the atmosphere, and explain how Anita Desai creates it.

1

When she came to the edge of the sea, she lifted the folds of her sari and tucked them up at her waist, then waded out into the waves that came rushing up over her feet and swirling about her ankles in creamy foam. She waded in till she came to a cluster of three rocks. One of them was daubed with red and white powder. It was the sacred rock, a kind of temple in the sea. At high tide it would be inundated, but now, at low tide, it could be freshly consecrated. Lila took the flowers from her basket and scattered them about the rock, then folded her hands and bowed.

Just then the sun lifted up over the coconut palms in a line along the beach and sent long slanting rays over the silvery sand to touch her on the back of her head. Enjoying their warmth, she stayed bowed for a little while, her feet still in the cold, whispering waves. The sun lit up the pink and mauve waves with sparkles. Far out, stretched along the horizon, was the fishing fleet that had been out all night, the sails like white wings, or fins, lifting out of the sea. They were anchored and still; they would not return before sundown.

2

The morning light was still soft as it filtered through the web of palm leaves, and swirls of blue wood-smoke rose from fires in hidden huts and mingled with it. Dew still lay on the rough grass and made the spider webs glitter. These webs were small and thickly matted and stretched across the grass, each with a hole in the centre to trap passing insects. Butterflies flew up out of the tussocks and bushes of wild flowers – large zebra-striped ones with a faint tinge of blue to their wings, showy black ones with scarlet-tipped wings, and little sulphur-yellow ones that fluttered about in twos and threes.

Then there were all the birds flying out of the shadowy, soft-needled casuarina trees and the thick jungle of pandanus, singing and calling and whistling louder than at any other time of the day. Flute-voiced drongoes swooped and cut through the air like dazzling knives that reflected the sun and glinted blue-black, and pert little magpie robins frisked and flirted their tails as they hopped on the dewy grass, snatching at insects before they tumbled into the spider's traps. Pairs of crested bul-buls sang from the branches. A single crow-pheasant, invisible, called out 'coop-coop-coop' in its deep, bogey-man voice from under a bush, and a pigeon's voice cooed and gurgled on and on. It was the voice of the village Thul as much as the roar of the waves and the wind in the palms. It seemed to tell Lila to be calm and happy and all would be well and all would be just as it was before.

Anita Desai

Death

Not only fiction and poetry use figurative language, of course. It can be equally suitable for some kinds of factual writing. We will conclude this discussion of style by looking at a piece by the American novelist, essayist and journalist, Norman Mailer, which describes an actual event. It is a description of a world championship boxing match which took place in the early 1960s, between Emile Griffith, the challenger, and Benny Paret, who was the current world champion, a fight which had a tragic ending.

The rage in Emile Griffith was extreme. I was at the fight that night. I had never seen a fight like it. It was scheduled for 15 rounds, but they fought without stopping from the bell which began the round to the bell which ended it, and then they fought after the bell, sometimes for as much as 15 seconds before the referee could force them apart.

Paret was a Cuban, a proud club fighter who had become welterweight champion because of his unusual ability to take a punch. His style of fighting was to take three punches to the head in order to give back two. At the end of ten rounds, he would still be bouncing, his opponent would have a headache. But in the last two years, over the 15-round fights, he had started to take some bad maulings.

This fight had its turns. Griffith won most of the early rounds, but Paret knocked Griffith down in the sixth. Griffith had trouble getting up, but made it, came alive and was dominating Paret again before the round was over. Then Paret began to wilt. In the middle of the eighth round, after a clubbing punch had turned his back to Griffith, Paret walked three disgusted steps away, showing his hindquarters. For a champion he took much too long to turn back around. It was the first hint of weakness Paret had ever shown, and it must have inspired a particular shame, because he fought the rest of the fight as if he were seeking to demonstrate that he could take more punishment than any man alive. In the 12th, Griffith caught him. Paret got trapped in a corner. Trying to duck away, his left arm and his head became tangled on the wrong side of the top rope. Griffith was in like a cat ready to rip the life out of a huge boxed rat. He hit him 18 right hands in a row, an act which took perhaps three or four seconds, Griffith making a pent-up whimpering sound all the while he attacked, the right hand whipping like a piston rod which had broken through the crankcase, or like a baseball bat demolishing a pumpkin. I was sitting in the second row of that corner – they were not ten feet away from me – and like everybody else, I was hypnotised. I had never seen one man hit another so hard and so many times. Over the referee's face came a look of woe as if some spasm had passed its way through him, and then he leaped on Griffith to pull him away. It was the act of a brave man. Griffith was uncontrollable. His trainer leaped into the ring, his manager, his cut man, there were four people holding Griffith, but he was off on an orgy, he had left the Garden[1], he was back on a hoodlum's street. If he had been able to break loose from his handlers and the referee, he would have jumped Paret to the floor and whaled on him there.

And Paret? Paret died on his feet. As he took those 18 punches, something happened to everyone who was in psychic range of the event. Some part of his death reached out to us. One felt it hover in the air. He was still standing in the ropes, trapped as he had been before, he gave some little half-smile of regret, as if he were saying, 'I didn't know I was going to die just yet', and then, his head leaning back but still erect, his death came to breathe about him. He began to pass away. As he passed, so his limbs descended beneath him, and he sank slowly to the floor. He went down more slowly than any fighter had ever gone down, he went down like a large ship which turns on end and slides second by second into its grave. As he went down, the sound of Griffith's punches echoed in the mind like a heavy axe in the distance chopping into a wet log.

Paret lay on the ground, quivering gently, a small froth on his mouth. The house doctor jumped into the ring. He knelt. He pried Paret's eyelid open. He looked at the eyeball staring out. He let the lid snap shut. He reached into his satchel, took out a needle, jabbed Paret with a stimulant. Paret's back rose in a high arch. He writhed in real agony. They were calling him back from death. One wanted to cry out, 'Leave the man alone. Let him die'. But they saved Paret long enough to take him to a hospital where he lingered for days. He was in coma. He never came out of it. If he lived, he would have been a vegetable. His brain was smashed. But they held him in life for a week, they fed him chemicals, and made exploratory operations into his skull, and fed details of his condition to The Goat. And The Goat kicked clods of mud all over the

---

1 Madison Square Garden in New York.

place, and spoke harshly of prohibiting boxing. There was shock in the land. Children had seen the fight on television. There were editorials, gloomy forecasts that the Game was dead. The managers and the prize fighters got together. Gently in thick, depressed hypocrisies, they tried to defend their sport. They did not find it easy to explain that they shared an unstated view of life which was religious.

Norman Mailer

The immediate aftermath of the fight was that there was talk of charging Griffith with manslaughter, and Griffith vowed never to box again. A decade later he was still world champion.

Write a stylistic analysis of the passage. You should try to find three examples of each of the following: simile, metaphor, personification. You should discuss as fully as possible the effectiveness of each image. In addition, you should discuss at least one example of each of the four figures of sound analysed in this chapter, and make some comments on the syntax.

Bibliography

Brett, R.L., *An Introduction to English Studies*, Edward Arnold, 1976
Desai, Anita, *The Village By the Sea*, Penguin, 1982
du Maurier, Daphne, *The Birds and Other Stories*, Longman, 1980
Mailer, Norman, *The Presidential Papers*, Penguin, 1968

Literature Writing Skills

14 Preparing Literary Texts

The literature part of the language and literature course involves writing essays on six different literature texts, in an average of 45 minutes each. Up until 1990, students were not allowed to take their texts into the exam, which meant that quotations had to be learnt by heart. The exam is now 'open book', so that there is less of an emphasis on memorisation. This does not make it easier, however! It means that you are likely to be required to engage in a more precise and detailed exploration of the text than was the case before the exam became open book. It also means that the annotation and preparation of your texts becomes more important than ever, and this is the focus of the chapter. Let us look first at the choice of texts offered for AEB English in the context of the syllabus as a whole.

The range of literature texts

The AEB English syllabus is unique in combining language and literature study in a single A level. This makes it the most broad-based of all the A-level English syllabuses, which is reflected in the examination board's policy for choosing set texts. While the choice of set texts on the purely literature paper (Paper 3) is conventional in the range of literary genres from which it is drawn – poetry, play, novel and short stories – the second paper is very different. It is a language and literature paper in the fullest sense: not only is it divided equally between language (comprehension and analysis) and two literature set texts, but there is a deliberate overlap between language and literature in the choice of questions for comprehension and the choice of texts. The comprehension exercise invariably includes a question requiring stylistic analysis in one form or another, and the set text list is likely to include genres which are normally thought of as being outside the realms of literature: a collection of journalism, a work of cultural/social analysis, a set of television monologues, as well as other genres on the margins of literature: an autobiography or an anthology of essays, for example. When you combine the range of options for textual study with the options, on the purely language paper (Paper 1), for writing your own short story or poem, you have a course which is far from being compartmentalised into one half language study and the other half literature.

In reality, of course, the genres of writing themselves overlap. Maya Angelou's autobiographical account of her formative years, *I Know Why The Caged Bird Sings*, often reads like a novel in the way that the characters are brought to life, and Angelou's personal development is vividly unfolded through her interactions with these characters. The language in which the book is written is often highly emotionally charged and poetic. Alan Bennett's set of monologues, *Talking Heads*, has many of the hallmarks of a stage play: an unfolding sense of each of the talkers' limitations and weaknesses and their lack of understanding of themselves; a perfect ear for the nuances of actual speech, as the talkers recount their conversations. William Hazlitt's essays are all carefully crafted little works of art.

Analysing literature texts

The principal purpose of studying literature at A level (in addition to gaining a qualification) is to develop an appreciation of the depth and subtlety of a range of writers within a variety of genres and historical periods, and to develop skills of analysis which will enrich your reading in the future. Some students tend to dislike 'pulling books to pieces' and would prefer to just enjoy reading a text without hunting for deeper meaning. This is a pity. Exploring works of literature in depth *should* be a stimulating experience, and, particularly with 'difficult' works, the sense of discovery that comes with the dawning of understanding should be a pleasure in itself. Background reading can often be an invaluable aid to understanding. A knowledge of relevant facts about a writer's life and ideas, for instance, can often unearth 'hidden' meanings and depths in a text, and this ought to make your reading more enjoyable. Let us look at an example of how background information can bring a complicated text to life.

The Sisters in James Joyce's Dubliners

This is one of the most difficult texts on the entire syllabus. On first reading, with no 'clues' to go on, it is likely to seem impenetrable. You're waiting throughout the story for something to happen, and nothing does!

If you *have* got some clues, however, then literary criticism can come to resemble detective work. Once you've got a lead, then you can work through the text looking for more clues and slowly working on your case, until it all comes together. A theme will have emerged, and, along the way, if you're lucky, a little insight into human beings and the world!

The Sisters, then. The story focuses on a boy's feelings about an old Catholic priest who has befriended him and who has just died, after suffering from a series of strokes which have left him paralysed. But what's the point of it? On the surface, there doesn't seem to be much. You need some background: historical, and particularly biographical, in this case.

The Sisters is the opening story in a collection of short stories written and set in Dublin at the beginning of the 20th century. At that time, the Catholic church and priesthood in Ireland was treated with the greatest veneration, and exerted considerable influence over people's lives. The author, James Joyce, as a child, was a devout Catholic. He was educated in a strict Catholic (Jesuit) school, and in his childhood he had an ambition to become a priest. By the time he wrote the story, however, he had rejected religion and come to view the Irish priesthood as a reactionary force, keeping people in ignorance and superstition, rather than as a source of spiritual enlightenment. Joyce himself stated that his purpose in writing the *Dubliners* collection as a whole was to highlight the shortcomings of his own country and countrymen. In a letter to a publisher which he sent with the first draft of *Dubliners* he wrote: 'My intention was to write a chapter of the moral history of my country and I chose Dublin for the scene because that city seemed to me the centre of paralysis'. So he had come to despise the powerful Catholic priesthood and he had set out to portray the paralysis of Dublin life.

Let us follow these leads through the story and see if we can make any final sense of it. We will focus on the priest and the reactions of the boy and others towards him. Since only the last two pages are quoted here, you may wish to read the complete story first, before you read on. It can be found on page 266.

There are clues to be picked up from the beginning of the story. In the opening sentence, we are told that the priest is certain to die, after suffering a third stroke. The child, who is narrating the story, whispers the word 'paralysis' to himself, with obvious reference to the priest's condition. The boy lives with his uncle and aunt and, during a conversation between his uncle and a visitor at the house, we are told that the boy used to spend a lot of time with the priest, who 'taught him a great deal' and had 'a wish' for the boy himself to become a priest when he grew up. When he is alone again, the boy imagines seeing 'the heavy grey face of the paralytic'. For the second time, therefore, the priest is associated with paralysis. This is, of course, a physical condition, but knowing of Joyce's intention to present the 'paralysis' of Dublin life, it ought to alert us to the possibility of a deeper, symbolic significance in the choice of the word. In his bedroom, on the threshold of sleep, the boy feels that the face is following him, and it begins to 'confess to me in a murmuring voice'. A curious role reversal is occurring here: it is the priest's job to listen to confessions, not the other way round.

Next morning, the boy goes round to the priest's house and discovers a notice on the door announcing the death of 'Rev. James Flynn'. The boy pictures what he would have done now if the priest were still alive: he would have taken in some snuff to him, which would have 'aroused him from his stupefied doze'. He goes on to picture how the priest would have lifted the snuff to his nose, with his 'trembling hand', and how 'little clouds of smoke dribbled through his fingers over the front of his coat'.

The smoke with which Catholic priests are normally associated is the smoke of incense, which rises up to the church roof. *This* priest is associated with stupefaction and smoke that dribbles downwards. Is there some symbolism in this? (Or are we reading too much into it?!) The boy becomes guiltily aware that he is experiencing 'a sensation of freedom, as if I had been freed from something by his death'. It is surely strange that the *death* of the priest should be associated in the boy's mind with freedom. He reminds himself that the priest 'had taught me a good deal'. Then, for almost a page of text, he reveals *what* the priest had taught him. It turns out to be things like 'the meaning of the different ceremonies of the mass and the different vestments worn by the priest' and giving the boy tests on 'the responses of the mass which he had made me learn by heart'. It is all ritual and rote responses. Nowhere is there any reference to a spiritual dimension. The boy tries to recall his dream of the night just gone and it seems to him that in the dream 'I had been far away, in some land where the customs were strange'. It seems like a dream of escape.

That evening, his aunt takes the boy to visit the house where the priest lived, with his two sisters, Eliza and 'Nannie'. He goes to see the corpse. The dead priest is lying with his hands round 'a chalice' (the cup for communion wine, which, according to Catholic doctrine, becomes transformed into the actual blood of Christ during the communion service). In the boy's eyes, 'his face was very truculent'. Eliza is asked whether he died peacefully, and she replies, 'He had a beautiful death,' and a few moments later: 'No one would think he'd make such a beautiful corpse.' This strikes a jarring note with the boy's impression of the corpse. Then the two sisters talk about their feelings towards their brother. This is the ending of the story.

– Ah, poor James! said Eliza. He was no great trouble to us. You wouldn't hear him in the house any more than now. Still, I know he's gone and all to that . . .
– It's when it's all over that you'll miss him, said my aunt.
– I know that, said Eliza. I won't be bringing him his cup of beef tea any more, nor you, ma'am, sending him his snuff. Ah, poor James!
She stopped, as if she were communing with the past and then said shrewdly:
– Mind you, I noticed there was something queer coming over him latterly. Whenever I'd bring in his soup to him there I'd find him with his breviary fallen to the floor, lying back in the chair and his mouth open.
She laid a finger against her nose and frowned: then she continued:
– But still and all he kept on saying that before the summer was over he'd go out for a drive one fine day just to see the old house again where we were all born down in Irishtown and take me and Nannie with him.
If we could only get one of them new-fangled carriages that makes no noise that Father O'Rourke told him about – them with the rheumatic wheels – for the day cheap, he said, at Johnny Rush's over the way there and drive out the three of us together of a Sunday evening. He had his mind set on that . . . Poor James!
– The Lord have mercy on his soul! said my aunt.
Eliza took out her handkerchief and wiped her eyes with it. Then she put it back again in her pocket and gazed into the empty grate for some time without speaking.
– He was too scrupulous always, she said. The duties of the priesthood was too much for him. And then his life was, you might say, crossed.
– Yes, said my aunt. He was a disappointed man. You could see that.

A silence took possession of the little room and, under cover of it, I approached the table and tasted my sherry and then returned quietly to my chair in the corner. Eliza seemed to have fallen into a deep reverie. We waited respectfully for her to break the silence: and after a long pause she said slowly:
– It was that chalice he broke . . . That was the beginning of it. Of course, they say it was all right, that it contained nothing! I mean. But still . . . They say it was the boy's fault. But poor James was so nervous, God be merciful to him!
– And was that it? said my aunt. I heard something . . .
Eliza nodded.
– That affected his mind, she said. After that he began to mope by himself, talking to no one and wandering about by himself. So one night he was wanted for to go on a call and they couldn't find him anywhere. They looked high up and low down; and still they couldn't see a sight of him anywhere. So then the clerk suggested to try the chapel. So then they got the keys and opened the chapel and the clerk and Father O'Rourke and another priest that was there brought in a light for to look for him . . . And what do you think but there he was, sitting up by himself in the dark in his confession box, wide awake and laughing-like softly to himself?
She stopped suddenly as if to listen. I too listened; but there was no sound in the house: and I knew that the old priest was lying still in his coffin as we had seen him, solemn and truculent in death, an idle chalice on his breast.
Eliza resumed:
– Wide-awake and laughing-like to himself . . . So then, of course, when they saw that, that made them think that there was something gone wrong with him . . .

James Joyce

Now see if you can tease out how this ties together with the impressions of the priest already discussed, by working on these questions. Try to pick out what you think are the key quotations.

1 What is the significance of the priest's longing to return 'to see the old house again where we were born'?
2 How do Eliza and the boy's aunt feel about James Flynn's vocation for the priesthood?
3 What was it that 'affected his mind'?
4 What is the significance of the priest suffering a kind of nervous breakdown over dropping a chalice that 'contained nothing'?
5 What is the significance of the last 14 lines?

Here is a possible interpretation. The priest's thwarted urge to take a trip out 'to see the old house again where we were born' shows him in a rather pathetic light. He was incapable of making even the simplest practical arrangements. Perhaps it also shows a deep-seated urge to escape back to a simpler time, when he was a child, before the heavy responsibilities of the priesthood began to weigh him down. If this is the case, then it could link in with the *boy's* urge to escape, which reveals itself in his dream. Certainly, the priest's sister and the boy's aunt feel that he was unable to cope with the duties of the priesthood.

In the final passage of dialogue, Eliza talks about her brother's breakdown. What 'affected his mind' was an accidental breach of ritual, which seems to have assumed massively disproportionate importance in his mind, so that he was unable to recover from the shock of it. This exaggerated concern over the details of religious observance recalls the 'teaching' which he gave the boy earlier in the story, and seems to confirm that Joyce is portraying a religion obsessed with ritual and devoid of any real spiritual significance.

Eliza's final remarks again tie in with earlier details in the story. The 'truculent' expression on the face of the corpse was earlier described by Eliza as 'beautiful'; again the priest is described by the boy as 'solemn and truculent in death', and Eliza now treats the fact that her brother was found 'laughing' as proof, in the final words of the story, that 'there was something gone wrong with him'. It is surely a grim, joyless religion which portrays gloom as beautiful and laughter as unnatural. Perhaps the repeated reference to the empty, 'idle chalice' on the breast of the priest at the end is symbolic: an emblem of a ritualistic religion, emptied of any spiritual meaning?

So what does the portrayal of the priest and his sisters finally signify? Even without going into all this depth it is easy enough to see that the priest is portrayed as a pitiful, inadequate character, associated throughout the story with gloom, paralysis and death. This tells us a lot about a particular character, but does it tell us more than this? To make a convincing case that the story *is* more than just a portrayal of a pitiful individual, you *do* need to work out the significance of the priest and his sisters' religious ideas to show the kind of religion that is being revealed in the story. Only then will it fully make sense. Father Flynn then becomes, in his emotional and physical paralysis (at least according to this analysis), a symbol of the *spiritual* paralysis of Dublin's religious life.

Making notes on the texts

As was remarked at the beginning of this chapter, the 'open-book' nature of this exam makes textual annotation especially important. Not only can you take your texts into the exam, but you can write any notes you want in them. Any of the white space in the texts, including the blank pages, can be filled with notes. Some students attempt to abuse this opportunity, as will be discussed later. The kind of notes you make in the white space can make a big difference to your success in the exam.

Let us consider approaches to making notes on the actual pages of text. There are two basic ways of making notes during lessons. You can either write notes straight into the text, or you can make notes on a separate sheet of paper first. There are advantages to both.

Making notes on sheets of paper

Since space is obviously limited in the text, you are likely to make fuller notes if you write them on paper and keep them in files, rather than making your notes directly into the text. You won't have to think about whether you can squeeze detailed explanations into the space available in the margins of the text. Some of what you write down in lessons will be background information anyway, which, once assimilated, won't be needed in the text.

The disadvantage, of course, is that you will have to transfer some of the notes you've made on paper into the text. Even this has its advantages:

- reading through your notes after a lesson is the best way of testing your understanding;
- you can then prune what you've written, and jot down the essentials into the text;
- you then have a working text for the exam.

In the exam, you need to be able to spot the essentials quickly; you won't have time while you're writing a 45-minute exam essay to read through masses of notes written into the text in tiny handwriting. One way or another, you'll eventually need to re-write your notes anyway.

Making notes directly into the text

The main advantage of this method is that you can make the notes directly against the section of text to which they apply. Identifying the relevant lines can be awkward if you write your notes separately, especially with a prose text. If you do write detailed notes directly into the text, it is important to write in pencil, even if the text belongs to you. When you are revising for the exam, it is best to simplify your notes, as explained above. This obviously means rubbing out the notes you made originally and rewriting them in a way which enables you to get straight to the essential points on any page of text. An alternative is to use highlighter pens to identify the key points, but abbreviated notes are probably easier to work from in an exam.

A disadvantage of writing notes straight into the text is that, because of the lack of space, there is a temptation to make only very abbreviated notes from the start, so that you lose some of the important detail or subtlety of the points being made.

General note-making strategy

Whichever method you use, it is important to develop some sort of strategy for initial note-making.

- You obviously can't hope to write down *everything* your teacher or fellow students say. You have to learn to be selective about what is important, and find ways of jotting down the points as succinctly as possible.
- 'Further advice on writing: note-making technique' on page 133 has a section on 'Making notes in lessons/lectures', suggesting systems of abbreviation, which you certainly ought to follow.
- You should get into the habit from the start of your course of underlining the key phrases in the text. When you are preparing the final version of your text, it is *essential* to have your potential quotes clearly highlighted. Selective use of highlighter pens can be a helpful way of doing this.

An example of annotation for the exam

It might be useful now to look again at the pages quoted earlier from Joyce's story *The Sisters*, this time as a section of text to be taken into the exam. This presentation should only be treated as a suggestion, and it must be clear that this is the *end* of the note-making process; much fuller notes should have been made when the text was first studied. This is an example of a pruned-down set of notes, for ease of recognition of the salient points in the exam itself.

– Mind you, I noticed there was something queer coming over him
latterly. Whenever I'd bring in his soup to him there I'd find him with his
breviary fallen to the floor, lying back in the chair and his mouth open.
She laid a finger against her nose and frowned: then she continued:

– But still and all he kept on saying that before the summer was over
he'd go out for a drive one fine day just to see the old house again
where we were all born down in Irishtown and take me and Nannie with
him. If we could only get one of them new-fangled carriages that makes
no noise that Father O'Rourke told him about – them with the rheumatic
wheels – for the day cheap, he said, at Johnny Rush's over the way
there and drive out the three of us together of a Sunday evening. He had
his mind set on that . . . Poor James!

– The Lord have mercy on his soul! said my aunt.

Eliza took out her handkerchief and wiped her eyes with it. Then she
put it back again in her pocket and gazed into the empty grate for some
time without speaking.

– He was too scrupulous always, she said. The duties of the
priesthood was too much for him. And then his life was, you might say,
crossed.

– Yes, said my aunt. He was a disappointed man. You could see that.

A silence took possession of the little room and, under cover of it, I
approached the table and tasted my sherry and then returned quietly to
my chair in the corner. Eliza seemed to have fallen into a deep revery.
We waited respectfully for her to break the silence: and after a long
pause she said slowly:

– It was that chalice he broke . . . That was the beginning of it. Of
course, they say it was all right, that it contained nothing, I mean. But
still . . . They say it was the boy's fault. But poor James was so nervous,
God be merciful to him!

– And was that it? said my aunt. I heard something . . .

Eliza nodded.

– That affected his mind, she said. After that he began to mope by
himself, talking to no one and wandering about by himself. So one night
he was wanted for to go on a call and they couldn't find him anywhere.
They looked high up and low down; and still they couldn't see a sight of
him anywhere. So then the clerk suggested to try the chapel. So then
they got the keys and opened the chapel and the clerk and Father
O'Rourke and another priest that was there brought in a light for to look
for him . . . And what do you think but there he was, sitting up by
himself in the dark in his confession-box, wide-awake and laughing-like
softly to himself?

She stopped suddenly as if to listen. I too listened; but there was no
sound in the house: and I knew that the old priest was lying still in his
coffin as we had seen him, solemn and truculent in death, an idle
chalice on his breast.

Eliza resumed:

– Wide-awake and laughing-like to himself . . . So then, of course,
when they saw that, that made them think that there was something
gone wrong with him . . .

[Handwritten margin notes:]
- desire for escape from responsibilities of priesthood. cf boy p. *
- pathetic & inadequate
- accidental breach of ritual
- nervous breakdown ∴ of breaking chalice
- cf p. * symbol of empty religion
- spiritual life offered to boy one in which grimness & death associated with "beauty", laughter an indication that "something gone wrong"

Preparing for the exam

However clearly you've annotated your texts and highlighted your quotes, there simply isn't time in the exam to keep looking at the text that you're writing about and searching for ideas and quotes – you only have 45 minutes to plan and write each essay. You need to be able to find the relevant passages and quotations in seconds. A strategy for final note preparation is needed.

Making summary notes

Your copies of the texts will probably contain quite a few blank pages before and after the text itself. You can use these pages. The most focused and systematic way of preparing for the exam is to draw up a list of likely question topics for each text and write summary notes with page or line references for the key ideas and quotations relating to each topic, in the blank pages. The notes should be as abbreviated as you can possibly make them. Here is an example of a set of question topics on a text:

Question topics on Shakespeare's *King Lear*

- Lear's personal development
- Parallels between Lear and Gloucester
- Parents and children
- Deception
- Portrayal and role of Cordelia
- Portrayal and role of Gloucester
- Portrayal and role of Edgar
- Portrayal and role of Edmund
- Portrayal and role of Kent
- Portrayal of Goneril and Regan
- Role of the Fool

Here is an example of a set of summary notes on one of these topics.

Portrayal and role of Edmund

Iii	1FF	Solil.: blasphemous malcontent.	
	23FF	Dupes Gl. Cunning, clever strategist.	(R)
	115FF	Solil.: wit and vigour.	
	131FF	Dupes Edg. Actor.	
	176FF	Solil.: ruthless manipulator.	(R)
IIi	20FF	Persuades Edg. to escape: opportunist & manipulator.	(R)
	36FF	Plot agst. Edg. completed.	
	45	Brazen liar and hypocrite.	
	71	High risk strategist.	
IIiii	1FF	Edg's solil.: adopts role of 'poor Tom'.	(R)
IIIiii	8FF	Encourages father's confidences and plans to betray them.	
IIIiv	45FF	Edg's meeting with L. on heath.	
	62	Meeting with Edg. tips balance of L's sanity.	(R)
IIIv	1FF	Given father's title by Corn. Hypocrisy and ruthless cunning.	
IIIvi	28FF	Gl. blinded and cast out through Edm's betrayal.	(R)

IVi	18	GI's self-discovery through blinding //^{s} L's through madness.	(R)
	66	GI's conclusion ab. life, through suffering, //^{s} L's (IIIiv33)	(R)
IVii	26	Gon. passionately in love with Edm.	
IVv	11	Sent to murder GI. Total villain.	
IVvi	1^{FF}	Edg. ('poor Tom') & blinded GI. on 'cliff'.	(R)
Vi	17	Coolly plays one sister off agst another.	
	57	Dilemma over R. & G's desire for him. Total cynicism.	
Viii	30	Commissions Capt. to kill L. & C. in prison. Inhuman cruelty.	(R)
	140	Courage & impetuous confidence in accepting Edg's challenge.	
	161	Repents and forgives unknown killer.	
	227	Bitter humour at news of deaths of R. & G.	
	238	Pathos in need to feel loved.	
	242	Slightly redeemed by final attempt to save L. & C.	
	256^{FF}	L's re-entry with dead C.	(R)

Explanation of abbreviations: ^{FF} = from this line forward;
Solil. = soliloquy; Gl. = Gloucester; Edg. = Edgar; agst = against;
L = Lear; Corn. = Cornwall; Edm. = Edmund; //^{s} = parallels;
ab. = about; Gon. = Goneril; R. & G. = Regan and Goneril;
Capt. = Captain; C. = Cordelia; (R) = role.

A few points need to be made about the summary note-making
technique illustrated above. As you will see, line references are given for
every point made. Some are followed by the abbreviation '^{FF}', others not.
The former has been used when the reference was to a whole section
(important lines of which should be highlighted in your text, of course),
and the latter when the point related to a specific line.

The exact nature of the notes you make will depend on the text and
the theme. In this case, the abbreviation (R) is added at the end of some
of the lines. This is to identify points which relate, wholly or partly, to
the *role* of Edmund.

This particular topic is complicated by the fact that an important part
of Edmund's role in the play is to initiate plot, theme and character
developments in sections of the play in which he does not figure. This
presents a problem. The solution found here was to identify moments in
the play when his earlier actions have helped to bring about particularly
crucial developments, rather than to include *every* development that
Edmund has influenced by his actions. Most summary notes should,
mercifully, be easier to make than this.

You cannot hope to be exhaustive in the notes you make with
reference to any particular question theme and you should generally avoid
repeating the same point in different episodes, since you are unlikely to
want to give more than one example of a point in an essay.

Ideally you should be preparing your summary notes throughout the
course. It will take a long time to write about ten sets of summary notes
on six or more texts. If you leave it until the last few weeks before the
exams, you probably won't finish them all. Then, of course, you'll get
questions on topics you didn't get round to preparing! You should find

that the process of going through the text several times, jotting down the main points and quote references for different potential question topics, is the ideal way to revise. You'll know a text really well by the time you've gone through it ten times, each time with a different specific focus.

If you are lucky, you'll get a question which relates directly to a topic on which you've made summary notes. In this case, your preparation for answering the question in the exam itself will involve selecting and organising points and quotes you've identified which are relevant to the particular question set. It's quite likely, of course, that your summary notes will *not* relate directly to either question set on a particular text. This doesn't mean that the time spent on making the summary notes is wasted. As pointed out already, the process *in itself* is the ideal way to revise, and it's highly likely that a question focused on a complete text will take in *aspects* of characters and themes you've summarised. Here are a couple more examples of sets of question topics on set books:

Question topics on
Dubliners

- Varieties of paralysis
- Epiphanies
- Self-delusion/self-awareness
- Portrayal of childhood and adolescence
- Portrayal of public life
- Significance of titles
- Presentation of family life
- Presentation of cultural life
- Entrapment/the urge to escape
- Characters who we can sympathise with
- Joyce's narrative technique
- Reasons for title *The Dead*

Question topics on
The Franklin's Tale

- Maistrye/sovereinetee
- Gentillesse
- Trouthe
- Fredom
- Rhetoric
- Courtly love
- Realism and convention in the portrayal of Aurelius
- Realism generally
- Presentation of Dorigen
- Impressions of the Franklin

Before leaving this subject, a note of warning should be sounded. The process described above has nothing to do with *copying*. Examiners' Reports frequently bemoan the ploy which some students adopt of filling the blank pages of their texts with model essays, in the hope that one of them will be set in the exam. This ploy never works. It is invariably obvious to the examiner when a student has reiterated a pre-prepared answer, because the question asked will never be so close to the previously written essay for it to read like an original answer and quite often it ends up being only marginally relevant.

A further warning. The use of summary notes does not mean stringing together pre-prepared sentences lifted from your marginal notes. If you attempt this, it will again be obvious to the examiner. You must always bear in mind that what the examiner is looking for is an honest, personal response, albeit an organised and convincingly illustrated one. But more of this in the next chapter.

Final revision

When you come to your final revision period for the exams, it is essential that you do a good deal more than merely reading through your notes. You would be well advised to draw up an overall revision scheme, in general terms, for the whole revision period, and then more detailed schemes for specific blocks of time, and a specific objective for each individual revision period. Try not to be over-ambitious about how much you can get through in a two- or three-hour spell, though: if you give yourself unrealistic goals, it can be demoralising.

But this book is not concerned with general study skills, so let us content ourselves with a few suggestions relating specifically to literature revision:

- re-read the text;
- read critical material and make notes on it;
- watch a good video or listen to a cassette of the text;
- collect a set of past exam questions or specimen questions, and write paragraph plans (ten minutes maximum) on selected questions;
- practise writing essays in 45 minutes, using your summary notes.

15 Writing Essays on Literature Texts

It is quite possible that 70 per cent of the marks available to you in the AEB English exam will be for essay writing, depending on whether or not you end up writing an essay for the continuous writing question on Paper 1. Certainly 50 per cent of the marks will be for essays. It is pretty important, therefore, that your essay-writing technique is sound.

If you have studied Chapter 1 (The Language Essay), you will have dealt already with the essential principles of essay writing. These apply whether the essay that you are writing is for language *or* literature. There are a number of requirements particular to literature essay writing, however, and it is the purpose of this chapter to explore them.

Understanding literature essay questions

Literature essay questions have a terminology all of their own and before embarking on an exploration of good literature essay practice, it is important that you understand the key examiners' phrases. The most basic phrases: 'Discuss', 'Consider', 'Examine', 'Comment on' are obvious enough. They all really mean the same thing: 'write about in a considered way, showing your own point of view'. The following pages look at some of the most important and less obvious terms that frequently appear on literature exam papers.

1 *Presentation* A common question in literature exams is this: 'Consider the presentation of . . .' (a character in a text). The word 'portrayal' is sometimes used instead of 'presentation'. What you are being asked to do in a question worded like this is to explain *what the character is like* and *how the impression of him/her is created*. You should therefore try to identify the various aspects of the character, and his/her behaviour towards other characters, and think of episodes and quotations to illustrate how these characteristics are brought out.

2 *Role*

Another common question is 'Discuss the role of . . .'. This is different from asking about the 'portrayal' or the 'character' of an individual in a literary text. Quite often, in fact, questions are set in terms of 'character *and* role'. You are *not*, therefore, expected to write at length about what the character named in the question is *like*, unless the question includes *character* as well as role.

There are three aspects of a question on 'role':
i)   how the character affects the *plot*;
ii)   how the character is used to bring out aspects of *(an)other important character(s)*;
iii) how the character is used to clarify *themes* of the story/play.

It is impossible to do this, of course, without *mentioning* what the character is like.

3 *Character/ caricature*

You may be asked a question such as this: 'To what extent do you think the characters in . . . are caricatures?' As with any question which begins 'To what extent . . .' or 'How far do you agree . . .?', it is unlikely that you will agree entirely with the contention being made in the question. It is perfectly possible and acceptable, though perhaps unlikely, that you will entirely *disagree*. The chances are, however, that the examiner is expecting you to agree to a certain extent, and give evidence to show why.

A question on caricature almost certainly presupposes that *some* of the individuals in the story/play *are* largely or entirely caricatures and some are not. The distinction is as follows: if someone is a caricature, it means that (s)he has one fundamental character trait, which is constantly dwelt on, in order to ridicule them; the alternative is a 'rounded' character, which means someone who is portrayed in a more complex way, with a variety of characteristics.

4 *Irony*

Irony is a favourite device of serious writers, and a common theme in exam questions, like this: 'Discuss . . .'s uses of irony'. There are different types of irony:
•   On a simple level, irony can mean a writer or a character stating one thing, but implying the opposite.
•   On a subtler level, it involves a character doing or saying something which has a quite different and opposite significance for the reader than that which the character imagines.
•   *Dramatic* or *tragic* irony involves a character doing something with good intentions, and setting off a chain of events which leads to tragedy.

5 *Sympathetic character*

A common question is 'To what extent do you find . . . sympathetic?' What you are essentially being asked to discuss here is whether and in what ways you find the character *appealing and likeable*, or the reverse. It may well be that the character inspires sympathy in the sense of pity, but you should not limit yourself to this meaning of the word 'sympathetic'.

6 Special characteristics

If you are asked to write about 'the special characteristics' of a prose writer, you are being asked to identify and illustrate the features of the work which you are studying which seem to you distinctive and special. There are many aspects of the work that you could focus on. Here are a few:

- Distinctive stylistic features, such as powerful or emotive language, frequent use of similes, complex vocabulary, unusual syntax.
- Distinctive mood and tone of writing.
- Use of features such as vivid descriptions, punchy dialogue, suspense, dramatic climaxes.
- Use of devices like irony, caricature, symbolism, satire.

7 How?/By what means?

Questions on prose texts and plays, as well as poetry, are sometimes phrased in such a way as to draw a distinction between *what* is revealed and *how* or *by what means* it is revealed. An example might be: 'Which character does . . . bring most fully to life in his novel and how does he do it?' Such a question *could* be answered simply by reference to relevant episodes and quotations, without drawing an explicit distinction between content and method. To get a high grade, however, the examiner will expect you to make at least some attempt to identify the writer's methods. Here are some possible 'means' you might mention:

- letting the reader into the private thoughts/feelings of a character;
- direct statement/judgement by an 'omniscient' narrator;
- indirectly, by inviting the readers to draw their own conclusions;
- dialogue;
- revelations made by characters;
- a climactic situation;
- comedy;
- symbolism;
- a 'sub-text' in which a character's impressions are at variance with the reader's;
- irony;
- satire;
- pathos.

A general approach to literature essay writing

Before looking in detail at the construction and presentation of a literature essay, we should consider some of the more important general qualities which the examiner will hope to find in your essays.

Personal response

There was a time when students writing literature essays were expected to adopt an impersonal stance, avoiding any reference to themselves. They were expected to argue their case with phrases like 'It can be seen . . .', or 'It should be recognised . . .'. This highly academic approach to essay writing is no longer expected; in fact, a personal response, a personal 'voice', using the pronoun 'I', is what the examiner is looking for.

It is *your* views which the examiner wants to read. He or she will not give credit for quoting second-hand opinions. This is not to say you should *avoid* reading literary critics; a good critic can help you deepen your response to literature, which is, after all, the principal objective of an A-level literature course. However, the examiner does not want to read the opinions of a literary critic in an exam essay. You should absorb and internalise the most stimulating ideas of the critics, but not quote them.

Consistency of style and response is important. Given the 'open-book' nature of the literature papers, there is bound to be a temptation to copy other people's phrases, which you have written down in the margins of your texts, into your essays. The probable result is that such borrowings will stand out from the rest, because they will be in a different style from yours. A sense of personal response is therefore lost, and it can hardly be stressed too strongly that it is a sense of personal response that the examiner is looking for.

A suitable register

The opposite extreme from the highly impersonal approach already mentioned is the highly colloquial approach. An essay is a formal exercise which demands a formal structure and a formal register. Slang and contemporary colloquialisms will create an impression of lack of control over your writing. To illustrate the point, here are some colloquialisms which frequently occur in A-level literature essays, with acceptable formal alternatives:

over the top	*extreme, exaggerated*
two-faced	*hypocritical*
off the wall	*foolish, absurd, etc.*
well out of it	*out of his/her depth, no longer in contention, etc.*
decides to go for it	*decides to take the risk*
tries to put it across to his readers	*tries to suggest to his readers*

Formal accuracy of expression *in general* is important. It is a mistake to assume that accuracy of grammar and sentence structure are not considered important in literature essays. Effective communication is a basic essential in any kind of essay, and technical accuracy is a vital aspect of it.

Writing a 'correct' answer

There is no such thing as a 'correct' answer to an English literature question. The examiner will not have any preconceived ideas of what he or she is looking for in your answer. This is not to say that whatever you write can never be wrong. If you display ignorance or obvious misunderstanding of the text, or your judgements are based on historical anachronism, then you will certainly not impress the examiner.

What is important is to produce a lively argument, well presented and carefully backed up from the text. This is what the next part of the chapter will deal with.

Structure and presentation of an essay

A sound knowledge of the text, and a thoughtful and personal critical response to it, are essential for a thoroughly successful literature essay. Organisation of your ideas into a clear essay structure is also of vital importance.

Basic essay structure

How many paragraphs should you write and how long should they be? This obviously depends on how much time you've got for the essay. In 45 minutes, however well prepared you are, you can hardly hope to write much more than two and a half sides. Less than two sides (depending on the size of your handwriting, of course!) is going to look rather short, but you're not being tested on the speed of your writing. So, working on the basis of a two-and-a-half-side essay, what would be a reasonable paragraph number?

Before answering this, let us consider what a literature essay entails. You will need to write an introduction and conclusion (it should hardly need saying), but what about the main paragraphs? Each main paragraph has to explore an aspect of the question, and the points made have to be illustrated by specific textual reference. There *must* be a clear theme or informing idea to each paragraph. To state an idea, develop it and illustrate it is almost bound to take close to half a side. In an essay of two and a half sides, therefore, with a brief introductory and concluding paragraph as well, we are talking about four or five main paragraphs.

Let us look at a question dealing with a text and theme that was explored in the previous chapter, and focus our study of essay organisation on this question. The text is James Joyce's *Dubliners*. This is the question:

'Joyce said of *Dubliners*: "My intention was to write a chapter of the moral history of my country and I chose Dublin for the scene because that city seemed to me the centre of paralysis." In what ways have you found this paralysis presented in the stories?'

A long question like this needs some sorting out! Before you do anything else, you need to make absolutely sure that you understand what the question is asking. This applies to any question. It would be a good idea to highlight the key words of the question, like this:

'Joyce said of *Dubliners*: "My intention was to write a chapter of the <u>moral history</u> of my country and I chose Dublin for the scene because that city seemed to me the centre of paralysis." In <u>what ways</u> have you found this <u>paralysis presented</u> in the stories?'

Once you have highlighted the key words, you can keep checking them while you are writing your essay, to make sure that you are not straying off into irrelevance.

The introduction

A brief introduction is all that is needed. You should not allow yourself to get bogged down trying to perfect your introduction. All that is needed is a few lines setting out your understanding of and approach to the question. Let us look at a couple of specimen introductions to the *Dubliners* question.

1 There are many kinds of paralysis in *Dubliners*. In this essay I am going to discuss the ways in which I have found this paralysis presented in the stories.

2 James Joyce wrote *Dubliners* in the first decade of the 20th century. It is a collection of short stories divided into four main sections: *Childhood, Adolescence, Maturity* and *Public life*, with a final story, *The Dead*, added after the original volume was completed. It is the first major work of one of the greatest writers of the century.

Neither of these introductions is satisfactory. Try to work out why, before you read on.

The first tells us nothing. The first sentence is an annoyingly obvious way to start an essay, and the second is merely a statement that the writer is going to answer the question. Something more than this is needed.

The second at least *says* something, but what it says has no direct bearing on the question. It is an introduction to the book, but not to the question. It is really no better than the first introduction. Here is a better effort:

3 Paralysis is present in *Dubliners* from the opening paragraph of the first story. In almost every story we encounter paralysed individuals, incapable of living life to the full, because of their own weaknesses or the pressures of a paralysed society, or both.

What makes this introduction better than the first two? – An attempt is made to set the theme of paralysis in the context of the book as a whole, and provide some sense of what the term means. This is all that is required in an introduction. Notice that although this introduction *refers* to the first story, it doesn't start analysing it. Your introduction must be *general*; you should leave specific analysis of and quotation from the text for the body of the essay.

The main paragraphs

The main paragraphs must *develop* an argument in such a way that the examiner can see clearly the way it is progressing. Each paragraph should focus on a specific aspect of the question. Let us look again at the *Dubliners* question, in terms of a developing essay. We are analysing the *ways that paralysis is presented* in the stories.

The simplest way to deal with the question would be to pick between three and five stories in which 'paralysis' seems to be present, and write a paragraph on each. The question, however, is really asking about *kinds* of paralysis, so simply writing about various stories is rather lacking in focus. An even worse approach would be to write in detail about one story, and then just leave yourself time to discuss a second one briefly, before winding the essay up. This approach lacks any sense of focus *or* development. It would be better to write three to five main paragraphs on different kinds of paralysis, perhaps using more than one story to illustrate each. Here is an example of a main paragraph:

In some stories, characters are paralysed by an obsession with money, to the exclusion of any real human concerns. In *After the Race*, Jimmy Doyle is so influenced by wealth and status that he only interests himself with people who possess both. He is thrilled to be in the company of the owner of an expensive racing car; his journey across Dublin in the car 'laid a finger on the genuine pulse of life'. Another of his companions on the journey is a 'brilliant pianist – but, unfortunately, very poor'; and therefore, by implication, not worth knowing. Jimmy thus appears arrogant and superficial, like so many of the Dubliners, with no values beyond commercial ones. At the other end of the economic scale is Leneham, in *Two Gallants*, whose dreams extend no further than marriage to 'some simple-minded girl with a little of the ready', and who spends his life sponging off his 'friends'. He is aware of his own 'poverty of purse and spirit', but is too paralysed by it to try to change his life.

What is noticeable about the opening sentence of this paragraph? It states the theme of the paragraph. This is a useful technique to adopt. It is called the *topic sentence*. Such an introductory statement of the theme makes it clear to the examiner (and to you!) what the paragraph is going to be about. The paragraph then goes on to show how the theme is developed in two stories, the first discussed in some detail, the second more briefly. Each point is stated and then related to (a) detail(s) of the story, into which quotations are fitted. The quotations are all short, and are slipped naturally into the illustrative statement. Each detail from the text is clearly related to the theme of the paragraph.

This is how the main paragraphs should be structured. The theme of each paragraph should be made clear from the outset and should then be kept in focus as the text is discussed and illustrated. You should never make assertions about a text without offering some kind of textual support. The point of the textual evidence must always be made clear; if there is any doubt about the relevance of an illustration or quotation, then the sense of development is lost. This is a very common failing in literature essays. Very little credit will be given for assertions about a character or theme which are not related to specific incidents or quotations from the text. Another common failing is to offer lengthy explanations of the story or poem or whatever, without clearly relating them to the question. Again, very little credit will be given for unfocused paraphrase.

The conclusion

As with the introduction, the conclusion only needs to be brief. It should round the essay off in a way which is satisfyingly definitive. Let us now look at a couple of specimen conclusions to the *Dubliners* question.

1 Therefore, to conclude, *Dubliners* presents paralysis in a range of forms: spiritual, emotional, social and material. Almost all the characters are affected by it.

2 There are other forms of paralysis in *Dubliners* also. In *Eveline*, for instance, the young woman of the title is literally paralysed by fear as she stands at the harbour where she is supposed to be escaping with her boyfriend to Buenos Aires and ends up stuck in the life she hates. So paralysis is everywhere in *Dubliners*.

Both of these conclusions are unsatisfactory. Why?

The first is boringly obvious. It is merely a summary of the themes of the four main paragraphs, in fact. There is no point in merely summarising what you have written. The 'range of forms' referred to is, in any case, far from definitive.

The second is hardly a conclusion at all. It is a continuation of the essay, with a hasty concluding sentence thrown in at the end.

Your conclusion must tie the whole essay together; ideally you should try to think of some *new* idea to round the essay off. Here is another possible conclusion to the essay.

3 Whatever form of paralysis people seem to be trapped by, the paralysis emanates from Dublin itself. It seems to spread like a blanket over the entire city, preventing people from pursuing or achieving any worthwhile goals. In the final story, *The Dead*, the snow which envelopes Dublin, with its associations of death, has spread 'all over Ireland'. Perhaps this is the final, all-encompassing symbol of paralysis.

This paragraph *does* bring in another story, but the comments on *The Dead* are linked in with the concluding idea, rather than standing on their own. They make a neat, definitive conclusion to the essay.

A sample essay

Let us now put all these aspects of literature essay writing together in a finished answer to the *Dubliners* question.

Joyce said of *Dubliners*: 'My intention was to write a chapter of the moral history of my country and I chose Dublin for the scene because that city seemed to me the centre of paralysis.' In what ways have you found this paralysis presented in the stories?

Paralysis is present in *Dubliners* from the opening paragraph of the first story. In almost every story, we encounter paralysed individuals, incapable of living life to the full, because of their own weaknesses or the pressures of a paralysed society, or both.

The opening story, *The Sisters*, sets the tone for the whole collection. In it we encounter an old priest, Father Flynn, who is literally paralysed through a succession of strokes. As the story develops, his paralysis takes on a deeper significance. The boy who narrates the story tells us that the priest 'had taught me a great deal', but when we learn a little later what it was the boy had learnt, it turns out to be things like 'the meaning of the different vestments worn by the priest' and 'the responses of the mass which he had made me learn by heart'. It is all external ritual and rote responses, with no spiritual dimension. At the end of the story, we discover that the priest had suffered a nervous breakdown through the shock of dropping an empty communion chalice, which is a mere accidental breach of ritual. The old priest, therefore, in his physical and emotional paralysis, has come to symbolise the spiritual paralysis of Dublin's religious life.

Emotional paralysis in various forms is a common feature of *Dubliners*. In *An Encounter*, a young boy meets a man who starts talking about 'whipping', and tells the boy 'that if ever he found a boy talking to girls or having a girl for a sweetheart, he would whip him and whip him.' He talks obsessively about 'how he would whip such a boy as if he were unfolding an elaborate mystery', which echoes the priest in *The Sisters* unfolding to the boy 'how complex and mysterious were certain institutions of the church'. Both the priest and the pervert are equally emotionally paralysed by their destructive obsessions. In *A Painful Case*, a reclusive intellectual called James Duffy is equally emotionally paralysed, unable to enter into a physical relationship with anyone, realising, too late, at the end of the story, that he is 'outcast from life's feast'.

The narrowness and pettiness of Dublin's social life and conventions is responsible for the paralysis affecting some characters. In *The Boarding House*, we find a man trapped into marrying, after sleeping with the daughter of the boarding-house owner, because of social pressures and the petty-mindedness of Dublin society: 'The affair would be sure to be talked of, and his employer would be certain to hear of it.' The priest 'magnified his sin', and Mrs Mooney, the boarding-house owner, threatened him with 'all the weight of social opinion' if he refused to marry her daughter. The fear or social disgrace is a form of paralysis from which few can escape.

In some stories, characters are paralysed by an obsession with money to the exclusion of any real human concerns. In *After the Race*, Jimmy Doyle is so influenced by wealth and status that he only interests himself with people who possess both. He is thrilled to be in the company of the owner of an expensive racing car; his journey across Dublin in the car 'laid a finger on the genuine pulse of life'. Another of his companions on the journey is 'a brilliant pianist – but, unfortunately, very poor'; and therefore, by implication, not worth knowing. Jimmy thus appears arrogant and superficial, like so many of the Dubliners, with no values beyond commercial ones. At the other end of the economic scale is Lenehan in *Two Gallants*, whose dreams extend no further than marrying 'some simple-minded girl with a little of the ready', and who spends his life sponging off his 'friends'. He is aware of his own 'poverty of purse and spirit', but is too paralysed by it to try to change his life.

Whatever form of paralysis people seem to be trapped by, the paralysis emanates from Dublin itself. It seems to spread like a blanket over the entire city, preventing people from pursuing or achieving any worthwhile goals. In the final story, *The Dead*, the snow which envelopes Dublin, with its associations of death, has spread 'all over Ireland'. Perhaps this is the final, all-encompassing symbol of paralysis.

An essay writing checklist

It might be a good idea to get into the habit of asking yourself questions while you are writing an essay, to check that you are on the right lines. Here is a checklist of such questions. You could perhaps go through the list again when you have completed the draft of an essay.

1 Does my introduction refer specifically to the question?
2 Is it clear what each paragraph is going to be about from the opening sentence?
3 Does everything I have written in a paragraph relate to the topic sentence of that paragraph?
4 Have I backed up each point I have made by reference to the text?
5 Are my quotations brief and clearly related to the point they are meant to illustrate?
6 Is there a clear structure and sense of development between the paragraphs in the essay?
7 Is each paragraph developed to full paragraph length?
8 Does my conclusion round off the essay without merely summarising it?

The use of quotations

There are a number of definite 'dos and don'ts' in the use and presentation of quotations in a literature essay. Since quotation is a fundamental aspect of literary analysis, it would be worth devoting a little time to ensuring that you understand the basic principles of the use of quotation.

If you have studied the specimen essay on *Dubliners* on pages 247 to 248, you will have seen how quotations can be built into an argument. Most of the quotations in this essay fit naturally into the statement which they are backing up, like this: 'At the other end of the economic scale is Lenehan, in *Two Gallants*, whose dreams extend no further than marrying "some simple-minded girl with a little of the ready", and who spends his life sponging off his "friends".' Quotations rarely need to be long: often a point can be successfully backed up by a quoted phrase of three or four words, or even one word, as in the sentence from the *Dubliners* essay. Two or three lines of quoted text would normally be the maximum length necessary for a point to be effectively illustrated.

Students are sometimes tempted to quote chunks of text in the forlorn hope that the quotation will speak for itself, and stand in the place of personal explanation. This is quite useless. Quotations should never take the place of personal comment, but should illustrate and supplement it, as part of a developing argument.

It is not always possible to simply fit a quotation into a statement, in the manner illustrated above, however. It may be necessary to make a point first, and then add the illustration. Here is an example. In an essay on Shakespeare's *King Lear*, an argument is being developed about the dramatic importance of the escape of a character called Edgar from his father's castle, and his adoption of the disguise of a mad beggar to avoid discovery. Edgar is hiding in a hovel on a heath. King Lear, who has run out onto the heath in a state of despair bordering on madness, because of his daughters' rejection of him, is persuaded to take shelter in the same hovel. The essay is making a point about the significance of the meeting which follows between Edgar and Lear.

'The subsequent meeting between the disguised Edgar and Lear, driven close to madness by the cruel and inhuman treatment of his daughters, seems to tip the balance of Lear's wavering sanity. He suddenly identifies with this "mad beggar", and addresses him, linking his suffering also with the cruelty of daughters, in an insanely obsessive manner:

"Didst thou give all to thy daughters?
And are thou come to this?" '

As you will see, the point is made, and the quotation offered to back it up – to 'prove' it. If you are using quotations in this way, there are dangers. The principal one is the failure to relate the quotation clearly enough to the point being made. This can usually be avoided if you take care to *contextualise* your quotes: in other words, make it clear what the situation is and who is speaking to whom. A very common weakness in literature essay writing is the failure to establish the context of a quotation within the text, so that it is left 'hanging', with insufficient reference to the preceding or succeeding comment, or to the text itself. Here is an example, based on the section from a *King Lear* essay discussed above:

'The subsequent meeting between the disguised Edgar and Lear tips the balance of Lear's wavering sanity:

> "Didst thou give all to thy daughters?
> And art thou come to this?" '

Without knowing who is speaking and why the reference to 'daughters' is significant, the quotation is meaningless.

A few other points might usefully be made with reference to the presentation of quotations. If a point is made and then a quotation is given to back it up, as in the above examples, the quotation should be separated from the comment by a punctuation mark. A colon is the best one to use, as illustrated.

The quotation from *King Lear* illustrates another minor but important point about presentation. If you are quoting two or more lines of blank verse or poetry, you should never use a prose layout, like this: 'Didst thou give all to thy daughters? And art thou come to this?' If the quotation is only two lines long, you can set it out with an oblique between the lines, like this: 'Didst thou give all to thy daughters?/And art thou come to this?' It is best, though, to set it out as lines of verse, as in the text.

There are two other very important 'don'ts' with reference to quotation which crop up every year in examiners' reports:

- Do not quote by referring to a page or line reference, without actually quoting the relevant words. (In fact, it is a waste of time to supply page or line references at all, since you cannot expect the examiner to look them up.)
- Do not just write the first and last words of a quotation, with a line of dots between, and a page or line reference, like this: 'Didst . . . this? (page 186)'. The examiner will not have time to hunt for all your references in his or her copy of the text, so the 'quote' will simply be ignored.

Writing a plan

With only 45 minutes to produce an essay on a literature text, should you risk spending some of it writing a plan? The planning of essays is discussed in Chapter 1, 'The Language Essay'. For the language essay, of course, you have one and a half hours. It is a different matter when you have half that time. You clearly cannot devote up to 20 minutes on the plan, as was suggested in Chapter 1, or anything like it. So should you just get straight into the essay?

The danger of writing a language essay without initial planning was again discussed in Chapter 1, and this applies to literature essays also: your essay *must* be clearly and coherently structured and some time needs to be put into thinking out a structure. If you practise writing essay plans on literature questions, you should be able to develop the ability to produce a skeleton plan in four or five minutes. You will have to think out the structure of your essay anyway, and it is safer to do it before you start rather than while you're writing the essay.

Of necessity, the plan will have to be brief. If we take the essay title explored earlier in this chapter, we can see how a five-minute plan can be produced. The title, in simplified form, is: 'In what ways have you found paralysis presented in *Dubliners*?' One way of writing a plan is just to jot down paragraph themes, like this:

Intro: Explain paralysis.
Par. 2:   Spiritual paral.: *Sisters.*
Par. 3:   Emotional paral.: *Encounter, Painful Case.*
Par. 4:   Social paral.: *Boarding House.*
Par. 5:   Money obsession: *After the Race, Two Gallants.*
Conc.:   final vision in *The Dead.*

Some people may find it useful to write down a spider-diagram-style plan, which they can add to while writing, like this:

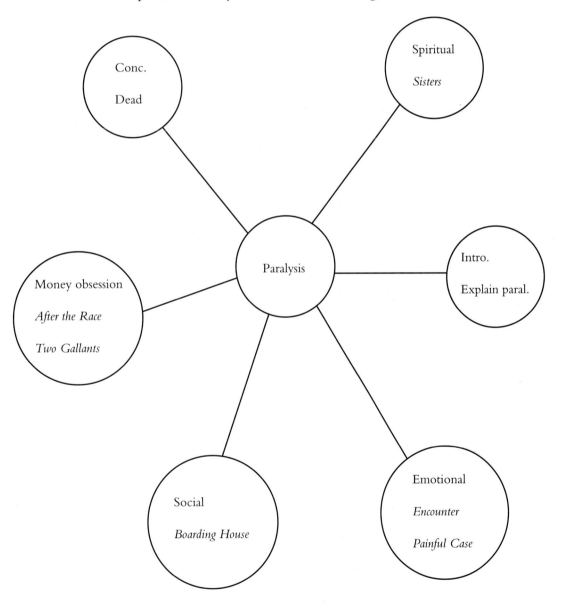

Writing an essay on a section of text

One of the questions on each of the set texts for the language and literature exam is almost certain to deal with a character or theme in the text as a whole. The alternative question is usually much more specific. You are likely to be required to engage in a detailed analysis of a section of text: a scene or a section of a scene from a play, an extract from a novel or autobiography, a single short story, essay or poem. This poses different kinds of problems, which we will now explore.

The importance of knowing the text

The depth of analysis required depends, obviously enough, on the length of the section of text you are asked to write about. This can vary from a single speech in a play or a short poem to a complete chapter of a novel or a complete short story. It is unlikely that you will be asked to write about a section of longer than ten pages. A passage of this length, however, can pose special problems. In 45 minutes you can hardly afford yourself the luxury of reading and trying to sort out a section of text with which you are only slightly familiar. You need to know the passage fairly well, and have the important details underlined, with marginal notes, to give yourself a fair chance of answering the question adequately. Much the same applies with even a very short piece of text. If you have only a slight acquaintance with the set poem or section of text, it is asking a lot of yourself to have to work it out and write convincingly on it within the time constraint of the examination.

Standard questions on sections of text

As with questions on whole texts, there are various standard questions which are set on sections of text. We will now look at some of them.

1 One of the commonest questions is along the lines of 'To what extent is (the passage) characteristic of the work as a whole? or 'What features of the style and content of the poem are characteristic of the poet?' or 'What aspects of the subject matter, ideas and style are typical of the writer?'

   Whether or not such a question specifically asks you to discuss the characteristic features of the *language* and *style* of the extract, you would be expected to do so. Some of the other features of a passage which show that it is typical might be:
   * the themes and ideas expressed in the passage;
   * the narrative techniques employed;
   * the dramatic or comic effects;
   * the uses of such devices as imagery or symbolism.
   You *must* make sure that you refer to illustrative examples from within the section of text *and* relate them to comparable examples from elsewhere in the text.

2 Another common question goes like this: 'Discuss the ways in which (a character) is presented' or 'Discuss the methods or techniques used to present (a character)'.

   If the text on which such a question is asked is a novel, then you will be expected to display your awareness of varieties of narrative technique:

- **omniscient narration:** the author makes *authoritative statements* about a character or situation which defines them for the reader;
- **unobtrusive narration:** the author simply presents a character and situation with no overt attempt to influence the reader;
- **caricature:** a character is presented *two-dimensionally*, to represent a single defining characteristic, or to highlight a theme;
- **realism:** a character is 'rounded', so that he or she displays both strengths and weaknesses, as in real life;
- through **other characters' judgements:** the reader can either accept or question these;
- through presenting a character in a situation of **crisis or conflict**, to which they react emotionally;
- through **characteristic dialogue** or **style of speech.**

3 A similar question is to ask you to *analyse (a writer's) narrative methods* in a section of text. Such a question will necessitate analysing the methods of presenting characters, so the above will apply. It will also require you to analyse the writer's style: including the uses of imagery and symbolism and of figures of sound appealing to the reader's emotions or imagination. A discussion of the structure may also be relevant: if the extract is straightforwardly linear and chronological in structure or not, for instance, or whether it builds up to a climax.

4 Questions on sections of text frequently require you to focus specifically on the language of the passage, poem or scene. You may be asked: 'How does the language reveal how (a character) thinks and feels?'

This kind of question necessitates a very detailed analysis of the language employed: particularly vivid or evocative phrases should be picked out and discussed, uses of imagery and figures of sound (explored in Chapter 13) should be analysed for their emotional or other impact, the tone of the language should be assessed.

5 A similar, but slightly less explicit question would be 'How are (a character's) emotions and experiences conveyed?'

This would again require a precise analysis of the character's uses of language. It would also need to take in aspects of the plot, such as the character's *actions* and *reactions to other characters*. If the text on which the question is set is a verse drama, the *rhythm* of the verse could be explored (whether it is smooth, or broken and disjointed, for instance).

6 A question along the lines of 'What is the impact of (an episode) and how is it achieved?' would once again require an analysis of the language and style. Other matters requiring discussion would be dictated by the nature of the text:

- If the episode is *dramatic* you would be expected to select especially dramatic moments and explain what *makes* them dramatic.
- If it is *touching*, you would need to identify moments of particular pathos.
- If it is highly *emotionally charged*, you would need to pick out moments when the emotional impact is especially strong.

Impact can come from moments of special illumination for the reader, when surprising discoveries are made, or important themes are brought out with particular force.

7 A very common question type is the two-part question, in which you are asked to explore the specified section in detail in the first part of the question, and then to relate the section to the rest of the text in some way. Typical examples of the second part of such questions are: 'How does (the extract) reveal ideas and themes in the work as a whole?' or 'What is the dramatic importance of (the scene) to the play as a whole?'

Such a broadening out of the question to take in the whole text requires skilful selection and illustration of key ideas and themes both from the section set and from other sections of the text. It may also involve discussion and illustration of the following:

- important revelations about central characters in the section set, which have been prefigured earlier;
- discussions of the plot developments which occur as a result of the episode.

The specimen essay which follows is of this two-part variety.

A specimen essay on a section of text

The scene on which the essay is set is printed in Appendix C. It is the second scene of Shakespeare's *King Lear*. Edmund is the illegitimate son of Gloucester, a leading nobleman in the realm ruled over by King Lear, who abdicated his throne in a dangerously divisive way in the opening scene. Edgar is Gloucester's first-born, legitimate son.

Find and re-read Act I scene ii. Show how you respond to Edmund in this scene, making reference to his uses of language. What is the dramatic importance of this scene in the play as a whole?

Edmund was briefly introduced in the opening episode of the first scene, where his father, Gloucester, was telling Kent of his embarrassment about his son's illegitimacy, and at the same time joking about it. Edmund appeared modest and deferential. Now a very different Edmund bursts onto the stage.

It is immediately obvious that Edmund is intensely resentful about the way he is branded 'bastard'. I can easily understand Edmund's resentment and bitterness. It obviously makes him passionately angry, as is shown in the obsessively repetitive way he speaks of it: 'Why brand they us/With base? with baseness? bastardy? base, base?' However, it is not his 'bastardy' which deprives him of inheriting his father's title, but the fact that he is younger than his legitimate brother. There is no justification for resentment over this, and, in fact, in the opening line of the soliloquy he seems to be rejecting religion and all the laws of society as he announces: 'Thou, Nature, art my goddess!' This makes me feel immediately suspicious of him. The sneering way he denigrates his brother's 'legitimacy', in the same obsessive style in which he talked of his own 'bastardy', while plotting his overthrow, almost makes my flesh creep: 'Fine word, "legitimate"!/Well, my legitimate'.

His plot is revealed in the next episode. Very cleverly, he ensures that his father sees the letter he has forged, implicating his brother in a murder plot against him, by pretending to hide it. While I admire the cunning way that Edmund dupes his father, I find the hypocritically deferential style he adopts in talking to his father, while pretending to defend his brother, disgusting: 'I dare pawn down my life for him, that he hath writ this to feel my affection for your honour'. Gloucester leaves, muttering about 'eclipses in the sun and moon' portending social collapse. Edmund picks up on this, and I find his wit and vigour, and the sense of his delight in his own cleverness, infectious, as he derides his father's astrological beliefs:

'An admirable evasion of whoremaster man, to lay his goatish disposition to the charge of a star.'

This is a highly imaginative and expressive use of language, with its contemptuous imagery of 'whoremaster' and 'goatish', and the mocking assonance in 'charge of a star'.

Edmund's quick-wittedness and opportunism is shown in the next episode, as he pretends to adopt his father's conviction that 'these eclipses' have been the cause of family divisions. He cunningly dupes Edgar into hiding in his lodgings till his father's 'displeasure' against him has abated. His final soliloquy destroys any lingering admiration I might feel for Edmund, however, as he gloats over the planned destruction of:

... a brother noble,
Whose nature is so far from doing harms
That he suspects none ...'

I cannot feel anything but disgust for such ruthless manipulation of his brother's goodness. By the end of the act, I can only think of Edmund as a cold-hearted villain and hope that his plot will rebound on his head.

An immediate result of the events of Act I scene ii is that Gloucester places complete trust in Edmund, which sets off a crucial chain of events. Gloucester decides to transfer the inheritance of his title to his 'loyal and natural boy', Edmund, and later in the play, he confides in Edmund the news he has heard of Cornwall and Regan's 'unnatural' treatment of Lear, sending Edmund to 'maintain talk with the Duke' while he goes off to 'relieve' Lear. The 'talk' which Edmund has with Cornwall is to betray his father, which leads to Gloucester being blinded and cast out. This in turn leads to the climactic meeting between the blinded Gloucester and the maddened Lear, who have come to similar conclusions about the cruel injustices of life. Their parallel discoveries about themselves and the nature of human existence forms a major theme of the play. When the country is invaded by an army from France to restore King Lear, Edmund, as a result of his treachery, is put in command of the English forces, which enables him to perform his final act of villainy in sending a captain to murder the imprisoned Lear and Cordelia. This leads to the ultimate climactic death scene of King Lear, with the strangled Cordelia in his arms.

The other effect of the events of Act I scene ii which has a far-reaching impact on the play's development is that Edmund is able to persuade Edgar to 'fly this place'. As a result, Edgar hides out on the heath, and adopts the disguise of 'poor Tom', a half-naked, mad beggar. The subsequent meeting between the disguised Edgar and Lear, driven close to madness by the cruel and inhuman treatment of his daughters, seems to tip the balance of Lear's wavering sanity. He suddenly identifies with this 'mad beggar', and addresses him, linking his suffering also with the cruelty of daughters, in an insanely obsessive manner:

'Didst thou give all to thy daughters?
And art thou come to this?'

Edgar's portrayal of himself in terms of inhuman degradation, in the scenes on the heath, adds considerably to the atmosphere of grotesquerie which characterises the central sections of the play.

In terms of both the main plot and the sub-plot, therefore, Act I scene ii is a major catalyst in the play. The chain of events set off by this scene finally comes full circle at the very end, with the killing of Edmund by Edgar, and the latter's elevation to the throne.

Analysis of the King Lear essay

The question specifically requires an analysis of Edmund's 'uses of language' as part of a personal response to the character. The answer attempts to analyse the imagery and figures of sound with which Edmund expresses himself, and his uses of repetition, as well as illustrating a more general contrast between his style of speech when alone and in the company of his father and brother. It does more than merely *identify* the various features of the language, however. To achieve a high grade, it is necessary to discuss the *uses* of imagery, etc., specifically in terms of the question. Thus, the examples of imagery are mentioned in terms of their *effect*: the 'contemptuous' effect of 'whoremaster man' and 'goatish disposition'. An example of assonance is quoted and discussed in terms of its 'mocking' effect.

Attempts are made throughout the first part of the essay to explain precisely the *feelings* which Edmund evokes, with phrases like 'almost makes my flesh creep' with reference to one quoted statement, and an explanation of the mixture of admiration and disgust felt at the duping of his father and brother. Brief quotations are used throughout to illustrate the points being made.

The second half of the essay, which broadens out to take in the rest of the play, is shorter than the first. This is as it should be. The *core* of this kind of essay is the detailed analysis of the episode. This should always form the bulk of the essay. A good rule of thumb would be to think in terms of devoting about a third of the essay to relating the episode to the rest of the text. Certainly it should never take up more than half.

The aspects of 'dramatic importance' of the scene which the second part of the essay focuses on are its importance in the development of the plot and themes of the play. Since there is so much that could be written about, in answer to the second part, it is essential to be concise, and to select only events and details of special importance. The summary notes on the 'portrayal and role' of Edmund (page 236) were extremely useful in selecting aspects of theme, plot and characterisation to mention.

A specimen essay on a poetry text

Finally, let us look at a question on a poetry text: *Selected Poems and Letters of John Keats*. The question focuses on Keats' *Ode to a Nightingale*. Here is the poem.

Ode to a Nightingale

1

My heart aches, and a drowsy numbness pains
  My sense, as though of hemlock I had drunk,
Or emptied some dull opiate to the drains
  One minute past, and Lethe-wards had sunk:

5   'Tis not through envy of thy happy lot,
        But being too happy in thine happiness,—
            That thou, light-winged Dryad of the trees,
                In some melodious plot
        Of beechen green, and shadows numberless,
10   Singest of summer in full-throated ease.

                                2

        O, for a draught of vintage! that hath been
            Cool'd a long age in the deep-delved earth,
        Tasting of Flora and the country green,
            Dance, and Provençal song, and sunburnt mirth!
15   O for a beaker full of the warm South,
        Full of the true, the blushful Hippocrene,
            With beaded bubbles winking at the brim,
                And purple-stained mouth;
        That I might drink, and leave the world unseen,
20   And with thee fade away into the forest dim:

                                3

        Fade far away, dissolve, and quite forget
            What thou among the leaves hast never known,
        The weariness, the fever, and the fret
            Here, where men sit and hear each other groan;
25   Where palsy shakes a few, sad, last gray hairs,
            Where youth grows pale, and spectre-thin, and dies;
                Where but to think is to be full of sorrow
                    And leaden-eyed despairs,
            Where Beauty cannot keep her lustrous eyes,
30   Or new Love pine at them beyond to-morrow.

                                4

        Away! away! for I will fly to thee,
            Not charioted by Bacchus and his pards,
        But on the viewless wings of Poesy,
            Though the dull brain perplexes and retards:
35   Already with thee! tender is the night,
            And haply the Queen-Moon is on her throne,
                Cluster'd around by all her starry Fays;
                    But here there is no light,
            Save what from heaven is with the breezes blown
40   Through verdurous glooms and winding mossy ways.

                                5

        I cannot see what flowers are at my feet,
            Nor what soft incense hangs upon the boughs,
        But, in embalmed darkness, guess each sweet
            Wherewith the seasonable month endows
45   The grass, the thicket, and the fruit-tree wild;
            White hawthorn, and the pastoral eglantine;
                Fast fading violets cover'd up in leaves;
                    And mid-May's eldest child,
            The coming musk-rose, full of dewy wine,
50   The murmurous haunt of flies on summer eves.

6
Darkling I listen; and, for many a time
　　I have been half in love with easeful Death,
Call'd him soft names in many a mused rhyme,
　　To take into the air my quiet breath;
55　Now more than ever seems it rich to die,
　　To cease upon the midnight with no pain,
　　　While thou art pouring forth thy soul abroad
　　　　In such an ecstasy!
　　Still wouldst thou sing, and I have ears in vain—
60　To thy high requiem become a sod.

7
Thou wast not born for death, immortal Bird!
　　No hungry generations tread thee down;
The voice I hear this passing night was heard
　　In ancient days by emperor and clown:
65　Perhaps the self-same song that found a path
　　Through the sad heart of Ruth, when, sick for home,
　　　She stood in tears amid the alien corn;
　　　　The same that oft-times hath
　　Charm'd magic casements, opening on the foam
70　Of perilous seas, in faery lands forlorn.

8
Forlorn! the very word is like a bell
　　To toll me back from thee to my sole self!
Adieu! the fancy cannot cheat so well
　　As she is fam'd to do, deceiving elf.
75　Adieu! adieu! thy plaintive anthem fades
　　Past the near meadows, over the still stream,
　　　Up the hill-side; and now 'tis buried deep
　　　　In the next valley-glades;
　　Was it a vision, or a waking dream?
80　Fled is that music:—Do I wake or sleep?

Specimen essay

Remind yourself of *Ode to a Nightingale*. Write about the features of the style and structure of this poem which you consider typical of Keats' poetry.

Intro.:　Keats' fame for creating sense-impressions.
Par. 2:　Creation of mood, through language.
Par. 3:　Alliteration, assonance, onomatopoeia.
Par. 4:　Verse-form.
Par. 5:　Summing up.

Keats is one of the truly great poets of the Romantic era. His fame rests primarily on the musical beauty of his language. Few if any poets of any era conveyed sense-impressions with the sensuous power of Keats, and this essay will attempt to illustrate his power.

　　One of the remarkable features of Keats' verse is the way in which he could create mood and atmosphere through his use of combinations of vowel sounds. This is illustrated in the opening lines of *Ode to a Nightingale*:

　　'My heart aches, and a drowsy numbness pains

My sense, as though of hemlock I had drunk,
Or emptied some dull opiate to the drains'

The effect of the 'um' and 'un' sounds, and the heavy vowel sounds in general, is to create a verbal impression of the 'numbness' and heartache the poet speaks of. This kind of enhancement of meaning through the sounds of the words is typical of Keats. In *The Eve of St Agnes*, a wonderfully vivid sense impression of coldness and bleakness is created in the description of the tombs:

'The sculptured dead on each side seem to freeze,
Emprisoned in black, purgatorial rails'

This is captured by the heavy sounds of 'sculptured' and 'purgatorial', combined with the long 'e' assonance of '*ea*ch side s*ee*m to fr*ee*ze', creating a brilliant verbal sense of 'freezing'.

The Eve of St. Agnes,
William Holman Hunt

Keats uses assonance, often allied to alliteration, to create a whole range of sensuous verbal effects. A particularly brilliant example of this is the evocation of the sense impression of a beaker of sparkling red wine in *Ode to a Nightingale*:

'O for a beaker full of the warm South . . .
With beaded bubbles winking at the brim'

We can almost see the bubbles, through the plosive alliteration of 'beaded bubbles' and the light 'i' assonance of 'winking at the brim'. The sense-impression is further enhanced by the onomatopoeic word 'bubbles' and the personification of 'winking'. Another quotation from *The Eve of St Agnes* will show how Keats could use assonance and alliteration to convey extraordinarily vivid sense-impressions, this time of delicious food:

'With jellies soother than the creamy curd
And lucent syrups tinct with cinnamon'

The alliteration in the first line followed by the repeated sibilants of 'lucent syrups',
together with the light 'i' alliteration in the last four words creates a quite mouth-
watering effect.

Keats' uses of onomatopoeia could also sometimes create wonderfully vivid and
precise sound-impressions, as in this line from *Ode to a Nightingale*:

'The murmurous haunt of flies on summer eaves'

We can almost hear the sound of the flies, through the onomatopoeic word
'murmurous', combined with the musical word 'haunt'. A very similar effect is created
in the ode *To Autumn*, in the line:

'Then in a wailful choir the small gnats mourn'

Again it is onomatopoeia of 'wailful choir' and 'mourn' accentuated by the assonance
of 'small' and 'mourn', which creates the verbal magic.

The verse form of *Ode to a Nightingale* is again typical of Keats. The poem consists
of eight stanzas, each of ten lines, with a basic ten-syllable iambic pentameter metre,
broken by a trimeter each eighth line. Keats generally employs a flexible iambic
pentameter metrical pattern. Within this overall structural regularity, however, there is
great fluidity. He frequently uses run-on lines to create particular effects in *Ode to a
Nightingale*, as in:

'. . . the breezes blown
Through verdurous glooms and winding mossy ways'

A sense-impression of the meandering movement of the 'breezes' is created partly by
the absence of a caesura. An even more brilliant example of the purposeful use of a
run-on line is in *To Autumn*, where the season is personified as a gleaner who:

'. . . dost keep
Steady thy laden head across the brook'

The slight pause in the flow of the statement, caused by the line ending, exactly
captures the sense of the gleaner cautiously keeping steady his load.

It can be seen from this essay that Keats was not only a brilliantly imaginative poet,
but also a poet of great skill and technical artistry. *Ode to a Nightingale* shows Keats at
his most dazzlingly evocative.

Final remarks

In a detailed analytical essay of the kind illustrated above, each point has
to be illustrated from the text and the quotation discussed. The basic
pattern is this:
- state the point;
- quote to illustrate the point;
- discuss the quotation.

If you look again at any of the points made in the essay, you will see how
this is done.

You should also bear the following points in mind:
- One of the commonest weaknesses of this kind of depth analysis essay
  is the failure to adequately analyse the text. There are always students
  who either paraphrase or quote a section of a poem, and simply add a

comment that they find it 'brilliant'. In the essay above, the word 'brilliant' is used of Keats' poetry, but it is followed by a precise analysis of *why* the detail under discussion is brilliant. There is really no point in quoting chunks of text anyway. As the essay shows, three lines of text is almost invariably enough to illustrate a point, and generally one or two lines will suffice.

- There is a danger, in the kind of essay illustrated above, of straying from the point of a paragraph. If the theme of the paragraph is Keats' uses of assonance and alliteration, for instance, and you quote a line which includes imagery, you should resist the temptation to go on to discuss the imagery. Your essay must have a structure, and the sense of structure is lost if you go off on tangents. You must be disciplined, and not allow yourself to follow interesting leads which take you away from the point at issue.

- You must also try to avoid getting bogged down on a single point. If you spend too long explaining each point you make, you will run out of time before you've had the chance to make many.

- If a question is in two parts, you must make sure that you allow yourself time to answer the second part reasonably fully. You must give a proper answer to all parts of a question.

- A summary of a poem, chapter or scene will gain very few marks. You must always read the question carefully, and do what it says. You will never be asked to tell the story.

- Try to avoid carelessness about the genre of a text: if it is a play, call it a play, not a 'book' (or a novel!).

- The examiner is looking for an informed personal response. Try to create a sense of personal engagement with the text, and show what you enjoyed about studying it.

Examiners' marking scheme for literature essays

Here is the AEB marking scheme for literature essays in the language and literature examination, together with the Board's notes for the guidance of examiners. The first two mark bands both approximate to a grade A, the next five reflect the standards necessary to gain grades B to N, and the last two may be considered to reflect work which would be ungraded.

23–25: Work of the highest standard to be expected in examination conditions. The candidate will demonstrate mastery of the shape and details of the text, and of the writer's style and intentions. The analytical approaches employed, and the well-considered comment, will demonstrate mature, informed understanding and personal response. There may be some originality in approach or organisation. Vocabulary and expression, handling of quotation and textual reference will match the quality of insight and argument.

20–22: Very good work, revealing thorough knowledge, perception, balance and cogency of argument. The candidate's writing will aptly demonstrate a high quality of thought and personal response. There will be evidence of the candidate's detailed knowledge of the text, and understanding of the writer's intentions and methods.

Answers will be conceptualised, showing real insight and 'flair'. Analytical skills will be firmly in place, and the handling of quotation and textual reference will be confident.

17–19: Good work, which clearly demonstrates the candidate's understanding and is supported by sound knowledge of the text and understanding of the writer's intentions. There will be some evidence of a conceptualised and analytical approach, though this may not be totally sustained nor developed into an overview. The candidate will be able to follow a line of argument, employing well-handled quotation or accurate reference, and offer an informed personal response. The writing will be focused on the essay topic, and the content and direction relevant to its demands.

14–16: Sound work, in which the candidate demonstrates textual knowledge and shows some understanding of a writer's intentions and methods. The writing will provide a personal response, though this may be somewhat limited and under-developed. There will be evidence of the beginnings of analysis, and an attempt to focus on the theme of the question. Specific details from the text, or a given passage, will be used to support some sustained discussion. Both details and discussion may be rather narrow, but relevant. The question topic will be adequately addressed. Argument may be attempted, but the form chosen to develop it may be by means of an illustrated list.

11–13: Acceptable work, which reveals an adequate knowledge of the text. A serious attempt, which demonstrates that the task has been understood, though the handling of it may be limited by the candidate's under-developed powers of analysis. Personal response may be simplistic, or show little independent thought. Understanding of a writer's purposes and techniques is likely to be on a limited level or may be patchy, but will be sufficient to enable the candidate to select some appropriate material to illustrate straighforward discussion. The response should cover more than one sound and relevant area of investigation, either within a set passage or in the text as a whole. Focus on the essay topic may be implicit within a narrative approach.

9–10: A basic response to the text and the task. The candidate will demonstrate sufficient knowledge of the text to select some relevant material or to refer to appropriate sections. Answers in this band will show that the response to the task is serious, and that relevant investigation has been attempted, but this is likely to be very limited. The writing may show a lack of independent thought or personal response. There will be very little evidence that the candidate is aware of a writer's crafting of material. The candidate will show an understanding of the task, even though the writing only achieves occasional direct and explicit relevance. The writing is likely to be characterised by narrative and/or description, limited powers of expression, and a lack of sustained discussion.

6–8: Responses in this band will show that the candidate has some superficial knowledge of the text, but will be a totally unsuccessful attempt to organise this knowledge to answer the question. The candidate's understanding of the demands of the task, and the material which has been studied, are both inadequate for successful work in this examination. An all-purpose, or wholly narrative approach, which fails to acknowledge the terms of the question, or which evades engagement with a set passage, should be placed in this category. Answers with some explicit relevance and a small amount of textual support should be in the band above this one.

2–5: There will be some evidence that parts of the text have been read, or that the candidate is in some way familiar with part or parts of the text. This bare minimum of knowledge is insufficient for any positive engagement with the task. The candidate may show a virtually total lack of understanding of both the text and the given task. Answers here may be very short or may include only one or two very generally appropriate points. Candidates who make a serious attempt to respond to the set task, even at a superficial level, should be placed in a higher band.

0–1: The candidate may be able to show some ability to write, but will not convince the examiner that he or she is familiar with anything in the set text.

General Guidance to Examiners

Marking must be positive. You should evaluate what a candidate offers, and the quality of the attempt to provide a *personal response* to the question. Avoid the temptation to have a 'set answer' in your mind to any question. Writing must be factually accurate, but a wide range of personal opinions is likely to be expressed to most of the questions set.

Each essay is marked out of 25, using the mark scheme which provides descriptors for different kinds of achievement. These should be used as a guide, but not as strict classification. Many essays will show characteristics of more than one band. You should make your decision on the given mark for an essay based on a careful estimation of its merits. It may help to think 'band', 'band minus' and 'band plus'. Work which appears to fit a certain band, but exhibits flashes of the qualities of the band above it, should be considered for the lowest mark in the higher band.

Be very careful not to award marks on the criterion of length alone, but look very carefully for the real achievements of candidates. A succinct, well-argued essay may appear brief, but have sufficient well-considered content for a high mark.

If a candidate provides an unfinished essay or set of notes, this should be evaluated and a mark awarded on the basis of the ideas and approach which is indicated. Such work cannot be awarded as high a mark as a finished essay, but proper credit must be given.

Please remember that what you are looking for and rewarding is the quality of thought and literary response. Candidates with very limited powers of expression are unlikely to be able to produce sustained discussion of a question, but there may be evidence of understanding and some flashes of personal response, which should be rewarded using the mark scheme criteria. Do not penalise candidates in this section of the examination for spelling or punctuation errors: these are fully covered in the mark schemes for the language section of the examination.

Appendices

Appendix A

Specimen answers to passages for summary

Summary exercise on pages 26–27.

New production of Shaw's *Mrs Warren's Profession* is at Citizens Theatre, Glasgow.

Director: Giles Havergal.

Set: very basic, expressing drabness.

Emphasis of production on acting.

Costume: modern, with only slight Edwardian hints.

Using actors who have mostly played before at Citizens Theatre.

Ann Mitchell plays Mrs Warren:

- wears a vaguely Edwardian hat with large birds' wings.

- employs Cockney accent.

Debra Gillett plays Vivie.

Michael MacKenzie plays Sir George Crofts.

Derwent Watson plays rector, Samuel Gardner.

Summary practice exercises on pages 35–39.

1 Educationalists frequently claim that there is too much violence in the mass media. The issue is complex. Violence and death have always featured in great art, and a distinction must be drawn between their treatment in serious programmes and those designed for a mass audience. Essentially, there are too many badly produced programmes relying on violence at peak viewing times, and competition for viewing figures almost certainly exacerbates the problem. Although only emotionally disturbed children are likely to actually learn violence from watching any particular programme, the repeated exposure to violence on television actually causes ordinary children to regard violence as normal and acceptable. If there are insufficient programmes expressing positive values, this acceptance is strengthened. Gratuitous lingering on violence increases the effect, and far too many programmes rely for their emotional impact on the scenes of violence, rather than on any message which the programme might be presenting.   (149 words)

2 a Based on a novel by E.M. Forster. Directors: Ismail Merchant and James Ivory. Cast: Judy Dench plays Eleanor Lavish, a novelist.

Helena Bonham-Carter plays the heroine.
Maggie Smith, Denholm Elliott and Simon Callow take other leading roles.
Several elderly English actresses play ageing English ladies.
Screenplay: Ruther Prawer Jhabvala.
Setting: Florence, and later, England.
Film is a period piece. Shows great care with costumes and interiors.
Forster's chapter headings used to introduce scenes.
Later scenes contain tea-parties and portrayal of social embarrassment.

b It concerns some English people whose visit to Florence early this century brings them spiritually to life. The romantic imagination of a female novelist and the barely concealed passion of another female character are portrayed.

It is also about social pressures constricting people, and the conflict between the splendour of Florentine architecture and the pettiness of English social life. There are moments of violence. The English scenes include tea-parties and episodes of social embarrassment, including an interrupted nude bathing scene. The film is partly a pastiche of film versions of the Edwardian era.   (94 words)

c The film has a genteel graciousness which is highly effective. It is a conscious period piece, and such great care is taken with the costumes and interiors that it seems almost museum-like. The Edwardian scenes are superbly constructed. The extreme care with which the directors attempt to capture precise details of the era, and the novel, gives the film a feeling of artificiality. However, every scene contains brilliant visual effects. The use of chapter headings is effective, though these tend to interrupt the flow of the action. The balance and control of the directors add power to passionate scenes. The tension of the film comes partly from the contrast between the magnificent setting of Florence and the carefully captured English dialogue, and there are some superb scenes of social embarrassment in the English scenes. The casting and acting of both major and minor parts is superb.   (146 words)

3 WHAT TO EAT AND DRINK DURING TENNIS TOURNAMENTS

Your success or failure in tennis tournaments may depend on what you eat or drink before and during your matches. Top players rely on snacking to boost their energy levels. So should you. This is what you should do.

- Before you go on court, drink $\frac{1}{2}$ to $\frac{3}{4}$ pint of water. Drink some water with a little salt added every ten to 15 minutes during the match. This stops dehydration, which is the real killer.
- Be careful with sweet drinks. They can MAKE you dehydrated. If you DO use soft drinks, swig some water afterwards.
- Take glucose for energy. Bananas are the best source. About one-fifth of their weight is carbohydrate, and they have a good sugar mix. Some of the sugars go quickly to the muscles to boost your energy and some go more slowly for a longer-lasting effect.
- Take special care to eat during long matches or if you are going on to play a doubles match as well as a singles.
- Eat as soon as you come off court, to keep up your energy supplies. If you do, you can start your next match with 20% to 30% more energy in your muscles than your opponent.

(199 words)

Appendix B

The Sisters

There was no hope for him this time: it was the third stroke. Night after night I had passed the house (it was vacation time) and studied the lighted square of window: and night after night I had found it lighted in the same way, faintly and evenly. If he was dead, I thought, I would see the reflection of candles on the darkened blind for I knew that two candles must be set at the head of a corpse. He had often said to me: *I am not long for this world*, and I had thought his words idle. Now I knew they were true. Every night as I gazed up at the window I said softly to myself the word *paralysis*. It had always sounded strangely in my ears, like the word *gnomon* in the Euclid and the word *simony* in the Catechism. But now it sounded to me like the name of some maleficent and sinful being. It filled me with fear, and yet I longed to be nearer to it and to look upon its deadly work.

Old Cotter was sitting at the fire, smoking, when I came downstairs to supper. While my aunt was ladling out my stirabout he said, as if returning to some former remark of his:

—No, I wouldn't say he was exactly . . . but there was something queer . . . there was something uncanny about him. I'll tell you my opinion . . .

He began to puff at his pipe, no doubt arranging his opinion in his mind. Tiresome old fool! When we knew him first he used to be rather interesting, talking about faints and worms; but I soon grew tired of him and his endless stories about the distillery.

—I have my own theory about it, he said. I think it was one of those . . . peculiar cases . . . But it's hard to say . . .

He began to puff again at his pipe without giving us his theory. My uncle saw me staring and said to me:

—Well, so your old friend is gone, you'll be sorry to hear.

—Who? said I.

—Father Flynn.

—Is he dead?

—Mr Cotter here has just told us. He was passing by the house.

I knew that I was under observation so I continued eating as if the news had not interested me. My uncle explained to old Cotter.

—The youngster and he were great friends. The old chap taught him a great deal, mind you; and they say he had a great wish for him.

—God have mercy on his soul, said my aunt piously.

Old Cotter looked at me for a while. I felt that his little beady black eyes were examining me but I would not satisfy him by looking up from my plate. He returned to his pipe and finally spat rudely into the grate.

—I wouldn't like children of mine, he said, to have too much to say to a man like that.

—How do you mean, Mr Cotter? asked my aunt.

—What I mean is, said old Cotter, it's bad for children. My idea is: let a young lad run about and play with young lads of his own age and not be . . . Am I right, Jack?

—That's my principle, too, said my uncle. Let him learn to box his corner. That's what I'm always saying to that Rosicrucian there: take exercise. Why, when I was a nipper every morning of my life I had a cold bath, winter and summer. And that's what stands to me now. Education is all very fine and large . . . Mr Cotter might take a pick of that leg of mutton, he added to my aunt.

—No, no, not for me, said old Cotter.

My aunt brought the dish from the safe and laid it on the table.

—But why do you think it's not good for children, Mr Cotter? she asked.

—It's bad for children, said old Cotter, because their minds are so impressionable. When children see things like that, you know, it has an effect . . .

I crammed my mouth with stirabout for fear I might give utterance to my anger. Tiresome old red-nosed imbecile!

It was late when I fell asleep. Though I was angry with old Cotter for alluding to me as a child I puzzled my head to extract meaning from his unfinished sentences. In the dark of my room I imagined that I saw again the heavy grey face of the paralytic. I drew the blankets over my head and tried to think of Christmas. But the grey face still followed me. It murmured; and I understood that it desired to confess something. I felt my soul receding into some pleasant and vicious region; and there again I found it waiting for me. It began to confess to me in a murmuring voice and I wondered why it smiled continually and why the lips were so moist with spittle. But then I remembered that it had died of paralysis and I felt that I too was smiling feebly as if to absolve the simoniac of his sin.

The next morning after breakfast I went down to look at the little house in Great Britain Street. It was an unassuming shop, registered under the vague name of *Drapery*. The drapery consisted mainly of children's bootees and umbrellas; and on ordinary days a notice used to hang in the window, saying: *Umbrellas Recovered*. No notice was visible now for the shutters were up. A crape bouquet was tied to the door-knocker with ribbon. Two poor women and a telegram boy were reading the card pinned on the crape. I also approached and read:

> July 1st, 1895
> The Rev. James Flynn (formerly of
> S. Catherine's Church, Meath Street),
> aged sixty-five years.
> R.I.P.

The reading of the card persuaded me that he was dead and I was disturbed to find myself at check. Had he not been dead I would have gone into the little dark room behind the shop to find him sitting in his arm-chair by the fire, nearly smothered in his great-coat. Perhaps my aunt would have given me a packet of High Toast for him and this present would have roused him from his stupefied doze. It was always I who emptied the packet into his black snuff-box for his hands trembled too much to allow him to do this without spilling half the snuff about the floor. Even as he raised his large trembling hand to his nose little clouds of smoke dribbled through his fingers over the front of his coat. It may have been these constant showers of snuff which gave his ancient priestly garments their green faded look for the red handkerchief, blackened, as it always was, with the snuff-stains of a week, with which he tried to brush away the fallen grains, was quite inefficacious.

I wished to go in and look at him but I had not the courage to knock. I walked away slowly along the sunny side of the street, reading all the theatrical advertisements in the shopwindows as I went. I found it strange that neither I nor the day seemed in a mourning mood and I felt even annoyed at discovering in myself a sensation of freedom as if I had been freed from something by his death. I wondered at this for, as my uncle had said the night before, he had taught me a great deal. He had studied in the Irish college in Rome and he had taught me to pronounce Latin properly. He had told me stories about the catacombs and about Napoleon Bonaparte, and he had explained to me the meaning of the different ceremonies of the Mass and of the different vestments worn by the priest. Sometimes he had amused himself by putting difficult questions to me, asking me what one should do in certain circumstances or whether such and such sins were mortal or venial or only imperfections. His questions showed me how complex and mysterious were certain institutions of the Church which I had always regarded as the simplest acts. The duties of the priest towards the Eucharist and towards the secrecy of the confessional seemed so grave to me that I wondered how anybody had ever found in himself the courage to undertake them; and I was not surprised when he told me that the fathers of the Church had written books as thick as the *Post Office Directory* and as closely printed as the law notices in the newspaper, elucidating all these intricate questions. Often when I thought of this I could make no answer or only a very foolish and halting one upon which he used to smile and nod his head twice or thrice. Sometimes he used to put me through the responses of the Mass which he had made me learn by heart; and, as I pattered, he used to smile pensively and nod his head, now and then pushing huge pinches of snuff up each nostril alternately. When he smiled he used to uncover his big discoloured teeth and let his tongue lie upon his lower lip – a habit which had made me feel uneasy in the beginning of our acquaintance before I knew him well.

As I walked along in the sun I remembered old Cotter's words and tried to remember what had happened afterwards in the dream. I remembered that I had noticed long velvet curtains and a swinging lamp of antique fashion. I felt that I had been very far away, in some land where the customs were strange – in Persia, I thought. . . . But I could not remember the end of the dream.

In the evening my aunt took me with her to visit the house of mourning. It was after sunset; but the window-panes of the houses that looked to the west reflected the tawny gold of a great bank of clouds. Nannie received us in the hall; and, as it would have been unseemly to have shouted at her, my aunt shook hands with her for all. The old woman pointed upwards interrogatively and, on my aunt's nodding, proceeded to toil up the narrow staircase before us, her bowed head being scarcely above the level of the banister-rail. At the first landing she stopped and beckoned us forward encouragingly towards the open door of the dead-room. My aunt went in and the old woman, seeing that I hesitated to enter, began to beckon to me again repeatedly with her hand.

I went in on tiptoe. The room through the lace end of the blind was suffused with dusky golden light amid which the candles looked like pale thin flames. He had been coffined. Nannie gave the lead and we three knelt down at the foot of the bed. I pretended to pray but I could not gather my thoughts because the old woman's mutterings distracted me. I noticed how clumsily her skirt was hooked at the back and how the heels of her cloth boots were trodden down all to one side. The fancy came to me that the old priest was smiling as he lay there in his coffin.

But no. When we rose and went up to the head of the bed I saw that he was not smiling. There he lay, solemn and copious, vested as for the altar, his large hands loosely retaining a chalice. His face was very truculent, grey and massive, with black cavernous nostrils and circled by a scanty white fur. There was a heavy odour in the room – the flowers.

We blessed ourselves and came away. In the little room downstairs we found Eliza seated in his arm-chair in state. I groped my way towards my usual chair in the corner while Nannie went to the sideboard and brought out a decanter of sherry and some wine-glasses. She set these on the table and invited us to take a little glass of wine. Then, at her sister's bidding, she poured out the sherry into the glasses and passed them to us. She pressed me to take some cream crackers also but I declined because I thought I would make too much noise eating them. She seemed to be somewhat disappointed at my refusal and went over quietly to the sofa where she sat down behind her sister. No one spoke: we all gazed at the empty fireplace.

My aunt waited until Eliza sighed and then said:

—Ah, well, he's gone to a better world.

Eliza sighed again and bowed her head in assent. My aunt fingered the stem of her wine-glass before sipping a little.

—Did he . . . peacefully? she asked.

—O, quite peacefully, ma'am, said Eliza. You couldn't tell when the breath went out of him. He had a beautiful death, God be praised.

—And everything . . . ?

—Father O'Rourke was in with him a Tuesday and anointed him and prepared him and all.

—He knew then?

—He was quite resigned.

—He looks quite resigned, said my aunt.

—That's what the woman we had in to wash him said. She said he just looked as if he was asleep, he looked that peaceful and resigned. No one would think he'd make such a beautiful corpse.

—Yes, indeed, said my aunt.

She sipped a little more from her glass and said:

—Well, Miss Flynn, at any rate it must be a great comfort for you to know that you did all you could for him. You were both very kind to him, I must say.

Eliza smoothed her dress over her knees.

—Ah, poor James! she said. God knows we done all we could, as poor as we are – we wouldn't see him want anything while he was in it.

Nannie had leaned her head against the sofa-pillow and seemed about to fall asleep.

—There's poor Nannie, said Eliza, looking at her, she's wore out. All the work we had, she and me, getting in the woman to wash him and then laying him out and then the coffin and then arranging about the Mass in the chapel. Only for Father O'Rourke I don't know what we'd have done at all. It was him brought us all them flowers and them two candlesticks out of the chapel and wrote out the notice for the *Freeman's General* and took charge of all the papers for the cemetery and poor James's insurance.

—Wasn't that good of him? said my aunt.

Eliza closed her eyes and shook her head slowly.

—Ah, there's no friends like the old friends, she said, when all is said and done, no friends that a body can trust.

—Indeed, that's true, said my aunt. And I'm sure now that he's gone to his eternal reward he won't forget you and all your kindness to him.

—Ah, poor James! said Eliza. He was no great trouble to us. You wouldn't hear him in the house any more than now. Still, I know he's gone and all to that . . .

—It's when it's all over that you'll miss him, said my aunt.

—I know that, said Eliza. I won't be bringing him in his cup of beef-tea any more, nor you, ma'am, sending him his snuff. Ah, poor James!

She stopped, as if she were communing with the past and then said shrewdly:

—Mind you, I noticed there was something queer coming over him latterly. Whenever I'd bring in his soup to him there I'd find him with his breviary fallen to the floor, lying back in the chair and his mouth open.

She laid a finger against her nose and frowned: then she continued:

—But still and all he kept on saying that before the summer was over he'd go out for a drive one fine day just to see the old house again where we were all born down in Irishtown and take me and Nannie with him. If we could only get one of them new-fangled carriages that makes no noise that Father O'Rourke told him about – them with the rheumatic wheels – for the day cheap, he said, at Johnny Rush's over the way there and drive out the three of us together of a Sunday evening. He had his mind set on that . . . Poor James!

—The Lord have mercy on his soul! said my aunt.

Eliza took out her handkerchief and wiped her eyes with it. Then she put it back again in her pocket and gazed into the empty grate for some time without speaking.

—He was too scrupulous always, she said. The duties of the priesthood was too much for him. And then his life was, you might say, crossed.

—Yes, said my aunt. He was a disappointed man. You could see that.

A silence took possession of the little room and, under cover of it, I approached the table and tasted my sherry and then returned quietly to my chair in the corner. Eliza seemed to have fallen into a deep revery. We waited respectfully for her to break the silence: and after a long pause she said slowly:

—It was that chalice he broke . . . That was the beginning of it. Of course, they say it was all right, that it contained nothing, I mean. But still . . . They say it was the boy's fault. But poor James was so nervous, God be merciful to him!

—And was that it? said my aunt. I heard something . . .

Eliza nodded.

—That affected his mind, she said. After that he began to mope by himself, talking to no one and wandering about by himself. So one night he was wanted for to go on a call and they couldn't find him anywhere. They looked high up and low down; and still they couldn't see a sight of him anywhere. So then the clerk suggested to try the chapel. So then they got the keys and opened the chapel and the clerk and Father O'Rourke and another priest that was there brought in a light for to look for him . . . And what do you think but there he was, sitting up by himself in the dark in his confession-box, wide-awake and laughing-like softly to himself?

She stopped suddenly as if to listen. I too listened; but there was no sound in the house: and I knew that the old priest was lying still in his coffin as we had seen him, solemn and truculent in death, an idle chalice on his breast.

Eliza resumed:

—Wide-awake and laughing-like to himself . . . So then, of course, when they saw that, that made them think that there was something gone wrong with him . . .

Appendix C

King Lear – Act I

SCENE II—[*The Earl of Gloucester's Castle.*]

Enter EDMUND, *with a letter.*

	Edm.	Thou, Nature, art my goddess; to thy law
		My services are bound. Wherefore should I
		Stand in the plague of custom, and permit
		The curiosity of nations to deprive me,
5		For that I am some twelve or fourteen moonshines
		Lag of a brother? Why bastard? Wherefore base?
		When my dimensions are as well compact,
		My mind as generous, and my shape as true,
		As honest madam's issue? Why brand they us
10		With base? with baseness? bastardy? base, base?
		Who in the lusty stealth of nature take
		More composition and fierce quality
		Than doth, within a dull, stale, tired bed,
		Go to th'creating a whole tribe of fops,
15		Got 'tween asleep and wake? Well then,
		Legitimate Edgar, I must have your land:
		Our father's love is to the bastard Edmund
		As to th'legitimate. Fine word, 'legitimate'!
		Well, my legitimate, if this letter speed,
20		And my invention thrive, Edmund the base
		Shall top th'legitimate—: I grow, I prosper;
		Now, gods, stand up for bastards!

Enter GLOUCESTER.

	Glou.	Kent banish'd thus! And France in choler parted!
		And the King gone to-night! prescrib'd his power!
25		Confin'd to exhibition! All this done
		Upon the gad!—Edmund, how now! What news?
	Edm.	So please your Lordship, none. [*Putting up the letter.*
	Glou.	Why so earnestly seek you to put up that letter?
	Edm.	I know no news, my Lord.
30	*Glou.*	What paper were you reading?
	Edm.	Nothing, my Lord.
	Glou.	No? What needed then that terrible dispatch of it into your pocket? The quality of nothing hath not such need to hide itself. Let's see: come; if it be nothing, I shall not need spectacles.
35	*Edm.*	I beseech you, Sir, pardon me; it is a letter from my brother that I have not all o'erread, and for so much as I have perus'd, I find it not fit for your o'erlooking.
	Glou.	Give me the letter, sir.
	Edm.	I shall offend, either to detain or give it. The contents, as in part I understand
40		them, are to blame.
	Glou.	Let's see, let's see.
	Edm.	I hope, for my brother's justification, he wrote this but as an essay or taste of

my virtue.

	Glou.	[Reads.] *This policy and reverence of age makes the world bitter to the best*
45		*of our times; keeps our fortunes from us till our oldness cannot relish them. I*
		begin to find an idle and fond bondage in the oppression of aged tyranny,
		who sways, not as it hath power, but as it is suffer'd. Come to me, that of this
		I may speak more. If our father would sleep till I wak'd him, you should enjoy
		half his revenue for ever, and live the beloved of your brother, EDGAR.—Hum!
50		Conspiracy! 'Sleep till I wak'd him,—you should enjoy half his revenue.' My
		son Edgar! Had he a hand to write this? a heart and brain to breed it in?
		When came you to this? Who brought it?
	Edm.	It was not brought me, my Lord; there's the cunning of it; I found it thrown in
		at the casement of my closet.
55	*Glou.*	You know the character to be your brother's?
	Edm.	If the matter were good, my Lord, I durst swear it were his; but, in respect of
		that, I would fain think it were not.
	Glou.	It is his.
	Edm.	It is his hand, my Lord; but I hope his heart is not in the contents.
60	*Glou.*	Has he never before sounded you in this business?
	Edm.	Never, my Lord. But I have heard him oft maintain it to be fit that, sons at
		perfect age, and fathers declin'd, the father should be as ward to the son, and
		the son manage his revenue.
	Glou.	O villain, villain! His very opinion in the letter! Abhorred villain! Unnatural,
65		detested, brutish villain! worse than brutish! Go, sirrah, seek him; I'll
		apprehend him. Abominable villain! Where is he?
	Edm.	I do not well know, my Lord. If it shall please you to suspend your indignation
		against my brother till you can derive from him better testimony of his intent,
		you should run a certain course; where, if you violently proceed against him,
70		mistaking his purpose, it would make a great gap in your own honour, and
		shake in pieces the heart of his obedience. I dare pawn down my life for him,
		that he hath writ this to feel my affection to your honour, and to no other
		pretence of danger.
	Glou.	Think you so?
75	*Edm.*	If your honour judge it meet, I will place you where you shall hear us confer
		of this, and by an auricular assurance have your satisfaction; and that without
		any further delay than this very evening.
	Glou.	He cannot be such a monster—
	Edm.	Nor is not, sure.
80	*Glou.*	—to his father, that so tenderly and entirely loves him. Heaven and earth!
		Edmund, seek him out; wind me into him, I pray you: frame the business
		after your own wisdom. I would unstate myself to be in a due resolution.
	Edm.	I will seek him, Sir, presently; convey the business as I shall find means, and
		acquaint you withal.
85	*Glou.*	These late eclipses in the sun and moon portend no good to us: though the
		wisdom of Nature can reason it thus and thus, yet Nature finds itself scourg'd
		by the sequent effects. Love cools, friendship falls off, brothers divide: in
		cities, mutinies; in countries, discord; in palaces, treason; and the bond
		crack'd 'twixt son and father. This villain of mine comes under the prediction;
90		there's son against father: the King falls from bias of nature; there's father
		against child. We have seen the best of our time: machinations, hollowness,
		treachery, and all ruinous disorders follow us disquietly to our graves. Find
		out this villain, Edmund; it shall lose thee nothing: do it carefully. And the
		noble and true-hearted Kent banish'd! his offence, honesty! 'Tis strange. [*Exit.*
95	*Edm.*	This is the excellent foppery of the world, that, when we are sick in fortune,

often the surfeits of our own behaviour, we make guilty of our disasters the sun, the moon, and stars; as if we were villains on necessity, fools by heavenly compulsion, knaves, thieves, and treachers by spherical predominance, drunkards, liars, and adulterers by an enforc'd obedience of

100 planetary influence; and all that we are evil in, by a divine thrusting on. An admirable evasion of whoremaster man, to lay his goatish disposition to the charge of a star! My father compounded with my mother under the dragon's tail, and my nativity was under *Ursa major*, so that it follows I am rough and lecherous. Fut! I should have been that I am had the maidenliest star in the

105 firmament twinkled on my bastardizing. Edgar—

Enter EDGAR.

and pat he comes, like the catastrophe of the old comedy: my cue is villanous melancholy, with a sigh like Tom o' Bedlam. O! these eclipses do portend these divisions. *Fa, sol, la mi.*

Edg. How now, brother Edmund! What serious contemplation are you in?
Edm. I am thinking, brother, of a prediction I read this other day, what should
110 follow these eclipses.
Edg. Do you busy yourself with that?
Edm. I promise you the effects he writes of succeed unhappily; as of unnaturalness between the child and the parent; death, dearth, dissolutions of ancient amities; divisions in state; menaces and maledictions against King and
115 nobles; needless diffidences, banishment of friends, dissipation of cohorts, nuptial breaches, and I know not what.
Edg. How long have you been a sectary astronomical?
Edm. When saw you my father last?
Edg. The night gone by.
120 *Edm.* Spake you with him?
Edg. Ay, two hours together.
Edm. Parted you in good terms? Found you no displeasure in him by word nor countenance?
Edg. None at all.
125 *Edm.* Bethink yourself wherein you may have offended him; and at my entreaty forbear his presence until some little time has qualified the heat of his displeasure, which at this instant so rageth in him that with the mischief of your person it would scarcely allay.
Edg. Some villain hath done me wrong.
130 *Edm.* That's my fear. I pray you have a continent forbearance till the speed of his rage goes slower, and as I say, retire with me to my lodging, from whence I will fitly bring you to hear my Lord speak. Pray ye, go; there's my key. If you do stir abroad, go arm'd.
Edg. Arm'd, brother!
135 *Edm.* Brother, I advise you to the best. I am no honest man if there be any good meaning toward you; I have told you what I have seen and heard; but faintly, nothing like the image and horror of it; pray you, away.
Edg. Shall I hear from you anon?
Edm. I do serve you in this business.   [*Exit Edgar.*
140 A credulous father, and a brother noble,
Whose nature is so far from doing harms
That he suspects none; on whose foolish honesty
My practices ride easy! I see the business.
Let me, if not by birth, have lands by wit:
145 All with me's meet that I can fashion fit.   [*Exit.*

Further Acknowledgements

The publishers would like to thank the following for permission to reproduce copyright material in this volume:

Text:
The AEB for permission to reproduce various marking schemes; the extract from Alfred Davey, *Learning to be prejudiced* reproduced by permission of Edward Arnold (1983); the extract from Brian Inglis, *The Forbidden Game* reproduced by permission of Curtis Brown Ltd on behalf of Brian Inglis. Copyright Brian Inglis 1975; the Associated Examining Board for the extract from D W Winnicott, *The Child, the Family and the Outside World*; Andre Deutsch Ltd for the extract from Norman Mailer, *The Presidential Papers* (1968); BBC Enterprises Ltd for the extracts from Rex Moorfoot, *Television in the eighties* (1982), Peter Black, *The Biggest Aspidistra in the World* (1972) and Janet Cohen, *File on Four*; Basil Blackwell for the extracts from Anthony Giddens, *Sociology* (Polity Press, 1990) and Kathy Myers, *Understanding Advertisers* (in *Language, Image, Media*, eds. Davis and Walton, 1983); extracts from the Authorized Version of the Bible (The King James Bible), the rights in which are vested in the Crown, are reproduced by permission of the Crown's patentee, Cambridge University Press; Davis Poynter for Cox and Dyson (ed.) *The Black Papers on Education* (1971); Faber and Faber Ltd for the extract from Robert Harris, *Gotcha! The Media, the Government and the Falklands Crisis* (1983); Gower Publishing Group for the extracts from Dennie Briggs, *In Place of Prison* (Temple Smith, 1975) and Thomas J Cottle, *Black Testimony: the voices of Britain's West Indians* (Wildwood House Ltd, 1978); The Guardian for Jenny Bryan, *Yes, do have those bananas* (26.6.92); Hamish Hamilton for the extract from Leon Radzinovicz and Joan King, *The Growth of Crime* (1977); Her Majesty's Stationery Office for the extracts from *Half Our Future: A Report of the Central Advisory Council for Education*, 1963 and The Official Report of the House of Lords and House of Commons Debates (Hansard); Ellis Horwood for the extract from Alan Burns, *The Microchip: Appropriate or inappropriate technology* (1981); The Independent for *Looking back, it doesn't seem quite so good*, (14.4.93), for Jonathan Glancey, *Curse of the Day-Glo Dazzlers*, for David Reynolds, *Whole-class teaching or group work?* (6.6.96), for Fran Abrams, *A school lesson in Taiwan* (6.6.96); John Wiley & Sons Ltd for the extract from Barrie Sherman, *The New Revolution* (1985); Kogan Page Limited for the extracts from Robert Allen, *How to save the world* (1980); the extracts from Tony Parker, *The Man Inside*, Betty Friedan, *The Second Stage*, and Betty Friedan, *The Feminine Mystique* reproduced by permission of Michael Joseph Ltd; the articles by Buchi Emecheta (1985), Anuradha Vittachi (1980) and Judy Gahagan, *Science on the Couch* (1988); New Internationalist; the extract from Michail Shallis, *The Silicon Idol*, and Rod Morgan, *The Oxford Handbook of Criminology* (1994) reproduced by permission of Oxford University Press (1984); the

extracts from Paul Harrison, *Inside the Third World: the anatomy of poverty* (1993), Susan George, *How the Other Half Dies* (1976), Edward Blishen, *The School that I'd like* (1969), David J Smith, *Racial Disadvantage in Britain: The PEP Report* (1977), and 'Advertising' by Frank Whitebread, in *Discrimination and Popular Culture* (ed. Denys Thompson, 1964), all reproduced by permission of Penguin Books Ltd; the extracts from Teresa Hayter, *The Creation of World Poverty* (1981) and Peter Fryer, *Staying Power* (1984) reproduced by permission of Drake Marketing Services on behalf of Pluto Press; Routledge, for the extracts from Janet Radcliffe Richards, *The Sceptical Feminist* (1980), Peter Conrad, *Television: The medium and its manners* (1982) and E Ellis Cashmore, *A dictionary of Race & Ethnic Relations*; SCM Press Ltd for the extract from David Bleakley, In Place of Work (1981); Screen for the extract from Beverley Brown, *British film censorship: an interview with James Ferman* (23.5.82); The Observer for H G Wells, *Our World in 50 years' time* and the front page of The Observer (9.12.90); Mirror Group Newspapers for the article by Frank Corless, *Brady's Xmas Feast*; The Spectator, for Peter Ackroyd, Pictures from Italy (19.4.86); The Sunday Telegraph Ltd, for the front page of The Sunday Telegraph (9.12.90); Victor Gollancz Ltd, for the extract from Christopher Evans, *The Mighty Micro* (1979); Guardian News Service Ltd, for the articles *Rainforest Factfile*, and *Still Papering Over the Cracks* by Yasmin Alibhai; Professor David Pearce for his article, *Options for the Forest* in *The Guardian*, (8.12.89); Bryan Magee, for the extracts from his article *Women's Rights and Wrongs* in *The Guardian*, (12.11.89); Manchester University Press for the extract from John Whale, *The Politics of the Media* (1977); Edward Arnold Publishers, for the extract from E M Forster, *Two Cheers for Democracy* (1972); The New Scientist, for Sanjay Kumar, *Too Many People Spoil the Planet* (6.11.93); News of the World, for the front page from The News of the World (9.12.90) and the extract from Sunday magazine; The Observer, for *Loggers in Rainforest Chainsaw Massacre* (8.9.96); Random Century for the extracts from Benjamin Spock, *Baby and Child Care* (The Bodley Head, 1979), Jonathan Gathorne-Hardy, *Love, Sex, Marriage and Divorce* (Jonathan Cape, 1981), Naomi Wolf, *The Beauty Myth* (Chatto & Windus, 1990); Random House Inc, for the extract from Paul Ehrlich, *The Population Bomb* (Ballantine Books, 1968); Sean Sweeney for James Joyce, *The Sisters*; Anthony Thwaite for Philip Larkin, poems from *Whitsun Weddings*; Times Newspapers for the extracts from The Times and the Sunday Times, and Keith Waterhouse for *I'm sorry, I'll write that again*. Copyright Times Newpapers.

Photographs:
Cover, p 48, Colin Taylor Productions; p69, Topham Picture Source; p88, Ecoscene; p103 left, John Birdsall Photography, right, Andes Press Agency; p128 Topham Picture Source; p147 top left, © John P Cavanagh/The Women's Press, bottom left, © Colin Tromp/Chatto and Windus, right, Topham Picture Source; p165, © David Simmonds; p219, © Kobal Collection; p259 Bridgeman Art Library.